THE FORMS OF THE OLD

D1086266

EZEKIEL

RONALD M. HALS

The Forms of the Old Testament Literature
VOLUME XIX
Rolf P. Knierim and Gene M. Tucker, editors

WILLIAM B. EERDMANS PUBLISHING COMPANY
GRAND RAPIDS, MICHIGAN

Copyright © 1989 by Wm. B. Eerdmans Publishing Co.
255 Jefferson Ave. S.E., Grand Rapids, Mich. 49503

Library of Congress Cataloging-in-Publication Data:

Hals, Ronald M., 1926-
Ezekiel / Ronald M. Hals.
p.   cm. — (The Forms of the Old Testament literature; v. 19)
ISBN 0-8028-0340-7
1. Bible. O.T. Ezekiel—Commentaries.
2. Bible. O.T. Ezekiel—Criticism, Form.
I. Title.   II. Series.
BS1545.3.H35 1989
224'.40663—dc19   89-1589
CIP

Contents

Abbreviations and Symbols

I. Miscellaneous abbreviations and symbols

cf.	compare
ch(s).	chapter(s)
cp	common plural
Diss.	Dissertation
ed.	editor(s), edited by; edition
e.g.	for example
Fest.	Festschrift
fp	feminine plural
fs	feminine singular
H	Holiness Code, Leviticus 17–26
ibid.	*ibidem,* in the same place
idem	the same
i.e.	*id est* (that is)
LXX	Septuagint
mp	masculine plural
ms	masculine singular
MT	Masoretic Text
NF	Neue Folge (in serial listings)
OT	Old Testament
P	Priestly source
p(p).	page(s)
tr.	translated by
v(v).	verse(s)
vol(s).	volume(s)
→	the arrow indicates a cross reference to another section of the commentary

II. Publications

AB	Anchor Bible
AnBib	Analecta biblica
ANET	J. B. Pritchard, ed., *Ancient Near Eastern Texts Relating to the Old Testament* (3rd ed.; Princeton: Princeton University, 1969)
ASTI	*Annual of the Swedish Theological Institute in Jerusalem*
ATANT	Abhandlungen zur Theologie des Alten und Neuen Testaments
BA	*Biblical Archaeologist*
BBET	Beiträge zur biblischen Exegese und Theologie
BEvT	*Beiträge zur evangelischen Theologie*
BHS	K. Elliger and K. Rudolph, eds., *Biblia hebraica stuttgartensia* (Stuttgart: Deutsche Bibelstiftung, 1977)
BHT	Beiträge zur historischen Theologie
Bib	*Biblica*
BibOr	Biblica et orientalia
BibS(N)	Biblische Studien (Neukirchen, 1951-)
BTB	*Biblical Theology Bulletin*
BWANT	Beiträge zur Wissenschaft vom Alten und Neuen Testament
BZ	*Biblische Zeitschrift*
BZAW	Beihefte zur Zeitschrift für die Alttestamentliche Wissenschaft
CBQ	*Catholic Biblical Quarterly*
ConBOT	Coniectanea biblica, Old Testament
EF	Erträge der Forschung
EHSS	Europäische Hochschulschriften
EvT	*Evangelische Theologie*
FB	Forschung zur Bibel
FOTL	The Forms of the Old Testament Literature
FRLANT	Forschungen zur Religion und Literatur des Alten und Neuen Testaments
HAT	Handbuch zum Alten Testament
HDS	Harvard Dissertation Series
HSM	Harvard Semitic Monographs
HTR	*Harvard Theological Review*
HUCA	*Hebrew Union College Annual*
IB	*Interpreter's Bible*
ICC	International Critical Commentary
IDB	*Interpreter's Dictionary of the Bible*
Int	*Interpretation*
IRT	Issues in Religion and Theology
JAOS	*Journal of the American Oriental Society*

JBL	*Journal of Biblical Literature*
JSOT	*Journal for the Study of the Old Testament*
JSOTSup	Journal for the Study of the Old Testament Supplement Series
LUÅ	Lunds universitets årsskrift
NCB	New Century Bible
OBO	Orbis biblicus et orientalis
OTL	Old Testament Library
OTS	*Oudtestamentische Studiën*
PEGLBS	*Proceedings Eastern Great Lakes Biblical Society*
RSV	*Revised Standard Version*
SBB	Stuttgarter biblische Beiträge
SBLMS	Society of Biblical Literature Monograph Series
SBS	Stuttgarter Bibelstudien
SBT	Studies in Biblical Theology
ThSt(B)	Theologische Studien (ed. Barth)
TLZ	*Theologische Literaturzeitung*
TOTC	Tyndale Old Testament Commentary
TTZ	*Trierer Theologische Zeitschrift*
TynB	*Tyndale Bulletin*
TZ	*Theologische Zeitschrift*
UUÅ	Uppsala universitetsårsskrift
VT	*Vetus Testamentum*
VTSup	Vetus Testamentum, Supplements
WMANT	Wissenschaftliche Monographien zum Alten und Neuen Testament
WZHalle	*Wissenschaftliche Zeitschrift der Martin-Luther-Universität Halle-Wittenberg*
ZAW	*Zeitschrift für die alttestamentliche Wissenschaft*
ZDPV	*Zeitschrift des deutschen Palästinavereins*
ZTK	*Zeitschrift für Theologie und Kirche*

Editors' Foreword

THIS BOOK is the seventh in a series of twenty-four volumes planned for publication throughout the nineteen-eighties. The series eventually will present a form-critical analysis of every book and each unit of the Old Testament (Hebrew Bible) according to a standard outline and methodology. The aims of the work are fundamentally exegetical, attempting to understand the biblical literature from the viewpoint of a particular set of questions. Each volume in the series will also give an account of the history of the form-critical discussion of the material in question, attempt to bring consistency to the terminology for the genres and formulas of the biblical literature, and expose the exegetical procedure in such a way as to enable students and pastors to engage in their own analysis and interpretation. It is hoped, therefore, that the audience will be a broad one, including not only biblical scholars but also students, pastors, priests, and rabbis who are engaged in biblical interpretation.

There is a difference between the planned order of appearance of the individual volumes and their position in the series. While the series follows basically the sequence of the books of the Hebrew Bible, the individual volumes will appear in accordance with the projected working schedules of the individual contributors. The number of twenty-four volumes has been chosen for merely practical reasons that make it necessary to combine several biblical books in one volume at times, and at times to have two authors contribute to the same volume. Volume XIII is an exception to the arrangement according to the sequence of the Hebrew canon in that it omits Lamentations. The commentary on Lamentations will be published with that on the book of Psalms.

The initiation of this series is the result of deliberations and plans that began some twenty years ago. At that time the current editors perceived the need for a comprehensive reference work that would enable scholars and students of the Hebrew scriptures to gain from the insights that form-critical work had accumulated throughout seven decades, and at the same time to participate more effectively in such work themselves. An international and interconfessional team of scholars was assembled and has been expanded in recent years.

Several possible approaches and formats for publication presented themselves. The work could not be a handbook of the form-critical method with some examples of its application. Nor would it be satisfactory to present an encyclopedia of the genres identified in the Old Testament literature. The reference work would have to demonstrate the method on all of the texts, and identify genres only through the actual interpretation of the texts themselves. Hence, the work had to be a commentary following the sequence of the books in the Hebrew Bible (the Kittel edition of the *Biblia hebraica* then and the *Biblia hebraica stuttgartensia* now).

The main purpose of this project is to lead the student to the Old Testament texts themselves, and not just to form-critical studies of the texts. It should be stressed that the commentary is confined to the form-critical interpretation of the texts. Consequently, the reader should not expect here a full-fledged exegetical commentary that deals with the broad range of issues concerning the meaning of the text. In order to keep the focus as clearly as possible on a particular set of questions, matters of text, translation, philology, verse-by-verse explanation, etc. are raised only when they appear directly relevant to the form-critical analysis and interpretation.

The adoption of a commentary format with specific categories for the analysis of the texts rests upon a conclusion that has become crucial for all form-critical work. If the results of form criticism are to be verifiable and generally intelligible, then the determination of typical forms and genres, their settings and functions, has to take place through the analysis of the forms in and of the texts themselves. This leads to two consequences for the volumes in this series. First, each interpretation of a text begins with the presentation of the *structure* of that text in outline form. The ensuing discussion of this structure attempts to distinguish the typical from the individual or unique elements, and to proceed on this basis to the determination of the *genre,* its *setting,* and its *intention.* Traditio-historical factors are discussed throughout this process where relevant; e.g., is there evidence of a written or oral stage of the material earlier than the actual text before the reader?

Second, the interpretation of the texts accepts the fundamental premise that we possess all texts basically at their latest written stages—technically speaking, at the levels of the final redactions. Any access to the texts, therefore, must confront and analyze that latest edition first, i.e., a specific version of that edition as represented in a particular text tradition. Consequently, the commentary proceeds from the analysis of the larger literary corpora created by the redactions back to any prior discernible stages in their literary history. Larger units are examined first, and then their subsections. Therefore, in most instances the first unit examined in terms of structure, genre, setting, and intention is the entire biblical book in question; next the commentary treats the individual larger and then smaller units.

The original plan of the project was to record critically all the relevant results of previous form-critical studies concerning the texts in question. While this remains one of the goals of the series, it had to be expanded to allow for more of the research of the individual contributors. This approach has proved to be important not only with regard to the ongoing insights of the contributors but also in view of the significant developments that have taken place in the field in recent years. The team of scholars responsible for the series is committed to following a basic design throughout the commentary, but differences of emphasis and even to some extent of approach will be recognized as more volumes appear. Each author will ultimately be responsible for his own contribution.

The use of the commentary is by and large self-explanatory, but a few comments may prove helpful to the reader. This work is designed to be used alongside the Hebrew text or a translation of the Bible. The format of the interpretation of the texts, large or small, is the same throughout, except in cases where the biblical material itself suggests a different form of presentation. Individual books and major literary corpora are introduced by a general bibliography referring to wider information on the subjects discussed and to works relevant for the subunits of that literary body. Whenever available, a special form-critical bibliography for a specific unit under discussion will conclude the discussion of that unit. In the outline of the structure of units, the system of sigla attempts to indicate the relationship and interdependence of the parts within that structure. The traditional chapter and verse divisions of the Hebrew text, as well as the versification of the *Revised Standard Version,* are supplied in the right-hand margin of the outlines.

In addition to the commentary on the biblical book, this volume includes a glossary of the genres discussed in the commentary. Many of the definitions in the glossary were prepared by Professor Hals, but some have arisen from the work of other members of the project on other parts of the Old Testament. Each subsequent volume will include such a glossary. Eventually, upon the completion of the commentary series, all of the glossaries will be revised in the light of the analysis of each book of the Old Testament and published as Volume XXIII of the series. The individual volumes will not contain special indices, but the indices for the entire series will be published as Volume XXIV.

The editors acknowledge with appreciation the contribution of numerous persons and institutions to the work of the project. All of the contributors have received significant financial, secretarial, and student assistance from their respective institutions. In particular, the editors have received extensive support from their universities. Without such concrete expressions of encouragement the work scarcely could have gone on. At Claremont, the Institute for Antiquity and Christianity has from its own inception provided office facilities, a supportive staff, and the atmosphere that stimulates not only individual but also team research. Emory University and the Candler School of Theology have likewise provided tangible support and encouragement. The editors are particularly indebted to Judith Streit Smith, a graduate student at The Iliff School of Theology and Denver University, for her assistance in the editorial work on this volume, and to Benjamin H. Hardaway III, of Columbus, Georgia, for his financial support of our work.

ROLF P. KNIERIM
GENE M. TUCKER

Preface

A commentary on a single book written as a part of a series is necessarily a compromise resulting from the attempt to do justice to two somewhat disparate aims. As part of a series this volume seeks to conform itself to what is typical of the entire OT, but as a commentary on Ezekiel it seeks to focus on the uniqueness of that one prophet. This same struggle, to integrate typicality and uniqueness, is the essence of all interpretation but especially of the form-critical method. It is only by understanding the typicality and extent of literary patterns that one can begin to appreciate uniqueness. The primary aim of this book is to show that Ezekiel's typicality is rooted in his heritage as a priest-prophet, and that his uniqueness grows out of his efforts to address, on the basis of that heritage, his distinctive audience in his particular time.

Whatever uniqueness characterizes my own study is the result of a dialogue with the scholars of preceding times. In the case of Ezekiel that means most especially Walther Zimmerli. I have absorbed so much over the years from using his works that I am often no longer aware of the extent of my dependence, although I have done my best to document my indebtedness. The area of my greatest departure from Zimmerli is in my reticence to undertake the restoration of a superior and less problematic original text by large-scale textual emendation. While I know that textual emendation is at times necessary, the format of this series has meant that no extensive text-critical discussions appear. For the most part, only final conclusions indicating departure from the text underlying the *Revised Standard Version* have been indicated.

The Bibliographies reflect the limited aim of the FOTL series, being restricted to issues of form-critical significance and to those works cited in my own analysis.

In line with what I consider the heritage of classical form criticism, my treatment of "genre" has tried to approach "structure" as the expression of the shape of a type of literature. Thus sections on structure and genre frequently have been combined. "Setting" I see as a broad area encompassing such matters as inherent mental process, orientation to an audience, and function. Because function and intention can overlap, the discussions of setting and intention have also occasionally been combined.

Finally I wish to acknowledge my specific indebtedness to particular institutions and individuals for their support of my work. Trinity Lutheran Seminary was of decisive help by granting sabbatical leaves in 1979-80 and 1985-86. The Aid Association for Lutherans undergirded both of these periods of study with generous financial grants, the second time giving me the Fredrik A. Schiotz Award. Additional grants were given by the Association of Theological Schools and Lutheran Brotherhood. I shall always remember both the School of Theology at Claremont in 1979-80 and Candler School of Theology at Emory University in 1985-86 with gratitude for their hospitality and stimulation. The editors of this series working at those two schools, Rolf P. Knierim and Gene M. Tucker, were especially helpful. But in the last analysis this volume would never have been completed without the patient skill of my secretary at Trinity, Melissa Curtis. Her ability and willingness to work at long range from overly rapid tapes and arcane scribbles and to squeeze her work on my manuscript in with her other duties have been a true delight.

Ezekiel

Chapter 1

The Book as a Whole

BIBLIOGRAPHY

D. Baltzer, *Ezechiel und Deuterojesaja* (BZAW 121; Berlin: de Gruyter, 1971); A. Bertholet and K. Galling, *Hesekiel* (HAT I, 13; Tübingen: Mohr, 1936); K. Carley, *Ezekiel Among the Prophets* (SBT II, 31; London: SCM, 1975); D. R. Clark, *The Citations in the Book of Ezekiel* (Diss., Vanderbilt, 1984); G. A. Cooke, *A Critical and Exegetical Commentary on the Book of Ezekiel* (ICC; Edinburgh: Clark, 1936); W. Eichrodt, *Ezekiel* (tr. C. Quinn; OTL; Philadelphia: Westminster, 1970); G. Fohrer and K. Galling, *Ezechiel* (2nd ed.; HAT 13; Tübingen: Mohr, 1955); G. Fohrer, *Die Hauptprobleme des Buches Ezechiel* (BZAW 72; Berlin: Töpelmann, 1952); K. S. Freedy and D. B. Redford, "The Dates in Ezekiel in Relation to Biblical, Babylonian and Egyptian Sources," *JAOS* 90 (1970) 462-85; J. Garscha, *Studien zum Ezechielbuch* (EHSS 23; Bern: Lang, 1974); M. Greenberg, *Ezekiel 1–20* (AB 22; New York: Doubleday, 1983); V. Herntrich, *Ezekielprobleme* (BZAW 61; Giessen: Töpelmann, 1933); G. Hölscher, *Hesekiel, Der Dichter und das Buch* (BZAW 39; Giessen: Töpelmann, 1924); F. Hossfeld, *Untersuchungen zu Komposition und Theologie des Ezechielbuches* (FB 20; Würzburg: Echter Verlag, 1977); C. G. Howie, *The Date and Composition of Ezekiel* (SBLMS 4; Philadelphia: Society of Biblical Literature, 1950); P. Humbert, "Die Herausforderungsformel 'hinnenî êlékâ'," *ZAW* 51 (1933) 101-8; W. A. Irwin, *The Problem of Ezekiel* (Chicago: University of Chicago, 1943); E. Kutsch, *Die chronologischen Daten des Ezechielbuches* (OBO 62; Freiburg: Universitätsverlag, 1985); idem, *Ezechiel* (EF 153; Darmstadt: Wissenschaftliche Buchgesellschaft, 1981); B. Lang, *Kein Aufstand in Jerusalem* (SBB; Stuttgart: Katholisches Bibelwerk, 1978); I. G. Matthews, *Ezekiel* (An American Commentary on the Old Testament; Philadelphia: Judson, 1939); H. G. May, "The Book of Ezekiel" (*IB* 6; Nashville: Abingdon, 1956) 41-338; J. W. Miller, *Das Verhältnis Jeremias und Hesekiels sprachlich und theologisch untersucht* (Assen: Van Gorcum, 1955); S. Park Joon, *Theological Traditions of Israel in the Prophetic Judgment Speeches of Ezekiel* (Diss., Princeton Theological Seminary, 1978); J. Pedersen, *Israel, its Life and Culture* (tr. A. Fausbøll; London: Oxford, 1959); T. M. Raitt, *A Theology of Exile: Judgment/ Deliverance in Jeremiah and Ezekiel* (Philadelphia: Fortress, 1977); K. von Rabenau, "Die Entstehung des Buches Ezechiel in formgeschichtlicher Sicht," *WZHalle* (1955/56) 659-94; idem, "Das prophetische Zukunftswort im Buche Hesekiel," in *Studien zur Theologie der alttestamentlichen Überlieferungen* (Fest. G. von Rad; ed. R. Rendtorff and K. Koch; Neukirchen-Vluyn: Neukirchener, 1961) 61-8; G. von Rad, *Old Testament Theology* (tr. D. M. G. Stalker; New York: Harper and Row, 1965) II; H. Reventlow, "Die Völker als Jahwes Zeugen bei Ezechiel," *ZAW* 71 (1959) 33-43; idem, *Wächter über Israel* (BZAW 82; Berlin: Töpelmann, 1962); P. Scalise, *From Prophet's Word to Prophetic Book: A Study of*

Walther Zimmerli's Theory of 'Nachinterpretation' (Diss., Yale, 1982); M. A. Schmidt, "Zur Komposition des Buches Hesekiel," *TZ* 6 (1950) 81-98; H. Simian, *Die theologische Nachgeschichte der Prophetie Ezechiels* (FB 14; Würzburg: Echter Verlag, 1974); J. B. Taylor, *Ezekiel* (TOTC; London: Tyndale, 1969); J. W. Wevers, *Ezekiel* (NCB; London: Nelson, 1969); D. R. Yates, *The Eschatological Message Concerning Man in the Book of Ezekiel* (Diss., Boston University, 1972); W. Zimmerli, *Ezekiel 1* (tr. R. Clements; Hermeneia; Philadelphia: Fortress, 1979); idem, *Ezekiel 2* (tr. J. D. Martin; Hermeneia; Philadelphia: Fortress, 1983); idem, "Knowledge of God According to the Book of Ezekiel," in *I Am Yahweh* (tr. D. W. Stott; Atlanta: Knox, 1982) 29-98.

Structure

I. The Message of judgment	1:1–24:27
II. The Prophecies against foreign nations	25:1–32:32
III. The Message of consolation	33:1–48:35

The book of Ezekiel has two major components, a collection of units expressing a message of judgment (1:1–24:27) and a parallel collection offering a message of consolation (33:1–48:35). These are separated by a largely unrelated block of prophecies against foreign nations (25:1–32:32). In addition to the obvious factor of the contrast in overall content, several other factors support this perception of the book's structure. (1) The fall of Jerusalem in 587 B.C. serves as the dividing point between the two parts of the prophet's message. The overwhelming preponderance of the units in chs. 1–24 announces this coming destruction (e.g., the symbolic acts in chs. 4–5 and 12:1-20; the prophecies in chs. 6–7; 14:12-23; 15–17; 19–24:24; and the vision in chs. 8–11), and similarly the bulk of the material in chs. 33–48 presupposes the occurrence of this catastrophe (e.g., 33:10, 24; 34:12, 28; 35:5, 12, 15; 36:2-4, 19; 37:11, 21; 38:8; 39:23, 28; 43:8). That Jerusalem's fall links precisely chs. 1–24 with 33–48 is indicated by the way a word mentioning the future arrival of a fugitive announcing Jerusalem's fall concludes chs. 1–24 (24:25-27), and the report of his actual arrival occurs in 33:21-22. (2) A number of passages seem to be paired as counterparts, one in chs. 1–24 with another in 33–48. Each of the two phases of Ezekiel's ministry has prefixed to it a section analyzing his role as that of a sentinel (3:16-22 and 33:1-9). The departure of Yahweh's glory as the climax of the vision in chs. 8–11 is balanced by its return in the course of the vision of 40–48 (43:1-9). The pairing of 6:1-7 with 36:1-15 and of ch. 18 with 33:10-20 are further instances. It must be noted, however, that this otherwise neat division is contradicted by the presence of several sections of consolation within chs. 1–24, e.g., 11:14-21, 16:53-63, and 20:40-44. How these apparently "out of place" sections are to be evaluated will be discussed as each specific section comes up for analysis.

Chapters 25–32 are not totally unrelated either to 1–24 or to 33–48. Many of the prophecies against foreign nations cite their attitude toward Jerusalem or behavior during its fall as a reason for the punishment announced. Similarly Yahweh's action in imposing punishment on other nations to set right the previous injustice is often presented as a first, negative step, necessary but not complete in itself. In fact, the large-scale subordination of the concern with other nations to Yahweh's predominant concern with Israel makes it clear that the treatment of foreign nations is not independent, either redactionally or theologically. A message about one of these nations is never presented from the perspective of the importance of that nation on its own, as a people to be considered in parallel to Israel. Moreover, these messages never have their theological rootage in a doctrine of creation on whose basis all nations stand equally as children of God. Far from it! The God of the prophecies against foreign nations is Israel's God, and even though he takes the sins of other nations with full seriousness, there is never a hint that Yahweh has some purpose for them which is independent of his purpose for Israel. The idea of Israel's election provides the ground for the wrathful judgment brought upon it and for the continuing hope promised to it, and this focus on Israel's election is never set aside in chs. 25–32. Even when other nations or their leaders are faulted for such sins as self-exalting hubris it is clearly Yahweh, the God of Israel, who levels this charge and not Yahweh as he could be conceived to be hidden behind the god of another people, e.g., the Tyrian Baal.

Further evidence that the structure detected is what is intended by the material itself comes in the manifest parallel between the book of Ezekiel and the books of the other two major prophets. Both the book of the eighth-century Isaiah and that of Jeremiah are similarly divided into an earlier message, a later message, and a collection of prophecies against foreign nations (cf. Isaiah 1–12, 13–23, and 28–32 and also Jeremiah 1–25, 26–45, and 46–51, the parallel being even closer in the LXX's arrangement of Jeremiah's message).

Genre

As the parallels with Isaiah 1–39 and Jeremiah indicate, Ezekiel 1–48 is to be classed as a PROPHETIC BOOK of rather typical structure. Although Ezekiel has been considered a bridge between prophecy and apocalyptic, this is at most only partially true. Visions and symbolism are indeed more prominent in Ezekiel than in most prophets (although cf. Zechariah), but Ezekiel's focus is almost totally on judgment within history. Admittedly his message of restoration, especially in chs. 38–39 and 40–48, contains much that is supra-historical in flavor, but this is not without analogy in other prophetic books (cf. Amos 9:11-15 or Isaiah 24–27). In any case it is not enough to demand a different genre label. Essentially any prophetic book contains the report of a ministry carried out within a community by the individual prophet whose name the book bears. The report of the activity—in the case of Ezekiel, both events and speeches are included—is rendered by those who have been drawn into this activity, whether as disciples, tradents, editors. The report is addressed to the community as a whole, but also especially to that circle most impressed with and affected by what it considers God's activity in and through this ministry. The report is preserved and shared as a response to this God who both spoke through the prophet and continues to speak through this preserved word. This perspective is effectively indicated by the shaping of the book so that it has a superscription but no conclusion. It is regarded as "the word of the Lord," which came via Ezekiel in specific, remembered circumstances, but which remains the Lord's word and continues to address his people long beyond those original circumstances.

There is, however, something else characteristic of Ezekiel's work and words that at least raises the question of whether or not some modification of the genre label is needed. Perhaps it ought to be called a prophetic book with a priestly orientation. The pervading flavor of priestly tradition and language is certainly present, but at bottom it is the manifest harmony of Ezekiel's priestly heritage with his prophetic calling which makes such a modification unnecessary. As the teacher of torah and the mediator of holiness, the priest—at least in Ezekiel's usage—functions as the one who seeks to sustain people in the realm of life rather than allowing them to succumb to the threat of death. The commandments of torah are given for life (Ezek 18:5-9; 20:11; see Lev 18:5), and holiness is the power that enables life, and the sanctuary is the place where both are found (J. Pedersen, *Israel*, III-IV, 299). To sustain life is precisely the way Ezekiel sees his prophetic calling throughout the book. "You shall surely die" is the sentinel's word intended to preserve life (3:18-21 and 33:1:9). Life out of death is what the post-587 B.C. exilic community knew it needed (33:10 and 37:11). False prophets are those who do not go up "into the breaches" à la Moses to offer their lives instead of those of their people (13:5, see Ps 106:23). In short, for Ezekiel priestly and prophetic ministry appear as entirely congruent, differing but in no fundamental disharmony. Thus it is entirely adequate to say of Ezekiel the priest that his words have been compiled into a prophetic book. His God is a persistent transforming presence whose identity and will are oriented outwardly so as to seek and enable the life of his people.

The genres of the individual units within the book as a whole, are much easier to label. The most frequently attested genre by far is the PROPHETIC PROOF SAYING, which appears sixty-one times. These appearances are widely scattered: twenty-nine in chs. 1–24, fifteen in chs. 25–32, and seventeen in chs. 33–48. However, the four major visions in the book (chs. 1–3; 8–11; 37:1-14; and 40–48), which constitute about one-third of the entire corpus, contain only three of the sixty-one occurrences. Elsewhere the proof sayings are used with almost any other type of material, occasionally determining the shape of large units, as in 34:17-31 or 38:3-23, but more usually playing a subordinate role, normally as the concluding part of a unit. The major units in the book have been edited rather thoroughly, being introduced almost invariably with the PROPHETIC WORD FORMULA. The large size of these major units gives the book its most distinctive trait and thereby determines a vital aspect of its study. Inasmuch as these major units are so much larger than in most other prophetic material, one must ask in each case about what factors have been responsible for this length and how this large amount of material has been organized.

Setting

Lack of evidence makes it extremely difficult to argue for any specific setting. Although in contrast to Isaiah 8:16 and 30:8 or Jeremiah 36 there is no mention of disciples or a writing down of a message, both of these factors must be assumed. Further, although no such liturgical appendices as Isaiah 12 and 33 are encountered, the question of a liturgical use of the traditions preserved in the book of Ezekiel is probably to be answered positively, assuming there were already in exile assemblies for worship and/or study (see Psalm 137 and already Ezek 33:30-33). Clearly the validation of Ezekiel's message of judgment on Jerusalem by the events of 587 B.C. would have decisively altered the reception the material was originally accorded (3:7) and would have added authority to the rest of his book. That no account is taken of the restoration of 539 B.C. as a fulfillment of Ezekiel's post-587 B.C. preaching suggests a relatively early date for the book's final form. To what extent Ezekiel may have functioned in the editing of his own material remains beyond the reach of present research, even though the short time-span makes such participation highly likely.

The frequent dates and strongly chronological arrangement of the book reflect a definite concern for what might be termed contextual accommodation. In very many cases a prophetic word is seen as not just reflecting a definite historical background, but as addressed to it, even called forth by it. Yet the very process of preservation presupposes also a certain detachability from this original background.

Intention

The existence of a book of specific compass bearing a prophet's name suggests that those who compiled it regarded it as a "complete" word from Yahweh. Similarly, implicit in the content of Ezekiel's message is the understanding that Yahweh had worked through this spokesman to indicate his commitment to a specific history. Preserving that message in a completed book would seem to indicate the belief that God's specific program of action had come to at least a relative conclusion. The arrangement of the book so as to connect both judgment and promise to the events of 587 B.C. reflects the dual purpose of reassuring those tempted to view these events as a defeat of Israel's God and of using that graphic fulfillment of Ezekiel's early message to enhance the strength of his later promises. In all this area, however, criteria for firm conclusions are exceedingly scarce, so that we are forced to depend almost totally on conjecture.

Nonetheless, it does seem necessary to conclude that the keeping, circulating, and rereading of these old words in the new form of a prophetic book is more than an expression of a concern to preserve the record of what once shaped a people's past. That mental process might lead to the storing up of archives, but the preservation of the word of the Lord through a prophet presupposes that the word in question is open to more than some remote kind of future significance. The reading and hearing of that word in worship presume that somehow it continues to serve as the vehicle by which the God of Israel addresses his people. As new events spoken of by the prophet took place, his message about them would be heard again, but now in a new light. After 587 B.C. bore witness to the truth of his message of judgment in chs. 1–24, Ezekiel was a partially vindicated prophet. After the return in 539 B.C. and the restoration in the years following, including the rebuilding of a temple, Ezekiel was again a partially vindicated prophet, although now in a different sense, inasmuch as the restoration which history brought corresponded far less closely to that which he had promised than did the doom he had proclaimed.

Since the process of the book's compilation overlapped the events of 587 B.C., we may assume (and in some cases the texts themselves reflect this) that the materials preserved were shaped in the light of their fulfillment. This seems not to have been the case with regard to the events of the restoration. Instead, the promises of a restored community are preserved in a kind of double way. Alongside those promises of a return to the land which were doubtless seen as having been fulfilled, there are also preserved those announcements which could only have been perceived as unfulfilled, e.g., Davidic leadership, reunification of Israel with Judah, and a new temple of a very precise sort. The specific ways in which this difference

6

was dealt with—or even the bare fact of its being recognized—are of course nowhere indicated within the text.

Beyond doubt some process of reinterpretation was at work here. In fact, the mere reading of a prophetic word in a later context always presupposes a sort of reinterpretation. Von Rad has written of how OT texts seem peculiarly open to such reinterpretation (*Old Testament Theology*, II, 360-62), but something more concrete than that must be seen here. The rereading of a passage from Ezekiel in the post-restoration period would have demonstrated that such a passage was not just open to reinterpretation, but that the passage would be seen as both requiring it and even perhaps modelling it. Such a reinterpretation was occasionally provided by literary updating, but chiefly it seems to have been a matter of the response called forth from the worshiping community. That might take the form of what has been called a doxology of judgment affirming "God is righteous," a prayerful "Amen" longing for further fulfillment, the affirmation of continuity within community in some such words as "His fidelity is everlasting," or simply the silent celebration of the ongoing experience of being addressed.

Bibliography

J. Pedersen, *Israel, its Life and Culture* (tr. A. Fausbøll; London: Oxford, 1959) III-IV, 299; G. von Rad, *Old Testament Theology* (tr. D. M. G. Stalker; New York: Harper & Row, 1965) II, 360-62.; U. Cassuto, "The Arrangement of the Book of Ezekiel," *Biblical and Oriental Studies* (Jerusalem: Hebrew University, Magnes, 1973) 227-40.

Chapter 2

The Individual Units of Chapters 1–24: The Message of Judgment

THE COLLECTION AS A WHOLE, 1:1–24:27

Structure

Within the structure of the book as a whole the material in chs. 1–24 seems to constitute Ezekiel's collected message of judgment as it climaxed in the fall of Jerusalem. Approximately thirty-three units of this judgment message occur. They are 1:1–3:15; 3:16-21; 3:22-27; 4:1–5:17 (a subcollection containing 4:1-3; 4:4-8; 4:9-17; and 5:1-17); 6:1-14; 7:1-27; 8:1–11:25; 12:1-28 (a subcollection containing 12:1-16; 12:17-20; 12:21-25; and 12:26-28); 13:1-23 (a subcollection of 13:1-16 and 13:17-23); 14:1-11; 14:12-23; 15:1-8; 16:1-63; 17:1-24; 18:1-32; 19:1-14; 20:1-44; 21:1-37 (a subcollection of 21:1-12; 21:13-22; and 21:23-37); 22:1-16; 22:17-22; 22:23-31; 23:1-49; 24:1-14; and 24:15-27. See the treatments of individual units for a discussion of the problem of unit boundaries. Also discussed there is the problem of the presence of a message of consolation already within 1–24.

That a deliberate collecting process has taken place is indicated by several factors: (1) the existence of subcollections grouped according to content, genre, or catchword; (2) the chronological ordering of the dates in 1:1-2, 8:1, and 20:1; and (3) linkages established within the current written form of the text, e.g., 3:23 to 1:4-28, 10:22 to 1:4-28, and 24:27 to 3:25-27.

Genre

Since no single comprehensive structural arrangement can be seen to exist by which each unit's precise place would be determined, it is best to speak simply of a COLLECTION. As is apparent in the structure of the book as a whole, this collection is focused on judgment units.

Setting

Clearly the collecting of material is an editorial task carried on by some preservers of tradition, perhaps beginning with the prophet himself, and probably involving a continuing group of disciples. The book of Ezekiel provides no hard evidence for such a process, but it remains a necessary assumption. The existence of subcollections composed of units grouped according to similar subject matter (e.g., 13:1-16 and 13:17-23), genre (e.g., 4:1-3; 4:4-8; 4:9-17; and 5:1-17), or catchword (e.g., 21:1-12; 21:13-22; and 21:23-37) suggests that the collecting process may well have involved a series of stages and covered a fairly extensive period.

Finally, while the structure of the book as a whole requires the existence of a collection of judgment units *within* the whole book, there seems to be no evidence that any such collection ever existed independently before its incorporation into the book as a whole. Although Ezekiel may well have done other preaching and perhaps other prophesying that was not preserved, the present collection is the result of selection and has been shaped by such factors as the independent preservation history of each unit, the desire to underline fulfillment (as in 12:1-16), and a pattern of balance over against chs. 33–48.

Intention

The relationship between chs. 1–24 and 33–48 implies that the fulfilled message of judgment is to undergird and legitimate the further message of the prophet. If a collection like 1–24 existed independently, it would leave open the possibility of its lending authority to further oral preaching. If, as seems more likely, the overarching plan of the entire book is responsible for the grouping of chs. 1–24, then specifically the prophecies against the foreign nations and the message of consolation were being authorized.

A problem is posed by the reinterpretation that occurs within certain units. (See the treatments of individual units.) This reinterpretation can certainly have taken place at any time during the growth of the book, but it may in itself be a deliberate expression of the intention of an earlier stage in the collection process, by which certain units were made to reflect *in themselves* the complete message of the prophet by expanding a judgment unit to include a dimension of hope.

THE ACCOUNT OF THE CALL OF THE PROPHET, 1:1–3:15

Structure

I.	Superscription to the book and introduction to the throne vision	1:1-3
II.	Report of the vision of the glory of Yahweh as preliminary to the prophet's call	1:4-28a
III.	Report of call and commissioning	1:28b–3:11
IV.	Report of the prophet's return to his people	3:12-15

The section 1:1–3:15, although a single unit, is so large that it will prove best to analyze each part separately. It must be borne in mind that each of these parts is only a subunit, i.e., never existed independently.

Genre

The entire unit is a VOCATION ACCOUNT in autobiographical prose. The most significant earlier parallels are Isa 6:1-8 and Jer 1:4-10. The greater size of the Ezekiel account in every respect is important, for it leads to the recognition of the typically greater size of units in Ezekiel in contrast with all other prophets. In each case it will prove necessary to investigate how this larger extent of material functions.

Setting

This account never functioned in its final form as oral tradition, as the mixing of first and third persons in 1:1-3 shows. Similarly the ending in 3:15b now serves as only a partial ending, functioning also as a transition to what follows. The literary nature of the final form is further shown by the extremely complex and apparently extensive elaboration which the description of Yahweh's glory in 1:4-28 has received. Comparing this section with the similar vision of Yahweh's glory in ch. 10 demonstrates the mutual harmonizing tendencies which influenced both final texts, reflecting a literary editorial process. Despite Zimmerli's valiant attempt to reconstruct the original form (*Ezekiel 1,* 100-108), the few hints in such a direction have not proved adequate to unravel the abundant complexities, even mysteries, of the text as we now possess it. That, however, the unit did originally exist in a more temporary, perhaps oral and probably considerably smaller, form, is suggested by the persistent emphasis on failure as the virtually certain result of Ezekiel's preaching. This rather esoteric emphasis would seem to make most sense within the group of those who shared in this fate. The absence of any reference to a more successful effort after the vindication afforded by 587 B.C. points toward the conclusion that the unit received its decisive orientation quite early.

It is fully clear that this account does not describe a purely private revelation, i.e., one aimed solely at the prophet himself and preserved as a kind of excerpt from a diary. While such a private character might seem a possibility for 1:4-28a, the account would then be left without a purpose. The continuation in 1:28b–3:11 is in itself proclamation, and of a most combative sort at that. To sum up: the vision exists only for the calling of a messenger; the messenger exists only for his message; and the message exists only for the apparently vain attempt of God to get through to his hardened people.

Intention

The account aims to affirm Ezekiel's authority in spite of the failure of his ministry, at least in the period before 587 B.C. (cf., though, 33:30-33 as reflecting a more pervasive failure). As subsequent analysis will show, this authority centers on two aspects: (1) Ezekiel's role as messenger, and (2) the identity of Ezekiel's God as the Yahweh of the Jerusalem temple.

THE SUPERSCRIPTION TO THE BOOK AND INTRODUCTION TO THE THRONE VISION, 1:1-3

Structure (preliminarily we present only a list of elements)

Date: year, month, and day	1aα
Location: exile, river	1aβ
Event: heavens opening	1bα
Consequence: that visions are seen	1bβ
Date: day	2a
Date: year according to Jehoiachin's exile	2b
Prophetic word formula	3aα
Patronymic with occupation	3aβ
Location: Babylon, river	3aγ
Hand of Yahweh revelatory formula	3b

Several problems suggest that a fairly complicated literary history lies behind these verses. The double dating (v. 1aα and v. 2), the double specification of the location (v. 1aβ and v. 3aγ), and the awkward juxtaposition of first person in v. 1 and third person in v. 3 are the major indications that a blending of at least two kinds of introductory material has taken place here.

Genre

The present text constitutes a fusion of both the introduction to the vision of 1:1–3:15 (vv. 1-2; 3b) and the SUPERSCRIPTION to the book as a whole (v. 3a). Interestingly, both Hag 1:1 and Zech 1:1 are prophetic book superscriptions which similarly prefix a date to the PROPHETIC WORD FORMULA. This contrast to the pattern of using the bare word formula as an introduction (see Hos 1:1; Joel 1:1; Mic 1:1; Zeph 1:1; and Jer 1:1 in the LXX) raises questions about a possible historical linkage of the editing of Ezekiel with that of Haggai and Zechariah. The HAND OF YAHWEH REVELATORY FORMULA in v. 3b is clearly, as the parallels show (3:22; 8:1; 33:22; 37:1; 40:1), a part of the beginning of the actual VISION REPORT and has only secondarily been separated from it (see below).

Setting

The parallels in 8:1; 20:1; and 24:1 suggest that vv. 1-2 and 3b were originally the typical first person introduction to the larger unit 1:1–3:15. When 1:1–3:15 later acquired the position of the first unit in a collection of Ezekiel's messages, making necessary a mention of the prophet's name, v. 3a was inserted as a kind of introduction to the book as a whole, requiring that v. 3b be changed to the third person. The body of the unit in the following verses, however, remains in the unaltered first person. Verse 2 may be an explanatory gloss giving the date which was originally in v. 1 before being replaced by the now cryptic figure thirty. (For details see the commentaries.) In our calendar the date given in 1:1 would fall near the end of June 593 B.C. (Zimmerli, *Ezekiel 1,* 115 and Kutsch, 45-54).

Intention

From our modern perspective one could say that the dating of a prophet's material aims at making clear the historical context within which it is to be understood. But to see that is to see only half of what this text and similar historical superscriptions to prophetic books as units intend. Because the word of Yahweh through the prophet is viewed as a powerful and effective force directed by Yahweh into a series of specific situations, it is impossible to grasp the message apart from its moment. The aim of the Lord whose word the prophet speaks is— as the message itself attests (see 12:21-25)—to bring about the accomplishment of that very word. And that accomplishment happened in this particular world of dates and places. These dates and places are not recorded that listeners might better understand the personal history of the prophet. The overwhelming absence of biographical detail reveals that such a concern is foreign to the text. Instead, it is for the meaning of the message that the history is essential. Manifest in the increased frequency and specificity of dating is an increasingly broader context of political history in which the word of Jeremiah, Ezekiel, Haggai, and Zechariah is active.

Bibliography

E. Kutsch, *Die chronologischen Daten des Ezechielbuches* (OBO 62; Freiburg: Universitätsverlag, 1985) 45-54; B. Lang, *Ezechiel* (EF 153; Darmstadt: Wissenschaftliche Buchgesellschaft, 1981) 19-21.

THE REPORT OF THE VISION OF THE GLORY OF YAHWEH AS PRELIMINARY TO THE PROPHET'S CALL, 1:4-28a

Text

Manifold and serious difficulties exist in the present text, and no widely acceptable solution has been proposed. Here a minimum list of conjectural emendations is offered, aiming to make reasonable sense of the passage while preserving its distinctiveness. The first word of v. 11 (*ûpĕnêhem,* "and their faces") should be deleted. In v. 13a probably read *ûbĕtôk* ("and in the midst of") for *ûdĕmût* ("and the likeness of") and *mar'eh* ("there was an appearance") for *mar'êhem* ("their appearances"). At the end of v. 15 read *lĕ'arba'tān* ("to the four of them") for *lĕ'arba'at pānāyw* ("to the four of its faces"). At the beginning of v. 18 delete *wĕgabbêhen* ("and their rims"). In v. 20 delete *šāmmâ hārûaḥ lāleket* ("where the spirit would go") as a dittograph. No attempt has been made here to resolve the confusion in the gender of suffixes.

Structure

I. Introductory description	4
A. Report of seeing	4aα
B. Summary description of what was seen	4aβγδb

What Ezekiel saw was a mysterious figure seated on a chariot throne provided with wheels and supported by weird creatures. Strangely, the key element, the figure on the throne, receives the least attention in space allotted. Instead, in order of decreasing amount of words we encounter first the "living creatures" (ten verses), then the wheels (seven verses), then the platform (four verses), and finally the figure on the throne (three verses). The whole scene is presented in a first person framework (vv. 4a, 15a, 24a, and 27a), with the introductory "behold" common to visions and dreams in vv. 4a and 15b. Each of the three parts of the vision preliminary to the description of the throne concludes with a reference to the manner of movement: creatures (v. 12), wheels (vv. 17-21), platform (vv. 24b and 25b). Even the possibly secondary element of fire amidst the creatures in vv. 13-14 concludes with a description of movement in v. 14. Besides mobility, the account stresses radiance. The overall description in v. 4 features brightness, fire, and gleaming bronze, and each successive element has at or near its beginning a similar feature: burnished bronze in v. 7 for the creatures, chrysolite in v. 16 for the wheels, crystal in v. 22a for the platform, sapphire in v. 26 for the throne, and gleaming bronze and fire in v. 27 for the figure on the throne (not to mention the fire of vv. 13-14).

After the preliminary overall description as a storm in v. 4, the creatures are characterized as human in appearance in v. 5, with each of the two exceptions to this humanness (note "but" at the beginning of v. 6) being introduced with *lĕ'eḥāt* ("each"). The subsequent description in vv. 7-11 follows a simple bottom to top sequence. On the other hand, the sequence of the major elements of the whole vision starts with the middle level (creatures), drops to the wheels ("upon the earth beside

14

the living creatures" in v. 15), and then moves upward, first to the platform, and then to the throne and the figure above it. Presumably the order intends to lead up to a climax.

Several factors strongly suggest that a complex literary development underlies the entire description. Some harmonization between chs. 1 and 10 seems highly likely, but, puzzlingly, the harmonization remains incomplete. The vision in ch. 1 is identified with that of ch. 10 by 10:15, 20, and 22. But, since in ch. 10 the throne is supported by "cherubim," it is necessary for 10:15 and 20 expressly to identify cherubim with living creatures. Moreover, since in ch. 10 the first face of the creatures is that of a cherub, and the ox of ch. 1 is unmentioned, again 10:22 finds it necessary to assert the identity of the faces in the two visions.

Further evidences of literary complications include: (1) repetitions, such as v. 9b and v. 12b, v. 24b and v. 25b, and (2) blending of masculine and feminine suffixes in vv. 5-25, even within the same verse (v. 10).

Rather than attempt to reconstruct a hypothetical, logically and grammatically consistent original on the basis of these complexities, it seems better simply to affirm a complex textual and literary history, doubtless resulting in part from the complexities of the content.

Eichrodt seems correct when he says that the description is not "the result of a conscious and calculated piece of construction" (p. 56), but rather reflects how even visionary perception is automatically influenced by the heritage of the perceiver. Naturally, any attempt to verbalize this perception would be similarly influenced.

Genre

The material is presented in autobiographical prose as a VISION REPORT of the presence type. This genre develops smoothly into a VOCATION ACCOUNT, and, although the vision report of vv. 4-28a never existed independently, in view of the large size of the entire vision it is convenient to analyze it separately as a relatively complete episode within the vocation account.

This account is much longer than the familiar parallels in Isa 6:1-8 and Jer 1:4-10, a difference characteristic of most units in Ezekiel. The basic structure of the vocation account, which moves from seeing to hearing, is, however, consistent in all three cases, even though the visionary element in Jer 1:4-10 is minimal. Again, the Ezekiel account differs from the others in the abundance of general, rather typical, THEOPHANY-style detail, but is similar in its reticence actually to describe the appearance of God. The heavy stress on the throne aspect, especially its transcendent radiance, corresponds to that in apocalyptic visions (e.g., Dan 7:9-10; 1 Enoch 14:9-25; and Revelation 4). But these latter differ in that their intent is to stress stable and even static characteristics, while Ezekiel continually returns to an emphasis on mobility.

Setting

Although, as indicated, the account never existed as a fully independent unit, its relatively great length does provide some clues about its setting within the prophet's mental heritage. Despite the more general beginning flavor of a storm theophany and some points of contact with Sinai tradition (e.g., Exod 24:10, 17; 19:9, 16, 18-19), the dominant characteristics soon focus virtually exclusively on the learned tradition of the Jerusalem priesthood. The overall label "glory of the Lord" (v. 28a) has strong ties to temple-rooted traditions (Exod 29:43; 40:34; 1 Kgs 8:11; 2 Chr 7:1; Psalm 24). The presence of God linked to the ark with its cherubim, and the fire glowing within a cloud of incense are the most obvious connections to the temple, but the use of "chariot" to describe the cherubim in 1 Chr 28:18 and the lions, oxen, cherubim, and wheels of the bronze stands of 1 Kgs 7:27-37 reveal intriguing additional points of contact. The seraphim of Isaiah 6 (even though these had six wings instead of the four of Ezekiel 1), the animal decorations of Solomon's throne (1 Kgs 10:19-20), the angelic Cherubim and Ophannin (wheels) of 1 Enoch 61:10 and 71:7, and the four living creatures of Rev 4:6-8 also exemplify an ongoing stream of tradition.

Intention

Clearly, a basic purpose of the entire portrayal of ch. 1 is the attempt to synthesize via symbolism the heritage of God's universal sovereignty and dwelling in heaven with the localization of his presence in Jerusalem. This attempt was doubtless characteristic of much similar symbolism (see Ps 76:2, 8). The most noticeable connections here to heaven as God's abode are the sky-blue color beneath the throne as a natural link to the heavenly ocean (see Exod 24:10) and the elements of a storm theophany in vv. 4, 13, 24, and 28. Psalm 18:7-15 reflects elements of a similar blending.

More precisely, this particular vision as a part of a vocation account aims to assure the despairing prophet, and through him his fellow exiles, that Yahweh's presence is not confined to Jerusalem. That God's presence is not thus confined is a powerful way of preparing for the following message of God's continuing purpose with the exiles. Presenting the appearance of God's glory in Babylon as identical to that known in the Jerusalem temple stresses both a sovereignty which moves in universalistic directions and a purpose which transcends and even embraces the political tragedies of the exiles' past, and this emphasis, in fact, even lays the basis for affirming God's purpose in the tragic events to come.

The heaven-centered aspect of God's throne and the deliberate linking up by the word "platform" *(rāqîaʿ)* with Israel's creation traditions are two relatively clear ways in which the account aims at communicating to the exiles an assurance of the broadest possible dimensions of Yahweh's rule. Still, the description of the vision is not to be seen as deliberately shaped to convey an understandable or reproducible message. Instead, its very obscurities and inadequacies bear witness that it is only an impression-centered sketch of the incomprehensible. It presents not a deliberate program of purposeful communication so much as an experience of great impact. Selected features of that experience seem to have triggered analogies in the prophet's mind, but the confusing nature of the whole attests to its essential indescribability. That later editorial elaboration has on occasion shown the existence of a more speculative orientation does not alter this assessment, for whatever elaboration and harmonization have happened have done relatively little to make the whole rationally comprehensible.

Bibliography

O. Keel, *Jahwe-Visionen und Siegelkunst* (SBS 84–85; Stuttgart: Katholisches Bibelwerk, 1977) 125-272; A. Low, *Interpretive Problems in Ezekiel 1* (Diss., Dallas Theological Seminary, 1985); T. Mettinger, *The Dethronement of Sabaoth* (ConB 18; Lund: Gleerup, 1982) 97-115; E. Vogt, "Der Sinn des Wortes 'Augen' in Ez 1,18 und 10,12," *Bib* 59 (1978) 93-96; E. Vogt, "Die vier 'Gesichter' *(panîm)* der Keruben in Ez," *Bib* 60 (1979) 327-47; A. D. York, "Ezekiel 1: Inaugural and Restoration Visions," *VT* 27 (1977) 82-98.

THE REPORT OF CALL AND COMMISSIONING, 1:28b–3:11

Text

In 3:6 it is necessary to read simply *'im* ("if") rather than *'im-lō'* ("if not").

Structure

I. Transition to address by Yahweh	1:28b
A. Report of seeing	28bα
B. Reaction: prostration	28bβ
C. Report of hearing	28bγ
II. Series of addresses by Yahweh	2:1–3:11
A. First address	1-2
1. Report of speaking	1a
2. Address as son of man	1bα
3. Instruction to stand	1bβ
4. Announcement of coming address	1bγ
B. Consequence	2
1. Spirit entered	2aαβ
2. Stood me up	2aγ
3. Report of hearing	2b
C. Second address	3-5
1. Report of speaking	3aα
2. Address as son of man	3aβ
3. Announcement of sending	3aγ
4. Destination: rebellious Israel	3aδ
5. Characterization: always rebellious	3b
6. Further characterization: stubborn	4a
7. Direction to speak, using messenger formula	4b
8. Result	5
a. Condition: whether listen or not	5aα
b. Characterization: rebellious	5aβ
c. Consequence: recognition of prophet	5b
D. Third address	6-7
1. Address as son of man	6aα
2. Encouragement to fearlessness	6aβγ
3. Metaphorical description of hostility	6aδ

2) Analogy: harder than stone	9a
3) Encouragement to fearlessness	9bα
4) Characterization: rebellious	9bβ
L. Eighth address	10-11
1. Report of speaking	10a
2. Address as son of man	10bα
3. Direction to take all my words	10bβγ
4. Commissioning formula	11aαβ
5. Direction to speak using messenger formula	11aγ
6. Condition: whether listen or not	11b

Ezekiel's prophetic vocation as an experience of hearing flows directly out of his foregoing vision, but no actual linkage to the content of ch. 1 is made. Instead, after a brief transition (I), the prophet is informed of his task and its difficulty in a series of eight addresses (II). In contrast to both Isaiah 6 and Jeremiah 1, no opportunity is provided for any response or objection by the prophet. Instead, the symbolism of eating the scroll might indicate a total union of the prophet with his message. Such interruptions and intercessions as 4:14; 9:8; and 11:13 modify this impression only to a slight extent. That the series of addresses is occasionally interrupted by consequences in II.B, F, H, and J is less significant than might appear, for the content of these sections is—apart from II.F—of minimal importance.

As a whole this section is written in an elevated prose whose use of parallelism (e.g., 2:3-4, 6a, 6b; 3:1, 3a, 7b, 8, 9b, 11a) borders on poetry. Further, II.K constitutes a sort of large-scale parallel or recapitulation of II.C and D, resembling the relationship of Jer 1:17-19 to 1:4-10. The apparent repetition of 2:3-5a in 3:10-11 is actually a kind of summary conclusion in which the central aspects of the prophet's task are reviewed while at the same time his assignment to Israel is now made specific in the case of the exiles (Zimmerli, *Ezekiel 1*, 132).

Genre

Within the larger structure of the prophetic VOCATION ACCOUNT this section serves as a kind of COMMISSIONING OF A MESSENGER. Although the customary elements— PROPHETIC WORD FORMULA, COMMISSIONING FORMULA with "Go and speak" and the identification of the addressee, and MESSENGER FORMULA —are not all present in the simplicity with which they appear in Jer 2:1-2, their equivalents are present. In fact, one could label Ezek 1:28b–3:11 a highly elaborated commissioning in which the identification of the addressee is the major focus of the elaboration. This structure is clear in both 2:1-7 and 3:4-11, but the intervening section in 2:8–3:3 adds a kind of act or sign of ordination. Like Isa 6:6-7 and Jer 1:9, this act serves to complete the setting apart and equipping of God's spokesman. In 2:5b we encounter a modified RECOGNITION FORMULA (→ the discussion at 5:13).

Setting

As personal experiences of the prophet, this audition and the accompanying vision of the scroll would have served as psychological equipment for his subsequent

19

activity. The prominent role of the messenger formula and the mention of "prophet" in 2:5 imply a function of authorization for the use of this material by Ezekiel's disciples, and the whole polemic tenor of the section implies that both prophet and disciples would encounter widespread challenges to Ezekiel's prophetic authority. The dispute about being "sent" in Jeremiah 26 in contrast to the use of that word in 1:7 in Jeremiah's vocation account along with the strengthening of the prophet over against his opposition in 1:17-19 further underline the similarity between Jer 1:4-10 and Ezekiel's commissioning. The prominence assigned to the people's refusal to listen suggests that this element of response to a prophet has moved from being an experience to be recorded (as in Isa 28:12; 30:9 and 15) to a standard element in the concept of the prophetic office. The "did not listen" motif is prominent in both Jeremiah (3:25; 7:13; 9:12; 11:8; 16:12; 17:23; 18:10; 19:15; 22:5; 25:3, 4, and 7) and the closely related Deuteronomistic History (see especially 2 Kgs 17:14 and O. H. Steck's discussion of the *Prophetenaussage* or statement about prophets, 66-72). Since both of these bodies of tradition stem from a time close to that of Ezekiel, there seems to be good evidence that this picture of a prophet as destined for rejection because of Israel's refusal to listen had become a standard motif by the time Ezekiel's message was shaped for preservation.

Intention

Beyond the undergirding and authorizing role this section would have played for both prophet and disciples, it also aimed at a broader purpose. The ominous tone of the references to opposition, especially the repeated wordplay characterizing the house of Israel as a "house of rebelliousness," enables the whole section to serve as an anticipation of and foundation for the subsequent record of Ezekiel's ministry, at least through ch. 24.

The intent of the report of eating the scroll is a matter of some dispute. Eichrodt is surely right in detecting here, not "a theory of prophetic inspiration," but "an assurance that the message . . . is independent of his own subjective judgments, and is divine in origin" (p. 62). However, Eichrodt's view of the eating as "a proof of the obedience of the person who has been chosen" (ibid.) is unconvincing. Nevertheless, there may well be an additional aim of anticipating Ezekiel's high degree of bodily involvement in his message. That we could find here information about Ezekiel's personality, such as his fondness for the message of doom because of its sweet taste or either the inherent toughness or gentleness of his spirit, is to be rejected in view of the nonbiographical and stylized character of the account.

Bibliography

N. Habel, "The Form and Significance of the Call Narratives," *ZAW* 77 (1965) 297-323; B. O. Long, "Prophetic Authority as Social Reality," in *Canon and Authority* (ed. G. W. Coats and B. O. Long; Philadelphia: Fortress, 1977) 3-20; O. H. Steck, *Israel und das gewaltsame Geschick der Propheten* (WMANT 23; Neukirchen-Vluyn: Neukirchener, 1967) 66-72.

THE REPORT OF THE PROPHET'S RETURN
TO HIS PEOPLE, 3:12-15

Text

In v. 12 read *bĕrûm* ("when . . . rose up") for *bārûk* ("blessed be"). In v. 15 delete *hayyōšĕbîm 'el-nĕhar-kĕbār* ("who dwelt by the river Chebar") as the secondary part of a conflate reading (Greenberg, *Ezekiel 1–20*, 71).

Structure

I.	Report of the departure of the glory of the Lord	12-13
	A. The prophet raised up by the Spirit	12aα
	B. Report of hearing the glory rise from its place	12aβb
	C. Sound of wings and wheels	13
II.	Report of the prophet's return to the exiles	14-15
	A. Translocation by the Spirit	14a
	B. Feelings	14bα
	C. Reason: the Lord's hand	14bβ
	D. Arrival at the river Chebar	15a
	E. Sat there seven days	15b

In brief fashion the vision itself is brought to a conclusion (I), and the prophet returned to his people (II) for the beginning of his ministry. Section I serves as a transitional link to the preceding (see 1:24, 28), as does II.C (see 1:3b). Subsections II.D-E serve as transitional links to the following (see 3:16a).

Genre

These verses constitute the conclusion of the VISION REPORT of 1:1–3:15.

Setting

This section never had an independent existence, having had always the function of bringing the vision report to an end and providing, at the same time, a basis for further units about the prophet here introduced.

Intention

The rapidity of the vision's conclusion stands in such contrast to both the vision itself and the account of the prophet's call and commissioning that several important implications can be drawn from what is not said: (1) from the absence of any report about a destination of the glory of the Lord it can be surmised that we may well hear more about this startling manifestation of God's presence in something that follows; (2) that nothing beyond the cryptically brief v. 14b is said about the response of the prophet to the vision implies that the account has the absolute minimum of biographical concern; and (3) that no mention is made of how Ezekiel ap-

21

peared to his fellow exiles during his vision indicates that no argument was intended about any overt legitimation of this prophet based on ecstatic behavior. Finally, that the entire section ends with the prophet's sitting for seven days in presumed silence indicates that he both has grasped and is operating in accord with his commission as a prophet, that is, as one who brings a message only when he has been given one to speak, and that the prophet's experience was perceived by him as so far beyond any of his previous experience or learning that he was for a considerable time powerless to come to terms with it. It is likely, then, that something is being deliberately taught about the nature of prophetic consciousness.

THE COMMISSIONING OF A SENTINEL, A METAPHOR FOR PROPHETIC ACCOUNTABILITY, 3:16-21

Text

In v. 20 read *miṣṣidqātô* ("his righteous deed") as in 18:24 and 33:18 for *miṣṣidqô* ("his righteousness"). In v. 21 read *hizhartā* ("you warn") for *hizhartô* ("you warn him") and delete the second *ṣaddîq* ("a righteous man").

Structure

I. Time specification	16a
II. Prophetic word formula	16b
III. Instruction to Ezekiel: his role as a sentinel	17-21
A. Address as son of man	17aα
B. Appointment as sentinel for Israel	17aβ
C. Pattern of function	17b
1. Whenever you get a word	17bα
2. You give a warning	17bβ
D. Analysis of responsibility	18-21
1. First case: warning the wicked	18-19
a. First subcase: warning not given	18
1) When I condemn the wicked	18aα
2) But you do not warn him	18aβ
b. Consequences	18b
1) He dies in his own guilt	18bα
2) But you are held responsible	18bβ
c. Second subcase: warning given	19a
1) If you warn the wicked	19aα
2) But he does not repent	19aβ
d. Consequences	19b
1) He dies in his own guilt	19bα
2) But you have saved your life	19bβ
2. Second case: warning the righteous	20-21
a. First subcase: warning not given	20aαβ
1) If a righteous man sins	20aα
2) And I put a stumbling block before him	20aβ

b. Consequences	20aγb
1) He shall die	20aγ
2) Delayed presupposition: because you did not warn him	20bα
3) He dies in his own guilt	20bβ
4) His former righteous deeds will not save him	20bγ
5) But you will be held responsible	20bδ
c. Second subcase: warning given	21a
1) If you warn a righteous man not to sin	21aαβ
2) And he does not sin	21aγ
d. Consequences	21b
1) He shall live because he took warning	21bα
2) But you have saved your life	21bβ

This unit is related to the preceding vocation account both in its subject matter, the prophet's role as a bearer of responsibility, and in its addressee, the prophet himself. While the vast majority of the book's units are addressed to the prophet himself, virtually all are directed, in contrast to this passage, *through* the prophet to his people (see, however, 3:22-27). On the other hand, sections I and II function to mark off this unit as separate from what has preceded.

After the brief labeling of the prophet's role in subsection III.B and the brief formulation of what that role involves in III.C, the bulk of the unit is in the form of two theoretical cases according to the two possible audiences the sentinel prophet might have to warn, wicked in III.D.1 and righteous in III.D.2. Each of the two cases is then in turn subdivided according to whether the prophet does in fact give a warning, III.D.1.c-d and III.D.2.c-d, or fails to do so, III.D.1.a-b and III.D.2.a-b. Each of these four subdivisions concludes with the statement of the consequences for both the prophet and the individual he was to warn.

Genre

As indicated, a strong legal flavor pervades subsection III.D. A death SENTENCE appears in III.D.1.a.1); the death penalty is discussed in III.D.1.b.1)-2), III.D.2.b.1), and III.D.2.b.5); a BLOOD RESTRICTION FORMULA appears in III.D.1.b.1)-2) and III.D.1.d.1)-2), and a kind of verdict of "unaccountability" (STATEMENT OF ACQUITTAL) appears in III.D.1.d.2) and III.D.2.d.2). The use of future time and the lack of concreteness throughout this material make it plain that we are dealing with hypothetical cases, but the traditional character of much of the terminology makes it equally certain that this hypothetical elaboration is formulated in the manner of actual laws and legal procedures. In view of the prominence of the priests in both the preservation and the implementation of Israel's legal traditions, Ezekiel's familiarity with and fondness for this terminology are eminently understandable.

Setting

However, a glance at the way in which the material in vv. 18-21 also occurs in other locations in the book makes it doubtful that the underlying setting of this passage is to be found in legal procedures. Instead the passage is most likely a redactional blending of material from two other locations. In 3:20-21 we can observe how material originally at home in ch. 18 (vv. 24 and 28) is employed to elaborate 3:17-19, which were in turn originally at home in 33:7-9. Both chs. 18 and 33 are self-contained units, of which the verses utilized in 3:17-21 are only minor parts.

It appears, then, that the unit 3:16-21 is a redactional expansion of 1:1–3:15 based on preexisting material. Perhaps v. 16a, which is not taken from elsewhere, was the original beginning of a following unit, either of 3:22-27 (Zimmerli, *Ezekiel 1*, 142) or of 4:1-3 (Fohrer, 28)

Intention

An editor noticed that 33:7-9 was relevant to the prophet's vocation. Since the sequence of items in the vocation account in 1:1–3:15 could not be disrupted by inserting 33:7-9, it was affixed—in a form expanded by material from ch. 18—to the end of the vocation account before the real beginning of the prophet's activity (Zimmerli, *Ezekiel 1*, 144).

By this insertion the current form of the text asserts that Ezekiel's ministry was characterized throughout by the same kind of pastoral accountability. Inasmuch as the major amount of divine warning is issued in chs. 4–24 rather than in 33–48, the insertion makes a well-grounded point. As instances such as 14:1 and 20:1 demonstrate, Ezekiel's ministry was marked by contact with individuals and not just with kings or groups. In this unit the subjective aspect of his calling receives attention in a way that supplements the objective emphasis of 2:1–3:11. Whereas there the possibilities of fearfulness and rebelliousness are alluded to, here it is the possibility of neglect of duty which arises, and the subject is treated with blunt force. The life and death of Ezekiel's people are directly linked to the prophet's own fidelity to his office. However, standing as the unifying factor behind the entire vocation account and its expansion here is the "divine will to save life" (Zimmerli, *Ezekiel 1*, 145).

Bibliography

See on 33:1-9.

THE ANNOUNCEMENT OF EZEKIEL'S DUMBNESS, 3:22-27

Structure

I. Preparation for a word from God	22-24a
A. Hand of Yahweh revelatory formula	22a
B. Direction to go to the plain for communication	22b
C. Compliance	23aα
D. Presence of the glory of the Lord	23aβγ
1. Glory was standing there (with introductory "behold")	23aβ
2. Same glory as seen by Chebar	23aγ

24

	E. Reaction: fell on face	23b
	F. Empowerment for communication	24a
	1. Spirit entered	24aα
	2. Stood me up	24aβ
II.	Instruction: pattern of Ezekiel's dumbness	24b-27
	A. Direction to stay in your house	24b
	B. Announcement of restrained behavior	25-26
	1. Address as son of man	25aα
	2. Bound with cords so that you cannot go out	25aβγb
	3. Dumbness	26aαβ
	4. Unable to reprove	26aγ
	5. Characterization: rebellious house	26b
	C. Exception	27a
	1. Mouth to be opened when revelation received	27aα
	2. Direction to speak using messenger formula	27aβ
	D. Result: let the hearer decide	27b
	1. Let the hearer hear	27bα
	2. Let the refuser refuse	27bβ
	3. Characterization: rebellious house	27bγ

A strangely long amount of preliminary material (I) leads up to the instruction (II), which is the essential content of this unit. As it stands, the preliminary material describes a revelatory experience similar to that in 1:1–3:15, but occurring at a different location, possibly that of 37:1.

The instruction itself (II.A) directs Ezekiel to remain in his house, and then follows this with a twofold announcement: (1) he will be bound with cords so that he cannot go out (II.B.2), and (2) he will be made dumb by God (II.B.3-4). To explain how the prophet could function as a prophet in spite of this dumbness, II.C indicates that God will open his mouth when he gives him a message. The fate of that message will then be up to its audience (II.D), but the ominous tone of II.B.5 seems to set the scene for failure.

Unusually, the prophet is addressed as son of man not at the beginning of this unit, but only after the direction in II.B.1.

Genre

Verses 22-24a form a narrative setting for the instruction of vv. 24b-27. Verse 22a is the HAND OF YAHWEH REVELATORY FORMULA, which normally introduces a vision. Verse 23aα is an interconnecting identification of the vision of God seen here with that reported in 1:1–3:15 (see 8:4). Such interconnecting linkages probably are quite late, presupposing the collecting of the material about the prophet into some kind of larger unity, whether that of the book as a whole (Zimmerli, *Ezekiel 1,* 157f.), that of chs. 1–24, or that of some other preliminary collection.

It is noteworthy that the description of the prophet's reaction and his subsequent empowerment in vv. 23b-24a is virtually identical with the earlier account in 1:28bβ and 2:2a. In fact, it can be noted in summary how virtually every subunit in this text can be linked with some other passage in the book as its possible point of origin, thus suggesting that these verses are a kind of editorial collage:

v. 22a	is to be linked with 1:3b; 8:1b; 37:1aα; 40:1bβ
v. 22bα	occurs frequently
v. 22bβ	is to be linked with 37:1aβγ
v. 22bγ	is to be linked with 2:1bγ
v. 23aα	indicates compliance
v. 23aβ	is to be linked with 1:28aγ
v. 23aγ	establishes an interconnecting linkage
v. 23b	is to be linked with 1:28bβ
v. 24a	is to be linked with 2:2a
v. 24b	is implicit in 14:1; 20:1; 33:30-33
v. 25aα	occurs frequently
v. 25aβγb	explains the situation underlying 14:1; 20:1; 33:30-33
v. 26a	is to be linked with 24:27; 33:21f
v. 26b	is to be linked with 2:5aβ, 6bγ, 7b; 3:9bβ; 12:2aβ, 2bγ, 3bγ
v. 27aα	is to be linked with 24:27; 33:21f
v. 27aβ	is to be linked with 2:4b; 3:11aβγ
v. 27bαβ	is to be linked with 2:5aα, 7aβ; 3:11b
v. 27bβ	is to be linked with the same verses as v. 26b above

Setting

Redactional operations seem to underlie the construction of these verses. By "redactional" is meant here the total process of collecting and arranging the deposit of the prophet's ministry, not merely its final stage. Probably on the basis of 14:1; 20:1; and 33:30-33, vv. 24b-25 picture all of Ezekiel's ministry as taking place from his house as a result of constraint imposed on him in some way. Similarly, on the basis of the one instance of dumbness and its removal in 24:27 and 33:21-22, vv. 26-27 describe a similar process as characteristic of the prophet's entire ministry (Eichrodt, 76-78).

Intention

Once again, then, as was the case in 3:16-21, an editor seems to have noticed that the subsequent content of the material describing the ministry of Ezekiel had implications about the basic, overall nature of that ministry. These implications should appear in connection with the vocation account, but the structure of that account did not permit literary interruption. As a result, this largely artificial unit was created, employing standard formulas or items known from other contexts as preliminaries and constructing instruction from God out of the implications together with some additional, frequently occurring, formulas and familiar items. To what extent either or both of these statements (vv. 24b-25 and 26-27) describe the totality of the prophet's daily life and to what extent they are to be limited to his functioning as a prophet can only be a matter for speculation. It is highly doubtful that they enable the diagnosis of some ailment.

It should be pointed out that this passage is one of the most difficult in the entire book and that the proposal made here is highly speculative. (For other possibilities, see Zimmerli, *Ezekiel 1*, 157-61 and Greenberg, *Ezekiel 1–20*, 120-21.)

Bibliography

M. Greenberg, "On Ezekiel's Dumbness," *JBL* 77 (1958) 101-5; E. Vogt, "Die Lähmung und Stummheit des Propheten Ezechiels," in *Wort—Gebot—Glaube (Fest.* W. Eichrodt; ATANT 59; Zürich: Zwingli, 1970) 87-100; R. R. Wilson, "An Interpretation of Ezekiel's Dumbness," *VT* 22 (1972) 91-104.

A COLLECTION OF SYMBOLIC ACTIONS, 4:1–5:17

Text

In v. 4:4a it is likely one should read *wĕnāśā 'tā* ("and you shall bear") for *wĕśamtā* ("and you shall place"), accompanied by changing *'ālāyw* ("upon him") to *'ālêkā* ("upon you"). In v. 5:4b the context makes it probable to emend *mimmennû tēṣē'-'ēš* ("from it shall fire go forth") to *wĕ 'āmartā* ("and you shall say").

Structure

I. First symbolic action: a model of the siege	4:1-3
A. Address as son of man	1aα
B. Directions for the action	1aβ-3bβ
1. First phase: a brick	1aβ-2
a. Take a brick	1aβγ
b. Draw a city on it	1b
c. Lay siege to it	2
1) Establish a siege	2aα
2) Build a siege work	2aβ
3) Erect a ramp	2aγ
4) Make camps	2bα
5) Set up battering rams	2bβ
2. Second phase: an iron plate	3abβ
a. Take an iron plate	3aα
b. Make it an iron wall	3aβγ
c. Set your face against the city	3bα
d. Press the siege	3bβ
C. Label: a sign for Israel	3bγ
II. Second symbolic action: the prophet lying on his side	4-8
A. First phase: left side	4-5
1. Directions	4
a. Lie on your left side	4aα
b. Bear the guilt of Israel	4aβ
c. For the days you lie this way	4b
2. Explanation to the prophet: one day for each year of punishment, 390 days	5
B. Second phase: right side	6
1. Directions	6abα

The unit begins unusually, for it lacks a prophetic word formula, although 3:16 may originally have immediately preceded 4:1.

The series of four symbolic actions is clearly demarcated, each section beginning with *wĕ 'attâ* ("and you"): 4:1, 4, 9; 5:1. The verses 4:1, 9 and 5:1 show further similarities in that they continue with *qaḥ* ("take"), as does 4:3a, the beginning of a subphase of 4:1-3. Verses 4:1 and 5:1 have the additional similarity of containing the address as son of man. Necessarily 4:4, the beginning of section II, differs because in this action no object is to be handled.

Genre

Symbolic actions are frequent in many prophetic books. Ezekiel's are somewhat different for several reasons: (1) they generally appear in LITERARY COLLECTIONS, e.g., 4:1–5:17 and 12:1-20; (2) they normally contain no mention of being carried out (12:7 and 24:18 are exceptions), and thus cannot be uniformly or strictly designated as REPORT OF A SYMBOLIC ACTION; and (3) they often pose questions of feasibility (e.g., 5:2 directs an action to be taken by the prophet in and around Jerusalem).

In line with the tendency toward larger units in Ezekiel, some symbolic actions are elaborated so extensively in the sections in which interpretation appears that the boundary between symbolic action and literary elaboration in another genre is crossed over. The fourth action, 5:1-17, is a clear example of this, as is 37:15-28.

The standard structure of a REPORT OF A SYMBOLIC ACTION is threefold: (1) Yahweh's instruction to perform the action, (2) the report of the execution, and (3) a word of interpretation. In addition, a question by the audience is often present, asking why this action was performed. As mentioned, the second part is omitted—not at all an unusual situation—in each instance in this collection, and the third part differs here in that only in the elaborational complexity of 5:7-17 is interpretation aimed at the prophet's audience. The instances in 4:5, 6bβ, and 8 are explanations aimed at the prophet himself. However, in 4:13 and 16-17 we do find interpretation which, although spoken to the prophet, is clearly suited for proclamation to the people. Thus, to summarize, sections I and II are made up almost entirely of directions to the prophet; III contains some interpretation—albeit addressed to the prophet; and only IV contains (5:7-12, 14-17) interpretation specifically addressed to an audience.

In this audience-directed material the genre of REPORT OF A SYMBOLIC ACTION is completely abandoned in favor of other genres more frequently employed in Ezekiel's preaching. Ezekiel 5:7-10 constitutes a modified PROPHECY OF PUNISHMENT against the people. While the typical structure of this genre involves a reason linked by lākēn ("therefore") plus the MESSENGER FORMULA to an announcement of punishment, the later prophets employ both lākēn ("therefore") and the messenger formula more extensively. Here 5:7 prefixes both the "therefore" and the messenger formula to the reason for punishment as well as using them in v. 8 as the familiar connecting link to the announcement. The appending of a further reason to the end of the announcement of punishment in v. 9b is a common type of expansion. In v. 10 lākēn ("therefore") seems to serve simply as a resumptive link introducing further elaboration of the announcement of punishment.

The announcement itself is ordinarily subdivided into Yahweh's intervention (usually in first person) and results or consequences of that intervention (normally in second or third person). It should be noted that the term "intervention" has the weakness of implying that Yahweh's judgment involves his breaking into an otherwise independently functioning continuity. Such an implication is a modern orientation foreign to the OT, and so is not to be drawn from the use of the term "intervention" as a traditional label for a genre element.

In 5:14-15 and 16-17 there are two instances of a modified PROPHECY OF PUNISHMENT against the people in which only the announcement appears and not the reason. Such a modification is especially understandable and appropriate in a position like that near the end of ch. 5 for two reasons. (1) The central focus of all four of these symbolic acts in chs. 4–5 is on the fact of punishment and the shape it will take, rather than on the reasons for it. In other places, e.g., ch. 16, the prophet can choose imagery in which the close and direct connection between guilt and punishment is seen to flow immediately from the logic of a single legal pattern, but the four symbolic actions here are all devoid of any inherent connection to a preceding guilt. (2) In the course of the preceding interpretative material in 5:5-13, the essentials of the reasons for punishment have already been sketched. In v. 6 is mentioned Israel's rebellion in disobedience and in vv. 9b and 11a their defiling abominations. Thus vv. 14-15 and 16-17 can add further punishments without in any way appearing ungrounded. These factors probably explain why the compilers of the tradition chose to group all of the interpretative material at the end of the collection of symbolic actions.

In 5:11-13 there appears for the first time that genre, frequently employed in Ezekiel, to which Zimmerli has given the name PROPHETIC PROOF SAYING (*Ezekiel 1*, 38-39, and "The Word of Divine Self-Manifestation," 99-110). In its simplest form this genre consists of a PROPHETIC ANNOUNCEMENT OF PUNISHMENT connected with the RECOGNITION FORMULA. This is the two-part PROOF SAYING. However, a three-part PROOF SAYING frequently occurs in which the announcement of judgment is preceded by a motivation or reason. The genre markers usually employed for these elements are: ya'an ("because") to introduce the reason, lākēn ("therefore") to connect the reason to the announcement, and the preposition bĕ ("when") prefixed to an infinitive elaborating the recognition formula. Thus the proof saying can appear as just a standard PROPHECY OF PUNISHMENT to which a recognition formula has been appended. In 5:11aδ the reason for judgment has a prefixed *ya'an* ("because"), an announcement of punishment follows in vv. 11bα-13a, and the recognition formula appears in v. 13bα, enlarged to become also a CONCLUSION FORMULA FOR DIVINE SPEECH, which is in turn elaborated with an infinitive clause in v. 13bγ. A number of modifications appear as well: (1) several other formulas occur at the beginning in v. 11aαβγ; (2) both "therefore" and the messenger formula are omitted before the announcement of punishment, possibly because of the other formulas at the beginning; and (3) the announcement includes the "No PITY" FORMULA in v. 11bβγ. Also, v. 12a is formulated as consequence, while v. 12b returns to the first person intervention of v. 11b, and v. 13 switches to the third person for the people, including the recognition formula, in contrast to both preceding and following.

The RECOGNITION FORMULA mentioned above is an exceedingly important and especially characteristic part of the book of Ezekiel. It is, again, Zimmerli who has contributed most to the analysis ("Knowledge of God According to the Book of Ezekiel"). He points out how the recognition formula involves first a verbal element, "you will know that . . . ," which is rooted in the legal sphere of "proving and demonstrating" (Gen 42:34), and often employs an infinitive with the preposition *bě* ("when") to indicate how the proof or sign of truth was to be brought (Zimmerli, *Ezekiel 1*, 37). Second, the formula includes the object clause "that I am Yahweh." Here Zimmerli points to the SELF-INTRODUCTION FORMULA as the root, seeing how Yahweh is described as actualizing his freedom anew in an action of self-revelation, even when it is an earlier knowledge to which his people are recalled, so that we speak of "recognition." In all, the formula occurs seventy-two times in Ezekiel, fifty-four times by itself, and eighteen others in which additional elements are added (ibid., pp. 38-39).

Five additional formulas are encountered for the first time in this unit. In 5:8aγ the CHALLENGE TO A DUEL FORMULA is used, in 5:11aβ the OATH FORMULA, in 5:11a the PROPHETIC UTTERANCE FORMULA, in 5:11bβγ the "No PITY" FORMULA, and in 5:13bβ, 15bβ, and 17bβ the CONCLUSION FORMULA FOR DIVINE SPEECH. The challenge to a duel formula, *hiněnî 'ālayik* ("Behold, I am against you"), was originally set in the report of a duel (1 Sam 17:45-49). In prophetic usage it serves simply to introduce a prophetic announcement of punishment. It is especially common (fourteen out of twenty OT instances) in Ezekiel and is normally preceded by the messenger formula. The oath formula, *hay-'ānî* ("as I live"), is simply the necessary modification of the old formula "as Yahweh lives" (Judg 8:19) required by the fact that Yahweh himself is now the speaker. The prophetic utterance formula *ně'um yhwh* ("utterance of Yahweh"), though probably originally at home in the VISION REPORT of a seer, is by the time of Ezekiel simply a marker of divine speech, whether used at the beginning, middle, or end of a unit. The "No PITY" FORMULA ("your eye shall not spare and you shall show no pity") is at home in the legal sphere of crimes so serious that they require a drastic penalty. Because of the destructive influence of such crimes, e.g., apostasy in Deut 13:9 (*RSV* 8), the community is admonished to have "no pity," lest through well-intentioned clemency the very basis of the community's existence be undermined. In Ezekiel the formula's use undergoes a grotesque twist so that it is not the pity of the family and friends of the criminal which is prohibited in order to protect against yet more serious consequences, but instead it is God's own pity which he disavows in order to establish the finality of his verdict of punishment upon his people (7:4, 9; 8:18; 9:10). The conclusion formula for divine speech, "I have spoken," is used to mark the end of a section of divine speech. As the expanded version, which adds "and I will do it," indicates, this formula stresses how Yahweh's word itself has the power to bring about its own realization (Zimmerli, *Ezekiel 1*, 28f).

The piling up of these formulas in 5:5-17, the occasional switch in person (v. 13) or number (v. 6b), the appearance of standard expressions familiar from other contexts (reproach and wild beasts), and some repetitions within these verses themselves (unsheathing the sword in vv. 2 and 12, executing judgments in vv. 8 and 15) have led commentators to conclude, probably correctly, that this passage reflects a process of gradual editorial expansion.

Setting

Research in the last fifty years has greatly clarified the understanding of prophetic symbolic actions. (See H. W. Robinson, "Prophetic Symbolism"; G. Fohrer, "Die Gattung der Berichte über symbolische Handlungen der Propheten"; idem, *Die symbolische Handlungen der Propheten;* and G. von Rad, *Old Testament Theology*, II, 95-98.) Instead of seeing symbolic action as a pedagogical addendum to the spoken word, it has become clear that the action is itself a powerful word. Symbolic actions constitute a creatively forceful prefiguring of future events, so that the future event begins to happen in and is guaranteed by the symbolic action. For this reason such actions were viewed as drastically important by the prophet's contemporaries (see Jeremiah 28). While older prophetic symbolic actions were often quite simple, even though not necessarily transparent in meaning, e.g., 1 Kgs. 11:29-39; Jer 13:1-11; 19, Ezekiel's actions are generally more complex. In 4:1-3, 4-8 and 5:1-4 there is an almost allegorical aspect to the way each item in the action has a symbolic significance. In 4:9-12 there is again an abundance of detail, this time not so that each item has a separate dimension of significance, but so as to portray all the more graphically the single reality of a siege diet. That a prophet should respond in protest to the directions he receives from Yahweh and that he should be granted an amelioratory revision of these directions are both unique items in the history of this genre in the OT.

And yet, while the concern with possible defilement in the preparation of food reflects the presupposition that this act was to be performed exactly as commanded, the directions about the preceding action in 4:4-8 make it highly dubious that any such action could possibly have been carried out. Over a year's time spent lying on one side is surely incredible! This is all the more the case when one ponders how the baking of vv. 9-15 could have been carried out in this position. It appears that either briefer ways of indicating the passage of time were used, or, perhaps more likely, only some part of a day was spent lying on one side. On the other hand, possibly what the present text attests is simply a later, speculative elaboration of the action in v. 4 in which the non-specific "number of days" was subsequently reinterpreted in a specifically symbolic, numerical way.

The prophecy of punishment comes out of the setting of oral preaching, especially as implied by the messenger formula. Still, the wording of both the reason for punishment and its announcement may and often does reflect a familiarity with and a borrowing from many other settings. The crime and punishment pattern of case law is one obvious and frequent possibility, but in an overall way the connection between reason and punishment has a much broader significance. This will be examined as the intention of a prophetic proof saying is treated below, for this latter genre is largely a specialized modification of the more general prophecy of punishment.

The many different formulas employed by the prophet, such as especially the challenge to a duel and "no pity" formulas, undoubtedly reflect, as pointed out above, distinctive sociological settings of their own. However, in their context in Ezekiel's preaching these formulas have been so totally removed from their original settings that those settings now serve only to provide a dimension of literary color to what the prophet says.

For several reasons it may be possible to make some conjectures even about the chronological setting of this collection. Naturally, it would seem that the actions in 4:1-3 and 9-17 must have been performed during the siege of Jerusalem, and much of the material in ch. 5 would similarly seem to reflect a time when the destruction of 587 B.C. was still only an ominous possibility. In addition, however, Zimmerli has made a proposal about 4:4-8 which may shed some light on the dating of the latter stages of the tradition-process which led to the book's present form. As do others, Zimmerli finds the reference to a parallel between Judah and Israel (in the sense of the Northern Kingdom) to be puzzlingly inappropriate. He conjectures that in the original form of this section the 390 days/years for the house of Israel referred to all Israel and dealt with the past guilt ('āwōn means both guilt and punishment) preceding 587 B.C. Only in the case of the 40 days/years is the reference to future punishment, and here Judah alone is appropriate. The chronological implication of his conjecture becomes apparent when he points out how 390 years plus 40 produces the same total of 430 years, which priestly tradition in Exod 12:40-41 had for the length of the sojourn in Egypt. This parallel would be particularly appropriate, for, as Ezek 20:35 shows, the prophet and his followers looked for a new exodus at the end of this sojourn/exile. Even the expression "wilderness of nations" in 20:35 shows the deliberate attempt to parallel the "wilderness of Egypt" in earlier tradition. Thus, in order for the number 40 to have any sense as an expectation for the duration of the exile, this material would have to have originated prior to 40 years after 587, i.e., 547 B.C. (Zimmerli, *Ezekiel 1*, 166-68).

Intention

A key element of these four symbolic actions, which can lead to a grasp of their essential message, is their detailed vividness. The meticulous way in which the account presents the minute elements of these actions fits well with the overall role of symbolic actions. Their stress is on power, not on clarification by illustration. In a way, they closely resemble magic, in that these deeds prefigure events with such inherent power that the coming events are actually herewith set into motion. And yet they differ from magical acts in one crucial aspect. It is neither in the scrupulously exact details nor in the authority and skill of the performer that their future-determining power is rooted. Instead, it is solely as the announcement of Yahweh's all-powerful will that these symbolic actions function. These words, like the rest of the prophet's proclamation, go far beyond any mere threatening of what they portray. Again, they simply announce in utter finality that future which the Lord of history has already determined. Thus, unlike Jeremiah, they see no possibility of "surrender and live" as an alternative to destruction (cf. Jer 38:17-28). That would reflect an open future, and these actions portray a closed and finally decided issue. Their goal is not a repentance that could still change things. The only repentance they seek is that which acknowledges guilt and accepts punishment.

That too is a kind of repentance, but is so powerless that it must have seemed akin to despair. At any rate, Ezekiel's audience was not willing to accept any such finality. Their confidence in their God is amazing—amazingly presumptuous and blindly false in Ezekiel's judgment. Other prophets proclaimed in this frightening moment a message of hope (cf. 13:1-16), and perhaps people even sat before Ezekiel expecting promises of Jerusalem's deliverance. Instead they heard a preaching which could only be perceived as the voiding of Yahweh's election of Jerusalem. On what basis could such an impossible view be set forth, above all in the name of Yahweh, the God who had promised through Isaiah that he himself would protect his Zion? So far only hints implicit in such terms as rebellion and wrath point to those aspects of Yahweh's purpose, which, according to Ezekiel, seem to rank above the promises of election. Clearly this is a theme to which the prophet must return. All that can be certain so far is that there is reflected in these symbolic actions a larger view—one which is capable of incorporating even such finality as Jerusalem's end within an overarching perspective, one that would include the extermination of a whole generation, like the forty years of earlier wandering, and then seem to imply the impossible possibility of a future even beyond the nation's destruction. But as yet this future is drastically hidden behind years of punishment.

A particularly intriguing feature of these symbolic actions is the way the prophet himself is physically involved in them. In the first action, in which the prophet behind an "iron wall" is ordered to "press the siege" against the city, Ezekiel's role might seem to be that of representing the attacking enemy, but later messages will show how it is really Yahweh whom the prophet represents in this respect, and that it is Yahweh who indeed is the attacking enemy. But for now it is the representational aspect of Ezekiel's role in the last three actions that is of concern. Once again in the second action 4:7 flashes a brief glimpse of the prophet as attacker, but for the remaining verses the prophet appears as bearer of guilt/punishment, even in a physical sense. In the final two actions the prophet's person is drawn even more forcefully into his message. The siege diet and the shaved head portray a prophet identified with his people to the point of literally embodying them in his distress. To draw a connection between this representative suffering and the bearing of guilt/punishment raises searching questions. The usage of *nāśā' 'āwōn* ("bear guilt") in Lev 10:17 and 16:22 shows that a substitutionary feature is in the forefront of priestly tradition. The background of Jeremiah's sufferings as the central focus of much of his book and the later strong similarity of the suffering servant role in Isaiah 53 reveal how an ongoing tradition is at work here. This will turn out to be only one of several instances in which Deutero-Isaiah seems manifestly to pick up and develop motifs inherited from Ezekiel.

One feature already encountered in chs. 1–3 reappears even more strongly in 4–5, the lack of any biographical concern. The prophet's reactions and feelings as well as the response he encountered are almost totally passed over. The account displays a certain coldness in its objectivity. Not a whisper of the emotional impact of all this on Ezekiel is audible, except in 4:14, where the possibility of ritual defilement provokes his outcry. Where are his anger and grief over the brutal suffering of his people which he portrays? They remain totally hidden behind the curtain of the account's objectivity. Just possibly the divine concession in 4:14 may reflect a faint flicker of God's mercy, but then the account does not permit the prophet even the opportunity of a "Thank you," and the cool curtain descends again. Is it just a modern, romantic fascination with the biographical which misses something here, or would an ancient audience already have found this silence about emotions disturbing?

Once the interpretative material in 5:5-17 is inspected, the aspect of emotionality is no longer missing, but now God's emotions surface. He challenges to a duel (v. 8); his personal involvement is stressed ("even I" in v. 8); the horror of cannibalism is announced as "what I have never yet done" and what I "never will do again" (vv. 9-10); pity is abolished (v. 11); and "anger" and "fury" to "satisfy myself" and "my jealousy" and even a flavor of gloating over the reproach to come appear (vv. 13-15). Here the cold objectivity is replaced with a hot-blooded proclamation of wrath rooted in sovereign jealousy. This too is an aspect which will surface even more prominently later (chs. 16 and 23).

One final part of the text's intentionality becomes apparent in the concern for the logical tie between guilt and punishment which characterizes the prophecy of punishment and especially its modification in the prophetic proof saying. The prominence of "therefore" and the "they shall know" of the recognition formula, particularly in its elaborated form (v. 13), reveal that this is a basic element of the prophetic heritage in which Ezekiel stands. Much of the fondness for legal genres on the part of the prophets can be understood only out of this concern that the objective guilt of their people should also become subjective, i.e., understood and accepted. And yet this tendency to trace the way the punishment fits the crime in a kind of divine *lex talionis* also reveals a concern at home in an entirely different kind of heritage. It is a wisdom concern to trace the order in events. Perhaps here, then, wisdom and prophecy have their closest point of contact.

Bibliography

G. Fohrer, "Die Gattung der Berichte über symbolische Handlungen der Propheten," *ZAW* 64 (1952) 101-20; idem, *Die symbolischen Handlungen der Propheten* (2nd ed.; ATANT 54; Zürich: Zwingli, 1968); G. von Rad, *Old Testament Theology* (tr. D. M. G. Stalker; New York: Harper and Row, 1965) II, 95-98; H. W. Robinson, "Prophetic Symbolism," in *Old Testament Essays* (London: Griffin, 1927) 1-17; W. Zimmerli, "Knowledge of God According to the Book of Ezekiel," in *I Am Yahweh* (tr. D. W. Stott; Atlanta: Knox, 1982) 29-98; idem, "The Word of Divine Self-Manifestation (Proof Saying), A Prophetic Genre," in *I Am Yahweh* (tr. D. W. Stott; Atlanta: Knox, 1982) 99-110.

TWO PROPHETIC PROOF SAYINGS INTRODUCED AS EXPRESSIVE ACTIONS, 6:1-14

Text

In v. 14 one should replace *mimmidbar diblātâ* ("from the wilderness of Dib-la[tha]") with *mēhammidbār riblātâ* ("from the wilderness to Riblah").

Structure

I. Prophetic word formula   1
II. Against the mountains of Israel   2-10
  A. Preliminaries   2-3bβ
    1. Address as son of man   2aα
    2. Directions for an expressive action   2aβb
      a. Hostile orientation formula against the
        mountains of Israel   2aβ
      b. Prophesy   2b
    3. Use the call to attention formula   3a
    4. Messenger formula   3bα
    5. Addressee: mountains and valleys   3bβ
  B. Two-part prophetic proof saying (2 mp)   3bγδ-7b
    1. Announcement of punishment   3bγδ-7a
      a. Summary   3bγδ-4a
        1) Intervention: I will destroy the high places
          with a sword   3bγδ
        2) Result: altars desolate and broken   4a
      b. Details   4b-7a
        1) Intervention   4b-5b
          a) I will put slain before the idols   4b
          b) I will put bodies before the idols
            (3 mp)   5a
          c) I will scatter bones around the altars   5b
        2) Results: doom for   6-7a
          a) Cities   6aα
          b) High places   6aβ
          c) Altars   6bα
          d) Idols   6bβ
          e) Incense altars   6bγ
          f) Works   6bδ
          g) Slain in your midst   7a
    2. Recognition formula (2 mp)   7b
  C. Elaboration in the form of a two-part
    prophetic proof saying   8-10
    1. Announcement of punishment   8-9
      a. Intervention: I will leave a remnant   8
      b. Result: escapees will remember and loathe
        themselves (3 mp)   9

Each of the two basic sections of ch. 6 (II and III) begins with an expressive action (vv. 2 and 11a), but the continuing development of both passages is shaped not by these actions, which are henceforth ignored, but by the familiar pattern of a two-part prophetic proof saying. In turn each of these two-part proof sayings is elaborated by a further two-part proof saying (II.C and III.D). New in this chapter over against the preceding proof sayings is the employment of a summary-and-then-details pattern in II.B.1 and III.C.1.a. The latter instance is especially clear, v. 11b listing sword, famine, and pestilence, and v. 12a supplying further details by connecting the "far off" with pestilence, the "near" with the sword, and the "survivors" with famine.

The structure of the chapter's development leaves many uncertainties. The figure of the "mountains of Israel" is addressed in vv. 3-5, but at v. 5b the addressee becomes the people. Only in v. 13 does the imagery of the mountains return, but no longer as addressee. The logic of the personal suffixes is also complex. Verse 5a interrupts an otherwise consistent 2 mp context and may be a late gloss. It is not attested in the LXX. Verses 8-10 deal with a 3 mp subject, but since future refugees are in mind, this still reflects a certain consistency. Verses 11-14 are all in the 3 mp, referring to the house of Israel, except for the 2 mp recognition formula in v. 13aα.

Since all those mentioned in vv. 11-14 die, it may be that this 2 mp has in mind Ezekiel's exilic audience, which alone is in a position to learn from the death of the Palestinians. Thus, apart from v. 5a there is a reasonable consistency.

Genre

The presence of the PROPHETIC WORD FORMULA in 6:1 and again in 7:1 but not in 6:11 reveals that the two REPORTS OF EXPRESSIVE ACTIONS and resulting PROPHETIC PROOF SAYINGS in ch. 6 have been regarded as a single unit by those responsible for the collection of chs. 1–24. In fact, the two have several similarities, as pointed out in the structural analysis. Still, they were originally two separate units, each one demonstrating the standard elements of a two-part proof saying, the announcement (II.B.1 and III.C.1) and the recognition formula (II.B.2 and III.C.2). In the first case, however, both the summary section of the announcement (vv. 3bγδ-4a) and the details section (vv. 4b-7a) break down clearly into the typical sequence of intervention and results. In vv. 11aδ-12 on the other hand, the results section precedes the intervention (v. 12b), and only the results section is broken down into summary-and-then-details. Because the word *'āḥ* ("Alas!," v. 11) is similar in import to the word *hôy* ("woe"), one could speak of vv. 11-14 as a rough equivalent to a WOE ORACLE, but this would be only a slight modification and would not really alter the section's basic shape as a proof saying.

The two elaborative portions (vv. 8-10 and 14) are also shaped as two-part proof sayings, standard in sequence in the first case (announcement—broken down into intervention and results—and recognition formula), apart from an expansion at the end in v. 10b which could be labelled an extended CONCLUSION FORMULA FOR DIVINE SPEECH. In the second case (v. 14) the announcement is confined to intervention only, v. 14a using heavily stereotypical language, as 35:3 shows.

Two formulas appear in ch. 6 for the first time, the HOSTILE ORIENTATION FORMULA in v. 2aβ and the CALL TO ATTENTION FORMULA in v. 3a. The former occurs nine times in Ezekiel and has faded from its original setting to be little more than a figure of speech (see Setting). The second formula is simply a natural development from ordinary conversation patterns and is common in both prophetic and nonprophetic material.

The phrase "mountains of Israel," although not a true formula, is a familiar designation for the land in Ezekiel (seventeen times), and in spite of the fact that it is used for the land as a whole and not just its mountainous areas, it does carry a particular flavor of illegitimate worship. Ezekiel 18:6 shows how standard this implication is. The idea of bringing about the defilement of illegitimate sanctuaries by the use of corpses is both a natural perspective for a priest in speaking about war and an effective *lex talionis* punishment for a fertility cult where the life-force was worshipped.

Setting

Expressive actions seem to be rather closely related to symbolic actions, for each adds power and emphasis to the prophetic word. The expressive actions appear, however, decidedly less powerful, perhaps having faded even further from an original background in magic. Setting one's face against an addressee might originally, as the instance of Balaam shows, have been a literal necessity for the delivery of a destructive word, but in Ezekiel it has become simply a formula (see 13:17; 21:2, 7; 25:2; 28:21; 29:2; 35:2; 38:2). Stamping one's foot, as 25:6 shows, probably functioned to "make a misfortune firm and irrevocable, and even increase its power" (Eichrodt, 97). In the case of both actions, as frequently, no report of compliance is recorded.

It is difficult to locate this material chronologically with any precision, but it seems likely that vv. 8-10 are an updating of an otherwise pre-587 B.C. message to fit an exilic scene. For an analysis that concludes for a very late date for this chapter, in the time of the Chronicler, see H. Simian. Of course, the choice of the name Riblah in v. 14 was doubtless motivated by the events recorded in 2 Kgs 25:6f. and 20f., being comparable to such modern sites as My Lai and Buchenwald, but this is already an elaborative verse, which could have come from almost any period of the developing tradition.

Intention

Even though the reformation of 621 B.C. may have eliminated much of the worship at local shrines, Ezekiel's approach to Israel's guilt is a standard one (see chs. 16, 20, and 23) which is not concerned with the details of fluctuating episodes. His analysis of the consistent guilt of his people is borne out by the account of Jeremiah 44. To a considerable extent the worship at the Palestinian hill shrines was intended for Yahweh, but prophetic tradition since the days of Elijah viewed the syncretistic worship, in which Yahweh was venerated with Baal rites, as apostasy. That for farmers fertility of field, flock, and family was indispensable is a commonplace, but it is just here that one of the unique dimensions of Yahwism surfaces most strikingly. The heritage of both the First Commandment and the prohibition of images was squarely against viewing the life-force as revelatory. With highest irony Ezekiel brands the shrines where life was celebrated as doomed to death. These places where holiness was supposed to center are destined for the severest form of ritual defilement, bones of corpses. For Ezekiel the true locus of sacrality is not between one's legs, but between the people and Yahweh and in the relationship that the covenant law called for between the members of the people. In line with the approximately contemporary tradition of the Holiness Code, true holiness is located in fidelity to the one who says "I am Yahweh."

Worship on the mountains persisted and triumphed for so much of Israel's history because it was shaped by the people's natural desires. Ezekiel scoffs at any diminishing of Yahweh's exclusive claim and views syncretistic rites as pandering to the people's wanton inclination. To combat this impulse toward apostasy Ezekiel uses coarse language, his word for "idols" probably being equivalent to terminology normally at home on the walls of public toilets.

That land, people, and religion are linked together by bonds at the deepest level is in no way ignored or denied in this scornful rejection of fertility shrines. With an approach to the unified character of the Palestinian ecosystem that seems almost modern, the prophet singles out the place of misuse and misunderstanding of agricultural blessings as the precise place where judgment and disaster will come. But for him this is not just an ironic natural order, it is the direct result of

Yahweh's fury, which in the violence of sword, famine, and pestilence brings doom upon his faithless people and their land. Even then God's purpose is affirmed to extend beyond doom in a bitter kind of repentance to which wandering exiles will come as they remember their God and loathe themselves for their evil folly.

Bibliography

H. Simian, *Die theologische Nachgeschichte der Prophetie Ezechiels* (FB 14; Würzburg: Echter Verlag, 1974).

THREE PROPHETIC PROOF SAYINGS ABOUT THE END, 7:1-27

Text

The text of ch. 7 is so difficult that every analysis must confess to extreme hesitancy. The problem encompasses untranslatable words, bewildering repetition, obscure allusions, and confusing organization. Already the LXX struggled helplessly with these problems, and neither its attempts nor recent proposals have succeeded in providing a secure basis for the reconstruction of the text.

Structure

I. Prophetic word formula	1
II. First two-part prophetic proof saying	2-4
A. Preliminaries	2aαβγ
1. Address as son of man	2aα
2. Messenger formula	2aβ
3. Addressee: land of Israel	2aγ
B. Announcement of punishment	2aδ-4bβ
1. Impersonal description: end has come	2aδb-3aα
2. Intervention	3aβγb
a. Wrath	3aβ
b. Judgment according to your ways	3aγ
c. Your abominations put on you	3b
3. "No pity" formula elaborated with recapitulation	4abαβ
a. "No pity" formula	4a
b. Intervention: requital formula	4bα
c. Results: your abominations	4bβ
C. Recognition formula (2 mp)	4bγ
III. Second two-part prophetic proof saying	5-9
A. Resumptive messenger formula	5a
B. Announcement of punishment	5b-9bβ
1. Impersonal description	5b-7
a. Disaster has come	5b
b. End has come	6

e) Prince	27aβ
f) People of the land	27aγ
4. Intervention: judgment according to ways	27bαβ
B. Recognition formula (3cp)	27bγ

Although textual problems make all judgments here tentative, sections II and III are so closely alike that they must be assumed to be some kind of doublets, though whether the product of the prophet's repeated return to this theme or of confused editorial preservation must remain undecided. Section IV is especially difficult in almost every regard. Its lengthy content reveals no clear structure or line of development. Instead it seems to ramble puzzlingly with no detectable continuity.

Genre

The chapter is plainly intended by the collectors of 1–24 to constitute a unit. The beginning with the PROPHETIC WORD FORMULA and the complete break between the ending and the start of the large vision complex of chs. 8–11 make this beyond dispute. In spite of the attempt of *BHS* to arrange the text as poetry, it seems better to regard it as elevated prose, characterized by occasional parallelism, but not by any consistency in either meter or parallelism.

The presence of the RECOGNITION FORMULA as an apparent ending in vv. 4 and 9 as well as in v. 27 implies that the chapter is a LITERARY COLLECTION of three PROPHETIC PROOF SAYINGS. That the content of II.B, III.B, and IV.A deals with the description of punishment to come supports this analysis, but the form of these three large sections is by no means simple or familiar. Instead of the typical pattern of PROPHETIC ANNOUNCEMENT OF PUNISHMENT (Yahweh's personal intervention followed by the results of that intervention), each of these sections is cast initially in an impersonal form, with no speaker identified and no audience indicated. While both II.B and III.B do soon turn to personal elements by employing in each case sections of intervention—the "NO PITY" FORMULA, and the REQUITAL FORMULA ("your ways I will put on your head") in vv. 4 and 9 with its stress on the fitting character of punishment—IV.A continues at great length in impersonal formulations. In fact, the few personal elements in IV.A.2 seem to interrupt whatever context is traceable, and also blend together, unusually for Ezekiel, both intervention and results in almost every verse. (The results appear in vv. 21b, 22aβb, 24aβ, and 24bβ.) The presence of occasional personal touches in all three impersonal sections ("upon you" in II.B.1, "against you" and "to you" in III.B.1, and "my wrath" and "the wrath of Yahweh" in IV.A.1.b) is more confusing than helpful, and these touches may perhaps be best described as transitional elements that connect the impersonal sections with the sections of intervention that follow in each case. That the recognition formula in both II.C and III.C is in the plural, while the preceding text has been in each case in 2 fs (see "land of Israel" in v. 2), is a further minor inconsistency. The shift to the plural is perhaps aimed at the surviving exiles. The overall impression of confusion is unavoidable, and no familiar pattern of organization seems discernible.

Only occasionally are there glimpses of a recognizable order, as in the listing in vv. 26b-27a of those leaders whose help will be of no avail. A number of aspects reflect the customary flavor of the "day of the Lord" tradition, even though that exact label occurs only in the LXX text of v. 10a. Like Isa 2:9-22 and Zephaniah 1, the passage starts with a concrete historical situation as its background, but then goes on to include features of a transcendent sort, like "the four corners of the earth" ("land" in *RSV* is an unlikely translation in view of the Akkadian parallel idiom) in v. 2. Other items typical of the day of the Lord tradition which Zimmerli notes (*Ezekiel 1*, 201f.) are standard words (end, day, wrath, has come, and near) and the use of an extreme contrast, like the light-darkness of Amos 5:20, in the picture of joyful shouting over against tumult in v. 7. To these could be added the battle panic imagery of vv. 14 and 17. In spite of the presence of this traditional day of the Lord language and the fondness for the word "end" in a central position, there is a distinct difference from the apocalyptic material of Daniel 8–12. There "end" has become "an apocalyptic category of time," whereas here it is still essentially a term of "threatening content" in the tradition of Amos 8:1f. (Zimmerli, *Ezekiel 1*, 204).

"Land of Israel" is a designation which occurs seventeen times in Ezekiel and nowhere else. It is certainly a standard expression, somewhat on the order of the Deuteronomic "land which the Lord your God gives you," even though it is not quite extensive enough to be designated a formula.

Setting

Once again this material seems to reflect a pre-587 B.C. oral proclamation. In view of the cryptic character of the term "my precious" in v. 22 it is unclear whether the city or the temple was meant, but in any case Ezekiel dealt extensively with both (see chs. 8–11 and 22:1-16). On the basis of 12:21-28 it can be concluded that in the time before 587 the prophet encountered great difficulty in convincing his hearers that the time of the fulfillment of his message of doom was near and would no longer be delayed. Most likely ch. 7 reflects further attempts on his part to overcome that resistance.

The apparently extensive literary elaboration, especially in vv. 10-27, suggests a period of complicated transmission. Still, some basic flaws in current research must be pointed out in this connection. Modern study is so comfortably accustomed to viewing the prophet as one who accuses a particular audience of specific transgressions and then goes on to announce a punishment coming within a limited historical horizon that it becomes difficult to deal with material not of this mold, especially a passage like this, which is largely impersonal and borders on the universal. The first reaction is either to emend a text until it is more typical or else to shove it aside as secondary and bordering on apocalyptic. Surely the developments in ancient tradition were more gradual, more complex, and less monolithic than this! The long-standing difficulty in packaging the day of the Lord material within a single neat framework of development should suggest caution.

Intention

The very aspect of impersonality, which at first glance seems weak because of its lack of specificity, turns out to have a peculiarly ominous power of its own.

The simple impersonality of such an expression as "the end has come" increases the aspect of finality. It is like the impersonal ringing of a bell or striking of a clock, which moves past all the fervor of every personal dialogue to the starkly neutral announcement: "Time's up!" Later apocalyptic does not have a monopoly on this message. Instead the proclamation of finality begins with this stark simplicity and then goes on to enhance its impact by adding new dimensions of personal color and specificity, this time of a transcendent sort. Each case invokes the horror of finality, and that is so great a horror that its communication requires every approach available. As will be shown later (Intention in 21:1-12), every attempt to minimize the dimension of finality or divine rejection or failure in the message of Ezekiel—or any prophet—by enclosing that message within a framework of a logically comprehensible, ongoing continuity is to be rejected in principle. The prophets were met with shock, puzzlement, anger, and violence. It is doubtful in the extreme that anyone ever sat down with Ezekiel to discuss how his message of "an end" was to be integrated within the broader perspective of an ongoing future. His message—and not just ch. 7—was far too clear for that!

Instead, his message, if accepted at all, must have led to blank despair. He aimed precisely at crumbling every previous ground for stability. In v. 10 he touches on the impersonal heritage of the automatic link between deed and consequence with the ripening of the blossom of injustice and violence into the flower of doom. Here indeed is a heritage of order, but it leads to no stability. And this chapter goes on to add an aspect of personal wrath to this inexorably impersonal finality. That divine wrath wipes aside every element of humanly created stability. The whole workaday world of business with its familiar structure of buying and selling is set aside with a solemn "No more!" (vv. 12-13). The false gods who can be so neatly and easily manipulated, for they are nothing more than the personification of such orders as the principles of sexuality or the rhythm of the stars, are exposed as useless. When the end comes they will be cast aside as useless encumbrances and evidences of shameful rebellion. Even all those trusted spheres of authority (prophets, priests, and the rest), whose traditions and charismata had given security for centuries, were now—for all their diversity—to be seen as united in impotence. These authorities had served as instruments through whom the guiding will of Yahweh had been mediated to his people. Now they stood before an immediate encounter with Yahweh. And they heard his words, "You will know that I am Yahweh, who smite" (v. 9bγδ).

The memory of the community's experience in 587 B.C., after the bald reality of its horror had begun to fade, drove them back to passages such as vv. 2-4 and 5-9. With the conviction to affirm that what had happened was fulfillment, they returned again and again to texts like these, for they found their own situation there. Only a simple elaboration—fully in accord with the text's original intention—was required to attest their acceptance of that message and the painful self-understanding that it made possible. That process of elaborating expansion was no casual editorial enterprise! It was the terror-struck acceptance of a challenge which could no longer be ignored. It was—and is—the challenge to a proper theological self-assessment by all who experience life as judgment.

THE REPORT OF A VISION OF JERUSALEM'S PUNISHMENT FOR THE ABOMINATIONS IN ITS TEMPLE, 8:1–11:25

Structure

Although 8:1–11:25 is at present arranged as a single unit, analysis of its structure reveals great complexities. To facilitate the treatment of the material, each section will be examined separately. The possible independent existence of the sections will be taken up in each case. The overall impression is that of a much looser unity than in 1:1–3:15.

Genre

As a whole, the account functions as a kind of grandiose PROPHECY OF PUNISHMENT against the people. Section I provides the four-stage reason for punishment and II the announcement of punishment. Section III is only loosely integrated into the preceding context. In 8:4 and 9:3 there is mention of the presence of the glory of Yahweh, but it plays no active role. The identity of the one speaking to the prophet in ch. 8 is that of "a man," distinct from Yahweh in some ways, but at the same time identified with Yahweh in vv. 6, 17-18. After 9:4 Yahweh is plainly the speaker, presumably from the glory mentioned in 9:3. The punishment is commanded to be carried out in 9:7-8 and is reported as accomplished in v. 11. Surprisingly, ch. 10 brings a new kind of reference to the glory. This time, instead of simply referring to the glory as a reality familiar from an earlier vision, only the cherubim are assumed as familiar, and the existence of the throne is introductorily described in 10:1. From then on in ch. 10 the narrative seems to follow two distinct directions. Verse 2 reports how the linen-clothed man of ch. 9 is directed to take coals from between the cherubim and scatter them over the city, and vv. 6-7 report how he does take the fire and go out. Here, however, this strand of narrative is dropped, and nothing is heard about the actual scattering of the coals or any results thereof. Instead, vv. 9-14 and 16-17 present a description of the appearance of the wheels and the cherubim closely akin to that in ch. 1. In 9:15a and 18-19 a narrative begins which seems to be leading up to the departure of the glory from the temple via the east gate, a narrative which finds its completion in 11:22-23. In 10:15b and 20-22 there appear interconnecting linkages which identify the vision of ch. 10 with that of ch. 1. Thus ch. 10 presents only a slight continuation of the announcement of punishment in ch. 9.

The DISPUTATION within a vision setting in 11:1-13 presents another reason for punishment, but makes no real connection at all to the preceding context, apart from the presence of the same number of men as in 8:16-18. Certainly it does not continue the account of judgment in process. That it is to be seen as a fifth abomination secondarily separated from the first four in ch. 8 is extremely unlikely in view of the totally different format in 11:1-13 as well as the noncultic character (note that there is no mention of "abomination") of the sin here. The remaining section of ch. 11 presents a message of hope essentially the same as 36:26-28, one that seems entirely out of place within a pre-587 B.C. setting. The logic of its location is that the confident attitude of the Palestinians reflected in the quotation of v. 15 is similar to the confidence indicated in the saying quoted in v. 3. The response to v. 3 in vv. 4-12, which announce the city's fall, is much more appropriate to a pre-587 scene, while the confidence of the Palestinians reflected by the quotation in v. 15 is more likely that of the post-587 population of the land. Thus it seems necessary to conclude that 11:14-21 is a redactional insertion aimed to provide from later tradition a partial answer to the prophet's protesting question in 11:13b.

The brief narrative of 11:22-23 is the apparent ending, as mentioned above, of that strand of ch. 10 that saw the essence of God's punishment for the sins committed in the temple as consisting in God's withdrawal of his presence.

The report of the prophet's return in 11:24-25 is, as it presently stands, the conclusion which balances the beginning in 8:1-3. Nevertheless, these two final verses are so indefinite that they really could originally have been designed to complete any account of a visionary trip to Jerusalem, even one not having the specific content now present in chs. 8–11.

Setting

It is plain from what has been observed so far that the overarching unity of chs. 8–11 is literary and editorial and not the reflection of the prophet's oral proclamation. Further it appears that—apart from 11:14-21—a pre-587 B.C. scene is presupposed. The loose nature of the unity imposed on these sections permits some observations about the character of the redactional process in this instance, observations which will have to be tested for validity as subsequent sections are examined. For now it seems evident that the traditions edited into this loose unity have not been subjected to the thorough sort of revision that would remove the rough spots that so obviously remain. This can only attest to a process which is extremely respectful of the traditions being preserved, so respectful that it refuses to undertake even the comparatively minor revision necessary to eliminate inconsistencies in person and number addressed or in the faces of the cherubim, or to eliminate inappropriate formulas, such as the prophetic word formula in 11:14. On the other hand, the presence of strands of material which lack a conclusion, such as the activity of the "man" of ch. 8 or that of the linen-clad figure of chs. 9–10, signals a process which was capable of fairly large-scale omissions. Not to be free to revise but to be free to omit may strike modern readers as unusual. The goal of study, however, is not to quarrel with ancient perspectives, but rather to discover and analyze them.

Intention

It is extremely difficult, in view of what has been said of the "silent" editing given these chapters, to establish their intention as an overall unit. It will prove easier to draw conclusions about the intention implicit in the smaller units. It does seem safe to conclude that the pairing of chs. 8 and 9 aims at the familiar logic that the punishment fits the crime. As has been repeatedly observed in smaller units, this is the same logic which is commonly present in a prophecy of punishment. Thus it seems fair to conclude that the later editorial process—whether carried out by Ezekiel himself or his disciples—demonstrates precisely the same perception of the intentionality of this period of the prophet's preaching as did the smaller, older units. While the earlier units made that logic quite clear in express words and abundant "therefores," the larger and presumably editorial context within chs. 8–11 is less overt about this *talio* logic. Chapter 9 follows ch. 8 without any specific tracing of the appropriateness of the judgment which begins at the sanctuary that has been violated in apostasy. The removal of God's presence in the departure of the glory in 11:22-23 does not assert with even a word the logic of withdrawal as a punishment. Even more, not a breath of allusion to the tradition in 1 Kgs 8:10-13 of the arrival of the glory points out that what has now happened is the "undedication" of the temple. It is left for 43:1-5 to bring the entire cycle of dedication, profanation, and reconsecration to its balanced conclusion. Thus once again there appears the same preference on the part of the tradition-connectors for silence and subtlety rather than insertion and explicit affirmation. This kind of redactional procedure demands of the reader an alertness and sensitivity which presuppose careful listening and a broad familiarity with older traditions.

Bibliography

E. Baumann, "Die Hauptvisionen Hesekiels in ihrem zeitlichen und sachlichen Zusammenhang untersucht," *ZAW* 67 (1955) 56-67; W. Brownlee, "The Aftermath of the Fall of Judah according to Ezekiel," *JBL* 89 (1970) 393-404; K. Carley, *Ezekiel Among the Prophets* (SBT 2/31; London: SCM, 1975); A. Graffy, *A Prophet Confronts His People* (AnBib 104; Rome: Biblical Institute Press, 1984) 45-52; M. Greenberg, "The Vision of Jerusalem in Ezekiel 8–11: A Holistic Interpretation," in *The Divine Helmsman* (ed. J. L. Crenshaw and S. Sandmel; New York: Ktav, 1980) 146-64; D. J. Halperin, "The Exegetical Character of Ezek. X:9-17," *VT* 26 (1976) 129-41; F. Horst, "Exilsgemeinde und Jerusalem in Ez viii–ix. Eine literarische Untersuchung," *VT* 3 (1953) 337-60; H. W. Wolff, *Das Zitat im Prophetenspruch* (BevT 4; Münich: Kaiser, 1937).

THE REPORT OF A VISION OF JERUSALEM'S WORSHIP ABOMINATIONS, 8:1-18

Text

In v. 2 it is necessary to read *'îš* ("a man") for *'ēš* ("fire"). In v. 16 *mištaḥă wîtem* is an accidental grammatical mistake for *mištaḥăwîm* ("worshipping"). In v. 17 *'appām* ("their nose") is a deliberate scribal euphemism for the original *'appî* ("my nose").

48

Structure

      2. Event: twenty-five men worshiping sun
        with their backs to the temple   16aεb
C. Summary question   17-18
    1. Renewed narrative introduction   17aα
    2. Question: did you see?   17aβ
    3. Address as son of man   17aγ
    4. Elaboration of question—in the form of a
       prophecy of punishment   17aδεb-18
      a. Reason   17aδεb
        1) Are these abominations too little?   17aδε
        2) They provoke me with violence   17bαβ
        3) They put the branch to my nose   17bγ
      b. Announcement of punishment   18
        1) Intervention   18a
          a) I will act in wrath   18aα
          b) "No pity" formula   18aβ
        2) Results   18b
          a) They will pray   18bα
          b) I will not listen   18bβ

The four scenes in II-IV are bound into a tightly integrated unity by a series of structural devices. Each scene moves in location from the north in the direction of the inner parts of the temple, reaching this destination only in scene four. The linguistic patterns are even more obvious. While the prophet's arrival for scene one is reported already in v. 3bβ, each subsequent scene begins with the visionary guidance formula "he brought me" (vv. 7a, 14a, and 16a). Then, as generally is the case throughout the book, the prophet is addressed as son of man in the first divine speech in each scene. Next, following the narrative description of the scene itself, in the size and detail of which there occurs considerable variety (scenes two and four being by far longer than one and three), always comes the question "Did you see . . . ?" (The participle is used in v. 6, but otherwise the perfect.) In each scene except the third this question is elaborated so as to amplify the description, and then each scene—with the appropriate exception of the last—is brought to its transitional conclusion with the refrain promise "You will see still greater abominations than these" (vv. 6bγ, 13, and 15b). Since no further scene is expected, the fourth closes with an announcement of punishment in v. 18.

This tight structure of the four scenes is not matched by the way the introduction is put together in vv. 1-4. The prophet's presence in his house with the elders sitting before him is not picked up at the conclusion in 11:24f. More disturbingly, the apparently divine "man" of v. 2, whose appearance reminds one of the figure of God in 1:27, is also abandoned midway in v. 3 as the report of visionary translocation switches over to employ "the spirit" as subject. The line of development crumbles still further as the latter part of v. 3 reports the prophet's arrival in a way which seems to anticipate the first abomination scene of v. 5b. As pointed out in the preliminary analysis of chs. 8–11 as a whole, the report of the presence of the glory in v. 4 belongs essentially with 9:3, ch. 10, and 11:22f. Finally, the feminine subject "spirit" is abandoned for a simple divine "he" for all the rest of the chapter, having thus functioned for v. 3b only.

Genre

Apart from the above-indicated confusion in the introductory verses, the entire chapter stays uniformly within the pattern of a VISION REPORT. However, once the brief elements of a presence vision in the introduction are set aside, the continuation does not fit well into the standard subtypes of a vision report. To an extent the four scenes constitute an event vision, but not as an anticipation of future results. Instead, as indicated earlier, ch. 8 offers an indictment of the abominations practiced in the Jerusalem temple, thus providing reasons for the announcement of judgment following in chs. 9–11. The "have you seen . . ." clauses appear, as 1 Kgs 20:13 and 28 demonstrate, as the equivalent of "because" clauses (Zimmerli, *Ezekiel 1*, 235). Verse 18 serves in part as the beginning of that announcement. In contrast to Isa 21:3-4 or Jer 4:19, this vision report omits any mention of the prophet's reaction. Since, as is frequent in Ezekiel, no report is made of the prophet's delivery of this message to an audience, any interaction between prophet and audience, such as occasionally appears in vision reports in other books, is missing here.

Setting

The structural complexities of vv. 1-4 suggest that an editorial blending of several prophetic traditions probably lies behind this first part of ch. 8. Apparently one tradition of a visionary trip to Jerusalem has been supplemented with material drawn from or created to link up to a vision of the glory of Yahweh, such as those in chs. 1 and 10. Presumably all these traditions would date from the period from 592 (8:1) to 587 B.C., but the combination could be later. The basis for any more precise hypothesis is uncertain. In any case it is highly unlikely that the chapter in its present form ever existed as an independent unit, since it is connected so closely to what follows.

The phenomenon of ecstatic, visionary experience in the case of Ezekiel is rather well attested (see 1:1-3; 3:12-14, 22-27; 37:1; and 40:1-4 and the use of the hand of Yahweh revelatory formula). Commentators have noted several points of contact in this regard between Ezekiel and Elisha (Carley, *Ezekiel Among the Prophets*).

Even though the four scenes of vv. 5-18 are much less complicated structurally, it is still difficult to pin down their setting. While it is possible that the types of cultic transgressions described there did in fact take place in the time around 592 B.C., the bizarre character of the access to scene two suggests either confusion in the text or a more fanciful kind of dream-vision. Digging through a wall in order to reach a door may simply be a graphic way of portraying the hiddenness of these transgressions.

It may be doubted that after the reform of 622/1 B.C. such overt apostasy would have been possible in the temple, but probably Ezekiel's account is not intended to describe just the circumstances of 592 B.C. or the stages of any single rite. More likely, along the lines suggested by chs. 19, 20, and 23, Ezekiel's portrayal in these four scenes was intended to characterize Israel's behavior throughout its past. Quite possibly the materials in these visionary scenes reflect a fusion of a multitude of actual observations by Ezekiel in preceding years, now doubtless heightened by their visionary context. Again it is to be assumed that the practices described by the prophet would have been viewed by other circles as minor and justifiable modifications and even enrichments of Yahwism undertaken under the influence of the emphases of other religions in areas where more traditional Yahwism had been judged lacking. Possibly an ecclesiastical court of today would assess the behavior in the temple as syncretistic rather than actually apostate.

Intention

A further point of contact between Ezekiel's message and that of much earlier prophecy, i.e., of Elijah and Elisha, is that Ezekiel condemns syncretism as rank apostasy. The only basic difference between Elijah's approach to Baal rites in 1 Kings 19 and Ezekiel's perspective here is that the foreignness of the infiltrating worship practices here is more obvious, coming not just from Canaanite worship, but from Egyptian and/or Babylonian practices. Ezekiel's visionary scenes pull the veil back to reveal the "mild accommodation" of supplementarily broadened Yahwism as blatant apostasy. Use of images, ceremonial mourning at the end of the agricultural year, and reverence for the sun all could be defended by segments of Jerusalem's population as a meaningful broadening of the concept of revelation, as a necessary recognition and affirmation of Yahweh's lordship revealed in the cycles of nature. Nevertheless, Ezekiel approaches any such attempted discussion from the heritage of the First Commandment and the accompanying prohibition of images. For him Yahweh's jealousy must brand all such modifications of worship as abominations. Perhaps as a priest actively involved in the preservation of Israel's legal heritage, these commandments represented, not at all housekeeping directions for good order, but the encapsulation of life-and-death experiences from the basic strata of Israel's existence vis-à-vis Yahweh. The passing reference to "violence," the sin of Noah's generation in Gen 6:11, in 8-17 is a subtle reminder to our generation that distinctions between cultic and social sins reflect a perspective basically at odds with Ezekiel's intention. For him as for the old legal tradition an "abomination" was an act which expressed a fundamental disavowal of loyalty to Yahweh. To attempt to evaluate the transgressions in this chapter—to which after all Ezekiel attributes Yahweh's wrathful destruction of Jerusalem—as ethically insignificant ritual would be like describing the early Christian martyrs, who went to their deaths rather than toss a pinch of incense on Caesar's altar, as liturgical fanatics.

THE REPORT OF A VISION OF JERUSALEM'S PUNISHMENT, 9:1-11

Text

In v. 8 one must read *wĕniš'ār* ("so that I was left") for the grammatically impossible *wĕnēšă'ar.*

Structure

I. Setting of scene for punishment	1-2
A. Summons to overseers	1

1. Report of a voice calling	1aα
2. Summons to approach	1aβ
3. With weapons	1b
B. Report of response	2
1. Six men come from the north gate (with introductory "behold")	2aα
2. With weapons	2aβ
3. A scribe with them	2aγδ
4. Took position by the bronze altar	2b
II. First phase: directions for punishment	3-6a
A. Glory of Yahweh had moved to threshold	3a
B. Summons to scribe	3b-4b
1. Report of summons	3b
2. Renewed narrative introduction	4aα
3. Go through Jerusalem	4aβ
4. Mark the faithful	4b
C. Directions to others	5-6a
1. Report of speaking	5aα
2. Go through and smite	5aβ
3. "No pity" formula	5b
4. Those to kill	6aα
5. Spare the marked	6aβ
6. Begin at sanctuary	6aγ
III. Second phase: results and further directions	6b-7
A. Report: began with elders	6b
B. Renewed narrative introduction	7aα
C. Further directions	7aβγδ
1. Defile the temple with corpses	7aβγ
2. Go forth	7aδ
D. Report of compliance	7b
IV. Third phase: intercession and response	8-10
A. Setting	8abβ
1. I was left during the smiting	8a
2. I fell on my face	8bα
3. I cried to Yahweh	8bβ
B. Intercessory protest: will you destroy all in your wrath?	8byδ
C. Response—in the form of a prophecy of punishment against the people	9-10
1. Renewed narrative introduction	9aα
2. Reason	9aβγδb
a. Israel's guilt is great	9aβ
b. Land and city are full of blood and violence	9ayδ
c. They say: Yahweh has left and does not see	9b
3. Announcement of punishment	10
a. "No pity" formula	10a
b. Intervention: requital formula	10b

V. Fourth phase: report of scribe's compliance—
with introductory "behold"   11

Essentially this brief chapter unrolls as a straightforward narrative. In contrast to all preceding units, the narrative dimension is heavily predominant. After the scene for the upcoming punishment is set in I, the punishment itself unfolds in two relatively uncomplicated stages, II-III. The final two sections, IV-V, are carefully integrated into the developing narrative, IV being set against the background of the carrying out of the direction ("while they were smiting") with which III concluded, and also further undergirding the punishment while it is being executed by summarizing the reason for it, even quoting from 8:12. Section V, though seemingly just a report of the next event, actually provides an indirect answer to the prophet's question of v. 8, for the action it reports is the conclusion of the sparing of a remnant.

Nevertheless, a few difficulties mar this otherwise direct narrative development. (1) It is textually uncertain whether v. 1 reports, as is more likely, a summons to the executioners ("Draw near") or announces their arrival ("They have drawn near"). No extensive difference would result from either choice. (2) As previously mentioned, the reference to the glory in v. 3a appears to indicate its preliminary movement toward departure and thus is part of a narrative strand which is not at all integrated into the rest of this chapter, but is continued in ch. 10 and 11:22f. (3) Even though the idea of marking and sparing a faithful remnant is fully incorporated into this narrative, no preparation has been provided for it. The preceding chapter indicated nothing but transgressions crying out for punishment, and thus the concern not to slay the faithful with the transgressors appears as unmotivated. This surprising focus on mercy may, however, be the very point of this part of the narrative, as will be considered below. (4) The most significant difficulty is the lack of any report, beyond the preliminary one of v. 7b, about the completion of the work of the destroyers. It appears impossible to assume that this item could ever have been deliberately passed over, for it is the central element for which the rest exists, and it is not replaced by anything remotely equivalent. There seems no choice but to conclude that it has been omitted as a result of the insertion of the material in ch. 10, a point to be examined more thoroughly later.

Genre

This chapter is to be classed as a DESCRIPTION OF PUNISHMENT. In contrast to other occurrences of this genre, almost no attention is devoted here to the direct portrayal of the effects of punishment on the people. There are two other somewhat unusual aspects: the destruction is carried out by personal, angelic (?) executioners rather than the familiar trio of famine, pestilence, and the sword; and the visionary aspect of this material is less prominent structurally than in ch. 8 (no reports of showing or bringing, and only two introductory "beholds"). Nonetheless, the chapter is closely linked to ch. 8, involving the same locale (the inner court of the temple, entered from the north), the same groups (beginning the destruction with the men "before the house" in v. 6; see 8:16-18), and the same reason for punishment ("abominations" in v. 4). From these extensive connections it can be concluded that ch. 9, like ch. 8, never existed independently.

Section IV is of particular interest form-critically. It not only illustrates the prophetic role as intercessor, using a questioning protest even in the midst of a vision, just as in Amos 7:2 and 5, but it also contains God's answer in the form of a PROPHECY OF PUNISHMENT against the people, even though in this instance the divine speech is not mediated by a prophet. The central hinge around which the typical prophecy of punishment pivots is "Therefore, thus has Yahweh spoken," i.e., the messenger formula. In vv. 9-10 no MESSENGER FORMULA appears because no messenger, i.e., no prophet, is involved. Still the pressure of the pattern is so strong that the familiar structure of reason and then announcement is followed anyway. In fact, the Lord even follows the familiar pattern of quoting the guilty in such a way that the punishment—in this case already announced—neatly fits the crime. Further, since the punishment itself is already underway, the intervention-results subpattern is reduced to the "NO PITY" FORMULA— especially appropriate in response to an intercession relying implicitly on God's mercy—and a REQUITAL FORMULA.

While the conclusion is normally the most decisive structural element within the narrative, its omission here does not prove to be serious, for the rest of the structure reveals what the conclusion must have been. The mention of "smiting" in v. 5 in the directions, in the first stage of results in v. 7b, and in the background for the prophet's intercession in v. 8a, leaves no possibility of any surprises. What else might have been a part of the ending of the unit beyond a report of the completion of the destruction is harder to say. A RECOGNITION FORMULA or a report of the end of the vision and the return of the prophet, as in 11:24-25, are possibilities, although it should be noted that the recognition formula is not otherwise used in chs. 8–10.

The mood of the narrative can be analyzed by noticing the techniques employed within it. The tone of finality dominates everything in the chapter. The double use of the "no pity" formula and the specification in detail that no considerations of age or sex are to limit the totality of the judgment are strong factors in the stress on finality. Another aspect emphasized through the narrative's development is that of irony. This appears in the way the shrine where life was imparted has become the starting point for death, the way the place of sanctuary within whose bounds the endangered could find refuge now not only becomes powerless to deliver, but is also judged to be a place of abominations and destined for defilement with corpses. Also bordering on irony is the way the destroyers and their actions remind one of the Passover in Egypt. As Zimmerli points out (*Ezekiel 1,* 246), the words "go through" or "pass through" (identical with "pass over") in vv. 4-5, "destroy" or "slaughter" in vv. 1, 6, and 8, and "smite" in vv. 5 and 7-8 are all deliberately parallel to the material in Exodus 12. However, since the idea of marking out those to be spared characterizes both Ezekiel 9 and the Passover account, more than irony is involved. In a strange way there is also opened here some kind of possibility for a future. While Ezekiel does speak elsewhere of a remnant, e.g., in 6:8-10 and 14:22f., the role of that remnant is left far more open here.

Setting

Chronologically the material in ch. 9 must be assigned to the time just before 587 B.C. In contrast to other passages, such as the mention of Riblah in 6:14 or the thinly veiled description of the fate of Zedekiah in 12:12f., no evidence can be adduced to show that the description of the city's doom has been influenced by the actual, later course of events.

A harder question is involved when one asks about setting in the sense of the mental process by means of which an account of doom like this would be passed on. With what attitude would generations of tradition-bearers preserve this portrayal of the finality and inescapability of God's judgment on Jerusalem and the temple? The scantiness of the account itself compels hesitancy here, but the question will have to be faced repeatedly in many following chapters. For now it will be sufficient to notice a stress on the appropriate necessity of the destruction. The divine response in vv. 9-10 to the prophet's intercession could very well have served to answer the continuing "why?" of the ongoing stream of scattered Judeans.

Intention

That the text intends primarily to proclaim the final end of Jerusalem as God's just response to the abominations carried out in his temple is clear. But in order to capture the precise flavor of this passage, some of the aspects of its mood must also be seen as part of its intention. The way the stages of the destruction unfold reveals that it is Yahweh's sovereign, but scrupulously fair, judgment that is being underlined. The failure of the prophet's intercession and the marking of the faithful for exemption from destruction approach the portrayal of divine justice from opposite sides, but they join together in depicting the sober and nonimpulsive nature of Yahweh's wrath. As the "no pity" formula asserts, to spare those guilty of these crimes would be in itself destructively unjust, because of the damage their apostasy causes to the rest of the community. But even the idea of a necessary death penalty is exceeded by the assessment given here. The extent of the guilt is such that purging is no longer appropriate. Instead the punishment must be collective, with the device of marking the faithful for remnant status as the way to avoid the injustice of blanket destruction. Thus, ironically, the community-oriented concern of the old, legal heritage of the "no pity" formula, once employed to justify the destruction of the few for the sake of the many, has now been twisted to justify the destruction of the community as a whole. That this should be the message of the prophet once thought by many to be the father of individualism is indeed a further irony.

Finally, the somewhat detached and objective character of the prophet's message is also noticeable in this chapter. In spite of Ezekiel's personal intercessory protest, no personal element is present in the sense of concern for an audience. There is a complete lack of any call for repentance, and not even an implicit "if only" or "should have" appears. Those who see the prophets as primarily preachers of repentance will have a difficult time with ch. 9. The manifestly climactic position of these verses as the consequence of the sins described in ch. 8 might have been expected to result in an overwhelming outburst of wrath and frustration, but such is not the case. Instead the absorption in descriptive detail reveals the centrality not of the fierce heat of anger but of the paralyzing chill of a sober, scrupulous concern for thorough justice.

THE REPORT OF A VISION OF THE GLORY OF YAHWEH, 10:1-22

Text

To improve the syntactical flow of v. 3 one should read *bĕbô'* ("in the coming of") for *bĕbō'ô* ("in his coming").

Structure

I. Report of seeing (autobiographical)   1aα
II. Overall description of throne as scene where action is
    to take place   1aβγδεb
    A. Location of throne: on platform (with
        introductory "behold")   1aβ
    B. Location of platform: on heads of cherubim   1aγ
    C. Color of platform: blue   1aδ
    D. Label of throne   1aε
    E. Indication of vision   1b
III. Direction to scatter fire over the city   2a
    A. Renewed narrative introduction   2aα
    B. Identification of addressee: a linen-clothed man   2aβ
    C. Direction about where to get fire   2aγδε
        1. Renewed narrative introduction   2aγ
        2. Among wheels   2aδ
        3. Under cherubim   2aε
    D. Direction to take coals   2aζ
    E. Direction to scatter coals over city   2aη
IV. Report of compliance, initial phase   2b
V. More detailed description of background scene   3-5
    A. Location of cherubim   3aα
    B. Time: when man went in   3aβ
    C. Location of cloud   3b
    D. Report of movement of glory   4a
        1. Glory lifted up   4aα
        2. New location   4aβ
    E. Accompanying phenomena   4b-5
        1. Cloud fills the temple   4bα
        2. Brightness fills the court   4bβ
        3. Sound of wings   5
            a. Extent of sound   5a
            b. Analogy for sound: like Shaddai speaking   5b
VI. Report of compliance, second phase   6-8
    A. Resumptive reference to earlier direction   6a
        1. Narrative reference   6aα
        2. Paraphrase of earlier direction   6aβ
    B. Continuation of narrative report of obedience   6b-7
        1. Position taken by man   6b

The attempt to analyze the structure of ch. 10 confronts one with extremely difficult problems. Description and action are combined in a puzzling blend. The action in III is preceded by unrelated description in II, and the continuation of III in IV is then abruptly broken off and separated from its further continuation in VI by more description. What is reported in VI is nowhere finished, but VII-VIII turn to further description closely linked to ch. 1. Section IX begins a narrative of the departure of the glory, but this is not picked up again until 11:22. Section X finishes the chapter, not by bringing the action any further, but with the assertion of the identity of the "living creatures" of ch. 1 with the "cherubim" of ch. 10, apparently attempting thereby to resolve the tension caused by significant differences between the otherwise closely related descriptive sections of the two chapters. A closer examination reveals these problems to be even more serious. They are extensive, complex, and not the result of any one cause. Space limitations permit only a brief summary of the problems. (1) In spite of the explicit identification in X of the vision of ch. 10 with that of ch. 1 and the extensive amount of repetition of material from ch. 1, disturbing differences remain. (The term *galgal*, "whirling wheels," in vv. 2, 6, and 13 is new over against ch. 1, and not only is the name used for the throne-bearing creatures different, but the listing of their faces in v. 14 clashes with 1:10. Even within ch. 10 the commonly used plural designation "cherubim" is puzzlingly replaced by the singular in vv. 2, 4, and 7.) (2) Tracing the movement of the glory involves a strange multi-stage shifting of location for no apparent reason (uncertainty about the meaning of the word *miptan*, "threshold," in vv. 4 and 18—see already 9:3—is a further complication). (3) The logic according to which the action develops is hard to trace. (The linen-clad man who marked the faithful for preservation in ch. 9 is now the instrument of punishment, while the six executioners are nowhere to be seen; the descriptive material, as mentioned, breaks the continuity of action—vv. 3-5 interrupting the connection between vv. 2 and 7, and v. 1 breaking the link between 9:11 and 10:2. Finally, there is no report of the scattering of the coals and the city's destruction.)

No convincing solution has been proposed to solve these problems, although commentators have undertaken all manner of drastic attempts. It seems necessary to conclude that an adequate base for any overall solution is simply not available. As was observed in a preliminary look at the setting of chs. 8–11, the occurrence of significant omissions in this complex blending of traditions undermines attempts at reconstruction. In keeping with this situation, a more modest path will be followed here, namely, to establish the purpose of each major segment or strand and to forsake the attempt to establish the sequence of the text's stages of growth as impossible for lack of sufficient evidence, and even as inappropriate in view of the nature of the tradition process. That process, as ch. 10 shows, must have involved repeated reflection upon the experience of a vision of Jerusalem's destruction. These reflections—which may well have resulted in a series of tradition units, some directed at an audience in proclamation and others more speculatively oriented—appear to have extended over an indeterminable period of time. These various units have been blended according to a procedure no longer fully recoverable, but characterized by three features: (1) editorial revision, which could be either minimal, as attested by the preservation of inconsistencies, or extensive, as indicated by the repeated, bold affirmations of the identity of the glory seen in ch. 1 with that of ch.

10; (2) a willingness to preserve traditions only partially, being free to omit even such presumably crucial elements as their endings; and (3) an approach to visionary material that did not feel the need to trace a single, consistent sequence of events, but instead preferred to convey the largely nonverbal content of this experience by a series of portrayals which, though placed one after another, are not necessarily intended as temporally or logically sequential.

As a result of this process, ch. 10 now has four major aspects, which it is not possible fully to synthesize because such a full synthesis never existed. First, it seems clear that ch. 10 affirms that Jerusalem's destruction was—as indeed it actually was—not just a matter of the sword (ch. 9), but of fire as well. The two portrayals now appear consecutively, but it is a misunderstanding of the material's horizon to approach it with questions about sequence (Wevers, 87). Second, the fall of Jerusalem is shown to the prophet in another way, somewhat parallel to the sword and fire traditions, as the departure of Yahweh's glory. Again this is not a third item in a sequence, but the single reality of 587 B.C. envisaged from what modern logic would consider a totally different perspective. It should be borne in mind throughout that, despite their detail, these scenes are not actual, historical observations, but reports of a transcendent experience in which the boundaries of time (including sequence) as well as space are described as fully surpassed. It is mental impressions that are recalled and interpreted, not a reel of movie film which is being edited. In the third place, ch. 10 embodies the affirmation that the glory which appeared to Ezekiel in ch. 1 as a demonstration of God's gracious concern for his exiled people is to be identified with the divine presence at Jerusalem's punishment. Since that punishment involved the abandonment of the temple in whose midst the glory of Yahweh was traditionally present, the two had—from one point of view— to be the same, even if the perception of that presence, necessarily colored by its activity, may have been experienced as having certain apparent differences. As this last observation implies, the final aspect of ch. 10 to be noted is its clear attestation of the differences between the visions of ch. 10 and ch. 1. No harmonization should attempt to remove these, and they should not be regarded as the result of carelessness (contra Wevers, 90). In spite of all the problems of textual transmission, which do abound in both chapters, it is undeniable that the two visions simply do differ. To an extent those differences have been harmonized within the tradition process, but to an extent they remain. The reasons for preserving these conflicting traditions may not be clear, but the existence of such significant amounts of material on both sides—both affirming the identity and attesting the differences—is scarcely good evidence for assuming an earlier form of the text where they were not present. To account for the later creation of these conflicting verses would surely be the more difficult task.

Genre

As in the case of ch. 8, the material in ch. 10 is manifestly presented as a VISION REPORT. However, here the shaping of the material is much more clearly in accord with standard subtypes than was the case in ch. 8. Extensive elements of a presence vision appear in the descriptive sections (vv. 1, 3-5, and 9-14), and the report of the destruction of the city, as revealed in the action of the linen-clad man taking fiery coals from among the cherubim to scatter them over the city (vv. 2 and 6-7), is plainly an event vision. As noticed earlier, the two types are blended in a puzzling way, which suggests the existence of two originally distinct traditions, one of each genre type. The movement of the glory toward the east as preparation for departure is another element of an event vision, the continuation of which appears in 11:22-23.

In contrast to ch. 9, the marks of a vision report are much more abundant in the form of such statements as "I looked" (vv. 1 and 9), "before my eyes" (vv. 2 and 19), "appearance" (vv. 9, 10, and 22), and introductory "beholds" (vv. 1 and 9). The pluperfect interconnecting linkage "I had seen" is also more frequent (vv. 15, 20, and 22) because of the prominence of the concern to identify the glory seen in the two visions.

Setting

A vision report gives expression to a private experience, but at the same time it must put that uniquely personal experience into words which will be understandable to others. The only way to do this is by employing words and concepts which belong to the common stock of the shared traditions of one's community. Further, even reflecting about a private experience requires utilizing the mental heritage of one's previous education. Ezekiel's heritage within the traditions of the Jerusalem priesthood in the light of which ch. 1 was formulated has already been explored. The vision in ch. 10 differs in that it has been incorporated within the larger context of chs. 8–11 in a way that has affected its shape much more extensively than was the case with ch. 1. The vision report of ch. 1 issued quite smoothly into the vocation account of chs. 2–3. In chs. 8–11, on the other hand, the situation is much more complicated for two reasons. (1) While ch. 1 was a vision report of the presence type, and thus could serve simply as the background for the vocation account of chs. 2–3, the glory in ch. 10 is, though still a revelation of Yahweh's presence, also an integral part of an event, namely, the withdrawal of God's presence from the temple. (2) While only a brief report of the glory's departure was necessary in 3:12-13 to complete its function within the larger unity of 1:1–3:15, the much more complex organization of 8–11, with the glory appearing in 8:4, 9:3, and 11:22-23 in addition to ch. 10, shows that the function of the vision report is not just as a preliminary to, but as an integrated aspect of, the larger unit's role as a message of judgment. The departure of the glory, which begins only in ch. 10, is the result of a motivation which is not even mentioned in ch. 10, but appears in ch. 8 and partially also in ch. 9.

That chs. 8–11 are the product of reflection which has repeatedly returned to the subject of Jerusalem's judgment is already clear, but this will become even more obvious when ch. 11 is examined. Nonetheless, it is already necessary to ask the question about the date and perspective of this complex process of reflection. Was the vision report of ch. 10 essentially complete before 587 B.C., or was it, like ch. 11, revised in the light of the prophet's later experience? As observed earlier, there was no evidence of such post-587 influence in ch. 9. It is hard to be as certain about ch. 10. The fact that the city was burned is scarcely reason to assume that the entire idea of coals of fire is a reflection of the experience of 587. After all, fire was a standard ingredient of and metaphor for prophetic announcements of punishment for centuries (see already Amos 1–2). And coals of fire were an almost automatic part of the picture of Yahweh's presence in his temple, even if they played a drastically contrasting role in Isaiah 6. However, the absence in ch. 10 of the conclusion of the report of the punishment by fiery coals means that some uncertainty will have to remain. It may even have been the case that the present shape of the glory material in chs. 8–11 silently reflects the anticipation of the promise of the return of the glory in 43:1-5. Because of the strongly attested links of ch. 10 to ch. 1, it is clear that ch. 10 entails a setting in which there was reflection about the consistency of grace with judgment. The absence of any express anticipation of ch. 43 in chs. 8–11 at least makes it clear that no expansion has resulted from the perspective of this later revelation, even though—as it has been necessary repeatedly to observe—the effect that the hope of the glory's return may have had on what may have been omitted must remain uncertain.

Intention

The account of the glory's departure from the temple is only partially present in ch. 10, its completion coming in 11:22-23. Therefore, an analysis of the significance of the departure idea will be postponed until the consideration of the later section.

Here the matter to be investigated is the relationship between the vision of God's presence and the role of the presence in the city's destruction. As was noted above, the fire common to portrayals of God's presence is a deliberately two-sided matter. The gracious reception of sacrifice and thereby the manifold aspects of cultic life are possible only by means of the altar fire. Expiation and consecration particularly are described in Isaiah's vocation account as happening via fire. But fire was equally the vehicle of punishment, as the account of the way "fire came forth from the Lord, and consumed the two hundred and fifty men" of Korah's party in Num 16:35 clearly demonstrates. This dual role for the fire of Yahweh's presence is not just a coincidence, it is a fundamental part of the understanding of holiness as both life-giving and death-dealing. Ezekiel's vision in ch. 1 gave powerful expression to the comforting message that Yahweh's presence was not confined to the Jerusalem temple. The appearance of the glory in Babylon was an assertion of a continuing gracious interest in and purpose for the exiles. Now the repeated assertion of the identity of the vision of ch. 1 with that of ch. 10 is an unmistakable message that the same divine presence is also at work in the destruction of Jerusalem. It is plain that the vision report deliberately raises the issue of the continuity between grace and judgment, between the way God's people cannot exist apart from his presence and the way that very presence at the same time must justly be the vehicle of their doom.

It would have been easy to minimize this contrast of a gracious presence and a destroying presence by a less extensive underlining of the identity of the glory of ch. 10 with that of ch. 1. But such is clearly not the intention of the chapter in its present form. While the surrounding material in chs. 8–9 and 11:1-13 is heavily focused on the just and appropriate nature of Jerusalem's destruction, it comes somewhat as a surprise to notice how minimal is the actual message of punishment in ch. 10. It appears only in v. 2aη. Verses 6-7 deal further with the burning coals, but their purpose is never again mentioned, and, as noted several times, the carrying out of the direction to scatter fire on the city is totally unmentioned. Finally, that the beginning of the glory's departure is recorded in vv. 18-19 plainly asserts that Yahweh's holy presence still exists. That that existence is not unrelated to his gracious concern for his people is immediately made explicit in the references to the appearance of the glory in Babylon in vv. 20 and 22. Thus, the glory has a gracious aspect in ch. 10 not only because of its connection to both ch. 1 and ch. 43, but also because it is given powerful stress even within ch. 10 itself. Such a strange and yet compellingly paradoxical affirmation of the continuity between grace and judgment is not unique to Ezekiel. It stands in fact in a solidly rooted line of tradition. The only destruction greater than that of 587 B.C. known to the OT is that of the flood. In it, too, there is a similar puzzling continuity between punishment and grace, as the ingrained character of human evil, which is the reason for the Lord's judgment in Gen 6:5-7, is also the reason for his gracious promise of an abiding future in Gen 8:21-22, given appropriately enough beside an altar with its sacrificial fire.

A DISPUTATION: THE CITY IS THE CALDRON, 11:1-13

Text

In v. 7b proper syntax makes it necessary to read *'ôṣî'* ("I will bring out") for *hôṣî'* ("to bring out").

Structure

I. Report of translocation	1aαβ
A. Lifted by the spirit	1aα
B. Brought to the east gate	1aβ
II. Sight	1aγb
A. Twenty-five men (with introductory "behold")	1aγ
B. Two specific men seen and named: Jaazaniah and Pelatiah	1b
III. Reason for judgment: quotation of wicked counsel	2-3
A. Renewed narrative introduction	2a
B. Address as son of man	2bα
C. Characterization of men: evil plans	2bβγ
D. Quotation	3
1. Introduction	3aα
2. Quotation proper	3aβb
a. Do not build houses	3aβ
b. It (city) is the caldron and we are the meat	3b
IV. Three-part prophetic proof saying, picking up the quotation	4-12
A. Preliminaries	4-5aδ
1. Transitional "therefore"	4aα
2. Direction to prophesy	4aβ
3. Address as son of man	4b
4. Spirit fell upon me	5aα
5. Renewed narrative introduction	5aβ
6. Direction to speak using the messenger formula	5aγδ
B. Message itself	5b-12

The report of translocation in v. 1 poses a question: Is what begins here a new vision report or a separated segment of what has preceded in chs. 8–10? The apparent connections in v. 1b to earlier scenes of chs. 8–11 turn out not to be real, for the Jaazaniah here has a different father from the one in 8:11, and the twenty-five men of 8:16 have nothing in common but the number, for no sun worship is mentioned in 11:1. Thus it is probably correct with Zimmerli (*Ezekiel 1,* 257) to see here "a thematically displaced parallel" to the vision of chs. 8–10.

The narrative interruption in v. 13 has provoked much discussion (see setting below), but it should be noted that it is still a part of the vision report.

Genre

Verses 1-12 present a DISPUTATION of a rather typical sort. A saying of a group within Israel is quoted and a response is given. Somewhat atypically, the first part of the quotation, v. 3aβ, is not picked up, but the second part is both revised in a hostile manner (v. 7) and denied (v. 11a) in a kind of divine veto (Horst, "Exilsgemeinde und Jerusalem," 342). There is no standard pattern for the shape of a prophet's response in such a disputation, but not surprisingly in view of the semilegal character of the whole genre, Ezekiel's response is shaped in the pattern of that genre he uses so frequently, a PROPHETIC PROOF SAYING. This time it is a three-part proof saying, with the reason in vv. 5b-6 as part one, "therefore" plus the MESSENGER FORMULA in v. 7aαβ as the transitional link, the announcement of punishment in vv. 7aγ-10a as the second part, concluding with the RECOGNITION FORMULA in v. 10b. Verses 11-12 function as recapitulation, with an announcement of punishment in v. 11 and an elaborated recognition formula in v. 12. The nature of the elaboration is to provide a reason for punishment, so that vv. 11-12 serve as a kind of second three-part proof saying, which may well be a secondary expansion employing the standard indictment about "the ordinances of the nations" known from 5:7. Already vv. 9-10 could be secondary, since the PROPHETIC UTTERANCE FORMULA at the end of v. 8 could mark the conclusion of the unit, although this formula does also often appear at the endpoint of a subsection of a prophetic announcement. Both sections, vv. 9-10 and 11-12, will be considered further under Setting below.

The lengthy preliminaries in vv. 4-5a introducing the proof saying in vv. 4-12 are rather unusual. The report of ecstasy, "the spirit of the Lord fell upon me," after the instruction to prophesy seems especially surprising in view of the ecstatic background of the vision itself, not only in 8:1 but also in 11:1. Of course, the whole idea of a prophet preaching in the midst of watching a vision is quite unusual, although see 37:4 and 9.

Further, the words of the twenty-five princes of the people are labeled in v. 2 as "wicked counsel." "Counsel" was the common designation for political advice given by those who held a position of respect (see Jer 18:18).

Finally, the prophet's intercession as a reaction to what he has seen is closely similar to his behavior in 9:8, where further parallels are given.

Setting

Since a disputation involves the response to a saying of the people, it would seem to be dependent upon something the prophet has actually heard. However, it has been shown that the prophets often invent such sayings for the purposes of their proclamation (see Wolff, *Das Zitat*). Since in 11:3 the prophet is told of the people's saying in the course of a vision, it is difficult to draw any conclusions about any actual element of skill at repartee which may have been involved. Zimmerli mentions the possibility of the prophet's hearing a report of this saying from someone from Jerusalem, and thereby being stimulated to this vision (*Ezekiel 1*, 260), but this must remain speculative.

In any case it seems likely that such a saying belongs to the period before the beginning of the final siege in 589 B.C. However, the references to judgment "at the border of Israel" seem suspiciously like an allusion to the events at Riblah, discussed above in connection with 6:14. The use of this phrase in both 11:10 and 11 is further support of its role as updating elaboration.

The strange report of the death of Pelatiah in v. 13a has been a favorite bit of evidence for those defending a Palestinian locus for Ezekiel's ministry. How could such a report be the product of anything other than a firsthand observation? The somewhat parallel situation of the death of Hananiah in Jer 28:17 is often mentioned. In each case there is a direct confrontation, and the powerful word of Yahweh finds its confirmation in the death of the prophet's opponent. But since this confrontation takes place in a vision and is thus not direct, Pelatiah would have been totally unaware of Ezekiel's vision unless he were told of it later. It is simply not known whether Pelatiah actually did die as reported here or not. As Zimmerli observes, to argue from a vision of Ezekiel toward his location or any unmentioned fulfillment of this vision in Pelatiah's death would be "arbitrary" (*Ezekiel 1*, 260). Moreover, to affirm, as Eichrodt does, that it would not make sense to preserve this vision report unless it had been proved true by a report from Palestine confirming Pelatiah's death (138), is to assign the phenomenon of unfulfilled prophecy a more serious role than the prophets themselves seem to have done.

Intention

The point of the quotation's first half about building houses must remain uncertain. It is not even possible to decide whether the reference is to "houses" in the sense of families or as actual dwelling places.

The second part of the quotation is clearer. The point of the people's regarding themselves as the flesh in the pot appears to have been to assert both their own worth in contrast to the exiles and their security within the city's protective walls. Their amazing confidence after the shattering experience of 598-7 B.C. is eloquent evidence of their "unwillingness to repent" (Zimmerli, *Ezekiel 1*, 260), and thus of their solidarity with the rest of the "rebellious house." The point of the divine revision of the saying is not fully clear in regard to the slain in the streets, although it may well be simply the claim that these unjustly slain were the people of genuine worth in Jerusalem (Eichrodt, 138). The point for those who give this "wicked counsel" is clearer. For them the message is that the pot will in their case serve not to protect its contents, but to hold them together for slaughter (Wevers, 94).

The death of Pelatiah serves as a precursor of the destructive power of the word of Yahweh through his prophet. Since the name Pelatiah means "Yahweh rescues a remnant," it is tempting to infer that his death implies the total rejection of any hope for the survival of a remnant. That thought is not unfamiliar in the prophetic tradition (see Amos 3:12 and Ezek 5:14). Still, it is difficult to be sure to what extent the name's meaning is a part of the text's intention.

PROPHECY OF SALVATION ABOUT THE EXILES, 11:14-21

Text

In v. 15 it is highly likely that one must read *rāḥ ăqû* ("they are far away") for *raḥăqû* ("go far away"). In v. 19a one should probably read *'aḥēr* ("another") for *'eḥād* ("one"). At the obscure beginning of v. 21 it is better to emend *wě'el-lēb* ("and to the heart of") to *wě'ēlleh 'aḥărê* ("and these . . . after").

Structure

At first glance the section vv. 14-21 appears more solidly and coherently structured than is actually the case. A minor complication occurs in v. 15, where the *RSV*'s translation obscures the fact that II.B.1 is a dangling subject which never receives a predicate. Section II.B.2 is not such a predicate, but rather is only a relative clause. If the word "are" is deleted from the *RSV,* a true picture of the verse emerges.

A much more serious problem exists in vv. 17-21. There, as the outline above indicates, the text is characterized by a puzzling alternation between second and third person forms. In the light of this the question of the structural nature of these verses will have to be examined further from the perspectives of genre and setting.

Genre

The presence of the PROPHETIC WORD FORMULA in v. 14 and the PROPHETIC UTTERANCE FORMULA at the end of v. 21 clearly marks off this section as an independent unit. That, of course, poses a serious problem, since the overarching unit of the vision which began in 8:1 does not end until 11:22-25. The conclusion seems inevitable that 11:14-21 is, like 11:1-13, a secondary incorporation of otherwise independent material within chs. 8–11. Logically, this second insertion is also made at the same place so that only the one interruption is necessary between the description of the glory in ch. 10 and the report of its departure in 11:22f. Verses 14-21 seem to have been inserted for two reasons. One reason certainly is the close parallel between the proud confidence indicated in the quotation in 11:3 and the similar mood reflected in the quotation in v. 15b. Nevertheless, what follows in vv. 16-21 is not a true DISPUTATION, but only a modified one which quickly issues in an announcement of salvation. The second and more complex reason for the placement of this section must have to do with its role as a contrast to the preceding context of doom. The discussion of this matter will take place below under Setting.

The pattern of a PROPHECY OF SALVATION is similar to that of a PROPHECY OF PUNISHMENT. The central element is an announcement encompassing intervention and results. While a prophecy of punishment normally prefixes a reason to the announcement, this is not usually the case in a prophecy of salvation. However, in the case of this prophecy of salvation, vv. 15-16 play the unusual role parallel to that of a reason for punishment which would then lead to an announcement. Here the quotation in v. 15 is given modified acceptance in v. 16 to stress that what has so far happened has indeed been Yahweh's doing. Then v. 17 announces Yahweh's further acts, contrasting them with past acts of punishment and leading to a message of hope through the link in v. 16b constituted by the reference to grace having already been shown in exile. The explicit references in vv. 17-18 to Israel's punishment and its cause, i.e., "out of the countries where you have been scattered" and "all its detestable things and all its abominations," make plain how this promise is shaped as the undoing of the past. Still, it becomes a much bolder sort of promise in vv. 19-20 where the transformation to obedience, to which the label repentance is normally given, is portrayed as God's own act ("I will give . . . put . . . take") rather than the people's action as it was in v. 18 ("they will remove"). Similarly, that the restored relationship between Israel and its God is expressed in the COVENANT FORMULA is not surprising, but that that formula should be cast in the future tense raises serious questions. These are largely content matters and will have to await the analysis of 36:22-38, where these same thoughts are expressed in lengthier fashion and within a more extensive context. In the shaping of this announcement of salvation here two additions appear, a second section of intervention in v. 19 and one of purpose in v. 20. This is only a slight and understandable variation from the standard shape, but the limitation imposed in v. 21 is quite unusual, and not just as a matter of form. In its content v. 21 seems to be quite inappropriate. After a promise of the gift of a new heart and spirit resulting in full obedience and restoration, it is hard to see the need to limit the scope of this promise to the obedient. After all, obedience here is the result of God's gift. This point also must be pursued further in ch. 36.

Another unusual aspect of this unit is the presence in both vv. 16 and 17 of transitional sections, "Therefore say, 'Thus the Lord has said.'" It is hard to put aside the suspicion that here is further evidence of the editorial joining of material from separate prophecies.

Setting

The occurrence of this section of good news (vv. 17-20) in the midst of a context concerned with announcing punishment and explaining its reasons (8:1–11:13) gives rise to one of the major issues in the study of Ezekiel. Can one conclude that Ezekiel's message before 587 B.C. included the proclamation of return from exile and spiritual restoration, or must one judge this passage and a few others like it to be post-587 expansions? Of course, it is not the concern of scholarship to decide what Ezekiel could or could not have said. The appropriate task is simply to try to understand any single passage within the context of the rest of the recorded words of the prophet. That certainly does not mean smoothing everything into one uniform picture. The unusual and even the unique can also be studied, but the context within which a surprise is presented is also significant. Thus the central issue to be pursued here is the understanding of these verses within their context, but the explanation of context must take into account both narrower and broader aspects.

The confidence of the inhabitants of Jerusalem expressed in v. 15b is, as was said above, the reason for the placement of this section. That confidence would be most natural in a pre-587 B.C. situation, and yet the description of the exiles as "the whole house of Israel" in that same verse reflects a point of view which seems to presuppose the deportation following 587 (see 11:5). Is there evidence within the book of Ezekiel about the mood of the people left in Palestine after 587? The key passage is 33:24f. There the survivors of the destruction of Jerusalem are presented as claiming exultantly, "the land is surely given us to possess." But there the speakers are identified as "the inhabitants of these waste places in the land of Israel," while in 11:15 the words "inhabitants of Jerusalem" are used. Both the factors of terminology and of mood, then, are difficult and inconclusive. Only this much is certain: In contrast to what Jeremiah 28–29 presents as the pre-587 exiles' high hopes for a speedy return, the Palestinians—both before 587 and after, at least according to Ezekiel—saw the deportation of their brothers on both occasions as final and rejoiced in the implications of their own preferential status.

It is necessary then to turn to yet another dimension of the context, i.e., how is this promise integrated into its context? Specifically, how far does what precedes vv. 17-20 reflect the glorious announcement contained therein? Here two parallel sections in 16:53-63 and 20:33-44 can be compared, for there too a unit centered on guilt and punishment goes on to speak of restoration. Essentially, then, the question faced is this: Did the promise of return begin before 587 B.C. or has it been added to these passages editorially after 587? The evidence is very strong that the vast majority of units in chs. 1–24 reflecting the time before Jerusalem's fall contain no promise like this one in ch. 11. More precisely, if this hope were a part of the prophet's pre-587 message, then it would obviously be of such decisive importance that all units not reflecting an awareness of this future would not merely be incomplete, they would actually be misleading! To speak of an end when the Lord had promised a return would be so incomplete as to be inadequate. Further, even within chs. 8–11, the significance of this promise at the end would have to have cast the preceding in an entirely different light—a dimension of intellectual and emotional context which the literary context in no way reflects. In chs. 16 and 20 the case is even plainer. The promise which comes at the end comes as a surprise, but not a surprise which penetrates into the mind and heart of the proclaimer. To speak this way to an audience would simply be impossible. The lack of an integration of the end with the beginning—and with the other messages—would seem incomprehensible, but not in a way that would lead to a praise of the surprising grace of God!

No, it is necessary to conclude that the element of promised return and restoration in 11:14-21, as well as in chs. 16 and 20, is the result of a post-587 editorial revision of the deposit of the prophet's pre-587 message.

Intention

It must be asked why anyone would insert a message of promise at the end of a section centering on punishment. Surely what would be illogical before 587 B.C. would not become less so just through the passage of time! No, the issue is to be approached differently, from the perspective of the larger context. The question of confusing the minds of pre-587 readers or listeners does not arise after 587, unless one assumes that the material in chs. 1–24 was preserved with the intent to enable the reconstruction of Ezekiel's earlier message. Manifestly, the presence of that later expansion in chs. 11, 16, and 20 reflects a lack of interest in such biographical reconstruction. Instead a different intention is revealed, one that reflects a different context. With the coming of Ezekiel's message of consolation in chs. 33–48, his earlier proclamation now became in a way obsolete. It could henceforth be read only from a perspective of historical curiosity. But this earlier message was preserved for a far different purpose. It found an ongoing use as authoritative tradition which continued to speak to the community in exile and even beyond. The expansions inserted in chs. 11, 16, and 20 are intended to enable those sections (surely among the largest and most comprehensive units within chs. 1–24) to serve as a kind of composite of Ezekiel's total message. Of course, all later use of chs. 1–24 would have to presuppose some historical perspective on the part of the users, but in these three largest units that historical perspective was made explicit, somewhat akin to the way a postresurrection perspective appears within a number of pericopes dealing with Jesus' ministry. If anything about this procedure is to be regarded as strange, it is that so little expansion was felt to be necessary and that so great a degree of historical perspective could be expected of later generations.

One further item requiring analysis here is the meaning of v. 16b, "I have been a sanctuary to them for a while in the countries where they have gone." It is not of great importance whether the Hebrew *mĕʿaṭ* ("a little") is understood temporally or otherwise ("in a small way"), but what is of significance is the prophet's point about God's favor shown to the exiles in Babylon. The brevity makes interpretation difficult, but the sentence seems to refer to the possibility of a limited sort of worship even in exile. Although describing the origin of the synagogue is not the prophet's aim, he does to an extent lay the groundwork for such an institution. More likely Ezekiel's focus is on the continuity provided by Yahweh's revelation of his word to the prophet as well as the visionary manifestation of his presence in the glory. No doubt the use of the covenant formula in v. 20 is to be contrasted with v. 16, with v. 20 describing a no longer limited relationship.

THE REPORT OF A VISION OF THE DEPARTURE OF THE GLORY OF YAHWEH (RESUMPTIVE OF CH. 10), 11:22-23

Structure

I. Report of the lifting up of the glory (based on 10:19)		22
A. Cherubim and wheels lifted up		22a
B. The glory was over them		22b
II. Report of departure of the glory		23
A. The glory went up from the city's midst		23a
B. It stood on a mountain to the east		23b

Section I is really only a transitional link to ch. 10 made necessary by the intervening insertion of the two units, 11:1-13 and 11:14-21. Actually, every word in v. 22 is already present in 10:19, so that it is presumably purely editorial, and only v. 23 advances the narrative.

Genre and Intention

As was noticed earlier when the VISION REPORT of ch. 10 was analyzed, vv. 11:22f. are really the conclusion of that vision, and thus do not represent a unit in themselves. The bulk of the vision report of which they are a part is of the presence type, but the action which takes place in 10:18f. and continues here reveals a shift in the direction of the event type. Still, it is not some earthly event which is prefigured here. It is rather solely a transcendent reality made visible to the prophet's eyes alone in order that he could, through seeing it, understand the deeper meaning of the visible events of the city's destruction. Whereas the report of the coming of the glory of Yahweh to fill his temple in 1 Kgs 8:10f. was the climax of the report of its dedication, this report of the departure constitutes the obviously ominous announcement of the reversal of the temple's consecration, in a way its desecration. That desecration is not the result of some offensive and hostile action by outsiders which damaged the temple's holiness, but instead it is the result of the voluntary and deliberate withdrawal by Yahweh himself from his temple so as to leave it without the source of its holiness.

To ordinary ancient Near Eastern religious perspectives this would be nearly incomprehensible. That an offended deity could punish his people for disobedience of his wishes was a normal enough idea, but that a deity would remove himself from his only earthly place of residence with no provision for an ongoing cultus would be unimaginable, a kind of divine suicide. There is, however, more involved in Yahweh's withdrawal than just the underlining of his distinctiveness, his lack of dependence on his worshipers. Because of his presence the Jerusalem temple, like the others in the ancient world, became a place where sanctuary, the right of sacred asylum, was available. This concept, its practice, and its terminology are familiar from texts such as Psalm 46 and 1 Kgs 1:51. The city as a whole also had a certain claim to inviolability because of this. The removal of the glory from the temple to indicate the cancellation of this claim was thus a kind of logical necessity as an accompaniment of the vision of God's destruction of Jerusalem in ch. 9.

Setting

While a dedication account would be used on the anniversaries of a temple's consecration, it seems initially quite unlikely that there would ever be celebrations of a temple's destruction. But it is in fact well known that later Judaism did observe such occasions (i.e., Tisha b'Ab), not in celebration, but in commemoration. How soon after 587 B.C. such observances began and to what extent they became widespread custom is not known, although Jer 41:45 and Ps 137:4 suggest a relatively early date. In any case, when such an occasion came to be a regularly practiced liturgical rite, this passage in Ezekiel would have made a highly appropriate pericope for use at it.

Within the book of Ezekiel, though, this passage functions in another way. There it serves as the foil for the visionary message in 43:1-9 of the return of the glory of the Lord to his temple to dwell there forever. Doubtless this vision of hope was separated by a number of years (40:1 implies a date of 573 B.C.) from that of chs. 8–11, and it seems unlikely that 11:22f. had any original connection to a message of hope.

THE REPORT OF THE PROPHET'S RETURN TO HIS PEOPLE, 11:24-25

Structure

I. Report of the prophet's return	24a
A. Return through translocation by the spirit	24aαβ
B. In a vision	24aγ
II. Report of the end of the vision	24b
III. Report of the prophet's delivery of his message	25

In contrast to the rather complex and fully detailed account of the beginning of the vision in 8:1-4, the end is presented in straightforward brevity. The return (I) to Jerusalem by means of translocation by the spirit balances 8:2f.; the mention of the cessation of the vision (II) corresponds to the description of the onset of ecstasy in 8:1b and the label "visions of God" in 8:3bβ. Finally, III indicates that proclamation took place. This is not the customary report of compliance, for no command to tell others had been recorded. Nevertheless, the content of chs. 8–11 makes it plain that this was no private revelation but was intended as a message to the community.

Genre

This small section constitutes the conclusion of the overarching VISION REPORT which has formed the background for all of 8:1–11:23, even though the earlier material in 11:14-21, as was noticed, was not originally part of any vision.

Setting

This two-verse conclusion was never an independent unit, but always served the function of bringing the larger unit of chs. 8–11 to its close.

Intention

While v. 24 does not go beyond the internal purpose of bringing the structure of the vision to a rounded conclusion, v. 25 has a broader implication. Attesting the approaching fall of Jerusalem and its causes to the exiles in Babylon makes sense only on the presupposition that they still have a part in the purposes of their God. Although only the secondary expansions in 11:1-13 and 14-21 specify that the exiles are henceforth to occupy the central place in Yahweh's plans, that fact was anticipated in the report of the movements of the glory and in the way the announcement of Jerusalem's fall was brought to an end without any indication of or preparation for an ongoing future for the survivors in Jerusalem. Thus the character of the content of chs. 8–10 and the return of the prophet to report this to the exiles provide the background over against which the later insertion of the units in ch. 11 comes to be a logical necessity.

TWO SYMBOLIC ACTIONS: 12:1-20

Text

In v. 3 delete *ûgĕlēh* ("and go into exile") as an inappropriate anticipation of what follows. The text of both v. 10b and v. 12b is quite confusing and presumably reflects serious scribal errors. In v. 14 it is advisable to emend *'ezrōh* ("his help") to *'ōzĕrāyw* ("his helpers").

Structure

I. First symbolic action: an exile's baggage	1-16
A. Prophetic word formula	1
B. Address as son of man	2aα
C. Explanatory background	2aβb
1. Characterization of community as rebellious	2aβ
2. Further characterization as blind and deaf	2bαβ
3. Summary characterization: rebellious	2bγ
D. Directions how to perform the action	3-6a
1. Resumptive address as son of man	3aα
2. General directions as an overall summary	3aβγbα

a. Prepare an exile's baggage openly	3aβγ
b. Move from one place to another	3bα
3. Explanation	3bβγ
a. Intent: they may see	3bβ
b. Problem: their rebelliousness	3bγ
4. Detailed directions	4-6a
a. First step: bring out your baggage openly	4a
b. Second step: go out openly at evening as is typical	4b
c. Third step: dig through the wall to bring it out	5
d. Fourth step: load up in the dark with face covered	6a
E. Label for action: a sign	6b
F. Report of execution of action	7
1. Report of overall compliance	7aα
2. Details of action	7aβγb
a. Brought out baggage by day	7aβ
b. Dug through wall at evening	7aγ
c. Brought out load openly in the dark	7b
G. Prophetic word formula	8
H. Address as son of man	9aα
I. Background for interpretation: people's asking	9aβγb
1. Rhetorical question: aren't Israelites asking?	9aβ
2. Characterization: rebellious house	9aγ
3. Quotation from Israelites: what are you doing?	9b
J. Directions for interpretation	10-12
1. Direction to speak using messenger formula	10a
2. General application: concerns prince and others in Jerusalem (text uncertain)	10b
3. Further directions for interpretation	11-12
a. Direction to speak	11aα
b. Overall label: sign for *you*	11aβ
c. Overall explanation: as I have done, so will it be done to *them*	11bα
d. Details	11bβ-12
1) Fate will be exile	11bβ
2) Prince will bring out baggage through the wall in the dark	12a
3) He will cover his face and not see (text uncertain)	12b
K. Two-part prophetic proof saying	13-15
1. Expressed in metaphor of net	13a
a. Intervention	13aα
b. Result	13aβ
2. Expressed historically	13b-14
a. Intervention	13bα
b. Result	13bβ-14

(Outline continued below)

The presence of the prophetic word formula in vv. 1 and 17 makes it plain that vv. 1-16 are a separate unit. That the prophetic word formula also occurs in v. 8 does not conflict with this conclusion, for the words "in the morning" in v. 8 show that the role of the formula here is merely to indicate the beginning of a new subpart of the text, occasioned by the lapse of time between the action and its interpretation. Because further structural issues are also linked to the analysis of the standard genre pattern, they will be discussed below.

Genre

Verses 3-16 clearly introduce the REPORT OF A SYMBOLIC ACTION. As was the case in chs. 4–5, a small subcollection of instances of this genre has been assembled in 12:1-20. For the connection between the two texts, vv. 1-16 and vv. 17-20, see the discussion of 17-20.

After developing rather normally according to the typical pattern for the report of a symbolic action in vv. 1–11, the structural logic inherent in this genre pattern begins to crumble in vv. 12-16. The typical pattern for the report of a symbolic action in its fullest form involves: (1) instruction from Yahweh to the prophet as to how to perform the action, (2) the report of the execution of the action by the prophet, and (3) its interpretation. In this passage it is remarkable to encounter at the very beginning in v. 2 a background characterization of the prophet's audience as rebellious, but the connection to this characterization in v. 3bβγ shows that this expansion of the usual pattern is deliberate.

The instructions in vv. 3-6a are set forth in the order frequently found in Ezekiel (see 6:3-7, 11f.; and 7:25-27), first an advance summary (v. 3aβγ) and then the details (vv. 4-6a). In a way that will turn out to characterize this unit, a strange double focus is found in these instructions: There is a stress on the fact of exile by describing the normal behavior of a deportee (see Isaiah 20), and in addition there appear some unusual, specific details about digging through a wall, darkness, and being unable to see. As suggested, this same double focus appears in the report of execution in v. 7 and in the interpretation in vv. 10-12. That in vv. 8-9 the people's questioning of the prophet's unexplained action should provide a transition to the interpretation is not unusual, as 24:19 shows. Furthermore, even though the reporting of the people's question within the divinely given announcement of interpretation rather than in the narrative account of the execution might seem strange, 21:12 (*RSV* 7) and 37:19 indicate that this too is not without analogy. It is, however, highly risky to attempt to draw biographical conclusions, as Eichrodt does (151), about the ambiguity of the prophet's action on the basis of the question in v. 9, for the question may simply be a stylized part of the genre pattern.

That no report is given of the prophet's execution of the command to speak in vv. 10f. is quite a common feature of OT narrative, but that the prophet should be told in v. 11 to speak in the first person about himself is unique in Ezekiel.

The double focus aspect of the interpretation reaches a high point when in vv. 10 and 12-16 the "prince" is specified as the subject of the message. The use of the term *maśśā'* ("oracle") is unique in this sense within Ezekiel. Further, the double occurrence of the command "say" in vv. 10 and 11 is unusual. All of these items combine to raise questions which are only made more serious in vv. 13-16. The switch to the divine "I" in vv. 13-15 and the occurrence of an elaborated RECOGNITION FORMULA in v. 15 reveal that vv. 12-15 are structured as a two-part PROPHETIC PROOF SAYING. However, even here the strange double focus noted above continues as the announcement of punishment in vv. 12-14 focuses only on the behavior of the unseeing prince, whereas the elaboration of the recognition formula deals only with the exiles in general. Finally, v. 16 is not at all linked to vv. 1-12, but seems to be connected only to v. 15, completing the thought of a possible remnant in the same spirit as 6:8-10. The occurrence of another recognition formula at the end of v. 16 gives it, too, the shape of a two-part proof saying, but also increases the impression of its being a secondary expansion.

Setting

The basic nature of a symbolic action is that of an especially powerful kind of proclamation, one which prefigures the event it announces. (For a fuller discussion of this general point about all symbolic actions → chs. 4–5.)

In this passage it is especially necessary to analyze the significance of the double focus mentioned above. That part of these verses which stresses the fact of exile as the future awaiting Jerusalem's inhabitants implies a pre-587 B.C. setting, and would draw effectively upon the memories of the 598/7 deportees, who with Ezekiel had experienced those very circumstances the prophet was reenacting "before their eyes." The switch in pronouns in v. 11 is precisely suited to this function, as the prophet is designated "a sign for you," i.e., the exiles in Babylon, about what will "be done to them," i.e., the people still living in Jerusalem but destined for deportation. The other part of these verses which centers on digging through the wall, darkness, and not seeing reflects a different background, that of the tragic fate of Zedekiah in 587. According to 2 Kgs 25:4-7; Jer 39:4-7; and 52:7-11, Zedekiah attempted to escape the fallen city by night, but was captured, brought before Nebuchadrezzar at Riblah, and blinded before being taken to Babylon. Zedekiah is consistently referred to by Ezekiel as "prince" rather than king, since he seems to have been regarded as a regent for Jehoiachin still living in exile.

While some scholars attempt to analyze this passage as a combination of two "sources," capable of being separated and reconstructed, it is more likely instead that these verses are just one more instance of post-587 "updating" of Ezekiel's earlier preaching. While it is possible that the prophet himself could be the one who editorially elaborated his own earlier material in the light of the actual shape of its fulfillment, the use of the term "oracle" not otherwise found in Ezekiel is against this. The way vv. 13-14 pick up 17:20-21 so closely may also support the assumption of a different editorial hand. The actual changes involved in this updating could well have been minimal, as Lang (21f.) points out, for the covering of the prophet's face, which was a mourning custom and thus appropriate in the setting of the city's fall, could simply have been made to take on a double meaning as it was given a new application by linking it to the prince unable to see. The actual reconstruction of an "original" version, as Zimmerli does (*Ezekiel 1,* 268), is perhaps more of a possibility here than in chs. 1–3 and 8–11, but still the problem of what may have been omitted from the pre-587 message in its updating for the post-587 situation casts a pall of uncertainty over the whole enterprise (see Eichrodt, 148-49).

Intention

The unit's original intention was to destroy false hopes, especially on the part of the exiles, that Judah would be able to break away from Babylonian domination. Eichrodt's idea (151) that the watching exilic audience might initially have misunderstood the prophet's actions to mean that he was acting out their own escape from Babylon is theoretically possible, but in the absence of any textual basis such an idea remains purely speculative. On the other hand, the shape of the action itself makes it certain that the 598/7 experience of the exiles themselves was being employed, through this deliberately reminiscent action, as an ugly paradigm linking the future with the past, and both together in the debilitating sphere of guilt and punishment. The public character of the action would have been a way of forcing an encounter with this message upon an unwilling audience.

The line in v. 3, "perhaps they will understand," stands in sharp contrast to the description of the rebellious house in v. 2, but no single item of a hopeful sort is present to suggest that this "perhaps" was anything more than a vain effort to bring about repentance, of the sort listed in Amos 4:6-12. The updating of this discouraging message by means of the even more discouraging fate of Zedekiah adds a yet more ominous cast to the text as a whole. The final expansion in v. 16 does nothing to ease this fateful mood.

As a whole the unit is thus one more reminder of the bizarre way false and foolish hopes could arise and become significant enough to require this sort of rebuke.

SECOND SYMBOLIC ACTION:
EATING AND DRINKING WITH TREMBLING, 12:17-20

Structure

(Continues the outline of 12:1-20)

II. Second symbolic action: eating and drinking   17-20
    A. Prophetic word formula   17

B. Address as son of man	18aα
C. Directions to perform the action	18aβb
1. Eat bread with quaking	18aβ
2. Drink water with trembling and fear	18b
D. Direction to speak to the people of the land	19aα
E. Directions for interpretation	19aβγδεζb-20
1. Messenger formula	19aβ
2. Subjects of concern	19aγδ
a. Inhabitants of Jerusalem	19aγ
b. In the land of Israel	19aδ
3. Content of interpretation in the form of a	
two-part prophetic proof saying	19aεζb-20
a. Announcement of punishment	19aεζb-20a
1) Results	19aεζ
a) Shall eat bread with fear	19aε
b) Shall drink water with horror	19aζ
2) Purpose: land may be emptied	19bα
3) Reason: violence of inhabitants	19bβ
4) Further results	20a
a) Cities laid waste	20aα
b) Land become a desolation	20aβ
b. Recognition formula	

Once again the presence of the prophetic word formula in vv. 17 and 21 demonstrates that these four verses constitute a unit. All aspects of structure may be treated with the analysis of the genre.

Genre

The unit comprises a REPORT OF A SYMBOLIC ACTION, although in not unusual fashion it is presented totally as instructions given to the prophet. Thus the usual pattern for this genre, which goes on to include the report of the execution of the action and its interpretation, is necessarily curtailed. No mention of execution occurs, and the interpretation comes only as instruction to the prophet about what he is to say.

The presentation of the interpretation is also somewhat unusual in that it comes as a two-part PROPHETIC PROOF SAYING following the mention of those whom the action concerns. This proof saying, made up of ANNOUNCEMENT OF PUNISHMENT and RECOGNITION FORMULA, is expressed in the third person throughout the announcement, shifting to direct address only for the recognition formula (see below under Setting). The announcement lacks any intervention, and strangely inserts a summary statement about purpose and reason between the first and second parts of the results. Both the overall brevity and the fact that both sections of results remain nonspecific contribute to a certain vagueness in the unit. Part one of the results does not go beyond the bare words used in the directions about the action to be performed, and part two employs only generalities about destruction.

Setting

While the *RSV* in v. 19 translates "say of the people of the land," this translation is the result of the belief that "people of the land" could refer only to the inhabitants of Jerusalem. However, as in 12:1-16, and especially in v. 11, it appears that a message *about* the Palestinians is being given *to* the exiles. "People of the land" is probably to be taken, as Würthwein argued in *Der 'amm ha'arez im Alten Testament,* to mean the "landed gentry," from which class the 598/7 B.C. deportees were quite likely drawn (see also Pope, *IDB,* I, 106). The very use of this description for landless deportees has, of course, a highly ironic flavor.

It is dubious if the label "inhabitants of Jerusalem" in v. 19, rather than "inhabitants of these waste places in the land of Israel" as in 33:24, is enough to determine that a pre-587 B.C. audience is in mind, although the similarity to 12:1-16 supports this. The parallel to 4:16, where "fear" and "horror" occur in the description of the siege diet, is further support of a pre-587 date, but it is also possible that this passage and 4:16-17 have been editorially assimilated to one another in language, even though depicting two separate symbolic actions.

To argue, as Zimmerli does (*Ezekiel 1,* 278), that the trembling involved was actually the result of the physical impact of ecstatic experiences, as in Jer 4:19-21, is possible to be sure, but is really without any clear basis in the text itself.

Intention

Once again this unit aims to quash false hopes of any escape from under the Babylonians' thumb. Thus it is closely parallel in intention to 12:1-16, and it is likely because of this similarity that the two have been linked together as a minor compilation of symbolic actions parallel to, but separated from, chs. 4–5.

Bibliography

B. Lang, *Kein Aufstand in Jerusalem* (2nd ed.; SBB; Stuttgart: Katholisches Bibelwerk, 1981); M. Pope, "'Am Ha'arez," *IDB,* I, 106; E. Würthwein, *Der 'amm ha'arez im Alten Testament* (BWANT 4/17; Stuttgart: Kohlhammer, 1936).

TWO DISPUTATIONS ABOUT DELAYED FULFILLMENT, 12:21-28

Structure

I. First disputation: "the days grow long"	21-25
A. Prophetic word formula	21
B. Address as son of man	22aα
C. Quotation of the popular proverb	22aβγb
1. Rhetorical question: what is this proverb?	22aβγ
2. Quotation of proverb: fulfillment is delayed	22b
D. Yahweh's response	23-25
1. Preliminaries	23aαβγ

a. Transitional "therefore"	23aα
b. Command to speak using messenger formula	23aβγ
2. Rejection of proverb	23aδ
3. Command to speak an alternative	23bα
4. Contrasting message	23bβγ-25baβ
a. Time of fulfillment is near	23bβγ
b. No more false visions	24
c. Self-introduction formula	25aα
d. When I will speak a word, it will be fulfilled, not delayed	25aβγ
e. My word will be fulfilled in your days	25baβ
5. Prophetic utterance formula	25bγ
II. Second disputation (elaborated below)	26-28

Once again the presence of the prophetic word formula in vv. 21 and 26 gives clear indication that vv. 21-25, by themselves, form a unit. Within the divine response to the popular proverb a carefully balanced arrangement is followed. As the proverb had spoken of "days" and "every vision," so these terms are picked up in the assertion of an opposite meaning. Instead of "days continuing to grow longer," they are now declared to "have come near." Instead of "every vision coming to nought," the claim is made for the fulfillment of every vision. Verse 24 shifts the subject briefly to those false visions which have been proclaimed, but only to remove this obstacle so that the final bold assertion of the speedy fulfillment of the word can be made.

Genre

As noticed earlier, a DISPUTATION typically presents a saying of the people to which Yahweh responds, usually by rejecting or radically revising the popular view. There is no prescribed pattern for the shape of the response, and the genre eventually undergoes major development in postbiblical times where it becomes a dominant pattern in Talmudic tradition. In Ezekiel the quotations from the people occur only within Yahweh's speech, but this is not a significant alteration in structure. In fact, like 18:1-3, vv. 22f. can be seen to be a rather stereotyped introduction to a disputation (Zimmerli, *Ezekiel 1*, 281).

Two additional formulas known from elsewhere in Ezekiel are employed here in modified form. At the beginning of v. 25 "I the Lord" is a reminder of the short form of the SELF-INTRODUCTION FORMULA, known from the laws of Leviticus 17–26, and the RECOGNITION FORMULA. In all these settings this formula constitutes an avowal of sovereignty. The words "I will speak the word and perform it" (v. 25bβ) constitute simply the common CONCLUSION FORMULA FOR DIVINE SPEECH transposed from the normal past tense into the future. Thus the power of traditional terminology patterns is observable in the way a new point is made by employing an old formula, even though the new point necessitates drastic revision of the old language.

The genre labels "proverb" and "vision" are encountered here, but not in any precise sense. "Proverb" is here not a specific kind of wise saying, but just a designation for a clever capsule. Similarly, "vision" is not employed in the narrow sense of something seen as opposed to heard, but as a broad label for prophetic revelation of any sort (see Isa 1:1; 2:1; Amos 1:1; Mic 1:1).

Setting

The passage provides one more illustration of the fantastically foolish confidence with which the Israelites, both in Palestine and in Babylon, viewed their future. Even while racing headlong toward the disaster of 587 B.C. and precisely in the face of strong prophetic messages of a coming doom, this popular confidence was apparently able to defuse those oracles of doom by branding them as old, as yet unfulfilled, and therefore powerless. As the events of 587 inescapably revoked that verdict, these disputations would have been preserved as evidence of the message's vindication, i.e., in a mood of "I told you so."

The precise background of the popular saying itself cannot be known. Zimmerli accurately summarizes the two alternatives: "either . . . the information about what was said by those who remained in the land came to him [Ezekiel] in the manner of Jer 29, or . . . he had in mind the whole history of . . . the contemptuous way Israel had always responded to its prophets" (*Ezekiel 1,* 281-82).

Intention

The popular saying reflects in its patronizing context a highly sophisticated attempt to neutralize the power of the prophetic word by lumping all prophecies together. The prophet is forced to admit the existence of "false vision or flattering divination," but unhesitatingly he fights off the attempted generalization and seeks to break through the defenses of his opposition by a bold assertion of fulfillment "in your days." As was always the case, no proof in advance was possible for the prophet, but the very placement of this unit alongside the message of 12:1-20 is a further ex post facto indictment of Israel's blind rebelliousness. Quite noticeably the focus of the unit in its context is not one which treats of the prophetic word in general. Instead, in this context the powerful word is seen only as the bringer of death, not life. Only as the setting shifted in the post-587 B.C. preservation of the tradition, within which the authentic word received its vindication, could there come once again a broader perspective within which one could dare again to think of a life-giving word and the possibility of a positive response (→ the elaboration of this idea in ch. 18).

SECOND DISPUTATION: "FOR MANY DAYS HENCE," 12:26-28

Structure

(Continues outline of 12:21-28)

II. Second disputation	26-28
A. Prophetic word formula	26
B. Address as son of man	27aα

82

C. Quotation of popular saying   27aβγb
  1. Introduction of quotation   27aβ
  2. Quotation proper   27aγb
D. Yahweh's response   28
  1. Preliminaries   28aαβγ
    a. Transitional "therefore"   28aα
    b. Command to speak using messenger formula   28aβγ
  2. Contrasting message   28aδbα
    a. No more delay   28aδ
    b. When I speak a word, it will be fulfilled   28bα
  3. Prophetic utterance formula   28bβ

In yet another instance the unit boundaries are clearly marked off by the prophetic word formulas in 12:26 and in 13:1, the prophetic utterance formula at the end of v. 28 confirming this.

Genre

This DISPUTATION is closely similar to the preceding one in both overall content and specific wording. However, it seems best in view of the clear differences that do exist between the two units to see them not as doublets created by the editorial process but as instances of a recurring return by the prophet to a common problem. Logically these two similar instances have been grouped in this small collection and linked appropriately to the related rebuking message of doom aimed at the rebellious audience of 12:1-20.

In this second instance the quotation of the people is introduced not with a rhetorical question as in v. 22, but with the direct observation of v. 27a. Also in this second instance the parallelism within the quotation puts the whole matter in a more elevated prose style.

The divine response in both units employs the same preliminaries, and v. 28aδbα expresses it in virtually identical words as those of v. 25aβγ, only with the clauses transposed in order. From this one would assume a single message from Yahweh was being applied by the prophet to two distinct, but similar, situations.

Setting

Again this passage reflects a time before 587 B.C., probably before the beginning of the siege in 589. The popular saying "the house of Israel" was most likely one that Ezekiel encountered among the Babylonian exiles, for it seems to be directed specifically against his own preaching in contrast to the more general orientation toward "every vision" in the preceding unit. Once the fulfillment of Ezekiel's message of doom was experienced, passages such as this would find their setting within a changed mood, one of vindication. Whether this new setting would have involved some new institutional context, such as fasts or other community ceremonies of lament and confession of guilt, will have to be discussed in connection with later chapters.

In its earliest oral setting the argument reflected in these verses reveals yet another attempt by the prophet's audience to raise a defense against the power of the prophetic word. In contrast to the more hostile claim in v. 22 that "every vision comes to nought," this section reveals a positive evaluation of the prophet's message, but one that blunts any impact of that message with the qualification that it concerns "times far off" (v. 27). Thus Ezekiel's audience could cheerfully affirm all he said, while at the same time incorporating everything into an intellectual perspective which effectively frustrated the prophet's intent. A similar situation existed in the way Jeremiah's announcements of punishment were seen as only a call to repentance on the basis of the case of Micah (Jer 26:17-19).

Intention

In response to this seeming endorsement of his message which actually denied its point there is little that the prophet can say. No arguments can touch their pious dodging of his proclamation. Instead he can only affirm that the fulfillment is at hand, that there will be no more delay. Thus the demonstration of who was correct was left to Yahweh's direction of history, and it was not long in coming.

Bibliography

A. Graffy, *A Prophet Confronts His People* (AnBib 104; Rome: Biblical Institute Press, 1984) 52-58.

TWO PROPHECIES AGAINST FALSE PROPHETS, 13:1-23

Text

In v. 2 one should probably read *hinnābē'* ("prophesy") for *hannibbā'îm* ("who prophesy"). In v. 11b the strange vocative *wĕ'attēnâ* ("you") should be deleted and *tĕbaqqēa'* ("will let break forth") revocalized as *tibbāqēa'* ("will break forth").

Structure

I. First prophecy: misleading the people		1-16
A. Prophetic word formula		1
B. Preliminaries		2-3aα
1. Address as son of man		2aα
2. Elaborated direction to prophesy		2aβγb-3aα
a. Direction to prophesy		2aβγ
b. Elaboration specifying prophets as false		2bα
c. Call to attention formula		2bβ
d. Messenger formula		3aα
C. First three-part prophetic proof saying		3aβ-9
1. Woe oracle as reason and announcement (2 mp and 3 mp)		3aβ-7
a. Pronouncement of woe to foolish prophets		3aβ
b. Series of accusations		3b-7
1) Prophets in 3 mp, except for v. 5		3b-6

84

a) They follow their own spirit	3bα
b) They have seen nothing	3bβ
c) Analogy: they are like foxes in ruins	4
d) You have not protected the people	5
(1) You have not stood in the breaches	5aα
(2) You have not built a wall	5aβ
(3) To serve as protection	5b
e) They make false claims	6
(1) They see falsely	6aα
(2) They use the prophetic utterance	
formula when not sent	6aβγ
(3) Yet they expect fulfillment	6b
2) Prophets in 2 mp	7
a) Accusatory question: haven't you	
seen falsely?	7a
b) You use the prophetic utterance formula	
when not told	7b
2. Transition to announcement (2 mp)	8
a. Transitional "therefore"	8aα
b. Messenger formula	8aβ
c. Summary accusation as reason:	
you have spoken falsely	8aγ
d. Transitional "therefore"	8bα
e. Challenge to a duel formula	8bβ
f. Prophetic utterance formula	8bγ
3. Announcement (3 mp)	9a
a. Intervention: my hand against them	
(with summary accusation in v. 9aβ)	9aαβ
b. Results: they shall be excluded	9aγδε
1) From the council	9aγ
2) From the register	9aδ
3) From admission to the land	9aε
4. Recognition formula (2 mp)	9b
D. Second three-part prophetic proof saying	10-16
1. Reason (3 mp)	10
a. They proclaim false peace	10a
b. They whitewash a wall	10b
2. Transition: direction to speak in response	11aαβ
a. Direction to speak	11aα
b. Addressee: whitewashers	11aβ
3. Series of announcements (2 mp)	11aγb-14bα
a. It will fall	11aγ
b. A great storm will come and they will all fall	11b-12a
c. People will mock daubers	12b
d. Transitional "therefore"	13aα
e. Messenger formula	13aβ
f. I will bring a great storm	13aγb
g. I will break down the wall	14a

(Outline continued below.)

Chapter 13 consists of two prophecies, vv. 1-16 and vv. 17-23, similar in both structure and content, grouped editorially into one larger unit by the use of the prophetic word formula only at the start of the first. Both deal with prophetic behavior unacceptable to the Lord, and each is made up of two prophetic proof sayings. In the first the focus is on male prophets proclaiming an inauthentic message, while the second section deals with female practitioners of a kind of black magic.

Genre

As noted earlier (5:11-13), a three-part PROPHETIC PROOF SAYING normally appears as just a standard PROPHECY OF PUNISHMENT to which a RECOGNITION FORMULA has been appended. That is, a prefixed reason is linked by *lākēn* ("therefore") and the MESSENGER FORMULA to an announcement, and then the entire unit is concluded with a recognition formula. Verses 1-16 consist of a pair of such units, vv. 1-9 and 10-16, but with certain minor departures. In place of the usual type in which reason precedes announcement, a WOE ORACLE in vv. 3aβ-9a appears, with the actual accusations or reasons for judgment coming in vv. 3b-7 and the announcement in v. 9a, v. 9aαβ presenting intervention, and v. 9aγδε results. As often, the announced punishment, exclusion from a future share in Israel, corresponds neatly to the crime of failing to protect the people so that they might have a future. It is disturbing that vv. 5 and 7-8 use the second person in direct address of the false prophets, while vv. 3b-4, 6, and 9a employ the third person. In parallel fashion the second prophetic proof saying in vv. 10-16 employs a third person reason in v. 10 and second person announcements in vv. 11-14. The announcements appear as results in vv. 11aγb-12 and v. 14bα, surrounding interventions in vv. 13aγb-14a. Then this second saying departs even further from the typical pattern by following the recognition formula in v. 14b with two verses in which an additional summary of announcements and reasons appears, once again blending second and third persons.

To salvage a consistent original text, Fohrer (68-73) groups the verses according to person into two parallel units. Zimmerli (*Ezekiel 1*, 290-91), on the other hand, sees the basic text in vv. 3, 5, 7a, and 8-9, to which the other verses have been added in a series of redactional developments. However, the material in vv. 7b, 11-12, and 15-16, which indeed seems to be secondary because of its repetitious content, is not consistently either second or third person, nor does it leave a consistent remainder. Thus it must be reluctantly concluded that available evidence does not enable us satisfactorily to reconstruct the text's editorial history. (See also the proposals of S. Talmon and M. Fishbane, "The Structuring of Biblical Books: Studies in the Book of Ezekiel.")

Setting

The words of both Jeremiah (see especially 6:14; 8:11; 23:9-40; 27–28; 29:8-9, 20-23, 31-32) and Ezekiel reflect that an important and extensive part of their activity involved opposition to other prophets, particularly ones preaching a message of nationalistic hope in the days immediately before 587 B.C. Ezekiel 13:1-16 clearly does reflect that kind of confrontation, the second person material perhaps stemming from actual prophet-vs.-prophet encounters. However, the material is not precise enough for us to decide whether it comes from a time immediately before the "day of the Lord" (v. 5) in 587 or a later time. Inasmuch as Ezekiel was already in exile since 598, a hope to "enter the land of Israel" (v. 9) would have been in order at either time. The use of the term Israel in vv. 2, 4, and 9 does not contribute to a decision about either date or locale, for Ezekiel always uses it to refer to the people of God as a whole (Zimmerli, *Ezekiel 2*, 563-65). That such encounters were really personal and individual in Ezekiel's case still remains likely, even though no textual evidence requires it. In any case, the editorial complexity of this text suggests that a considerable amount of generalizing has taken place.

Intention

This unit remains remarkably "objective" throughout. No reference at all is made to Ezekiel's own "genuine," and therefore superior, psychic experiences. But at the same time there is not given any fundamental "truth" which could be employed as a standard over against which to evaluate the work or words of others. Instead, it is mainly from the angle of responsibility that false prophets are denounced. Of course, the falsity of their message is a serious matter, but it is the intent of their preaching rather than its inaccuracy that is seen as decisively significant. Prophets are always vulnerable to being left in the lurch by a God who changes his mind, but Ezekiel's words do not even raise this possibility. Prophets who invent a message on their own and pass it off as revelation from God are always guilty of a fraudulent misuse of authority, but even that matter of speaking "presumptuously" (Deut 18:22) is not Ezekiel's primary concern here. It is the twofold failure of intent that is branded as most serious. A prophet's responsibility is to speak the true word of God in order that people may not be misled and in order that they may have a chance to change (Lam 2:14). While Ezekiel's adversaries are charged with having "seen nothing" (v. 3) and following "their own minds" (v. 2) and "their own spirit" (v. 3), when "the Lord has not sent them" (v. 6) and "has not spoken" (v. 7), the burden of his indictment lies elsewhere. By their false message they have given hope and security to a people facing judgment. False peace and whitewashed walls lead people to miss the purpose of God, and thereby to miss out on their only chance for life in the midst of the death being brought upon them. This is the one side of the failure of intent. The other side lies in what Ezekiel's opposing prophets had not done. They "have not gone up into the breaches, or built up a wall for the house of Israel" (v. 5). In Ps 106:23 it is observed that Moses "stood in the breach," i.e., put his life at risk in intercession for the people whom God had entrusted to his care. Evidently, Ezekiel sees prophets as called to a Mosaic office, of which intercession was an automatic part. Certainly that is how Ezekiel himself lived (9:8 and 11:13). To miss one's calling in this way is a far more tragic failure than any inaccuracy of prediction. Perhaps there is a further subtle reference to this idea of the failure to follow the prophetic calling in v. 9aαβ. This idea of the hand of Yahweh being upon his prophet finds expression in the hand of Yahweh revelatory formula (1:3). By a play on the word "upon" or "against" this very phrase is now made to express in 13:9a God's punishment on those who forsake their prophetic calling and thereby receive not ecstasy, but exclusion.

SECOND PROPHECY: MAKING BLACK MAGIC, 13:17-23

Text

In v. 18a one should likely read *yād* ("hand") for *yāday* ("my hands"). In v. 18b the interrogative *hanĕpāšôt* ("souls?") is to be read for *hannĕpāšôt* ("the souls"), although this may be just an uncommon vocalization. In v. 20a one should delete *lĕpōrĕḥôt* ("for birds"), and in v. 20b the difficult *'et- nĕpāšîm* ("souls") should be changed to *'ōtān ḥopšîm* ("them free").

Structure

(Continuation of outline of 13:1-23)

II. Second prophecy: making black magic	17-23
A. Preliminaries	17-18aαβ
1. Address as son of man	17aα
2. Hostile orientation formula	17aβ
3. Appositional preliminary accusation	17aγ
4. Direction to prophesy	17b
5. Direction to speak using messenger formula	18aαβ
B. First three-part prophetic proof saying	18aγδε-21
1. Woe oracle as reason	18aγδε-19
a. Pronouncement of woe to practitioners of black magic	18aγδε
1) Those who use bands	18aγ
2) Those who use veils	18aδ
3) Purpose: to hunt souls	18aε
b. Accusation	18b-19
1) Rhetorical question: will you control life and death?	18b
2) You have profaned me	19aα
3) For a profit	19aβγ

4) Purpose	19aδε
a) To kill those not destined to die	19aδ
b) To keep alive those not destined to live	19aε
5) Means: by your lies	19b
2. Transition	20aαβ
a. Transitional "therefore"	20aα
b. Messenger formula	20aβ
3. Announcement	20aγδεζ-21a
a. Intervention	20aγδεζ-21aαβ
1) Lord is against magic bands	20aγδε
2) I will tear them away (suffixes are used eccentrically in vv. 20a-21aα)	20aζ
3) I will set souls free	20b
4) I will tear off veils	21aα
5) I will deliver my people	21aβ
b. Result: they will no longer be your prey	21aγ
4. Recognition formula (2 fp)	21b
C. Second three-part prophetic proof saying	22-23
1. Reasons	22
a. You have improperly opposed the righteous	22a
b. You have supported the wicked	22bα
c. Result: blocking the wicked from a chance to change	22bβ
2. Transitional "therefore"	23aα
3. Announcements	23aβγbα
a. Result: you will not mislead anymore	23aβγ
b. Intervention: I will deliver my people	23bα
4. Recognition formula (2 fp)	23bβ

This section addresses female prophets rather than male, but the pattern of organization is remarkably similar to the preceding. Both vv. 1-16 and vv. 17-23 contain two three-part prophetic proof sayings, with a woe oracle employed in the first saying in each case. A few additional verbal similarities also appear in both sections.

Genre

As indicated above, vv. 18-21 contain a WOE ORACLE, with the accusations or reasons for judgment coming in vv. 18b-19 (apart from a preliminary one-word labeling in v. 17a of these prophets as speaking from "their own minds"). The announcement of God's action in response comes in vv. 20aγδεζ-21a, following the typical pattern of intervention in vv. 20aγδεζ-21aαβ and result in v. 21aγ. Apart from a few gender irregularities, the material consistently refers to these prophets in the second person feminine plural.

Setting

The known popularity of manipulative magic in Babylon helps somewhat to understand that it is some form of syncretistic practice here under attack, but the exact nature of either of the two practices mentioned is unknown (but see Greenberg's theory of "cushions," 239f.), and no evidence helps us to decide for a date either before or after 587 B.C. The colorful vividness of the language suggests that we do have here the record of a direct confrontation.

Intention

Once again it is a twofold failure of intent which is at the center of Ezekiel's attack. As in vv. 1-16, the focus is primarily on misleading people by giving them false security and thereby denying them an opportunity for a life-saving repentance. Secondarily here, in contrast to vv. 1-16, the profit-making aim of the false prophets and the accompanying profanation of the Lord (vv. 18b-19) are also mentioned.

Bibliography

W. Brownlee, "Exorcising the Souls from Ezekiel 13:17-23," *JBL* 69 (1950) 367-73; F. Dumermuth, "Zu Ez XIII 18-21," *VT* 13 (1963) 228-29; S. Talmon and M. Fishbane, "The Structuring of Biblical Books: Studies in the Book of Ezekiel," *ASTI* 10 (1975-76) 131-38.

AN ADAPTED LEGAL CASE: WHEN IDOL-WORSHIPERS INQUIRE OF THE LORD, 14:1-11

Structure

I. Narrative setting	1
II. Prophetic word formula	2
III. Preliminaries	3-4aαβγ
A. Address as son of man	3aα
B. Accusatory identification of audience	3aβγ
1. They have taken idols into their hearts	3aβ
2. They have set iniquity before them	3aγ
C. Reproachful rhetorical question: should inquiry be permitted?	3b
D. Transitional "therefore"	4aα
E. Direction to speak using messenger formula	4aβγ
IV. Three-part prophetic proof saying	4aδεζηb-8
A. Case of inquiring idol-worshiper (serves as reason)	4aδεζηb
1. Crime	4aδεζη
a. Identification: anyone of the house of Israel	4aδ
b. Specification of crime	4aεζη
1) Has taken idols into his heart	4aε
2) Sets iniquity before him	4aζ
3) Yet comes to a prophet	4aη
2. Punishment: the Lord will answer	4bα
3. Summary reason: because of his idols	4bβ
B. Purpose for Israel	5
1. That I may reach their hearts	5a

2. They are estranged from me	5b
C. Transition	6aαβγ
1. Transitional "therefore"	6aα
2. Direction to speak using messenger formula	6aβγ
D. Call to repentance	6aδb
1. Turn from idols	6aδ
2. Turn from abominations	6b
E. Announcement in the form of legal punishment	7-8a
1. Identification	7aαβ
a. Anyone of the house of Israel	7aα
b. Or a resident alien	7aβ
2. Specification of crime	7aγδεbα
a. Separates himself from me	7aγ
b. Takes idols into his heart	7aδ
c. Puts iniquity before himself	7aε
d. Yet comes to a prophet to inquire	7bα
3. Punishment: all intervention	7bβ-8a
a. I the Lord will answer	7bβ
b. Hostile orientation formula	8aα
c. I will make him an example	8aβ
d. I will excommunicate him	8aγ
F. Recognition formula (2 mp)	8b
V. Additional case of a disobedient prophet	9-11
A. Case of a disobedient prophet	9-10
1. Specification of crime: a deceived prophet gives an oracle	9aα
2. Explanation: I have deceived him	9aβ
3. Punishment	9b-10
a. Intervention	9b
1) I will stretch out my hand	9bα
2) I will destroy him from my people	9bβ
b. Result: his punishment will be like that of the inquirer	10
B. Purpose	11
1. That Israel may no longer go astray	11aα
2. That they may not defile themselves	11aβ
3. That the covenant may be restored: covenant formula in future tense	11bα
4. Prophetic utterance formula	11bβ

This section is undoubtedly a single unit, for it has a prophetic word formula in v. 2 near the beginning, closes with the prophetic utterance formula in v. 11bβ, and is followed by a new unit beginning with another prophetic word formula. The narrative setting in v. 1, which reminds one of that in 8:1, describes the scene for all of vv. 2-11 and is totally unconnected with vv. 12-23. In what seems at first glance like needless repetition, the guilt of the inquirers is described three times— vv. 3aβγ, 4aδεζη, and 7aγδεbα; their punishment is described twice—vv. 4bα and 7bβ-8a; and the entire situation is connected twice to the Lord's purpose for Israel—vv. 5-6 and 11abα. Further, while vv. 4-8 have the familiar overall shape of a prophetic proof saying using the language of a legal case, vv. 9-11 seem to be a peculiar extension of that case beyond the usual end marked by the recognition formula. It is Zimmerli's accomplishment ("Die Eigenart der prophetischen Rede des Ezechiel") to have explained how all of this fits consistently together by clarifying the generic usage.

Genre

The shift to impersonal terminology in vv. 4 and 7-8a reveals that material from a different setting has been incorporated within the normal structure of a three-part PROPHETIC PROOF SAYING. Examination of parallel material in the Holiness Code (H), Leviticus 17–26, makes it plain that it is a sacral law which has been incorporated. The introduction of the legal case with "any man of the house of Israel" occurs in virtually that form in Lev 17:3, 8, 10, and 13; 20:2; and 22:18. Even the elaboration of that introduction appearing in 14:7 in Ezekiel, "or of the strangers that sojourn in Israel," appears in all but the first of the H passages. Also the punishment, "cut him off from the midst of my people," in v. 8 is found in closely similar wording in the first five of the H texts. The use of the expression "bear their punishment" in v. 10 is another instance of the use of the terminology of sacral law (see Num 5:31).

As a priest, Ezekiel might be expected to utilize sacral legal formulations, but the precise way in which he does this needs to be spelled out. Appropriately, the legal case provides both the accusation and the announcement of punishment, but the overarching purpose of God requires that the sacral legal language be interrupted in vv. 5-6. In v. 5 the crime of idolatry is extended to all "the house of Israel," and in v. 6 the same "house of Israel" is called to turn from idols. When the legal case language is resumed in v. 7, this now serves only to introduce the legally specified punishment of excommunication, which brings the case to its conclusion, as shown by the use of the RECOGNITION FORMULA. Throughout, the legal aspect of the unit is characterized by the familiar *talio* pattern, according to which those whose crime is seeking an ORACLE from the Lord (→ ORACULAR INQUIRY) in spite of their idolatry, receive their punishment by means of the Lord's actually giving them what they seek, an oracle—only in this case one of judgment. However, in typical case-law style a further subcase appears and requires additional legal elaboration, namely the case of a prophet who mistakenly does grant the original request for an oracle. In vv. 9-10 that subcase is presented, the crime in v. 9aα and the punishment in vv. 9b-10. The punishment links both prophet and inquirer together in the sacral SENTENCE that they "bear their punishment," again a judgment calling for excommunication. Once again in v. 11 even this subcase is integrated into God's larger purpose for the purging and restoration of his people, climaxing this time with the COVENANT FORMULA in v. 11bα rather than the recognition formula.

Setting

There is nothing specific in this section which allows us definitely to fix either its locale, Jerusalem or Babylon, or its date, before or after 587 B.C. Zimmerli (*Ezekiel*

1, 306) suggests that "the complete indifference to the actual situation of Jerusalem and the individualizing of the divine judgment against specific idolaters and specific prophets" argue for a Babylonian context, and that idol-worship became a more severe temptation for exiles once the fall of Jerusalem crushed their hopes for a quick return. However, the most such arguments can give us is a certain degree of likelihood.

Intention

There is a strong element of irony in the selection of the particular legal terminology which gives this unit its distinctive flavor. Both the "cutting off from the midst of my people" of v. 8 and the "bear their punishment" of v. 10 are formulaic language envisaging a specific legal outcome, excommunication. In the first case, excommunication is the perfectly natural consequence for the idol-worship which breaks the bond that united Israel as the people of Yahweh. While Deuteronomy 13 sees the death sentence as the more appropriate punishment for apostasy, that perspective has in mind a time when Israel could function more as a political state, while Leviticus 17–26 sees Israel more as a cultic community, held together by a common allegiance in worship. In any case, though, excommunication is conceivable as a punishment only for a small minority of individuals within the group. In high irony Ezekiel documents the particular crime he discusses as extending to the "house of Israel, who are all estranged from me through their idols" (v. 5). To threaten excommunication as the punishment for the whole community is grotesque. What would be left? This is not a case of a poor choice of metaphor by the prophet. Repeatedly we have seen and shall see again that Ezekiel does view his entire people as united in guilt and standing under a judgment of rejection. Nevertheless, he persists in avowing a vast consistency of divine intent and purpose. None of this tragedy is described as having somehow slipped out of divine control. Even a disobedient prophet is being deceived by Yahweh (v. 9aβ, see 1 Kgs 22:22-23). In shocking consistency the ultimate conclusion is logically drawn: The people have to go in order to save the people! What became a sarcastic joke about the goal of the United States in Vietnam is here given bald expression. In order to be saved Israel must be destroyed. Certainly such an extreme formulation must have triggered opposition in response, and we can expect to encounter evidence thereof in Ezekiel's preaching.

After two units in which an initial section closing with the recognition formula was extended into a second section climaxing in the same formula (13:3-9 and 10-14, 13:18-21 and 22-23), it is provocative to find in 14:1-11 a similar pattern, except that the second section ends in the covenant formula expressed in the future tense. Does this not suggest that the essential content of God's restoration of his people may be equivalently expressed in either way? The proof that results in insight ("and you shall know") is aimed at nothing other than the restoration of peoplehood.

Bibliography

R. Mosis, "Ez 14,1-11—ein Ruf zur Umkehr," *BZ* 19 (1975) 161-94; W. Zimmerli, "Die Eigenart der prophetischen Rede des Ezechiel," *ZAW* 66 (1954) 1-26.

THE CASE OF INTERCESSION: EVEN THE MOST RIGHTEOUS COULD NOT HELP, 14:12-23

Text

In v. 16 the copula should be prefixed to *šĕlōšet* ("three"), so as to read *ûšĕlōšet* ("and . . . three"). In v. 22 one should likely change *hammûṣā 'îm* ("who will be brought out") to *môṣî 'îm* ("who bring out").

Structure

I. Prophetic word formula	12
II. Preliminary: address as son of man	13aα
III. Three-part prophetic proof saying	13aβγδb-23
A. Theoretical legal case of divine judgment, as reason	13aβγδb-20
1. Basic case as background for subcase	13aβγδb
a. Crime: a land's guilt	13aβ
b. Punishment	13aγδb
1) I stretch out my hand	13aγ
2) I break the staff of bread	13aδ
3) I send famine	13bα
4) I cut off man and beast	13bβ
2. Subcase: presence of three famous righteous men	14-20
a. Preliminary assessment of inescapability	14
1) Condition: presence of three men	14a
2) Result: could only save themselves	14bα
3) Prophetic utterance formula	14bβ
b. Detailed explanation of subcase	15-20
1) First possibility: wild beasts as punishment	15-16
a) Situation: I send wild beasts	15aα
b) Results	15aβb
(1) They bereave the land	15aβ
(2) Desolation takes over	15b
c) Assessment: potential for deliverance denied	16
(1) Condition: presence of three men	16aα
(2) Lord's oath of denial	16aβγδb
(a) Oath formula	16aβ
(b) Prophetic utterance formula	16aγ
(c) Oath	16aδb
α. They could not deliver their own children	16ad
β. They could deliver only themselves	16bα
γ. Result: desolation	16bβ
2) Second possibility: sword as punishment	17-18
a) Situation: sword	17abα

2. Specification: that I have not acted without cause	23bβ
3. Prophetic utterance formula	23bγ

There are some strange elements which mar the otherwise smooth logic of this unit's development. After leading up fairly briefly in a general case (v. 13) to the subject of the inescapability of God's judgment, by far the largest amount of space is spent in highly repetitious fashion spelling out *three* kinds of divine punishment as inescapable (vv. 14-20) even for the children of outstanding past righteous heroes. But in this lengthy section the treatment remains general, even universal ("land"). Only in vv. 21-23 is a connection to Jerusalem made. But when that connection is made in v. 21, *four* acts of judgment are specified: sword, famine, wild beasts, and pestilence, the second being previously mentioned only in the introductory section in v. 13. Finally, after stress on the impossibility of escape in vv. 13-20, survivors strangely become the focus of attention in vv. 22-23.

Genre

The presence of the PROPHETIC WORD FORMULA in 14:12 and 15:1 marks this text as a unit, and the RECOGNITION FORMULA — albeit modified—in v. 23b suggests the structure of a PROPHETIC PROOF SAYING. The usual pattern of a three-part prophetic proof saying, though, is formidably stretched by the lengthy reason section III.A, employing legal language for nearly eight verses. Unusually, the dominant emphasis is clearly placed on the subcase III.A.2.b in which a strictly followed pattern appears three times over. This is no previously existing pattern, but one created ad hoc for the shock value of its negative assessment. The actual announcement in III.C is relatively brief and again seems to reflect both an emphasis and a structure peculiar to Ezekiel (see 6:8-10 and 12:16).

The structure of an OATH appears more fully here than is the case where only the OATH FORMULA is used, as in 5:11. The apparently puzzling construction by which "If . . ." is used as a way of saying, "I swear that . . . not . . . ," is accounted for by the supposition of an unexpressed self-curse. Instead of saying, "I swear that if X happened, then may Y happen," one says more simply, "I swear (i.e., "as the Lord lives") if X . . . ," thereby not putting into words the fearful reality invoked as a curse upon oneself. On a few occasions, as in Job 31, the actual self-curse is expressed, thus strengthening the oath to its fullest potential. The PROPHETIC UTTERANCE FORMULA is used to punctuate key parts of the structure of the whole unit: marking the boundary between the end of the preliminary presentation of the subcase in v. 14 and the subsequent beginning of the detailed explanation; marking the oath in each of the three possibilities explored within the subcase; and marking the end of the entire unit.

Setting

It is evident that Ezekiel encountered much opposition based on the popular belief in the certainty of Israel's election. Earlier Amos 3:12 shows how a disputation saying could function to shock those who believed any divine judgment could only be partial. Jeremiah 15:1-3 attests how at about the time of Ezekiel's beginning ministry it could become necessary to shock an audience by denying the delivering power of intercession, even by famous heroes like Moses and Samuel. In close similarity to the role of the preceding unit in asserting the inescapability of judgment because of the negative factor of apostasy, this unit stresses the impossibility of any hope for escape because of the ineffectiveness of any positive factor. One should assume that Noah, Daniel, and Job were all known in popular tradition as heroes in stories with a positive outcome, not just as people of exemplary righteousness. The language of "four sore acts of judgment" (v. 21), i.e., "sword, famine, evil beasts, and pestilence," is both heavily traditional and linked to ceremonies of covenant curses (Lev 26:21-39).

Because vv. 22-23 speak of "survivors," whereas vv. 13-20 deny a meaningful survival, it has often been suggested (e.g., Wevers, 114) that these verses are a post-587 B.C. addition. In opposition to this, it must be noted that vv. 22-23 do not speak of those who have been delivered (vv. 14, 16, 18, 20), but only of "survivors" who serve as evidence to prove the fulfillment of the predictions of doom. The parallel to the "remnant" in Amos 3:12, which only served to enable a death certificate, is striking. That Ezekiel's fellow exiles should be "consoled" by this suggests the familiar mood of a doxology of judgment. "I have not done without cause" would be extremely close to the acknowledgment "righteous art thou" in Jer 12:1 (von Rad, *Old Testament Theology*, I, 357-59).

Intention

In Gen 18:22-33 Abraham is presented as demonstrating how seriously he takes the promises of God by his intercession for Sodom. The appeal is made there on the ground of God's righteousness. The presence of as few as ten righteous would secure the deliverance of even this epitome of all evil cities. Ezekiel 14:12-23 presents the exact opposite in intention, viz., to demonstrate how serious are the announcements of God's judgment. The repetitious buildup of emphasis in each case aims at a similar numbing effect: Jerusalem, just like Sodom, is hopelessly doomed. No avenue of hope has been left unexplored, and God's justice must simply be acknowledged. To see in this stress on how "God's judgment remains inexorable" a reason to "hope ... for the unchangeability of the divine covenant promise" (Zimmerli, *Ezekiel 1*, 316) seems perhaps to open the door to confusion. It is not the function of this passage in its original oral setting to lay the groundwork for any kind of hope, even in the God who brings life out of death. The original aim is rather to chop down a false reliance that clings to some path of escape. No, the judgment is absolutely inescapable. To be consoled about the fall of Jerusalem because it was a just punishment is not immediately a basis for hope. Rather, like ch. 8, it compels a sigh of acquiescence, "Not without cause." Only in the ongoing liturgical use of this material in following years could the possibility arise of undergirding unfulfilled promises by means of fulfilled threats. But long before such a perspective could develop in theological reflection, Ezekiel was to comfort his hearers with an even bolder message of hope (ch. 37).

Bibliography

G. von Rad, *Old Testament Theology* (tr. D. M. G. Stalker; New York: Harper, 1962) I, 357-59.

AN ANALOGY: THIS VINE IS USELESS, 15:1-8

Structure

This section is manifestly a unit by itself, beginning with the prophetic word formula, ending with the prophetic utterance formula, having a consistent common subject, and being followed by the beginning of a separate unit with a new prophetic word formula.

Genre

Although the unit is given the typical shape of a three-part PROPHETIC PROOF SAYING by the utilization of the RECOGNITION FORMULA near the end (v. 7b), the rest of the arrangement is rather unusual. The employment of the vine metaphor in vv. 2-6 serves to provide a consistent linguistic image for both the accusatory reason in vv. 2-5 and the first part of the announcement of judgment in v. 6. After the initial announcement is made by applying the vine image to Jerusalem, the analogy is discarded apart from the use of fire as the means of destruction in v. 7a. The concluding part of the unit is also unusual in that the recognition formula is elaborated, this time with nothing bearing the flavor of the distinctive content of the preceding (as, e.g., in 14:23b), but simply with the FORMULA OF HOSTILE ORIENTATION modified into a temporal clause. Finally, the appearance of a summary conclusion using the two normal parts of a prophecy of punishment, reason and announcement, only this time in reverse order, is very close to 13:15-16.

It seems inappropriate to designate the use of the vine image in vv. 2-6 as a parable, if that label is to have any more precise meaning than "metaphorical discourse." The absence of any distinctively parable-style formulaic introduction or conclusion supports this judgment. The more accurate label indicating function would be that of a DISPUTATION (→ Setting).

The logic underlying the vine image is reasonably consistent, but not completely so. The application of the analogy in v. 6 does not elaborate the uselessness of Jerusalem, but picks up instead the relatively incidental item of the burning of vine branches which have been pruned off (Wevers, 118).

In the history of critical study much has been made, especially by Hölscher, of the poetic form of this text. Actually, as recent commentators are clear (see Zimmerli, *Ezekiel 1*, 318), this poetic form can be achieved only by drastic emendation. Although parallelism of sorts does occur, e.g., in v. 3, it is much more accurate to class the text as elevated prose rather than poetry.

Setting

From frequent examples, e.g., Ps 80:9-20 (*RSV* 8-19) and Isa 5:1-7, we know that the figure of the vine was used to give popular expression to the idea of Israel's election by the Lord. Because of the great importance of viticulture in Palestine, this figure gave expression not only to a faith conviction about God's choice, but to an evaluation of Israel's worth and even security. This whole complex of popular belief must have resulted in strong opposition to any prophetic preaching of a message of the rejection and destruction of Jerusalem. In taking issue with this popular confidence, Ezekiel makes it clear that the approaching doom is also the Lord's choice.

From the fact that Jerusalem's doom is still to come, the unit must be assigned to a date shortly before 587 B.C. That Jerusalem and its inhabitants are consistently spoken about in the third person, whereas the recognition formula speaks in direct address, fits precisely with Ezekiel's prophetic function in the midst of exiles in Babylon. To attempt to identify historically the two ends or two burnings with the fall of Samaria and of Jerusalem or any other specific events is a textually unwarranted allegorizing.

Intention

A mocking tone pervades the unit. To switch the discussion of the value of a vine from its fruit to its wood is deliberately and perversely to "stack the deck" in favor of a hostile verdict. Although the rhetorical questions give a flavor of objectivity to the prophet's discussion, it is plain that he actually intends no kind of dispassionate evaluation, but rather a scornful rejection. He seeks to destroy a popular fantasy, a "deceptive counterpart to a genuine faith in Yahweh's call" (Eichrodt, 196), for this delusive presumption has exploited God's promise so as to shut God's people off from the warnings that might have saved them, and even now stops their ears from hearing and heeding the redemptive purpose which underlies God's judgment. The only way to penetrate this false faith is by the shocking employment of the very imagery by which the dignity and privilege flowing from the Lord's gifts of grace had traditionally been expressed.

Bibliography

E. Baumann, "Die Weinranke im Walde. Hes. 15:1-8," *TLZ* 80 (1955) 119-20; G. Hölscher, *Hesekiel, der Dichter und das Buch* (BZAW 39; Giessen: Töpelmann, 1924).

AN ANALOGY: JERUSALEM, AN UNGRATEFULLY AND DISGRACEFULLY UNFAITHFUL WIFE, 16:1-63

Text

The following emendations have been adopted: in v. 6b *ḥăyî* (the second "live!") is omitted as a dittograph; the last two words of v. 15 are omitted as unintelligible; v. 16b is omitted as incomprehensible, possibly an exclamatory gloss; in v. 19a the final word is omitted as an incomprehensible gloss.

Structure

I. Prophetic word formula		1
II. Preliminaries		2-3aαβ
A. Address as son of man		2a
B. Directions		2b-3aαβ
1. Make known abominations		2b
2. Speak using messenger formula		3aα
3. Addressee		3aβ
III. Prophecy of punishment in figurative language (in direct address)		3aγb-43
A. Reason for punishment: Jerusalem's history of misbehavior		3aγb-34
1. Jerusalem's bad ancestry		3aγb
2. Her faithless ingratitude		4-34
a. The Lord's amazing care of her		4-14
1) Her neglected condition at birth		4-5

100

a) Heading and time reference:
"And as for your birth, on the
day you were born" 4aα
b) Evidence of parental neglect 4aβγb
  (1) Umbilical cord not cut 4aβ
  (2) Not washed with water 4aγ
  (3) Not rubbed with salt 4bα
  (4) Not swaddled 4bβ
c) Summary analysis 5abα
  (1) Omission of caring deeds reveals
    absence of love 5a
  (2) Exposure reveals contempt 5bα
d) Time reference, "on the day you
were born" (inclusio picking up v. 4aα) 5bβ
2) The Lord's amazingly gracious care:
first stage, childhood 6-7
a) Circumstance: his passing by 6aα
b) Her predicament seen 6aβ
c) His purpose as command: "Live"
and "grow up" 6b-7aα
d) His response as report: "I made you
like a plant" 7aβ
e) Results: her sexual maturation 7aγδb
3) The Lord's amazingly gracious care:
second stage, marriage 8
a) Circumstance: his passing by 8aα
b) Observation: the age for love 8aβ
c) Action 8aγδbαβ
  (1) Claimed as bride 8aγδ
  (2) Oath sworn 8bα
  (3) Covenant made 8bβ
d) Prophetic utterance formula 8bγ
e) Summary conclusion: "you
became mine" 8bδ
4) The Lord's amazingly gracious care:
third stage, beautification of the bride 9-14
a) Cleansing 9
b) Clothing 10
c) Jewelry 11-12
d) Summary 13
  (1) Jewelry 13aα
  (2) Clothing 13aβ
  (3) Food 13aγ
  (4) Generalization: regal beauty 13b
e) Resultant lofty reputation 14abα
f) Source: splendor from me 14bβ
g) Prophetic utterance formula 14bγ
b. Her shameless whoring 15-34

In its present state ch. 16 is one extremely long unit. In the course of the barest of preliminaries (II), an accusatory and legal note (Zimmerli, *Ezekiel 1*, 336 and Greenberg, 273f.) is struck in v. 2b, identifying Jerusalem as the accused and employing the familiar priestly label "abominations" as the charge. In III this charge is elaborated in great detail in the pattern of a prophecy of punishment addressed to the city, but employing the figure of a grossly faithless wife. While the major part of III is devoted in III.A to the spelling-out of the charge, after the briefest of transitions (III.B), another long section (III.C) announces the punishment to be imposed. In III.C.4 the pattern of accusation and punishment is summed up as wrath-engendering lewdness which demands requital. Here again is that synthetic perspective which sees deeds as inescapably linked to their consequences.

Within that summary in v. 43 the actual structure of the preceding accusation is further attested in the way Jerusalem's sin is specified as consisting in a failure to remember the days of her youth. Subsection III.A.2 spells out—again in great detail—how Jerusalem's early history reveals her gross ingratitude. In a series of three stages the Lord's amazingly gracious care is described (vv. 6-7, 8, 9-14) as a foil over against which later the shocking misbehavior of his wife can be made to stand out even more vividly. In fullest exaggeration Jerusalem is portrayed as totally lacking from birth even the simplest forms of elementary child care (vv. 4-5). God's electing grace is then described as consisting in two occasions on which he passed by and first commanded, "Live, and grow up" and then at the later visit entered into a marriage covenant with this still completely neglected waif. In fantastic generosity the Lord continued this pattern of one-sided graciousness by heaping upon his bride every kind of beautiful ornament so that her beauty was royal, resplendent, and internationally acclaimed (vv. 9-14). The foil character of this section is highlighted at its end with the concluding observation that it was a perfection *bestowed by God* (v. 14bβ). Verse 15 at the beginning of the next section picks up the idea of the given character of Jerusalem's beauty and identifies the young bride's shame as being rooted in a self-centered and ungrateful trust in her own beauty, which then finds expression in her whoring behavior, described in language that brings to mind words such as "wanton" and "nymphomaniacal." These are indeed appropriate words, for the young bride's actions are both perverse and self-destructive.

After the general description of Jerusalem's shameless whoring (vv. 15-16), a series of sections presents specific details of her disgusting behavior. The element of ingratitude in response to God's gracious gifts dominates the first two such sections, vv. 16-19 and vv. 20-22. In vv. 16-19 this motif appears in a series of repetitions, "you took," in each of which there appears Jerusalem's wanton misuse of the Lord's gifts for idolatrous purposes. In vv. 20-22 attention focuses on the grotesque misuse as fertility sacrifices of the children the Lord had given her, but the perverse character of Jerusalem's behavior is in v. 22 reconnected to God's preceding graciousness with the thought of how she failed to remember her desperately helpless past. This last thought comes in an obvious structural parallel, anticipating the summary reappearance of that same idea, as already pointed out, at the end of the announcement of punishment in v. 43.

After an interruptive cry of lament with the prophetic utterance formula in v. 23b, the specification of Jerusalem's transgressions resumes. While that prophetic utterance formula is often used in this gigantic unit as a marker of the end of subsections (see vv. 14b, 19b, 23b, 30a, and 43b), it is not so used in the case of every subsection, v. 34 being a clear case of the end of a subsection not so marked. Whether literary-critical conclusions about the secondary character of some sections can be supported by this absence of the formula is uncertain. It is true that vv. 30-34 do raise a separate theme, the bizarre fact that this whore must pay her "customers" in reversal of the standard practice. Still, although vv. 30-34 are to an extent thematically aside, they are at the same time linked to vv. 24-29 (see how v. 31 connects with v. 24). However, vv. 24-29 themselves are a departure from the preceding in that here Jerusalem's whoring is political, i.e., trusting in political alliances with neighboring powers rather than in the Lord. The previous infidelity had been seen as religious apostasy, but even then links clearly exist in the present text connecting vv. 24-29 with vv. 15-23 (see v. 27's link to v. 15). In addition, vv. 24-29 display structural peculiarities of their own, v. 27 being an anticipation of the announcement of punishment, which does not properly begin until v. 36, and vv. 28-29 being linked to each other by a threefold stress on insatiety as a characteristic of Jerusalem's selfdestructive lack of both fidelity and self-control. While Zimmerli and others seek to smooth out these peculiarities by the assumption of an editorial process of expansion performed upon a detectable original core, the available evidence to support such efforts is so small and disputed that no proposed literary reconstruction has been convincing. Once again the path of wisdom seems to be to stay with the present shape of the text as an endpoint, noting possible theoretical earlier stages, but not making those earlier stages the point of departure for investigation unless a preponderance of evidence suggests that action.

Following the brief transition from accusation to announcement in v. 35, and a preliminary review in v. 36 of the reason for the punishment, vv. 37-42 present the actual announcement of punishment in the customary alternation of intervention and results. Also highly typical is the *talio* logic followed in vv. 37-38, by which the whore, whose nakedness had been uncovered before her lovers, will find suitable punishment, when at the hands of those very lovers she is stripped bare so that her nakedness is exposed to all. Already in the formulation of this punishment it is clear that not just religious apostasy is in mind as Jerusalem's sin, but, when her lovers are gathered together against her from every side, a strong flavor of a political punishment for a political transgression is present. Similarly in vv. 39-41 a military-political doom is again described by allusions to bringing up a host, cutting to pieces with swords, and burning houses. And yet that military-political aspect is woven intimately together with another *talio* of stoning as the appropriate punishment for an adulterous wife (vv. 38, 40, and 41). Even the idea of the whore who paid her customers reappears in v. 41. Thus it would not be possible to recover some simpler original core in which the complicating ideas of accusation in vv. 16-34 were eliminated, without performing the most drastic sort of literary surgery upon the entire corresponding section of announcement in vv. 36-43.

One surprising lack of continuity between the earlier accusations and the later announcements comes in v. 42. This discontinuity lies not in the balance of crime and consequence, but in the description of God's emotions. While God's feelings find no express mention in the extremely objective portrayal of his gracious kindness to and even marriage with this abandoned girl, and while only one word, "to provoke me to anger," at the end of v. 26 departs from the steadily objective focus on Jerusalem's horrid behavior, v. 42 focuses solely on God's emotions. It is of course true that Jerusalem's emotions are repeatedly touched on in vv. 15-34, but astonishingly the Lord's feelings are not. This is all the more striking when it is recalled that in the compact summary in v. 43 the verb "enraged" does single out the emotional aspect. Nevertheless, the coherence of vv. 35-43 with the preceding in the present state of the text is in other respects exceptionally tight. For example, the accused Jerusalem is never even named in vv. 35-43. Her identity is simply carried over from the preceding. Thus vv. 35-43 could never have had an independent existence.

Sections IV and V extend the metaphor of Jerusalem as the Lord's faithless wife used in vv. 3-43 by the use of a related figure, that of Samaria and Sodom as Jerusalem's sisters, even though Jerusalem herself is never actually named in IV and V. Since v. 45 plainly picks up v. 3, and since in neither IV nor V are the sins of Jerusalem ever identified by more than generalities ("corrupt" in v. 47, "abominations" in vv. 51 and 58, "sins" in vv. 51-52, "wickedness" in v. 57, "lewdness" in v. 58, and "breaking the covenant" in v. 59), it is most likely that both of these sections had no independent existence, but have always been what they are now, elaborations expanding upon vv. 3-43. Section IV expands by taking up in vv. 44-45 the theme of bad blood which flows in Jerusalem's veins because of her parentage. This thought moves readily and naturally to Samaria in vv. 46a and 51 as Jerusalem's older sister, but rather surprisingly also to Sodom in vv. 46b and 48-49 as a younger sister. Also somewhat startling in view of the prominence in the chapter of the metaphor of sexual misbehavior is the way Sodom's sin is described without any such sexual dimension. Also unexpected is the way no specific sin of Samaria is mentioned at all. A new and especially caustic development in this section is the way unfavorable comparison with her sisters now becomes the way in which Jerusalem is accused (comparison to both sisters in vv. 47 and 51b-52 as an envelope, with comparison to Sodom alone in vv. 48-50 and Samaria alone in v. 51a). However, rather than issuing in an announcement of specific, appropriate punishments, section IV does not go beyond a condemnation to disgrace and shame for having made her evil sisters appear righteous by comparison. This heavy preponderance of accusation after punishment had already been announced in III.C is further indication of the expansionary role of IV.

Verses 53-57, on the other hand, proceed in a totally new direction in developing the accusatory comparison by some sort of announcement. Quite unexpectedly vv. 53 and 55 announce a restoration of all three sisters. This seemingly completely unanticipated message of hope is nonetheless made the vehicle of condemnation in vv. 54 and 56-57, in that the restored Sodom and Samaria are public evidence of Jerusalem's greater (v. 54) or at least similar evil (vv. 56-57). Thus the net effect of the restoration is simply further baring of guilt (v. 58).

A new messenger formula in v. 59a introduces section V as yet another expansionary announcement, this time one which picks up and builds upon the idea of covenant from v. 8. However, while the covenant in v. 8 was clearly one of marriage, vv. 59-63 again make no specific use of the marriage metaphor. The only remotely possible allusion to sexual misbehavior is the reference to "shame" in vv. 61 and 63. Instead, after an introductory statement "I will deal with you as you have done," which leads one to anticipate a message of suitable punishment as in vv. 38-42 above, there appears in vv. 60 and 62 a surprising promise, as in vv. 53-58, this time a promise of the establishment of an everlasting covenant. Once again, nonetheless, just as in vv. 53-58, this apparent message of hope is developed in vv. 61 and 63 as further ground for Jerusalem's shame. For the only time in the chapter, the recognition formula appears in v. 62b, thus giving V the vague shape of a two-part prophetic proof saying. This also makes section V seem only a loosely related, secondary expansion of the preceding, being of course, as stated, dependent upon both III for the covenant idea and IV for the imagery of an older and a younger sister.

Genre

As already noted, in its present state all of ch. 16 is one extremely long PROPHECY OF PUNISHMENT against the people with expansionary elaboration in vv. 44-63. How should its metaphorical dimension be formulated? In some ways the whole chapter is an ALLEGORY, for this faithless wife *is* Jerusalem. However, no real section of interpretation is given in which the imagery is explained, as in 17:11-21. Rather, in the accusation material a wealth of detail appears, some of which, e.g., the marriage covenant, had a clear point of symbolic correspondence to the history of God's people, while the majority, e.g., umbilical cord, clothing, etc., constitutes items with no specific symbolic role. Further, in the accusation material, but especially in the announcement of punishment, a number of nonfigurative items appear, e.g., sacrifice of children, burning of houses, etc. Thus, it seems necessary to conclude that the prophecy of punishment cannot properly be called allegorical, just one which extensively employs the metaphor of a faithless wife (Zimmerli, *Ezekiel 1*, 334f.). While many, following Gunkel (*Das Märchen im Alten Testament*, 113-15), have tried to find in ch. 16 the adaptation of a known folktale (→ STORY) about a "foundling child who is preserved from disaster by the intervention of a beneficent power and brought to prosperity and happiness" (Eichrodt, 202), any such connection is at best highly tenuous. At the most such a folktale provides nothing more than a starting point, and, more importantly, the largely nonmoral world of the fairy tale or MÄRCHEN (see Jolles, 218-46) is rapidly left behind as soon as the distinctive flavor of ch. 16 begins to receive attention in vv. 15-34.

When one proceeds to inquire into the atypical elements which make this particular instance of the genre of prophecy of punishment unique, the answer comes in a way which is nonetheless typical—of the book of Ezekiel. It is the crassness of this chapter that marks it off from similar passages in Hosea, and even in Jeremiah. The crudity of expression and of imagery, the overdrawn extensiveness of the portrayal of Jerusalem's wanton, insatiable, stubbornly persistent whoring comes close to being simply gross, or at least grotesque. The reason for this will be considered when the chapter's intention is examined.

Setting

In its present state ch. 16 definitely reflects a literary rather than an oral setting. However, it is highly likely that prophetic direct address lies behind the passionate vividness of much of the material. Zimmerli points to the legal background inherent in "make known" in v. 2, citing parallel usage of this term in 20:4 and 22:2 (*Ezekiel 1*, 336). Since the same root also occurs prominently when priestly duties are described in 22:26 and 44:23 and also receives much attention in Hosea (see H. W. Wolff, " 'Wissen um Gott' bei Hosea als Urform von Theologie"), we may have here a more or less technical label for the prophet's function as a legal accuser. (This juridical flavor appears even in the elaboration in vv. 44-58, where the legal terminology for established guilt is reflected in vv. 52 and 58; see Zimmerli, *Ezekiel 1*, 164 and 352; see also 14:10.) This would strongly undergird arguments that an originally oral presentation lies behind the present text. However, that this present state is the result of a literary development, and not just the recording of an oral activity, seems beyond doubt. Most especially sections IV and V reflect the technique of the reapplication of a related figure and the picking up and redirection of individual items of imagery. These are the techniques of literary expansion, not of oral presentation. While such a conclusion is suggested even by the complexity of the structure itself, with its backtracking from announcement in vv. 35-43 to renewed, though modified, accusation in vv. 44-52, another argument is even more forceful. While vv. 3-43 lead up to the announcement and the justification of the *forthcoming* fall of Jerusalem in 587 B.C., the remainder of the chapter in essence presupposes that fall. Once again such an updating of prophetic material could well have happened relatively soon after 587, and it could well have been done at the hand of or under the direction of Ezekiel himself.

Inasmuch as the same imagery of sexual misbehavior is employed in another extended metaphor in ch. 23, it is natural to wonder about possible dependence of one chapter upon another. Scholarly investigation has led to no firm results. Since the focus in ch. 23 is totally upon whoring behavior with the nations, i.e., political infidelity, it has often been proposed that the presence of this motif in ch. 16 is the result of the influence of ch. 23. Such an approach, though, is an oversimplification, for it assumes that influence can only come from literary material known to us. Certainly other influences in the process of tradition history are equally likely, if not more so. Whether the sexual metaphor in ch. 16 was in some original version limited to the worship of other gods, i.e., cultic or spiritual infidelity, cannot be demonstrated. The text simply does not provide a clear basis for deleting vv. 26-29 as an intrusion. As the text is now, the political and cultic dimensions are interwoven and interconnected in both the accusation and the announcement of punishment, and the prehistory of that blending can only be the subject for conjecture, not for literary reconstruction. The blending may well go back to the oral stage of preservation, if not to that no longer capturable first moment when the prophet delivered the oral message that was the starting point out of which our present text eventually developed as a literary precipitate.

To try to be more precise is exceedingly difficult, and the literary-critical attempts to isolate earlier and later strata are, as indicated above, uncertain and unconvincing. At least this much is certain: The attempt to reconstruct a basic oral core by searching out a poetic original is a wishful romanticism which does not take seriously enough either the present text as the end point of a tradition process or the immensely speculative character of all reconstruction techniques. Not only is any reconstructed core in itself only a hypothetical reality, but the explanation of why such a beautiful and logical original text should have been subjected to such insensitive elaboration requires us to postulate a chaotically careless procedure of preservation which is in itself totally without any support other than the assumption which requires it. (See the summary of Zimmerli's work by P. Scalise, 65-92.)

It is instead more profitable to ask how this literarily elaborated end product functioned. In response to this question a few proposals can be risked. First, the prophet's career itself, reaching beyond 587 B.C. as it did, suggests that pre-587 material presented earlier as God's powerful word would increasingly raise the question, "Of what significance is such a word now, beyond its fulfillment?" As has been seen before (see 6:8-10 and similar passages), it is characteristic of this book to press for the shameful confession that God was just in the punishment he sent. Thus the chronological setting underlying these updating sections does not extend down to the time of any post-exilic restoration, but merely to the continuing post-587 exile in which Ezekiel himself functioned for over a decade and a half. Consequently, neither the expansion in IV or that in V takes us beyond a message of "be ashamed and bear your disgrace" (vv. 52, 54, 61, and 63).

Intention

Already the first oral presentation lying behind the chapter seems likely to have had an aim closely similar to that of the present vv. 1-43. That intention was broadly to trace Judah's corrupting Canaanization, which could so aptly be described as a wife's infidelity, back to Israel's beginning. In a way similar to that of chs. 20 and 23, Ezekiel's goal here is broad historical analysis. The intention is to penetrate into the cause and effect pattern underlying this twilight time in the history of the people of God. Extremely large-scale theological structuring lies behind this analysis. No attention is paid to individual historic incidents in their uniqueness. No concern is given to the political options available in a given historical moment, nor to the whole question of the extent to which Canaanization in worship may well have been simply an unconscious and unreflected syncretism. Instead, every part of the chapter's development is directed toward the construction of a pattern of the absolute contrast between God's unmotivated graciousness and his people's shameless apostasy. This is a process of theological abstracting by which each side of the analysis magnifies the extent of its counterpart. God's grace appears the greater in the light of his partner's madly consistent, self-destructive rebellion, and Israel's sin appears all the more offensive as the betrayal of such amazing, freely given love (→ ch. 20).

The theme of the unmotivated character of the Lord's election of his people is highlighted by the description of how he "passed by" and spoke the powerful words that rescued his partner from total helplessness and doom, and then endowed her with such an abundance of gifts that she reached royal status. Clearly the mental process underlying this use of the metaphor of a faithless wife is not one aiming at realistic portrayal of a common human problem. No attempt whatsoever is made to create the least element of sympathy for this woman. Obviously Ezekiel wished solely to portray an intellectual reality, but to do so with such power that it might move via its emotional dimension beyond the sphere of the purely intellectual into the deepest levels of self-understanding. To accomplish this all stops are pulled out. Israel's behavior is described as gross, perverse, shockingly offensive, and simply disgusting. Repeatedly the idea is used that his partner's behavior is so bizarre as to be incomprehensible to the whole world, and even such an extremity of evil that Sodom would look good in comparison. Such words as total depravity come to mind as labels for that which is here conveyed by savagely powerful imagery. But the imagery is not the only instrument by which this theologizing (→ THEOLOGICAL REFLECTION) is expressed. The root of this shameful whoring is labeled in v. 15 as false trust, an insightful analysis of the root of sin which appears only in 33:13 additionally, and there in a much more theoretical context. While the imagery aims at producing a self-understanding which issues in shame and embarrassment, there is also, as is so typical of Ezekiel, a distinct element of rationality aiming at the intellectual insight, which is led in horror to comprehend, to recognize, and even to accept the extent of one's folly. Moreover, because it is all at bottom a historical survey (→ HISTORY), it must be understood as an attempt to bring about that powerful

111

kind of remembering of which Deuteronomy speaks. The essential difference between Ezekiel's historical surveys and Deuteronomy's sermonic reflecting lies only in the extent of the imagery. Both are the theological reflections of profound and creative minds motivated by a passionate concern, seeking to reach their audiences by extreme means which, while bordering on the excessive as in Deut 7:7 or 9:4-7, or as in Ezekiel 16, still demonstrate the power of theology to become proclamation.

While the expansion in section IV is closely akin to the intention of the preceding material in its aim to shock by the illustration of a Sodom made to appear righteous by Jerusalem's disgusting behavior, section V moves a step beyond this. While a considerable element of stunned amazement over the extent of her own wickedness is still intended by vv. 53-58, section V in vv. 59-63 focuses on memory in a slightly different way. Now that memory which had been missing (v. 43) in Jerusalem's shameless folly is explicitly present, triggered by the Lord's remembering his covenant (v. 60), and it is to play a key role. Alongside the recognition formula (v. 62), coming both before it in v. 61 and after it in v. 63, Jerusalem's remembering is the only element Ezekiel describes as a link between her grievous past and her forgiven future.

Bibliography

H. Gunkel, *Das Märchen im Alten Testament* (Tübingen: Mohr, 1917); A. Jolles, *Einfache Formen* (2nd ed.; Tübingen: Niemeyer, 1968); P. Scalise, *From Prophet's Word to Prophetic Book: A Study of Walther Zimmerli's Theory of "Nachinterpretation"* (Diss., Yale University, 1982); H. W. Wolff, " 'Wissen um Gott' bei Hosea als Urform von Theologie," *ET* 12 (1952-53) 533-54.

A FABLE: THE EAGLE, THE CEDAR, AND THE VINE, 17:1-24

Structure

I. Prophetic word formula	1
II. A fable	2-10
A. Preliminaries	2-3aαβ
1. Address as son of man	2aα
2. Direction to use figurative speech	2aβ
3. Addressee: house of Israel	2b
4. Direction to speak using messenger formula	3aαβ
B. The fable proper	3aγδb-10
1. The first eagle	3aγδ
a. His great size	3aγ
b. His fancy plumage	3aδ
2. His deed	3b-5
a. Locale: Lebanon	3bα
b. First act: cut off cedar top	3bβ-4a
c. Second act: took it to a merchant city	4b
d. Third act: started a new plant from "the seed of the land"	5

The organization of the chapter is quite clear. This is so in spite of the un-usual second appearance of the prophetic word formula in the middle of the unit. That formula in v. 11 is not used, as it is on almost every other occasion, to intro-duce a new unit, but here only to introduce a major new section within a unit. After the fable is set forth (II), the prophetic word formula functions to introduce its in-terpretation as though it were an entirely new section. (See 12:8 as a similar usage.)

Actually, another sort of break has already taken place in the chapter before v. 11, and once again it is a formula that calls attention to it. While the figurative language of the fable is developed consistently from v. 3 to v. 10, the messenger formula at the start of v. 9 signals the shift from the description of past events in vv. 3-8 to a focus on an undecided future in vv. 9-10. However, again this apparent structural break reflects a definite logic inherent in the use of the fable form. The fable itself is *addressed* to an audience, one vv. 2-3 make plain. While that addres-see seems to vanish from the scene in the face of the objective narrative in vv. 3-8, in v. 9 the addressee reappears as the actual point of the fable surfaces.

Similarly in the interpretation (III), a break comes in v. 16, this time signalled by the oath formula. Verses 12-15a here follow the narrative of the fable in provid-ing the historical decoding of the figurative language in narrative form, vv. 12-13 resuming in their "and he took" that same word from vv. 3 and 5. Verse 15b again allows the addressee to reappear as the rhetorical questions of vv. 9-10 are picked up. Once the addressee has surfaced again, vv. 16-18 return to the familiar pattern of an announcement of punishment as would be typical of a prophecy of punishment. In vv. 19-21 the same thoughts of punishment are presented again, this time marked off by "therefore" plus the messenger formula, in the style most typical of Ezekiel, that of a two-part prophetic proof saying.

Section IV manifestly goes on to something not in any way anticipated in vv. 1-21, a message of hope. To make this possible, a new scene is loosely attached to the fable's end, one which simply bypasses the questions about an undecided future and the message of judgment which grew out of them. In v. 22 a new beginning is described whose stress on the high and lofty (v. 23) is in marked contrast to the low and humble of the preceding (vv. 6 and 14). Also totally different in vv. 22-24 is the way the figurative language is left uninterpreted, but its structure as a two-part prophetic proof saying is still highly characteristic of Ezekiel.

Genre

A narrative in which plants and animals function as characters, such as vv. 3-10, is by definition a FABLE. Beyond that, however, the interpretations provided in vv. 11-21—and already the obviously symbolical character of the personnel and actions within vv. 3-10—make it plain that we have here a fable with rather extensive allegorizing elements. While some of the details, such as the colors of the plumage, do not receive or lend themselves to any specific symbolical significance, many items do. While the word "allegory" appears in the *RSV,* the Hebrew word *mašal* does not have that precise meaning, being used for proverbs, comparisons, and varieties of figurative language (see 12:23; 16:44; 18:2; 21:5; 24:3). In v. 2 the designation RIDDLE is used alongside *mašal* and is also a label from the heritage of wisdom literature (see 1 Kgs 10:1; Ps 49:5; 79:2; and Prov 1:6). The essence of a riddle is its intent at the same time both to conceal and reveal, and thus to entice its interpreter to search for meaning. This essential dimension is manifestly present in vv. 3-10, even though the label "riddle" would be inappropriate because of its narrower connotations, such as the question/answer pattern, which are not a part of ch. 17. Further, while some scholars, e.g., Zimmerli and Greenberg, see full poetic structure in vv. 3-10, it seems more accurate in light of metric difficulties to label this material elevated prose, that is, prose enhanced by repeated use of parallelism even though a strict metrical structure is not discernible. That some preexisting poem lay behind the present text is a proposal without any real support.

As noticed above under Structure, the fact that this fable and its interpretation are a part of a prophetic proclamation, i.e., addressed to an audience as the communication of a message from God, affects the organization. As a result, the interpretation in vv. 11-21 is shaped specifically as judgment preaching, that is, interpretation aimed at convincing the hearers of the just consequences of infidelity, and not just as curiosity-satisfying analysis. This addressee-oriented element was seen to be especially prominent in vv. 15b-18 and 19-21. The appearance of the RECOGNITION FORMULA in v. 21b strongly supports this analysis.

Although the genre of vv. 22-24 as a secondary expansion of the fable is discussed under Structure, the final line of that section calls for additional comment. The CONCLUSION FORMULA FOR DIVINE SPEECH, "I the Lord have spoken," appears already in v. 21, but in v. 24 it is elaborated by the words "and I will do it." This elaboration, which also occurs in 22:14, 36:36, and 37:14, seems to be simply an underlining of the power inherent in the prophetic word, but it should be noted that of these four occurrences, all but 22:14 appear as the conclusion of a message of hope. The unelaborated formula, on the other hand, in all but one instance appears as the conclusion of a message of doom.

Setting

Such wisdom genres as fables and riddles customarily reflect a setting in which the relatively timeless truths of moral instruction and social advancement are taught and learned. When the prophet borrows such material for the proclamation of God's judgment upon unfaithful behavior, a major change in setting takes place. When the continuing unfaithful behavior demonstrates itself in political maneuvering and rebellion in specific, known, historical circumstances, that change becomes complete, for out of this historical knowledge we are able virtually to pinpoint the occasion on which the message was preached.

The aspect of an undecided future apparent in vv. 9-10 and 15b makes it evident that the preaching of this message must have taken place before that siege which began in January 588 B.C., when Nebuchadrezzar, the first eagle, took vengeance on Zedekiah, the seed of the land he had installed in 597. The second eagle was likely Psammetichus II (594-588 B.C.), and the Pharaoh of v. 17 who did not give effective help was Apries (or Hophra) whose abortive expedition into Palestine succeeded only in bringing about the brief temporary lifting of the Babylonian siege. Although these facts would all be equally known to residents of Palestine or to Jewish exiles in Babylon, the labeling of the city of Babylon as "the city of merchants" in "a land of trade" (v. 4) might reflect the exiles' greater familiarity with circumstances in Mesopotamia. Similarly, the description of the eagle's colored plumage in v. 3 may conceivably reflect the glazed tiles of Babylonian art.

Although vv. 11-21 speak from the assurance of Zedekiah's doom, the details of the description of his punishment make it unlikely that this section reflects a time after 587 B.C. In v. 20 Zedekiah is threatened with being brought to Babylon for judgment, but the episode of his blinding at Riblah is not mentioned at all. This is in sharp contrast to 12:1-16 where this episode does seem to be presupposed. Accordingly, 17:11-21 may well come from the same time as vv. 1-10, just before the Babylonian siege in 588.

The expansion of the fable in vv. 22-24 reflects an entirely different setting. We have moved from a stinging political allegory to a mythological tree, a *Weltbaum*. This section promises a glorious future of worldwide acknowledgment for Israel's Lord in language that borders on apocalyptic (Wevers, 139). Israel's return from exile and the exaltation of the Davidic dynasty are seen as the result of God's action. That God "will take" a cedar top and plant it on a mountain height in Israel is a deliberate contrast to the eagle's taking of vv. 3, 5, 12-13 and to the lowliness of the vine in vv. 6 and 14. The apparent peaceful character of this exaltation is in some ways similar to Isa 2:2-4, but that passage is also exceedingly difficult to date. To see in the skillful appropriateness of the way the verses link up to the rest of the chapter some indication of Ezekiel himself as the author, rather than some presumably less insightful disciple as Eichrodt does (229), is to adopt a romantic view of the prophet's relation to his disciples which unnecessarily belittles the subsequent bearers of the prophetic tradition.

Intention

The wisdom flavoring of the passage reflects its goal of establishing Zedekiah's folly in his rebellion. A closely similar section appears in 21:30-32 (*RSV* 25-27). Of particular significance is the way the root of Zedekiah's sin—and of course that of his party—is analyzed as being mistrust. The passage presents a kind of "theopolitics" (see Buber, 134-41), which a more secular interpreter might classify as astute, political, common sense. But the prophet is worlds away from such a detached perspective. For him the wrong of anti-Babylonian alliances is not political, but theological. Isaiah 31:1-3 expresses a similar perspective. The rebellion against Nebuchadrezzar is seen, according to this analysis, as being essentially a rebellion against Yahweh, for it stresses that it is Yahweh's oath which has been violated. This analysis may reflect a ceremony in which the vassal swears allegiance to his overlord by invoking the vassal's own gods, although such a procedure is disputed (Greenberg, *Ezekiel 1–20*, 321f.). In any case Nebuchadrezzar's role is not taken as far as it is in Jer 25:9 or 27:6, where he is viewed as Yahweh's servant carrying out his divine verdict of judgment. Instead, it is rather Zedekiah's evil folly which God directs back upon his own head (v. 19). The riddle dimension shows itself in the way the listener is led by the figurative speech to the recognition that, just as Nebuchadrezzar did not let a covenant-breaker go unpunished, so Yahweh cannot ignore the rebellious way in which Judah's king has despised "my oath" and "my covenant" (v. 19).

In vv. 22-24 this theocentric point of view is carried still further. The controlling factor in history is even more plainly seen as God's all-powerful word (cf. v. 24 with v. 21). The theme of the Great Reverser in v. 24 is an old element in Israel's picture of God (see 1 Sam 2:7; Ps 18:28; 75:8 [*RSV* 7]; 147:6), but it is also one which finds new life in the apocalyptic hope of the overthrow of the mighty and the exaltation of the lowly (see Luke 1:51-53 and Revelation 18).

The hope in vv. 22-24 has a clear messianic aspect. It has associations with the "Branch" imagery, not so much as it is rooted in 2 Samuel 7, but as its transcendent dimensions are anticipated in Isa 11:1-10 and as God's surprising reversal of appearances is foreseen in Zechariah 3 and 6 and in Luke 1:78-79. The promise is one of God's free act, which arises not from any proud attempt to attain political sovereignty by juggling alliances, but from his own decision to act in a way similar to the course of political overlords, although out of a transcendent power which will summon forth universal recognition and submission.

Bibliography

M. Buber, *The Prophetic Faith* (tr. C. Witton-Davies; New York: Harper, 1960) 134-41; M. Greenberg, "Ezekiel 17 and the Policy of Psammetichus II," *JBL* 76 (1957) 304-409; K. von Rabenau, "Die Form des Rätsels im Buche Hesekiel," *WZHalle* gesellschafts- und sprachwissenschaftliche Reihe 7,5 (1958) 1055-57.

A DISPUTATION: THE ONE WHO SINS SHALL DIE, 18:1-32

Text

Only a few relatively minor emendations are required: in vv. 10b and 18a *'āḥ* ("brother") is to be omitted, and in v. 17a *mē'āwel* ("from wrong") is to be read for *mē'ānî* ("from a poor man").

Structure

3) Keeps my commandments	9aβ
e. Declaratory verdict	9baβ
1) He is righteous	9ba
2) He shall live	9bβ
f. Prophetic utterance formula	9bγ
2. A wicked son	10-13
a. Statement of case	10-11a
1) Begets a wicked son	10a
2) Who does/does not any of	
these (following)	10b-11a
b. List of violations	11b-13aαβ
1) Does eat on the mountains	11bα
2) Does defile his neighbor's wife	11bβ
3) Does oppress the poor	12aα
4) Does rob	12aβ
5) Does not restore a pledge	12aγ
6) Does lift his eyes to idols	12bα
7) Does abomination	12bβ
8) Does get interest	13aα
9) Does take increase	13aβ
c. Verdict	13aγbα
1) Rhetorical question: shall he live?	13aγ
2) Answer: no	13bα
d. Summary formulation of disobedience:	
did abominations	13bβ
e. Further formulations	13bγδ
1) Shall be put to death	13bγ
2) His blood is on him (blood	
restriction formula)	13bδ
3. A righteous grandson	14-18
a. Statement of case	14
1) Begets a son	14aα
2) Who sees his father's sin	14aβ
3) Does not act so	14b
b. List of obligations	15-17aαβ
1) Does not eat on the mountains	15aα
2) Does not lift his eyes to idols	15aβ
3) Does not defile his neighbor's wife	15b
4) Does not oppress	16aα
5) Does not take a pledge	16aβ
6) Does not rob	16aγ
7) Feeds the hungry	16bα
8) Clothes the naked	16bβ
9) Withholds his hand from wrong	17aα
10) Does not get profit from loans	17aβ
c. Summary formulation of obedience:	
walks in my statutes	17aγ
d. Verdict	17b

The chapter's structural development is highly complex, but still fully logical. In fact, it is so patiently and painstakingly logical that the reader may well find the slow build-up of details a distraction which tends to obscure the overall line of argument. Essentially the chapter consists of a disputation in which the prophet quotes a popular saying (v. 2b, see Jer 31:29) and then presents the Lord's lengthy response objecting to this proverb (II.B), arguing against it (III), and drawing a very different conclusion (IV). In III the full complication becomes apparent, as a series of legal cases is cited as the Lord's counterargument: three major cases in III.A and two supplementary cases in III.C separated by a brief return in III.B to direct confrontation and the restatement of God's counterprinciple (compare v. 20 with v. 4). The supplementary cases turn out to have a particularly crucial role in the Lord's counterargument, and this is developed in a resumption of direct confrontation in III.D.1 and 3 and in the restatement of the two supplementary cases in III.D.2. The conclusion (IV), however, presents not so much the logical superiority of the Lord's position as an impassioned summons to repentance, indeed based on the preceding logic (compare v. 23 with v. 32), but reflecting a strongly admonitory mood.

Genre

As indicated above, the overarching pattern of the chapter shows it to be a DISPUTATION. For an unconvincing attempt to derive the chapter's underlying structure from cultic legal procedure in cases dealing with death sentences, see H. Schulz, 163-87. In a disputation the prophet presents an argument of the people as captured in a proverb (v. 2b) and then interpreted in a protest (vv. 25 and 29) about the unfairness of the Lord's justice. It is, though, the shape of the Lord's response, his counterargument, that is responsible for giving this particular disputation its highly atypical shape. The presentation of the counterargument employs at considerable length two borrowed genres, both of which show striking contacts with Ezekiel's personal heritage as a priest. His utilization of legal forms has already been noticed in 14:1-11, and this same characteristic predominates here in the way hypothetically postulated legal cases are used as a vehicle for the Lord's logic. The patient repetition of the characteristics of a righteous person in III.A.1 and 3 reminds one forcefully of modern legal jargon: "if, the contrary not withstanding, the party of the first part. . . ." The thoroughness of the bearer of the priestly legal tradition shows in the way a three-generation alternating sequence of a righteous man, a wicked son, and a righteous grandson is employed to demonstrate—admittedly with some logical overkill—that a new generation can be different, and that the proverb's crass affirmation of cross-generational consequence is not the Lord's way. That aspect of the counterargument is avowed as a general principle in v. 4 and then again as a kind of q.e.d. in v. 20. (The closeness to Deut 24:16 is to be noted.) Additional logical overkill is introduced when, above and beyond the essential counterargument denying that guilt continues from one generation to the next, the focus shifts in vv. 21-29 to the further logical point that change—either for good or ill—can take place within a single generation. Once again legal cases are used to establish this point. In the cases set forth the appropriate legal language is employed: (1) for the classification of the individual ("righteous" and "wicked" are the technical terms for "innocent" and "guilty," see 1 Kgs 8:31-32); (2) for describing the death sentence as verdict, "he shall surely die" (v. 13); and (3) for the disavowal of responsibility by the community in the execution, "his blood shall be upon himself" (v. 13), the BLOOD RESTRICTION FORMULA. However, for those cases which climax in a STATEMENT OF ACQUITTAL, something most unusual happens. In place of the expected, and presumably customary, "he shall not die" (see vv. 17, 21, and 28), these cases concluded by a verdict of acquittal are provided with a specially created formulation, one patterned as the deliberate counterpart to a death sentence. "He shall surely live" (vv. 9 and 17) is of course not a "sentence" at all, though one might attempt to capture its generic derivation in a pun by calling it a "life sentence." But the prophet has in mind far more than a play on words. That further aspect of his goal is made clear by the second borrowed genre he utilizes, that of an ENTRANCE LITURGY.

From the fact that certain practices were specifically characteristic of worshipers using particular sanctuaries, and from the shape of Psalms 15 and 24, it seems likely that there was a ceremonial question/answer pattern employed for those entering the Jerusalem temple. Essentially the pattern of this ritual involved three parts: (1) the question by the one seeking entrance (e.g., Ps 15:1); (2) a list of obligations, largely of an ethical sort (e.g., Ps 15:2-5a), designed to be recited as incumbent upon those worshiping at this place; and (3) an assurance of blessing (e.g., Ps 15:5b) pronounced upon those affirming the required obligations. The lists of such obligations in the OT were selections of items which, as we know from legal collections, were intended to mark off Israelites as the Lord's people. Naturally, the focus of such items would be, and in fact was, on matters of behavior which were either distinctive of Israel (e.g., disavowal of fertility rites) or likely to be neglected as burdensome or inconvenient (e.g., no interest on loans). Thus the underlying stress is on an avowal of loyalty. Quite possibly the Decalogue and other series of commandments were employed in such entrance liturgies. The list Ezekiel 18 uses in vv. 6-8a and 15-17aαβ clearly singles out such obligations inherent in Israel's peoplehood. The list of violations in vv. 11-13aαβ is manifestly an artificial ad hoc creation derived from the list of obligations. No one ever felt the need for a listing of ways to violate the standards of loyalty to God, and that list—as was observed—is simply part of the logical overkill inherent in the chapter's legal style. Variations in the lists within ch. 18 do not argue for Ezekiel's own creativity (Greenberg, *Ezekiel 1,* 343) any more than variations among series of commandments within Israel's legal corpora show the creativity of particular legal redactors. Such an approach is romantic and inconsistent with the process of legal tradition. The very formulation of the cases reflects not Ezekiel's creativity, but his consistent conformity to the patterns of priestly legislation (see the placement of *kî,* "for," in vv. 5, 18, and 21; the similarity to 14:9; and Zimmerli's comments in *Ezekiel 1,* 302 and 375).

A subordinate aspect of this entrance liturgy which turns out to be crucial for understanding the meaning of ch. 18 is the terminology of classification: righteous and wicked. As pointed out above, this terminology is the ancient equivalent for our legal language of innocent or guilty. However, psalmic usage shows that "righteous" or "wicked" were terms with a cultic significance as well. "Righteousness" (*RSV* "vindication") is the way the concluding assurance of blessing in Ps 24:5 speaks of those who commit themselves to the obligations listed. Psalm 1 is typical of the way the loyal and the apostate are categorized as righteous and wicked, and Ps 118:20's speaking of "the gate of the Lord" and how "the righteous shall enter through it" is a further example of how "righteous" comes to be the label or classification for those who go in the temple gate and thereby affirm their loyalty.

Setting

It is immediately to be noted that both of the "borrowed" generic elements in this chapter, the legal cases and the entrance liturgies, coincide quite emphatically in the outcome to which they lead. Acquittal as a legal verdict and admission to the Lord's sanctuary find expression in the label "righteous," and more precisely in that kind of "righteousness" which is tantamount to life as opposed to death. As seen above, the opposite of a death sentence is the assurance of life, "he shall surely live" (vv. 9 and 17). The ritual commitment of oneself to obedience to the law is repeatedly characterized as the way of life (Deut 30:15, 19; Lev 18:4-5; von Rad, "Righteousness and Life," 253-54). What the sanctuary cult has to offer is precisely "life" (see Amos 5:4, 14 and Pedersen's words that "holiness never lost its true nature as the force on which life depended and from which it was renewed," *Israel,* III-IV, 295; see also Ps 16:11; 36:9). That declaratory formulas such as "he shall surely die/live" or "he is righteous" are specially priestly, as many following von Rad have supposed, is no longer so likely, as Hutton has pointed out *(Declaratory Formulae).*

For Ezekiel's audience, being "dead" was their own self-description (see 37:11 and 33:10). In the traditional pattern of a disputation, the prophet takes the people's very words and uses them to bring a contrasting message, in this case one that affirms a new possibility, "turn and live" (v. 32). Whether this exilic self-understanding as being "in death" was something which surfaced only after the destruction of the city and temple, as its use in chs. 33 and 37 might support, or whether such a despairing view of exile was already current during the few years of Ezekiel's pre-587 B.C. ministry, is nearly impossible to decide. True, the sins listed in ch. 18, especially "eating upon the mountains," refer to abuses identified with Israel's behavior in Palestine, but that in no way implies that pre-587 sins—

particularly such a basic one as apostasy—would not be prominent in post-587 reflection. Jeremiah 44 provides strong evidence to the contrary. Furthermore, the hope of life out of death (v. 32) cannot be viewed as necessitating a pre-587 date, for the surprising message of a hope for life out of death and the return of post-587 exiles is exactly what 37:1-14 offers.

That this pairing of cultic and legal terminology involving righteous/wicked and life/death could be borrowed by a prophet, especially a prophet who was a priest, is in itself easily conceivable, but in actuality such a borrowing was already widely attested in another circle, that of wisdom literature. Psalm 1 and Ps 32:10-11 do not remind us of their cultic roots when they employ this particular terminological pairing. Rather we recognize here a major characteristic of wisdom literature, its patterns of classifying behavior and consequences, and its function as motivation for obedience. Proverbs 6:20-35 and the whole of Proverbs 7 use the instance of sexual infidelity as death-producing behavior, and if Boström is correct that the "strange woman" there is a reference to Astarte worship, then the parallel to the apostasy of the immediately pre-587 B.C. Israel in Ezekiel and Jeremiah 44 would be even closer. In any case, it is their basic rootedness in human existence itself that makes fidelity and life or faithlessness and death such natural and automatic candidates for transplanting from one life-setting to another. Ezekiel 3:16-21 and 33:10-20 are simply further instances, the first having already been discussed, and the second being reserved for subsequent analysis.

Intention

It used to be generally claimed that Ezekiel 18 seeks to move from the older doctrine of collective responsibility to the new insight of individual responsibility. Enough has been said here already to make it plain that this chapter does not really function on any such abstract or theoretical level. To allow use of theoretical cases to convince one that the purpose is to discuss a theory is to be as seriously misled as if one were to understand a defense lawyer's use of legal precedents as showing he was seeking to make a legal point, thereby forgetting his basic aim of securing his client's acquittal. The nature of ch. 18 as a disputation is critical to grasping its meaning. It does present an argument, but an argument with a clear, specific, pastoral goal. Apart from that goal, the argument would be a matter of doctrinal theory, but the argument clearly never intends to function apart from its practical goal.

Some in the prophet's community see their fate as deportees constituting a challenge to divine justice. Perhaps they were young people who served essentially as hostages in Babylon, used to insure the loyalty of their fathers, who occupied positions of leadership in Jerusalem. It may well have been true that the pro-Egyptian policies of their fathers had led to the exile of their minor and politically innocent children, thus justifying their use of the proverb in v. 2. But Ezekiel's point is not made by any theoretical challenge. He does not oppose one theory with another, however more enlightened. Instead it is Ezekiel's point that the whole matter of the challenge posed by the fact of exile has been misperceived. He affirms that the meaning of their exile is a challenge to them—a challenge to repent (Schenker, 459, 462f., 466f.).

For us the heritage of revivalist tradition makes it natural to assume that the preaching of repentance is the normal and natural place where any preacher—especially one with ambitions to be viewed as a prophet—would begin. But what is missed by such a seemingly natural and even traditional approach is the dimension of mood. The mood of the chapter is a response to the perspective from which Ezekiel's partners in argument speak. They speak out of cynical resignation (Zimmerli, *Ezekiel 1*, 382). They speak mockingly, disillusioned by their fate. For them there is no point to concerning oneself with the God of Israel. Their use of the proverb is defensive, a way of excusing themselves from responsibility, and probably a preparation for an assimilation into their environment which would end in apostasy. That what they do next does not matter is defended by the claim that what they had done in the past did not matter. The mood of the prophet's response is, of course, much more directly available for analysis. As has been noted, the prophet's mood has often been misunderstood because of the legal and ritual style employed. Nonetheless, the evidence for the nontheoretical dimension is clear. The aspect of logical overkill is an attempt to drive the partners in this dialogue inescapably toward a confrontation of the most untheoretical sort, a confrontation with the will of God. Furthermore, that will of God is set forth in language that moves forcefully beyond the level of desire for behavior to desire for people's lives. "Have I any pleasure in the death of the wicked?" (v. 23) and "I have no pleasure in the death of anyone" (v. 32) are only slightly different in structure and not at all different in content from "There is joy before the angels of God . . ." (Lk 15:10).

Similarly, the mood inherent in the prophet's conclusion, "turn and live," needs careful and precise analysis, lest it be heard as simply a "summons" or even a "demand" for repentance. Once again the simplistic model of revivalist preaching lies dangerously close. Just because a word is grammatically in the imperative mood does not make it a "command." "Turn" in vv. 30 and 32 is indeed imperative in form, but what follows in each case is decisive for accurately capturing the mood. "Lest iniquity be your ruin" is a motive clause in the form of a warning, which makes it plain that "turn" here is more precisely to be heard as an appeal. And "live" at the end of v. 32, although grammatically simply a second imperative, is clearly also a motivation, actually a promise, which transforms the mood of "turn" into that of an invitation (see Wolff, "Das Thema 'Umkehr'"). The parallel with the clearly similar imperative "live" in 16:6 is striking. Thus, far from opposing one theory to another, the chapter more basically opposes one mood to another. Cynical resignation is opposed by an affirmation of the possibility of transformation, even by the invitation to life out of death.

Bibliography

G. Boström, *Proverbiastudien* (LUÅ, N.F. Avd. 1, 30, 3; Lund: Gleerup, 1953); J. B. Geyer, "Ezekiel 18 and a Hittite Treaty of Mursilis II," *JSOT* 12 (1979) 31-46; A. Graffy, *A Prophet Confronts His People* (AnBib 104; Rome: Biblical Institute Press, 1984) 58-64; R. Hutton, *Declaratory Formulae: Forms of Authoritative Pronouncement in Ancient Israel* (Diss., Claremont Graduate School, 1983); P. M. Joyce, "Individual Responsibility in Ezekiel 18?" *Studia Biblica 1978* (JSOTSup 11; Sheffield: JSOT, 1979) 185-96; H. Junker, "Ein Kernstück der Predigt Ezechiels," *BZ* 7 (1963) 173-85; B. Lindars, "Ezekiel and Individual Responsibility," *VT* 15 (1965) 452-67; J. Pedersen, *Israel, its Life and Culture* (tr. A. Fausbøll; London: Oxford, 1959); G. von Rad, " 'Righteousness' and 'Life' in the Cultic Language of the Psalms," *The Problem of the Hexateuch and Other Essays* (tr. E. Trueman

Dicken; New York: McGraw-Hill, 1966) 243-66; A. Schenker, "Saure Trauben ohne stumpfe Zaehne," *Mélanges Dominique Barthelemy* (OBO 38; Fribourg: Éditions Universitaires Fribourg Suisse, 1981) 449-70; H. Schulz, *Das Todesrecht im Alten Testament* (BZAW 114; Berlin: Töpelmann, 1969); H. W. Wolff, "Das Thema 'Umkehr' in der alttestamentlichen Prophetie," *ZTK* 48 (1951) 129-48; W. Zimmerli, "'Leben' und 'Tod' im Buche des Propheten Ezechiel," *TZ* 13 (1957) 494-508.

A DIRGE OVER A LIONESS AND A VINE, 19:1-14

Text

The first two words of v. 7 ("and he knew his widows") are so obscure as likely to be corrupt. No proposed emendation is fully satisfactory.

Structure

I. Direction to conduct a dirge	1-2aα
A. Address as "you"	1aα
B. Direction proper	1aβb-2aα
1. Genre to be employed: "a dirge"	1aβ
2. Subject: "princes of Israel"	1b
3. Direction to speak	2aα
II. Dirge over a lioness	2aβ-9
A. Exclamatory introduction of figure (direct address, "your mother, what a lioness")	2aβγ
B. Elaboration of metaphorical figure: rearing cubs	2aδb
C. Narrative about her first cub	3-4
1. She raised one cub	3a
2. He became a terrorizer	3b
3. His fate	4
a. Nations captured him	4a
b. Took him captive to Egypt	4b
D. Narrative about her second cub	5-9
1. Her despair over first failure	5a
2. She sent a second cub forth	5b
3. His activity as a terrorizer	6-7a
a. Prowling	6a
b. Preying	6b
c. Destroying cities	7a
4. Consequences	7b-9
a. Land appalled	7b
b. Nations took action	8a
c. They captured him by nets and pits	8b
d. They brought him helpless to the king of Babylon	9abα
e. Purpose: to still his voice	9bβγ
III. Dirge over a vine	10-14a

Even though lacking the prophetic word formula at the beginning, ch. 19 is plainly a separate unit, linked neither to what precedes nor to what follows. A possible redactional connection to ch. 17 may exist in the way both chapters treat the subject of Judah's royal house and some of its particular members. Chapter 19 is framed by vv. 1 and 14b, both of which—like 32:2 and 16—use the genre label which identifies the unit framed thereby as a lament, or more precisely a dirge. What is surprising is the way the metaphor changes with vv. 10-14a from that of a lioness and her cubs to that of a vine and its branches. The possible implication of this switch will be pursued below.

Genre

The DIRGE is one of the best-known and most clearly recognizable of Israel's literary genres. From OT occurrences we learn its name *(qînâ)*, its meter (3:2), and its sociological context—performed by expert women, usually in the presence of the corpse. That ch. 19 is not an actual dirge, but a prophetic adaptation thereof, is the necessary result of the "deceased" subject being not a single specific person, but a nation's royal dynasty. The most frequent stylistic features of an actual dirge, the use of exclamatory "how" or "alas" and the employment of imperatives calling for mourning, are also missing. The reason for these stylistic departures lies in the need and intent of the prophet's adaptation. The exclamatory "What a lioness" in v. 2 is in a way an equivalent to the standard "How," but its aim here is less to express grieving despair than it is to begin the "then-now" contrast, also a stylistic feature highly typical of the genre. The summons to mourning is missing, because the prophet views the dynasty's fall as not just a tragedy to bring grief to all patriotic citizens, but a disaster resulting from misdirected national ambition and pride. The first metaphor (vv. 2-9) sets this forth in remarkably objective fashion, omitting any evaluation of the aggressive attempts of the lioness or her cubs. In the second metaphor the use of the vocabulary of exaltation, "towered aloft" and "height," gives a subtle judgmental tone, but this section is also remarkably objective.

The actual stinging severity of the prophet's modification of a familiar genre becomes apparent only when attention is given to its traditio-historical background. The metaphors of both lion and vine were of noble heritage in Israel. The royal tribe of Judah is called a lion's cub in Gen 49:9, and the symbol persisted for many centuries. "To catch prey" and to "devour men" are natural developments of this metaphor to express political aggression and dominance. However, "pit," "hooks," and "net" are also traditional language, but from the vocabulary of the hunt, in which the point is not the awesome power of the king of beasts, but his degradation by the skill of the hunters. "Cage" in v. 9 is literally "neck stocks" and seems to be an instance where metaphorical language is abandoned in favor of actual political, factual description of a captured rebel king, just as is the case with the reference to "the land of Egypt" in v. 4 and to "the king of Babylon" in v. 9. In any case it is the switch to degradation that is decisive. That the glory of Judah's monarchy could come to such an end in the mouth of one speaking for Israel's God can only mean the cancellation of earlier prophetic promises affirming the everlasting character of the Davidic house (e.g., 2 Samuel 7 and the use made of the Nathan promise in Psalms). The other dirges used by Ezekiel are notably more hostile and scoffing, especially those dealing with foreign nations in chs. 27, 28, and 32. Ch. 19 is vastly more restrained and subtle.

The metaphor of the vine in vv. 10-14a is also from a noble tradition in Israel, as noticed in examining ch. 15, but, as observed there, it is normally used to express the election of Israel as a people rather than its royal house. To compensate for this partial inappropriateness, references to a ruler's scepter have been introduced in vv. 11 and 14, thus making the dynastic application more apparent. The similarity to the first section is discerned more readily when it is pointed out how "water," "fruit," "branches," and "boughs" are drawn from the imagery of productivity, that for which a vine is inherently destined, while "plucked up," "dried up," "stripped off," "withered," and "consumed" are vocabulary at home only in the failure and removal of a vine. Once again it is more than the tone of tragedy and frustration that comes through here; it is just like the first section, for it is the appalling note of rejection of choice, cancellation of destiny, and extermination of potential continuation that becomes noticeable.

Zimmerli points out that the envelope of divine direction to conduct a dirge in v. 1 and the report of realization in v. 14b reminds one of the pattern of instruction/compliance and other formulas in Priestly materials (*Ezekiel 1,* 398).

Setting

As indicated above, the dirge belongs properly to the setting of a funeral. When prophets borrowed this kind of language, they necessarily effected great changes in it. While one might think the change from the death of a person to the use of death as a metaphor would eliminate the poignancy of the grief involved, that proves in general not to be the case. The death of a nation, as in Amos 5:1-2, can be extremely moving. When an element of political mockery is introduced, as in Isa 14:12-21 or Ezekiel 27, 28, and 32, then of course grief is replaced by scorn, even though the emotional intensity may remain high. In ch. 19 it is another sort of transformation inherent in the shift from a personal death to a political metaphor that proves to be of decisive importance: the use of this metaphor in order to make veiled allusions to specific historical personages. While the overall subject of concern in the dirge is the dynasty, the details become at times so specific that particular members of the dynasty must be in mind. But, because the specific historical details are mingled with standard metaphorical elements, the emotional content is lowered somewhat as the element of riddle is introduced, i.e., as the mental process of decipherment replaces a part of the shock of bereavement. Interpreters through the years have struggled with this matter of deciphering precisely which Judean kings were meant in the various parts of the chapter. Virtually all agree that the reference in v. 4b to being brought to Egypt means that the first cub must be Jehoahaz. Beyond here, though, the unanimity vanishes. While "they . . . brought him to the king of Babylon" in v. 9 suggests Jehoiachin, others argue for Jehoakim or Zedekiah on the ground that the three months of Jehoiachin's rule were not enough for the aggressive behavior described in vv. 6-7. Still the element of stylization in this portrayal weakens any such objections, and the identification of the second cub as Jehoiachin seems most likely. It is quite possible, though, that these verses making the switch in metaphor from lioness to vine (vv. 10-14a) may be a kind of updating in which Zedekiah's latest political ambitions were in mind. Nonetheless, the major focus in vv. 9-14a is on the dynasty as a whole rather than on any one member. Yet other scholars (see Fohrer, 106) have pursued the process of decipherment one step farther, taking the references to "your mother" in vv. 2 and 10 more literally, and seeing here an allusion to the office of queen mother *(gĕbîrâ)*. This is supported by the fact that Jehoahaz and Zedekiah were in actuality sons of Hamutal and the mention in 2 Kgs 24:15 that "the mother of the king" was deported. However, that passage refers to a different woman, the mother of Jehoiachin. Probably the attempt to identify the queen mother is best seen as the allegorical pushing of a metaphor beyond its original intent. In any case the chronological setting of vv. 1-9 is pre-587 B.C. and even vv. 10-14 could be seen as from that same time, if the past tense of the verbs could be viewed as the so-called "prophetic past" (Greenberg, *Ezekiel 1–20,* 359).

Intention

To conduct a dirge beside the hospital bed of a still living patient would be incredibly crass. Something of that dimension of bizarre crudity is inherent in prophetic dirges. It is not nearly enough to see in ch. 19, as Eichrodt does, a warning (255). Something much stronger is present here, the pronouncement of judgment on Judah's royal house and the cancellation of 2 Samuel 7's divine undergirding of the Davidic dynasty. Thus the aim of using a dirge comes close to that behind the use of symbolic actions, almost a kind of semimagical, power-displaying pre-enactment.

More precisely, the lack of exact detail is deliberately the sort of stylization to be expected in dirges. Of course Jehoahaz could not have acquired such a great reputation as a fierce king in the three months of his sovereignty! That is not the point. Rather the pretentious hopes—and even faith—of both people and king are crudely rejected with a brutal finality. Similarly, the "overkill" (Greenberg, ibid., 355) in the picture of the vine's fate, when it is uprooted, thrown down, dried up, and finally burned, is just a dramatic expression of the decisiveness of God's rejection. Finally, when a note of fulfillment is sounded in v. 14b, "and it became a dirge" (ibid., 349), the element of a doxology of judgment is plainly detectable.

Bibliography

W. Brownlee, "Two Elegies on the Fall of Judah (Ezekiel 19)," in *Ex Orbe Religionum (Fest. G. Widengren* I; Leiden: Brill, 1972) 93-103; H. Jahnow, *Das hebräische Leichenlied im Rahmen der Völkerdichtung* (BZAW 36; Giessen: Töpelmann, 1923) 197-208; M. Noth, "The Jerusalem Catastrophe of 587 B.C. and its Significance for Israel," *The Laws in the Pentateuch* (tr. D. Ap-Thomas; Philadelphia: Fortress, 1967) 260-80.

THEOLOGICAL REFLECTION: THE HISTORY OF ISRAEL AS GUILT AND GRACE, 20:1-44

Text

In v. 37 it is better to read the second to the last word *bĕmāsōret* ("in the bond") as *bĕmispār* ("by number") and to delete the last word as a dittograph.

Structure

I. Narrative setting	1
A. Date	1aα
B. Situation: inquiry by some elders	1aβb
II. Prophetic word formula	2
III. Preliminaries	3-5aαβ
A. Address to the prophet	3aαβγ
1. Address as son of man	3aα
2. Direction to speak to the elders using messenger formula	3aβγ
B. What the prophet is to say	3aδb
1. Reproachful theoretical question: do you come to inquire?	3aδ
2. Oath formula	3bα
3. Refusal to permit inquiry	3bβ
4. Prophetic utterance formula	3bγ
C. New address to the prophet	4-5aαβ
1. Proposal of judgment	4
a. Rhetorical question as premise	4aα
b. Address as son of man	4aβ
c. Direction to accuse as conclusion	4b
2. Direction to speak using messenger formula	5aαβ
IV. An extended divine analysis showing the pattern in the events of Israel's history (all first person)	5aγ-44

131

a) Not to bring them to the glorious land	15b
b) Because of disobedience	16
(1) Disobedience of ordinances	
and statutes	16aαβ
(2) Profanation of sabbaths	16aγ
(3) Because of their idols	16b
C. Third event: admonition to the second generation	
in the wilderness	17-26
1. God's activity	17-20
a. His withholding of punishment	17
b. Admonition to the second generation	18-20
1) Report of God's speech	18aα
2) Admonition against behavior of fathers	
(statutes, ordinances, and idols)	18aβγb
3) Self-introduction formula	19aα
4) Exhortation to obey the Lord's statutes	
and ordinances	19aβb
5) Exhortation to sabbath-hallowing as a	
sign of relationship	20abα
6) Recognition formula (2 mp)	20bβ
2. Israel's response	21a
a. General: next generation rebelled	21aα
b. Specific: they rejected the commandments	21aβγδ
1) Statutes and commandments intended	
for life	21aβγ
2) They profaned the sabbaths	21aδ
3. God's response	21b-26
a. God's decision to act in wrath in the wilderness	21b
b. Report of his withholding	22aα
c. His change of mind to avoid profanation of	
his name in view of the nations	22aβb
d. Further lifting up of the hand	
in a threatening oath	23-24
1) Report of lifting up of the hand	23a
2) Contents of oath	23b-24
a) To scatter them among the nations	23b
b) Because of disobedience	24
(1) Disobedience of ordinances	
and statutes	24aα
(2) Profanation of sabbaths	24aβ
(3) Because of their fathers' idols	24b
e. Report of punishment	25-26
1) God gave them bad statutes and ordinances	
(not intended for life)	25
2) He defiled them through the sacrifice	
of their firstborn	26a
3) Intention: recognition formula (3 mp)	26b
D. Application of this past to Israel's present	27-44

Ezekiel 20 is one of the most strictly, even forcefully structured units in the whole book. Like chs. 16 and 23, it gives a survey of Israel's history, and, also like those two other chapters, its structure reveals a prophetic message in which old tradition and radical reinterpretation are present. Logically, the interpreter's primary task is to analyze the character and intent of the reinterpretation. Nonetheless, it is appropriate to some extent to examine which particular traditions are employed, at least as far as our knowledge makes this possible.

Under the heading of "judging" his people (v. 4a), which is elaborated in legal style (see 16:2 and 22:2) as making known "the abominations of their fathers" (v. 4b), three major events in Israel's past are taken up and presented in a strongly stereotyped pattern (IV.A, B, and C). So forceful is the stereotyping that each event is presented as consisting of the same three parts, in the same sequence, and in nearly identical words (IV.A.1, 2, and 3; IV.B.1, 2, and 3; and IV.C.1, 2, and 3). The events themselves, the Lord's choosing of Israel in Egypt (IV.A.1), his revealing himself in commandments in the wilderness (IV.B.1), and his handling of the second generation in the wilderness (IV.C.1), are not that similar, either in tradition or inherently. But they are deliberately forced into a pattern which demonstrates with almost monotonous consistency how the Lord's gracious, life-affirming acts met first with his people's rebellion, a key word from the call vision of chs. 2–3 (IV.A.2.a, IV.B.2.a, IV.C.2.a), then with Yahweh's decision to respond in wrath (IV.A.3.a, IV.B.3.a, IV.C.3.a), and finally with the changing of his mind to act in mercy "for his name's sake" (IV.A.3.b, IV.B.3.b, IV.C.3.bc). In the case of the second two events, further threats (IV.B.3.c and IV.C.3.d) qualify this decision to act in mercy. Thus in spite of large inherent differences in these three phases of Israel's history, Ezekiel imposes a uniformity upon them that is so strictly carried out that the differing details of the individual events become only illustrative instances of the underlying pattern of guilt and grace, or to be more precise, grace, guilt, and new, stubbornly persisting grace.

While it might appear from this survey that the focus is on Yahweh's triumphantly persistent grace, in actuality the overall impression is a different one. Since the events being reviewed are, according to their place in old tradition, customarily presented under the heading of saving acts, any introduction at all of Israel's guilt into such a survey constitutes a drastically negative reinterpretation. Ezekiel's reinterpretation is spectacularly negative for several reasons, particularly his statement that Yahweh gave his people bad laws as punishment (vv. 25-26), and the heavily negative way in which he applies this past history to Israel's present in IV.D. Of the three points made in this application, the first two are again negative. The section IV.D.2 reconnects to the situation which originally triggered the whole oracle (III.A and B) by rejecting the idea that the Lord could be inquired of by Israel, and IV.D.3 goes even further. There the language of a new exodus, i.e., another *saving* act of God after the pattern well known in old traditions, is used to announce a new *judgment* in the wilderness. Only after this stunningly negative aspect does a positive dimension of this new exodus emerge in IV.D.4. And even there the concluding verses return to the theme of Israel's guilt, speaking of the loathing with which the restored people will remember their past and how in summary all this will reveal the underlying way in which Yahweh deals with them "for my name's sake, not according to your evil ways, nor according to your corrupt doings" (v. 44).

A few comparatively small items within this tightly unified structure remain problematic. (1) The offering of firstborn by fire in v. 26 is elsewhere a sin linked to Israel's life only in Canaan, but Ezekiel's drastic rewrite here has it precede the entry into the land reported in v. 28, a fact which has led some commentators, e.g., Eichrodt, to rearrange the sequence of verses. (2) The thought of Israel's proposed idolatrous assimilation to the nations in v. 32 is not specifically said to be the content of the inquiry of vv. 1, 3, and 31, but that seems its most likely interpretation. (3) The exhortation to Israel in v. 39 to go and serve idols is puzzling, but it seems to serve as a transition from the preceding announcement of punishment to the following promise, perhaps affirming God's triumph even over Israel's persisting sin.

Genre

In a way the entire chapter presents one large three-part PROPHETIC PROOF SAYING. The historical survey in vv. 5-26 serves as the reason for the three announcements in vv. 27-44, the last two of which end with RECOGNITION FORMULAS (vv. 38b, 42, and 44abα). Actually, though, Ezekiel's large-scale expansion of this particular genre has moved it far along the road toward something entirely different. Though still structured as divine speech by the use of MESSENGER and UTTERANCE FORMULAS (vv. 3aγ, 3bγ, 5aβ, 27aδ, 30aγ, 31bβ, 33aβ, 36bβ, 39aβ, and 44bγ), OATH FORMULAS (vv. 3bα, 5aβ, 6aα, 15a, 23a, 31bα, and 33aα), and first person discourse for God throughout, this chapter nevertheless comes close to being essentially a new literary type, THEOLOGICAL REFLECTION, albeit presented as divine speech.

Lest this be thought a more far-reaching classification than it really is, it must be observed that no separation can be made here between the prophet's thoughts, i.e., his own theological reflection, and the word revealed to him by Yahweh. The nature of the material does not permit such a distinction, and it is to be doubted that the nature of the prophet's experience of revelation would be appropriately described by any such dichotomy. Still the impression persists that familiar genres of prophetic speech are here so far extended that they are beginning to crumble.

The shape of Ezekiel's analysis of Israel's history (→ HISTORY) is, of course, not fully an ad hoc creation. It follows the familiar pattern of the credal recitation of those saving acts of the Lord on which Israel's existence was based. Such recitations are familiar to us from so-called credo passages, such as Deut 6:21-23; 26:5-9; Ps 135:8-12; 136. Their age and the antiquity of the pattern they reflect is a matter of dispute, but they certainly predate Ezekiel. In the selection of the three specific events in this chapter there is a measure of arbitrariness. As has been noted, the entry into the land is not given its customary prominence, and the separation of the wilderness community into a first and second generation is highlighted in a way not found in any other short historical summary. Still, all of these matters are minor indeed in comparison to the way the purpose of the analysis differs so markedly from that of the usual recitation of Yahweh's saving acts. It is not enough to note that already Amos 4:6-11 parodies the pattern of a list of saving acts by substituting a list of judging acts, for Ezekiel does indeed stick with saving acts. It is actually the point made from the list that is grotesquely different. Ezekiel 20 is a much more graphic parody, for here he declares "the great events of this very history as stations in the way of the frightful sins committed by Israel" (Zimmerli, *Ezekiel 1*, 407). Thus the very basis of Israel's existence, the sequence of the mighty acts of God she confesses, is now made into an accusation which cancels that very basis. In a truly horrifying perversity, the very life-enabling commandments of God's law are made into "statutes that were not good and ordinances by which they could not have life" (v. 25). However, Ezekiel's message is not and never was complete at the end of the survey of the three events. Possibly the point of introducing the people's thought in v. 32, that they could now be like the nations, intends precisely to deny that God's mighty acts with Israel are at an end. Instead, there is a new act portrayed in vv. 33-38 without which this history was never complete. While there is this general connection in logic between v. 32 and vv. 33-38, the connection is not so explicit in either wording or logic as to give vv. 32-44 the form of a DISPUTATION as Zimmerli proposes (*Ezekiel 1*, 414). Instead, there is a considerable break between v. 32 and vv. 33-38, as Ezekiel begins to describe Yahweh's new act. This next act is described in vv. 34-35a as a new exodus, using the familiar trio of verbs, brought out (*hôṣî*), gathered (*qibbeṣ*), and brought in (*hēbî*), as well as the standard terminology of "a mighty hand and an outstretched arm" (v. 33). This will, however, come before us more fully in ch. 34.

In contrast, though, to the hope-bringing role of a new exodus in ch. 34 and in Deutero-Isaiah, Ezek 20:33-38 uses this language to describe a judgment in "the wilderness of the peoples." Indeed, this judgment is not totally destructive in that it results in a purging out of the rebels, who although "brought out," "shall not enter the land of Israel" (v. 38). Thus once again the element of hostile parodying looms large in this survey of God's acts. Ezekiel's original proclamation of this message in 591 B.C. may well have ended at this point (→ Setting). In linking the thought of a new exodus as judgment in the wilderness with the judgment of the fathers on the way out of Egypt (v. 36), he may have in mind such episodes as the instances of rebellion in Numbers 11–20 and Exodus 16–17. In the current form of the text, however, vv. 40-44 go on to portray, using the same three verbs (bring out, gather, and bring in), a positive new exodus which eventuates in a restoration of acceptable worship on "my holy mountain" (v. 40). Since these final verses constitute a kind of condensation of Ezekiel's later message in chs. 34–36 and 40–48, this may indicate, as has been suggested with regard to chs. 8–11 and 16, that an expanded version of ch. 20 has been created as an updating of this message later in Ezekiel's ministry. This will be explored further under Setting.

In yet another way the shape of Ezekiel's survey grows out of the tradition lying behind it. He takes the SELF-INTRODUCTION FORMULA, "I am the Lord your God," in v. 5b as a capsule of what Israel's election means, following the pattern of Exod 20:2. Then he goes on to employ this same phrase in vv. 7b and 19a, following the usage of the Holiness Code in Leviticus 17–26 to indicate the essential role of the commandments as markers of Israel's belonging to the Lord. But then with his incorporation of this self-introduction formula into the RECOGNITION FORMULA, Ezekiel enables his announcements both of judgment and of promise to serve as striking demonstration of the continuity in Yahweh's purpose. Even further, Yahweh's binding of Israel to himself by means of his name logically includes both the risk of the profanation of that name by Israel's disloyalty, and Yahweh's motivation to act "for the sake of my name." Surely this blending of memory and analysis is the same intellectual process inherent in theological reflection.

In any such survey of God's acts in which past events are not just described but expressed in divine speech, a variety of older genres will be utilized in passing. Where this utilization is crucial to the structure of the survey, e.g., the self-introduction formula, these genres have been given attention. In other cases, such as the specific commandments alluded to in vv. 7, 12, and 26 or the admonition in vv. 18-20, it seems unnecessary to explore those genres in any detail.

Setting

Chronologically the chapter is dated in 591 B.C., about one year after chs. 8–11. The narrative setting of a group of elders coming to inquire of the Lord through Ezekiel is clearly parallel to 14:1-11. Exactly what such inquiry would involve is not possible to determine, but it seems natural that the inquirers hoped for some prophetic message of good news, only to have this hope harshly rejected by Ezekiel. It has, however, also been understood in a far different way. Fohrer and others have argued that "what is in your mind," namely, idol worship (v. 32), provides the clue needed to understand what the inquiry of v. 31 was about. These scholars theorize that, despairing of continuing in a situation of inability to worship Yahweh in

Babylon because of being cut off from his temple, the elders proposed the construction of an image of Yahweh. Chapter 20, in this theory, is Ezekiel's sharp rejection of the request, especially in claiming that such an act would only continue their ancestors' history of apostasy (Fohrer, 108). While such a reconstruction of the setting is possible, the mere following of v. 31 by v. 32 is hardly an adequate basis for such a radical proposal.

The theological context of this bold chapter can only be approached by a tentative kind of speculation, but the question is so important that a preliminary answer must be attempted. Looking back as we do from a perspective that sees the fall of Jerusalem in 587 B.C. as an outcome fully to be expected in view of the misguided politics and vain hopes of the Judean leadership, it is hard for us to reconstruct the attitude of confidence with which they made their revolutionary plans in those years preceding Jerusalem's destruction. A variety of evidence in both historical and prophetic texts makes it plain that these hopes were of two sorts. One was rooted in what we would call practical politics, the hope for military aid from Egypt and the plan for a coalition of revolutionary nations. Jeremiah 27:1-11 clearly reflects this international political hope, as an enterprise undertaken through kings and envoys. Freedy and Redford (480) suggest that news of an Egyptian victory in the Sudan and of an upcoming triumphant visit to Palestine prompted the elders to hope for successful Egyptian opposition to Nebuchadrezzar, possibly issuing in the repatriation of the exiles. A second sort of hope was based on what we would call religious fanaticism, the confidence that the God of Israel would miraculously deliver his people and his city from their enemy. Jeremiah 21:1-10 and 27:12-22 show how this hope was fed by the promises of prophets. Jeremiah 29 and Ezekiel 13 demonstrate that also the exiles heard and trusted in the siren voices of these promising prophets. Moreover, that trust had as its foundation the tradition of Zion's inviolability, certain Zion Psalms (46, 48, and 76), and a good bit of the preaching of Isaiah. Both Jeremiah and Ezekiel responded with anger and scorn to this popular religious hope, Jeremiah directly to the royal house in Jerusalem and in public preaching, but also in response to inquiry (Jer 21:2; 37:17; 38:14). The dearth of biographical material in the book of Ezekiel makes it impossible for us to reconstruct precisely the ways in which Ezekiel responded to the vain hopes of his people for a favorable word from the Lord. Passages such as 11:1-12 and 11:15 show that Zion-centered hopes were known and discussed in his community, and his disputation sayings show how sharply he took issue with such hopes. Chapters 16 and 20 plainly belong within the context of the prophet's rejection of a trust based on the past election of Israel by Yahweh and his delivering acts in her history.

Once the fall of Jerusalem in 587 B.C. did take place, the reactions of the people both in Jerusalem and in Babylon were diverse. Amazingly, some factions persisted in military violence, apparently seeking to continue the Davidic line (Jeremiah 41). Others seem to have been bewildered and sought prophetic guidance from a now vindicated prophet like Jeremiah (Jeremiah 42). Some in Babylon were overcome by despair (Ezek 33:10), speaking of their existence as only a form of death. Many doubtless were simply assimilated into the surrounding culture. While it is hard to be sure, "the thought 'Let us be like the nations . . . and worship wood and stone'" (20:32) could reflect this kind of despair. Some, however, did continue to consult the prophetic voice, as the very existence of the book of Ezekiel attests.

The latter part of ch. 20, i.e., vv. 27-44, seems to reflect two different moods on the part of both prophet and audience. Initially vv. 27-31a lead up to the refusal of v. 31b, "I will not be inquired of by you." But vv. 33-44 go further and in themselves imply two differing moods within their audience. Verses 33-38 affirm that God is not done with his people, but will act further in a purging judgment, a message which presumably would be accepted by a group of penitent hopefuls. Verse 39 seeks manifestly to burn the bridge of continuity behind those who refuse this message. Then vv. 40-41 bring the surprising promise of a restoration of acceptable worship in Jerusalem, while vv. 42-44 move even further along in this perspective, speaking of the shame-filled memory of the restored.

It is, of course, theoretically possible that all of these diverse perspectives—and even diverse groups holding them—could have been addressed at one time in one large-scale prophecy by Ezekiel, and this is indeed the surface impression given by the present shape of ch. 20. In view, however, of the extreme brevity within vv. 40-44 in which such crucial matters appear as the new worship—in a new temple?—and the return to the land of Israel, it seems far more likely that we have here an updating of an initial message of judgment in the light of the subsequent message of promise now known more fully from chs. 33–48. As discussed earlier in connection with 11:14-21 and 16:53-63, the later updating of these older messages of judgment is not at all a matter of correction or alteration, but of reinterpretation, answering the question about the ongoing significance of a fulfilled message of judgment. Essentially, the answer given in 20:33-44 is the affirmation that God will not allow his purpose to be frustrated, but will act further, even though it is only through a people hopelessly mired in longstanding guilt that he can act. But more about this under Intention.

Traditio-historically the chapter exhibits some particularly strong links to specific streams of tradition. A setting within priestly tradition is especially clear from the close ties to the nearly contemporaneous Holiness Code material (Leviticus 17–26). The use of the self-introduction formula at the end of a commandment as in vv. 7b and 19a and the reference to the commandments "by whose observance man shall live" (vv. 11b, 13aβ, and 21aδ) and conversely to commandments "by which they could not have life" (v. 25b) are items vividly reminiscent of the Holiness Code in general and Lev 18:5 in particular. However, as befits Ezekiel's late place in the development of Israel's traditions, a variety of other contacts exists. Contacts to P tradition appear in both the stress on the sabbath as the sign of Israel's peoplehood and the closeness of the language of election to Exod 6:8. Contacts to Deuteronomic tradition appear in the use of the word "choose," in the role of Yahweh's oath in describing his election of Israel, and in the terminology of "a mighty hand and an outstretched arm." The stress on God's concern for his honor before the nations as in the golden calf episode in Exod 32:12 (see also Num 14:13-19) is a link to older pentateuchal traditions. Similarly, the stress on the rebellion in the wilderness shows a use of the tradition preserved in the Numbers 13–14 account of the spies (Coats, *Rebellion in the Wilderness*). Even the key verb "searched out" in v. 6 is the one characteristic of the spy story in Numbers.

Not surprisingly, links to major subsequent streams of tradition also appear in ch. 20. The whole negative shape of Israel's history is very close to the Deuteronomistic history, finished after 561 B.C. Deutero-Isaiah may well be adopting Ezekiel's language about "for my name's sake" in Isa 48:9-11. Finally, the way in which the pattern can be extended from the past into the future has some analogy to the apocalyptic idea of a future already fixed in heaven.

Intention

The rather sober, even casuistic style in which Israel's past is surveyed in ch. 20 tends to mask the violence with which the survey handles its material. The chapter is a tremendous *tour de force*! True to the normal intent of any historical survey, the selection of material aims to demonstrate and make evident a comprehensive understanding of the pattern followed by these events. But, while it is indeed normal for such a survey to press and distort events in order to make them fit the presented pattern more closely, the analysis in this chapter affirms a position of such fierce one-sidedness that both its underlying conclusion and the manner in which it uses its evidence are uniquely shocking within the entire OT. In a kind of historical affirmation of total depravity, the account describes Israel as having been totally and consistently rebellious from the beginning.

Although Jacob is mentioned in v. 5, the entire patriarchal period is basically passed over without mention, perhaps because it would be hard to force that material into a pattern showing only rebellion. Nonetheless, when Israel in Egypt is made the point of departure for the survey, it is also made—in a way nowhere attested in the Scriptures—the beginning of rebellion. Similarly, God's decision in Egypt even before the exodus to act in wrath, which is then modified for his name's sake (vv. 8b-9), is unknown anywhere else. One can only conjecture that the golden calf episode in which such possibilities are considered has been pushed back into Egypt in order to show that faithlessness was always typical of God's people. Further, it is starkly idiosyncratic that God responded to his people's subsequent disobedience of his commandments by giving them bad laws as a punishment. Where else are God's laws ever seen in such a light? One can only conjecture that the mistakenly and syncretistically literal interpretation of such commands as Exod 34:19, "All that opens the womb is mine" (see also Exod 22:28), which ignored the subsequent clarification, "All the firstborn of your sons you shall redeem" (Exod 34:20), was viewed as some kind of divine hardening of Israel's own heart, a shockingly bold affirmation of divine all-causality outdoing even Micaiah ben Imlah (see 1 Kgs 22:19-24) in seeing no problem in a false word from Yahweh which aimed at Israel's doom.

Why such a massively and distortingly artificial rewrite of Israel's history? Certainly the reason is to be found in the cyclical framework into which the history is forced. In a vast oversimplification the history of the people of God is analyzed as having always consisted of only two elements: the rebellious disobedience of God's chosen people and God's persistent, self-motivated grace. This pattern is not really as foreign as might appear, at least within Christian circles. It is highly reminiscent of certain dogmatic treatments of original sin. In those too, all God's people bring to history is their complete and total depravity. When observation might threaten to contradict this affirmation by pointing to good anywhere, the response is simple and thoroughgoing: all the good works of unbelievers are just so many splendid sins. And correspondingly all true good works are completely the result of God's almighty grace powerfully working in people totally without any merit or worthiness of their own. It is certainly not the purpose here to evaluate this kind of systematic theology, rather merely to notice the underlying goal it reflects. Its intent is clear beyond all doubt: to exalt the grace of God. Statements about the essentially sinful character of human behavior are not intended as moral evaluation, but as doctrinal affirmation, to attest the point that salvation is *sola gratia,* by grace alone. This affirmation is made—and has significance—only over against a tradition which affirms salvation as to some extent a matter of human deserving. The parallel with Ezekiel 20 is rather extensive. Ezekiel's God chose Israel out of pure grace. Israel was then already, and has continued to be ever since, a rebellious house. Undaunted by this first rebellion, God's grace persisted again and again, only to be met by persistent rebellion. Greater grace encountered only greater guilt. Plainly the purpose of this survey is not some appropriately balanced assessment of the extent of Israel's unfaithfulness in the wilderness. Traditions of individual fidelity about that period exist—those about Moses, Caleb, and Joshua—but they are ignored here, not because of oversight or unfairness, but solely in order to make a single point, that the existence of God's chosen people continues not by any sort of right, but only because of God's stubborn grace. Once again, such a point is made—and has significance—only over against a tradition which affirms the continuing existence of God's people as to some extent a matter of right. In both cases a theological *tour de force* is involved, and in order to make the intended point fully, an extreme, one-sided, and to some extent distorted, position must be taken. Still the point being made is one both Ezekiel and seventeenth-century orthodoxy felt to be essential to the survival and existence of the people of God.

Ezekiel is a theologian and he pays the price inherent in that calling. He takes an extreme position, even when it makes him seem arbitrary and unsympathetic. But it should not be thought that the emotional dimension of his proclamation is either incidental or accidental. As has been seen before (see chs. 2–3 and 16), there is a deliberate attempt to incorporate the emotional side of this material as a part of the revelation it conveys. This shows here in the way God is portrayed as changing his mind. The decision to cancel Israel's election is not one which is located at some specific point on the scale of God's anger. There is no 212°F at which divine blood boils, and beneath which there is safety. Instead God's decisions switch back and forth. He will destroy Israel, because their behavior calls for that. Then he changes his mind, not because Israel has changed, but because of his own overarching purpose. There is never any averaging out or homogenizing of these two contrasting elements. Rather, the two continue throughout each stage of Israel's history: Israel does what it always does, i.e., rebels; and the Lord of Israel does what he always does, i.e., acts for his name's sake. Note that the Lord is not said to forgive or to specify one more chance. Rather the tension that endangers the continuation of Israel's history arises precisely because of God's determination to act for his name's sake.

It is not enough that Yahweh does not destroy his people, for their mere existence does not accomplish God's purpose. If Israel continues in persistent, unchanging rebellion, God must *change* Israel so that she does honor his name and not just profane it. Thus the climax of the chapter in vv. 27-44 speaks exactly of how Israel is to be changed. It will be by judgment, but not the destructive judgment announced as the end in ch. 7. This is to be a purging judgment by which the Israel that profanes Yahweh's name is removed. It is no longer determinable with certainty if Ezekiel in his original message of 591 B.C. went on to any announcement of a positive hope—though this analysis suggests he did not. But the present text presents a message which is in obvious harmony with that of chs. 34–37, where the transformation of Israel which God promises to bring about is spelled out in much greater detail. One should note already here, though, that v. 41 speaks of how "I will manifest my holiness among you in the sight of the nations," a precise counterpart to the previous stress on the profanation of God's name and in clear continuity with chs. 33–48 as a whole. That another such link between past and future is to be found in the use in v. 40 of the verb *dāraš* ("to require"), the same verb used previously in the sense "inquire," as Zimmerli maintains (*Ezekiel 1*, 417), is far less certain.

The major continuity which is definitely present is not just one of terminology, but of theology. In the case of every event in Israel's history it is God's action alone that created a positive future. It is only as an expression of divine all-causality that a future can be spoken of—either in judgment or in grace. As noted before, the typological correspondence of God's earlier acts to his future acts in the language of a new exodus is the language which Ezekiel like others selects to express this continuing all-causality: "I will bring you out . . . gather you . . . bring you in." But in a unique, additional homiletical touch, Ezekiel seizes upon the traditional motifs of wilderness and judgment, located following the going out from Egypt, in order to make his message of a new wilderness and a new judgment to come after the going out from Babylon both more appropriate and also more frightening. It is therefore totally wrong that Zimmerli (*Ezekiel 1*, 406) should speak here of how "there is hidden implicitly the call of the 'freedom to repent.'" The text speaks not at all of repentance, but of solidarity in guilt and continuity in stubborn grace. Chapter 20 does not face at all the same audience mood that ch. 18 did. Here the only link between past and present is not "you can" but "I will."

Bibliography

G. Coats, *Rebellion in the Wilderness* (Nashville: Abingdon, 1968) 231-41; K. S. Freedy and D. B. Redford, "The Dates in Ezekiel in Relation to Biblical, Babylonian and Egyptian Sources," *JAOS* 90 (1970) 462-85.

A COLLECTION OF SWORD PROPHECIES, 21:1-37
(*RSV* 20:45–21:32)

Structure and Genre

I.	The sword of the Lord against all flesh	1-12
II.	The sword is sharpened and polished	13-22
III.	The king's decision at the crossroads	23-37

The prophetic word formulas in 21:1, 13, and 23 make it immediately apparent that this chapter is not one single unit but several. Upon a closer look, though, ch. 21 still reflects a kind of overarching unity that marks it off from the larger units that precede it in chs. 16, 17, 18, 19, and 20 or the smaller, more diverse units that follow in 22:1-16, 17-22, 23-31. A still closer look reveals additional similarities and differences. Chapter 18 is a true unit, all coming from one time and demonstrating a singularity of logic and purpose throughout. Units such as chs. 16 and 20 cannot be said to be completely unified, because updating in later verses appears within them. Still this updating presupposes and builds upon the older material with a consistency of content and imagery within each chapter. The bond uniting the sections of ch. 21 is weaker, confined to the presence of the same figure of speech, "sword," in each subunit. Thus ch. 21 must be designated a catchword-based collection (→ LITERARY COLLECTION). In this regard, ch. 21 reflects a closer relationship to chs. 17 and 19. In ch. 17 it is the fable genre, with its speaking of birds and trees, that provides the basic link between 17:1-21 and 22-24. This unity is powerful enough to enable a switch in message from judgment to hope without totally destroying the bond between the subunits. In the case of ch. 19 commonality of genre again provides the unifying bond. Verses 1-9 and 10-14 are both dirges, and that unifying factor is strong enough to permit the metaphorical switch from lioness to vine without completely bursting apart the unity.

Clearly the unity within ch. 21 is of a much weaker and more fragile sort. This becomes fully evident when one glances at the complexity within all three subunits in ch. 21 (see the subsequent analysis for details). The important matter now is to identify what illumination the lesser unity within ch. 21 can shed upon the process of the growth of the book of Ezekiel. Two observations suggest themselves immediately. (1) Such a minor sort of bond uniting inherently quite diverse material reveals that the process of assembling the tradition of Ezekiel's proclamation was neither automatic nor easy, requiring sometimes, as here, the using of surface, minimal similarities as a starting point. (2) This process of assembly did not begin *de novo* with the original units of Ezekiel's preaching, for each part of ch. 21 reflects a lengthy process in regard to date of material and presumably also in regard to the earlier circulation and acceptance by the community.

Setting

Further reflection on the process of preservation in this so-called editorial phase raises questions about the intellectual perspective implicit here. The use of catchwords as a technique of organization appears elsewhere in biblical literature, and is perhaps most at home within wisdom literature. To discover inherent, even hidden, order by analysis is of course what underlies ancient wisdom, for this is what enables one to establish a mastery over otherwise apparently random matters. To capture a certain area from the realm of chaos by penetrating to its own inner order is the underlying perspective of all science, and the imposing of an even somewhat arbitrary principle of order is the sort of hypothesis-proposing with which the order-seeker begins. But this aim of mastery and organization was not just some abstruse private delight. It is how teaching others proceeds. The mental process of the organizer is immediately linked to that of the teacher. To group a series of prophecies under the catchword of "sword" was thus not only a way of organizing by grouping for purposes of memory by analogy and a way of passing on the contents of these prophecies, it also served the intellectual and theological understanding. Such a keyword grouping was a first step toward the proper

144

pre-understanding of what Ezekiel's message truly was in the eyes of his disciples. Perhaps even the concluding part of the third subunit, the prophecy against Ammon, is placed there in order to make clear how far this one dimension of the prophet's message can and must go, namely to a view of God's control of history that extends beyond the scope of Judah, its citizens and refugees.

When one asks what must necessarily have been the presuppositions of an editorial process like this, certain other conclusions immediately force themselves upon one's mind. Such a collection makes sense only in the light of the fulfillment of the prophet's message. Only after 587 B.C., and in the case of vv. 35-37 perhaps only after 562, was the assembly of this collection meaningful. Only in the light of the remembrance of the resistance Ezekiel's preaching had encountered was it practical to group the material which fiercely sought to break through that resistance. But with such conjectures, we have moved into the area of reconstructing the intention behind such a collection.

Intention

Quite a number of purposes could be involved in organizing the collection that is ch. 21. A historian would note that it provides some insight into the political how and why of Jerusalem's fall, and the modern mind would immediately leap to the possibly political aim of avoiding the repetition of such disasters. But all such ideas are far too modern and not in any way the expression of the text itself. While ch. 20 could end with an avowal of guilt in the concept of self-loathing (20:43) to follow future remembering, such a notion does not appear in ch. 21. Instead, it seems that the collection itself intends to be simply an additional affirmation of that which is affirmed within each of its subunits, the tracing of Yahweh's work by confessing it. The "sword" may be in the hand of the king of Babylon, and it may be a terrifying prospect, but from beginning to end it is Yahweh's sword. To affirm that is what Ezekiel's prophecies here collected did, and to make that claim yet one more time is what the collecting seeks to do. This is what is assumed under the labels "disciple" and "school."

Finally, to follow up on the question of a possible future as raised by vv. 35-37, there is a dimension of this collection which points to an openness to the further acts of this same Lord. By placing this collection within that of chs. 1–24 and before those in 25–32 and 33–48, a certain perspective for approaching the reading of ch. 21 has been provided. But then from another angle one could realistically contend that such an openness to the future acts of Yahweh is inherent as soon as the affirmation of his sovereignty appears within a context of the preservation of a message for future generations.

THE SWORD OF THE LORD AGAINST ALL FLESH, 21:1-12
(*RSV* 20:45–21:7)

Text

Only one minor emendation is required: in v. 7 read *miqdāšām* ("their sanctuary") for *miqdāšîm* ("sanctuaries").

Structure

2. Result: terror   12bγδεζ
3. Affirmation of finality (impersonal)   12bη
4. Prophetic utterance formula   12bθ

Despite the presence of the prophetic word formula in v. 6, the internal connections between vv. 1-5 and 6-12 suggest that the entire text is a single, if highly complicated, unit. In an unusually complex three-stage way, a message of judgment is delivered against Jerusalem. The first stage (I-IV) centers in a vague announcement of punishment (II) against "the forest of the south" (Zimmerli's translation, *Ezekiel 1*, 424) threatening a fire from Yahweh bringing unquenchable results, but the prophet rather surprisingly reports that the message is not accepted because it is perceived as an allegory. As the second stage another announcement (V-VII) centers in a word about the sword of Yahweh, a message presented to clarify the first, but certainly not much more specific and nearly as vulnerable to being perceived as an allegory. The third stage (VIII) is the expressive action of sighing by the prophet centering on the terror which would result from this divine action to come.

Genre

As pointed out above, this brief unit is itself a kind of collection of three sub-units, all presented as attempts to communicate a message of doom about Jerusalem. To a certain extent the second subunit constitutes the interpretation of the first. As Zimmerli has shown (ibid.), Jerusalem in v. 7 identifies who is meant by the obscure "forest of the south" of v. 2; "righteous and wicked" in vv. 8-9 explain the "green tree" and "dry tree" of v. 3; and v. 9 links up—albeit still obscurely—to vv. 3-4. In this way III and VII are related to each other somewhat as 17:1-10 and 17:11-21. In each of the subunits here (both the two-part PROPHETIC PROOF SAYINGS and the EXPRESSIVE ACTION) there is uniformly a stress on the results rather than on God's action. The divine action itself appears only in vv. 3bγδ, 8aδb, and impersonally in 12bβ—a total of only eleven words describing God's action. Virtually all the rest focuses on the terror which will result. The terror appears prominently in stages one (v. 3bε) and three (v. 12bγδεζ), a total of nineteen words. This aspect makes the unit seem strangely unusual.

    Zimmerli is correct (*Ezekiel 1*, 421-22) that the prophet's personal involvement, especially his grief, has only a superficial resemblance to Jeremiah's suffering. Here the prophet's suffering is "swallowed up" in the divine word which orders it forth. Unlike Jeremiah's case, Ezekiel speaks not at all of his own grief. Nonetheless, the report by the prophet of the lack of response by his hearers reveals a different kind of prophetic suffering.

    Prophetic sign actions and the related expressive actions were examined in chs. 4–6 and 12. The closest formal parallels are to 12:9 where the audience is quoted (see also 24:19 and 37:18). Minor items of form-critical significance appearing here which have already been examined also include the CHALLENGE TO A DUEL FORMULA in v. 8aγ (see on 5:8) and the impersonal announcement in v. 12b (see on 7:1-

27). This last item, which Zimmerli calls a "binding divine affirmation" (*Ezekiel 1,* 422), appears significantly also in 39:8. Actually "divine affirmation" is not an appropriate label, for the expression "it is coming and will happen" (Zimmerli's translation, ibid., 421) is fully impersonal. The combination of impersonal finality, the possible universalism of "all flesh," uncomprehended allegories, terror, and symbolic sighing gives the unit a slight apocalyptic flavor, so that the links to chs. 7 and 39 are indeed significant. Still, the brevity of the whole does not enable one to speak of more than a slight flavor.

Setting

Since Jerusalem and the temple are warned of doom, they must not yet have fallen. Thus the text would date from 589 B.C. or earlier. Although directed toward the Palestinian realities, it is unlikely that these words were delivered in Palestine. Rather they represent more of Ezekiel's attempt to get through to his Babylonian audience about that which they refuse to hear, viz., the warning of Jerusalem's fall. In the prophet's complaint in v. 5 about being passed off as an allegorizer, we must recognize yet another of the ways Ezekiel's rebellious audience insulated itself from the full impact of his word (see 12:21-28).

Intention

Yahweh's word through his resisted prophet seeks to confront that resistance in a variety of ways. The clarification of vv. 1-5 by vv. 6-10 is one such way, but the presence of vv. 11-12 shows that simple reiteration remains the major way in which this deliberately "hard of hearing" audience is addressed. If the same message repeated in different words is not enough, then different literary forms are employed. Is this an attempt "by all means [to] save some"? In fact, the text speaks not at all about saving. Instead the concentration centers on the terror that should—and will!—be experienced by them from the prospect of Yahweh's decisive act against his own sanctuary. Once again, our age is tempted to leap to the conclusion that repentance must be the prophet's goal. But the text itself shows us that we find repentance there only because we think it must be there. In actual fact, the text's stress on finality strongly suggests that repentance was not within the prophet's perspective here. He stresses the terror ahead as a counter to the security his listeners feel about Jerusalem and the temple (see Eichrodt, 291). Like the Rabshakeh's audience in 2 Kgs 18:27, people are being addressed who stand before the inevitable but refuse to face it. And, like Hezekiah's well-trained servants in 2 Kgs 18:36, Ezekiel's listeners are not moved by the threats of terror, for they are well-trained—this time well-schooled in the hope-filled traditions of which 2 Kings 18 was a key part. Just as Jeremiah's message of "terror on every side" produced smiles on the faces of those who facilitated their resistance to it by mocking its monotony, so Ezekiel's hearers defended themselves from his words by nodding their heads and saying of the "maker of allegories," "He's at it again." And it worked!—until the pain of the divine frustration burst forth in the fury of fire and sword.

THE SWORD IS SHARPENED AND POLISHED,
21:13-22 (*RSV* 21:8-17)

Text

The textual obscurity of this unit makes any analysis of it uncertain in the extreme. Not only are two lines (vv. 15b and 18a) incomprehensible and beyond translation, but much of the rest is so corrupt that virtually every line is rendered uncertain by the conjectures necessary to make any sense of it (see Zimmerli, *Ezekiel 1*, 426-31). Quite possibly the problematic state of the text's preservation is a direct consequence of its highly imaginative and subtly allusive poetic form. In any case, the interpretation set forth here is done with a maximum of hesitancy and tentativeness.

Structure and Genre

I.	Prophetic word formula	13
II.	Preliminaries to stage one	14abα
	A. Address as son of man	14aα
	B. Direction to prophesy	14aβ
	C. Direction to speak using messenger formula	14aγδ
	D. Direction to speak repeated	14bα
III.	Highly poetic announcement of punishment: stage one	14bβ-18
	A. Description of the preparation of the sword (impersonal)	14bβ-15
	1. Key words: sharpened and polished	14bβ
	2. Elaboration of key words	15a
	a. Sharpened for slaughter	15aα
	b. Polished to be like lightning	15aβ
	3. Incomprehensible insertion (first person)	15b
	B. Description of the delivering of the sword (impersonal)	16
	1. Delivered to the polisher	16a
	2. Key words (sharpened and polished) again	16bα
	3. Delivered to the killer	16bβ
	C. Direction to the prophet to lament (direct address)	17
	1. Direction to lament	17aα
	2. Address as son of man	17aβ
	3. Identification of target as Israel	17aγδbα
	4. Direction to lament by gestures	17bβ
	D. Incomprehensible observation (impersonal)	18a
	E. Prophetic utterance formula	18b
IV.	Preliminaries to stage two	19aαβ
	A. Address as son of man	19aα
	B. Direction to prophesy	19aβ
V.	Highly poetic announcement of punishment: stage two	19aγb-22a
	A. Direction to attack with gestures (direct address)	19aγbα
	1. Clap hands	19aγ

149

In the midst of such obscurity and uncertainty one need not surrender completely to despair of any meaningful analysis, but one must proceed with utmost caution. In such situations form critics always fall back upon the basic questions of their approach, i.e., "Who speaks?," "Who is addressed?," and "What is the mood?" The answers to these questions promise at least a starting point. The PROPHETIC WORD FORMULAS in vv. 13 and 23 confirm that we have here a single unit. The contents together with the preliminaries in vv. 14a and 18a, the PROPHETIC UTTERANCE FORMULA in v. 18b, and the CONCLUSION FORMULA FOR DIVINE SPEECH in v. 23b show that the single unit is divided into two subunits related in metaphor and terminology, III and V, as stages one and two. Each stage contains mainly matter expressed in an impersonal form, but some first person and some second person material is to be found in each stage. The structural analysis of both stages here is based on these differences in speaker and addressee. Further, the analysis of the grammatical and emotional mood of the verses enables us to supplement this analysis by isolating some descriptions and some lamenting. Thus stage one seems to break down into two impersonal descriptions of matters naturally connected with a sword, its preparation and the role of the person to use it, plus a call to the prophet to lament, flowing from the identification of the sword's target as Israel. Stage two is similarly a mixture of impersonal material, first person speech, and direct address. Here, however, the situation is even more complicated. While the prophet is addressed in v. 19abα, the sword itself is addressed in v. 21 (see Jer 47:6-7). While the object of the sword's use is identified— only in general terms in both v. 19bβγδ and v. 20a—the first of these is impersonal and the latter is expressed in the first person (presumably for Yahweh). Then surprisingly the lament of v. 20b returns to the impersonal. Finally, while the sword is called upon to attack in v. 21, Yahweh himself announces his joining in that attack in v. 22b.

In summary, the text consists essentially of contemplation of a sword. That contemplation triggers reflection and response on the part of both God and prophet. The mood of the contemplation moves from fascination to horror and lament in stage one, and from sober direction and observation to hostile attack in stage two. Because no specific presentation of results appears, the whole must be classified as essentially functioning as an ANNOUNCEMENT OF PUNISHMENT.

Setting

Because of the strongly imaginative character of the text, especially the fascination with words such as "sharpen" and "polish," the prominence of gestures, and the unusual direct address to the sword itself, scholars have felt challenged to propose settings that might explain this imaginativeness. These proposals have run the gamut from sword dance to incantation. In spite of the corrupt state of the text, it is clear that such proposals are justified only as suggestions about the background of the present text. The text itself does demonstrate a reveling in the pleasure of sounds and images, but it does not provide an adequate basis for identifying some one ritual as necessarily the setting of this particular text.

The original background of much of ancient dealing with weapons was magical. One sang or pictured only victory, only the successful use of one's weapons. What made such use magic was mainly the attempt thereby to predetermine the success of tomorrow's battle or hunt. However, the personification of a sword or the description of its functioning as that which happens by itself may be further aspects of magic. There is also a natural link between powerful, efficacious words and impressive eloquence, between captivating, repetitious style and the primitive verbal power of a spell. In the specific case of the sword, there is a given night-before-battle setting which persists in military circles to this day. As a way of insuring cleanness, and therefore effective performance, all of the soldier's equipment is polished. In the quiet night before the battle, when anticipation and nervousness prevent sleep, the routine chores of polishing bring a soothing concentration upon readiness. And when marching forth to battle in the morning's sunlight the shining weapons overwhelm the enemy with their "awe-inspiring splendor" (see Sennacherib's Taylor-Prism, *ANET,* 287). The clapping of hands is less clearly a part of this background, but it was probably linked to the rhythmic dimension of poetry, just as the use of repetition and refrains. In any case it was not likely to have been, as it is today, an expression of vengeful joy. Nor should one pedantically ask how a person holding a sword could at the same time clap hands (Eichrodt, 295).

Intention

Ezekiel's use of this ancient imagery has a clear point of contact with the intent inherent in magic. Just as magic sought to guarantee the outcome of a battle, Ezekiel's words seek to reveal the predetermined destruction of the city and people of Yahweh. Horrifyingly, it is Yahweh himself who establishes this outcome of doom and who employs his prophet to bring its ugly truth before his people in the eloquence of skillful poetry. But precisely that point, that the doom is from Israel's own God, is the focus of this text. Lamenting may well be the only appropriate response to such proclamation, for the flavor of fixity is so strong that any possibility of seeking to change it by petition, intercession, or repentance can only seem totally irrelevant.

THE KING'S DECISION AT THE CROSSROADS AND ITS CONSEQUENCES, 21:23-37 (*RSV* 21:18-32)

Structure

I. Prophetic word formula 23
II. Report of symbolic action about choosing a road 24-28

1. Order: return (the sword) to its sheath	35a
2. Intervention	35b-36
a. Judgment in the land of birth	35b
b. Fiery wrath	36a
c. Delivery into the hands of the wicked	36b
3. Results	37abα
a. Fuel for fire	37aα
b. Blood in the land	37aβ
c. Not remembered	37bα
D. Conclusion formula for divine speech	37bβ

Both the use of a single prophetic word formula in v. 23 and the connected content of the three sections (II, III, and IV) indicate that this material is editorially seen as a single unit. Of the three subunits, II is the clearest in both structure and content, leading up to the identification of Jerusalem as the next target of the king of Babylon. Subunit III does not continue the imagery of the symbolic action, but instead picks up in v. 29 the legal language of v. 28. That this is an artificial, editorial linkage is shown by the fact that the nation's sins are the subject of v. 29, whereas the prince of Judah and his sins are the subject of the remainder of the subunit. Subunit IV connects back logically to II, answering the question: What will become of the Ammonites, if Babylon chooses to take the road leading to Jerusalem rather than the one to Rabbath Ammon? The content is, however, much less clear, since it is difficult to be sure whose fate is described in the announcement (IV.C). One would naturally expect to hear of the fate of the Ammonites, who should not feel that their initial escape from being Nebuchadrezzar's first target will mean more than a temporary respite. Confusingly, though, the text of the prophecy addresses Yahweh's sword and does not mention any nation. Further, directing the sword to return to its sheath sounds more like the cessation of destruction than its anticipation. Thus it is unclear whose punishment is announced in vv. 35-37. If the sword in all these prophecies is the sword of the king of Babylon as in v. 24, then vv. 35-37 could refer to the subsequent punishment of that nation in its own land after its role as the Lord's tool was finished. This would then parallel Isaiah's treatment of Assyria as the rod which exalted itself against the one who wielded it in ch. 10. The generalized character of the remaining content of the announcement does not enable a decision.

Genre

The REPORT OF A SYMBOLIC ACTION in vv. 24-28 is typical of those elsewhere in Ezekiel, in that it consists totally of instruction from Yahweh. No report of the carrying out of this instruction appears, nor any reaction by the viewers. The interpretation, as is normal for Ezekiel, becomes simply a second part of the divine instruction. As will be seen under Intention, the reality-effecting power of the sign-action appears here in a somewhat unusual way, in that the event prefigured is only a decision, not the actual execution of it. Also unusual is the conclusion in v. 28, where (if the 3 mp subject in mind is the people of Jerusalem) an alternate understanding of the meaning of the event symbolically portrayed is described only to be rejected.

The problem of the switch from plural to singular at the beginning of vv. 29-32 has already been pointed out and identified as editorial, and the genre pattern of the remaining verses supports this. By itself v. 30 is a full and fitting addressing of the announcement which follows in vv. 31-32. The double appearance of the messenger formula in vv. 29a and 31a is to be explained, as frequently in the book of Jeremiah, as the drawing of what was traditionally the prophet's word (v. 30) within the bounds of Yahweh's word proper, inasmuch as the Lord himself provides the prophet with the "label on the envelope" as well as the message within.

Verses 33-37 display the typical pattern of a PROPHECY OF PUNISHMENT, but the complications of content are so serious that the structural clarity is of little significance.

Setting and Intention

Any treatment of the setting of this unit must give priority to the editorial process underlying it. Editorial logic rather than any recurring life situation is responsible for the shape the text now has. The place to begin is at vv. 24-28, for the situation is the clearest there. As so frequently, the prophet had to confront an audience whose firm trust in the promises given to Jerusalem made them unwilling and unable to hear his message of God's fixed decision to destroy Jerusalem at the hand of the Babylonians. When in Babylon the precise war plan of Nebuchadrezzar would come up for discussion, these firm believers seem to have persisted in their beliefs that somehow something would happen to prevent Jerusalem's destruction. Naturally, the longer Jerusalem could endure, the more likely such an escape would be, and to be scheduled at the end of the list of rebellious vassals to be chastised would certainly imply a tiny bit of hope which could be grasped. The symbolic action of the sign at the crossroads is the attempt to demonstrate even more forcefully to these believers that their faith in Yahweh's power and control was not as thoroughgoing as that proclaimed by Ezekiel. He proclaimed a Lord whose power and control are at work even in the pagan divination by which the military schedule was determined. True enough, this divination was "false" and impotent, but Yahweh was nevertheless at work in it—but to destroy his city rather than to spare it. But this whole matter goes far beyond the question of who is the sharper theologian, whose formulations are superior. What is addressed by Ezekiel's proclamation is the unpreparedness of the Judeans, both in Jerusalem and in exile, for judgment. Ezekiel's ministry and the editorial preservation of it have an immediate pastoral concern, to bring his hearers beyond dreams of deliverance to the acceptance of judgment. Only thereby does survival become any sort of possibility.

The function of subunit two is governed by the same editorial purpose. The legal language of indictment and apprehension (see Num 5:13-15 and Zimmerli, *Ezekiel 1*, 445) at the end of the subunit was made the bridge to the following subunit—albeit awkwardly as shown above—so that the grounded character of the Lord's decision to reject both city and monarchy could be pointed out yet one more time.

The chronological setting of these two sections must certainly have been in 589 B.C., i.e., before the siege of Jerusalem actually started. Thus, when v. 33 refers to the reproach made by the Ammonites, a new and later time is presupposed. There can be little doubt, in view of 25:3 and 6, that the reproach in question refers to the behavior of Ammon in 587 B.C. at the end of the Babylonian siege. The function of this final subunit is only in part to supply an answer to a curiosity about the fate of the city at the end of the road not chosen, i.e., Rabbath Ammon. Although interpretation is uncertain because of the problems outlined above, this section in one way or another seeks to follow the sword of the Lord in the hand of Nebuchadrezzar to the end of its role, to the moment of its return to the scabbard. Much of the language here is extremely intriguing. What was understood by "final punishment" in v. 34? Is an apocalyptic flavor recognizable in that expression, a flavor amplified in the references to "my indignation," the mysterious instrument of judgment, and the "no more remembered" of what follows? One could even move back to the end of v. 32 and ask if "until he comes whose right it is" constitutes a deliberate allusion to Gen 49:10. Although textual brevity and obscurity make confidence beyond reach, there seems to be no real evidence that any such apocalyptic or even Messianic meanings were intended. Most likely the message is simply that Babylon's role in Yahweh's plan is a brief and limited one, and that there is an appropriate place in divine judgment for it too. That is not a message to be scorned as chauvinistic or bloodthirsty, but it is one that is fitting only as a later editorial expansion. For the audience of 589 B.C. it would have been a distraction from the central message of the preceding.

A PROPHECY AGAINST THE OFFENSES OF THE BLOODY CITY, 22:1-16

Text

The logic of its placement requires that *wĕniḥaltî* ("and I shall be profaned") be read in v. 16a instead of *wĕniḥalt* (2 fs).

Structure and Genre

I. Prophetic word formula		1
II. Preliminaries		2-3aαβ
A. Address as son of man		2aα
B. Proposal of judgment		2aβb
1. Rhetorical question as premise		2aβ
2. Direction to accuse as conclusion		2b
C. Direction to speak using messenger formula		3aαβ
III. Three-part prophetic proof saying		3aγδb-16
A. Brief prophecy of punishment as advance summary (direct address)		3aγδb-5
1. Accusation by a series of pairings of crimes and consequences		3aγδb-4aαβγδ
a. First pair (blood and destiny)		3aγδ
b. Second pair (idols and uncleanness)		3b
c. Third pair (blood and guilt)		4aαβ
d. Fourth pair (idols and uncleanness)		4aγδ
2. Assessment: you have brought your destiny		4aεζ

The prophetic word formulas in vv. 1 and 17 make it plain that this text is to be seen as a unit, definitely separated in content from vv. 17-22. Still, the structural development within vv. 2-16 is complex and a bit unusual. An advance summary in III.A is unusually prefixed to an otherwise typically arranged three-part PROPHETIC PROOF SAYING. ACCUSATION, ANNOUNCEMENT OF PUNISHMENT, and RECOGNITION FORMULA come logically in order in III.B, C, and D, with the PROPHETIC UTTERANCE FORMULA marking the end of the accusation. However, the direct address of the city as feminine has only partially penetrated from III.A into what follows. Section III.B seems to be a series of accusations based on a list of commandments (see Hos 4:2 and Jer 7:9 for other passages presupposing such a list). The list is largely in the third person plural, except for vv. 8 and 12b, where the feminine direct address returns. These particular verses are located each at the end of two of the three subsections of the list of commandment violations, the subsections each beginning with "in order to shed blood." Apparently the traditional character of the list of commandments, which has close resemblances in most instances to Holiness Code material, is so strong that it resisted being phrased in feminine direct address. One can, though, risk the suggestion that the particular commandments whose violations now appear in the third person were originally formulated impersonally, i.e., "one who . . . ," while the other instances reflect an original direct address, which has only been changed to the feminine.

The announcement of punishment and even the following recognition formula are both consistently formulated in feminine direct address. Further, the announcement in v. 13 picks up both "blood" from v. 3 and elsewhere and "unjust gain" from v. 12, thereby reiterating and concluding the preceding. Zimmerli also suggests that "days" in v. 14 is a deliberate linking up to that same word in v. 4 (*Ezekiel 1,* 459), but the very common character of that word makes this suggestion much less certain.

No content principle for the organization of offenses in vv. 6-12 is detectable, and it is evident that modern categories such as ritual and ethical do not correspond to ancient ones. Thus, when Eichrodt proposes deleting v. 8 because of "the sudden shift into the second singular feminine and the insertion of such purely ritual matters among anti-social crimes" (308), he is on shaky ground with both of his reasons.

Setting and Intention

A legal heritage stands behind much of this text. It begins by raising the issue of "judging," and then goes on to base its indictment on a heritage of traditional commandments. But we can be more precise than this. It is particularly the priestly dimension of law within which this text is to be understood. As noted in connection with 16:2 and 20:4, language about making known abominable deeds stems from priestly legal terminology, but it is the specific function of the idea of "blood" that the language of these verses forces us to explore. From the law about shedding human blood in Gen 9:4-6 (P) to the attention paid to blood in the first Holiness Code pericope in Leviticus 17, especially v. 4, it is striking how crucial a concern priestly law has with blood. Priestly tradition concerned itself with both the crime of bloodshed and its consequence of bloodguilt. In 22:13 the text speaks of "your blood," but actually means "the blood shed in you" as well as the "bloodguilt incurred by you." In words about "uncleanness" (vv. 3-5) and "become guilty" the text uses terminology which envisages the consequences of disobedience as a sphere of corruption and harm into which one entered (Zimmerli, *Ezekiel 1,* 456), and it would be a priestly, legal pronouncement as verdict (see Hutton, *Declaratory Formulae*) by which that disastrous entry would be established. Of course, such priestly procedures were traditionally directed at the care of individuals, but here it is the whole city of God whose guilt is affirmed. When, then, the center and locus of holiness has become defiled, where could one turn for help?

Another shocking aspect of this text's heritage is the way it picks up in "bloody city" a label scoffingly applied by Nahum to Nineveh a few decades earlier. This could only raise the same hackles as the comparison of Jerusalem to Sodom in ch. 16. The prophet returns to this label in 24:6 and 9. It must have seemed to his audience that Ezekiel as a priest and a prophet was one who missed the point of both offices. Transgressions undoubtedly occurred, but it was the job of both priest and prophet (see ch. 13) to bring about the restoration of the transgressor and deliverance from guilt or harm. Even when a priest or prophet might point to manifold sins, the natural question, "What must be done?," was assumed to have an answer in the area of ceremonies and intercessions. That is what priests and prophets are for! To get the answer, "You must be scattered," was not only inappropriate, it was unfair. If individuals transgress, individuals must bear consequences, not the entire community. To apply laws for individual members of the community to the community as a whole was not possible. After all, such laws were given as the instrumentality of life. Thus Ezekiel must have faced an audience which looked at him in bewilderment. He spoke for a God who was turning the instrumentality of life into the vehicle of death, and the end he announced could only lead to the profaning of God in the sight of the nations.

Yet it was just such a desperate God that Ezekiel's words attested. But this God was also desperately consistent. In his laws he had laid claim to every area of his people's lives, and the expression of allegiance was to be measured not just by affirmations, but by implementation. As in ancient times, the meaning of "I am Yahweh your God and you are my people" was to find expression much more in how one treated others than in what sacrifices one offered. In fact, to mistreat others was to enter into the sphere of guilt and uncleanness which prevented ritual contact with God.

What this comes down to is a "radical sharpening" (Zimmerli, *Ezekiel 1,* 459) of the will of God. It is a sharpening in that it works with the commandments in such a way that they cut through and penetrate into every area of life, especially those wherein security was customarily to be found. They cut so deeply as to threaten the death of the one addressed. Yet this is "radical" in still another way, for it goes back to the root of the relationship between the Lord and Israel. The commandments were signposts marking out the Lord's possession. Each commandment marked out an aspect of life as belonging to the Lord. The refrain "I am Yahweh" accompanies the laws in the Holiness material, because the laws are equivalent to the statement, "You are my people." If the examination of his people revealed that they were denying and disavowing the basis of their existence, that they had forgotten him (v. 12), then they would have to learn in some new way to recognize anew what it means that "I am the Lord."

Bibliography

G. R. Driver, "Linguistic and Textual Problems: Ezekiel," *Bib* 19 (1938) 60-69; R. Hutton, *Declaratory Formulae: Forms of Authoritative Pronouncement in Ancient Israel* (Diss., Claremont Graduate School, 1983).

AN ALLEGORY: ISRAEL IS DROSS, 22:17-22

Text

The simplest solution to the apparent confusion in the use of the metallurgical figure is to follow G. R. Driver's suggestion in *Bib* 19 (1938) 69 and read *sîg mikkesep* ("dross without silver") for *sigîm kesep* ("dross . . . silver") in v. 18b. The presence of a comparison in v. 20 makes it probable that the first word be read as *kiqĕbuṣat* ("as one gathers [silver]") rather than *qĕbuṣat* ("gathering of [silver]").

Structure

I. Prophetic word formula	17
II. Preliminary: address as "son of man"	18aα
III. An allegorical description addressed to the prophet	18aβb
A. Israel is dross	18aβ
B. They are other metals	18bα
C. They are not silver	18bβ
IV. Transitional "therefore" and messenger formula	19aαβ
V. A message to the people, interpreting the allegory in a three-part prophetic proof saying	19aγb-22
A. Reason for punishment	19aγ
B. Transitional "therefore"	19bα
C. Announcement of punishment	19bβ-22a
1. Intervention	19bβ-21
a. I gather you into Jerusalem	19bβ
b. Analogy	20
1) As metals are gathered for melting	20a
2) So I will gather you in wrath to melt you	20b
c. Summary: I will gather, blow, and melt	21
2. Results: analogy	22a
a. As silver is melted	22aα
b. So you will be melted	22aβ
D. Elaborated recognition formula	22b

Marked off by the prophetic word formula at the beginning in v. 17 and again in v. 23 following the concluding recognition formula and a change in the figure of speech, this section is beyond dispute a unit in itself.

Genre and Setting

Very much after the fashion of ch. 15, here Yahweh takes up another familiar allegory from Israel's traditions, that of the smelting furnace. This figure of speech usually had the positive purpose of interpreting some experience of national suffering as having served to purify the people, just as precious metal is obtained from impure ore by the use of the refiner's fire. The figure was a fairly frequent one in the prophets: Isaiah used it in 1:22-25, Jeremiah in 6:27-30, and Deutero-Isaiah in 48:10. It was used specifically of both the bondage in Egypt and the exile in

Babylon. Ezekiel picks up this rich and familiar tradition, but modifies it in such a way as to skew its meaning from a message of the positive interpretation of past disaster into a totally hopeless announcement of new disaster. While elsewhere Yahweh's purpose was healthy if painful, here it is simply pointless.

From the very beginning it is made clear to both prophet and people that Israel is dross, the impurity which is removed from the valuable metal. When after that the metaphor proceeds apace to talk of gathering, blowing, and melting, that is evidently nothing but folly. One does not refine impurities, one gets rid of them. Nonsilver-bearing metals are not like ore, a candidate for refinement and purification; they are by definition totally without potential. To put them in the furnace, according to the prophet, is not a hopeful step. They will, of course, melt, but in a fully useless way. The word "refine" is nowhere mentioned here. The fire is not the instrument of stern but productive purification; instead it represents nothing but anger and wrath.

Intention

To the people of Judah at a time about 589 B.C., near the beginning of the siege of Jerusalem, the prophet brings a message interpreting their upcoming experience. It will be an occasion when the Babylonians will indeed make things hot for them. Nevertheless, the prophet speaks strongly of the Lord as the one who is behind and active in bringing and gathering the refugees from other Judean cities into Jerusalem. But from the start the figure is turned on its ear—to mix a metaphor. Once it is said that Israel is dross there is no point in any process at all. The text frighteningly chooses the metaphor of fire simply because Jerusalem will be burned. Moreover, where hopeful listeners might ask, "Will the fire be the end?" thereby facing the terrifying possibility of a future in which God might say, "No," the prophet bluntly affirms that God's "No" lies not somewhere in the future, but has already been spoken. The people of God, purified in the furnace of Egypt, once were spoken of as precious, even though perhaps needing purification. Now there exists no more people of God in Jerusalem, and there is nothing that could be done to get such a people out of Jerusalem's inhabitants. Bronze, iron, lead, and tin are what they are; they are not silver and can never become silver. To say that is not to threaten judgment or implicitly to call for repentance. It is simply to announce an interpretation of what is happening and about to happen which from the outset leaves it totally devoid of any positive value.

A PROPHETIC EXPLANATION: ALL LEADERSHIP CLASSES ARE CORRUPT, 22:23-31

Text

In v. 24 the use of the metaphor of rain makes it likely that *muṭṭārâ* ("rained upon") be read for *mĕṭōhārâ* ("cleansed") and *gušĕmâ* ("showered upon") for *gušmāh* ("its shower"). Because prophets are mentioned in v. 28, it is highly likely that the listing of various leaders requires reading in v. 25 *'ăšer nĕsî'êhā* ("whose princes") for *qešer nĕbî'êhā* ("a conspiracy of its prophets").

160

Structure

I.	Prophetic word formula	23
II.	Preliminaries	24aαβ
	A. Address as son of man	24aα
	B. Direction to speak	24aβ
III.	Prophetic explanation of punishment	24aγb-31
	A. Metaphorical address to land as not rained upon	24aγb
	B. Survey description of behavior of all leadership classes	25-29
	1. Princes: greedy and oppressive	25
	2. Priests: pervert or ignore duties	26
	3. Officials: destroy for gain	27
	4. Prophets: give false messages	28
	5. People of the land: oppress the vulnerable	29
	C. Summary report of failure of leadership (in divine speech)	30
	1. I sought one who would act on behalf of the people	30a
	2. I did not find any	30b
	D. Report of judgment (in divine speech)	31abα
	1. I acted in wrath	31a
	2. Requital formula	31bα
	E. Prophetic utterance formula	31bβ

Once again formulas and uniformity of subject mark off a clear unity within which the position of III.B is central.

Genre

Perhaps for want of a more precise label, Zimmerli characterizes this text as a "sermon" against all classes of society (*Ezekiel 1,* 466-67). Surely, "sermon" is too broad a label, especially since—apart from the "land" in v. 24a—no one is addressed directly. It is still a prophetic type of speech in that God is the speaker throughout, but it looks back upon the causes of divine judgment already performed, rather than announcing them in advance. Thus I propose the designation PROPHETIC EXPLANATION OF PUNISHMENT. While many writers see here an examination of five groups as representatives of all social classes, that view is both impossible and inappropriate. It is impossible because the term "people of the land" is not a reference to citizens in general, but to a leadership stratum (see among others Pope in *IDB* I, 106). It is inappropriate because the context, as will be shown, is from beginning to end an indictment of leaders for their failure.

The address to the land in v. 24aγ is particularly apt, since after 587 B.C. no significant group remained. The metaphor of not having received rain should be seen as pointing out that no help had been perceived from that source from which help might have been expected, viz., the leaders of the community. In vv. 25-29 each segment of the leadership is examined consecutively: princes (or possibly kings in Ezekiel's terminology), priests, officials, prophets, and "people of the land." In each case the key to understanding the logic inherent in the particular charges is that the intent is to show failure to do one's duties. Princes are supposed to protect, not plunder. Priests are to administer Yahweh's *torah,* not do violence to it, to distinguish properly between holy and profane, etc. Officials exist to maintain life, not destroy it for gain. Prophets are to expose transgression, not cover it up (see 13:1-16), to speak only genuine words from the Lord. And the people of the land are to uphold social order, not pervert it (see the language for the wicked in ch. 18). Thus vv. 25-29 are an indictment of failed leaders presented in stereotypical language, inverting the job description of each group. Sometimes this inversion is done by an ironic play on words, such as using the noble, dynastic image of "lion," but looking not at the nobility of the "king of beasts," but at the plunderer a lion can be. In most instances, though, the prophet seems to have switched a table of duties into the negative. Finally, the summary of misbehavior in v. 30 specifies God's inability to find any responsible leader who would undertake that representative role through which health and protection might come. It is interesting that the metaphor selected for this responsible action, to "stand in the breach," is that which Ezekiel employed for the prophetic office in 13:5. It is clear, then, that leadership groups are the focus from beginning to end in 22:23-31. To see the "order of precedence" in the sequence of these groups, as Eichrodt does (312), is probably more than the evidence can establish.

Setting

That Ezekiel in these verses is dependent upon preceding prophetic tradition would be likely from the outset, considering his constant use of tradition, but especially so here, since by definition categorization follows patterns. Thus, it is only to have been expected that similar indictments of leadership groups appear in Mic 3:11, Jer 5:31, and Zeph 3:3-4. The link to Zephaniah is, as has been repeatedly noticed, particularly strong, twelve of the key terms in Zeph 3:3f being picked up in Ezekiel. The relationship could chronologically be one of dependence by Ezekiel, but in view of the stereotypical way in which lists of duties are handled here, such lists may well have been common legal language. The key word (*za'am,* "indignation") for Yahweh's wrath in both Zeph 3:8 and vv. 24 and 31 here seems to be one prophets used especially for "Yahweh's intervention in judgment" (Zimmerli, *Ezekiel 1,* 467), and one which became in apocalyptic a kind of *terminus technicus* (ibid.).

Intention

Zimmerli's influential treatment of this text starts from the right perspective, noting that it is a reflection about history, purposefully examining what happened and why. But he goes on to speak of this aim almost totally within the sphere of "remembering" (*Ezekiel 1,* 469f.) as opposed to the forgetting or suppressing of history. Actually, the text itself speaks not at all of remembering or forgetting, and it would be more accurate to see here the marshalling of evidence. Just as prophets frequently present evidence in advance to justify an announcement of divine judgment, so here in a mood akin to that of the doxology of judgment (see von Rad, *Old Testament Theology* I, 357-59) the evidence supporting the fitting character of God's judgment is reviewed after the fact. The focus on the failure of the leadership is a way of analyzing God's decision and proclaiming it, somewhat similar to the assessments of the Deuteronomistic historian about certain kings—especially Jeroboam I and Manasseh. In his more spacious framework the historian could look at both the good and the evil and strike a balance, whereas Ezekiel here ignores and even denies the presence of any good leadership. God simply allows the misdeeds of the leaders to come upon their heads and thereby destroys them in wrath. To see here, on the other hand, a concern that the people of Israel "abstain from offending in the future" (Eichrodt, 316) is to introduce an idea fully and automatically natural for us, but one which is intimated by not a single word in this text.

Bibliography

G. R. Driver, "Linguistic and Textual Problems: Ezekiel," *Bib* 19 (1938) 69; R. Hutton, *Declaratory Formulae: Forms of Authoritative Pronouncement in Ancient Israel* (Diss., Claremont Graduate School, 1983); M. Pope, "'Am Ha'arez," *IDB* I, 106; G. von Rad, *Old Testament Theology* (tr. D. M. G. Stalker; New York: Harper, 1962) I, 357-59.

AN ALLEGORY: THE TWO LEWD SISTERS, 23:1-49

Text

The final word of v. 5 ("warriors") must be moved to the start of v. 6. The pattern of vv. 3 and 8 suggests that in v. 21b we should read *bĕ'aśśôt* ("when . . . handled") for *ba'śôt* ("when . . . did") and *lĕma'ēk* ("to press") for *lĕma'an* ("for the sake of ").

Structure

I. Prophetic word formula	1
II. Preliminary: address as son of man	2a
III. Allegory of Oholah and Oholibah: a prophecy of punishment	2b-27
A. Reason	2b-21
1. Background	2b-4
a. Two sisters	2b
b. Both lewd in Egypt	3
c. Their names	4aα
d. Married me and bore children	4aβ
e. Their names interpreted	4b
2. Oholah's history: a prophetic explanation of punishment	5-10
a. Reason: was unfaithful with Assyrians	5-8
1) Summary in advance	5
2) Details spelled out	6-7
a) Attractive soldiers	6

Although the prophetic word formulas in 23:1 and 24:1 point out clear boundaries, the presence of a new report of divine speech in 23:36 creates a problem. That problem is best faced by recognizing that vv. 36-49 are a lengthy, separate, new treatment of the same subject as vv. 1-27, this time largely in the third person, whereas the earlier section had begun in the third person (vv. 2-20) only to switch to direct address for its climax (v. 21 seems to begin this direct address one verse too early). Rather oddly vv. 44-49 return to speak of both sisters and an impending judgment, thereby creating a peculiar blending of the events of 722 and 587 B.C. Further investigation reveals that vv. 28-35 are a series of smaller additional units, fairly clearly linked in content to the preceding, and all in direct address. Some parts of VIII are hopelessly corrupt in text, and in both VII and IX the text alternates for no discernible reason between description and direct address, with some gender confusion as well.

Genre

Although the textual corruption near the end makes for some uncertainty, the classification of the chapter as a whole is not in doubt. The basic section, vv. 2b-27, is an allegorical PROPHECY OF PUNISHMENT. Although the prophet is not commanded to preach this section, the direct address at the end makes such a use overwhelmingly likely. Actually, the allegorical elements within the entire chapter are so transparent that the explanations given in vv. 4b and 33b are scarcely necessary and perhaps glosses. Fohrer is hardly correct in seeing the amputation of nose and ears in v. 25 as an allegorical reference to the deportation of Jerusalem's leading citizens (136).

As often in Ezekiel, the length of the unit allows room for development which tends to alter somewhat the normal shape and role of the genre. The development in this case shifts the emphasis from the actual announcement of the coming event of the fall of Jerusalem to the analysis of what it is within the people of Judah and Jerusalem that brought this outcome about. In some ways then, as in ch. 20, the material moves toward becoming THEOLOGICAL REFLECTION. This shows in the bold way in which the analysis skips from Egypt to the Assyrian age, and like ch. 20 views Egypt as the place of the beginning of Israel's evil.

In the process of this enlarging of the unit some secondary elaboration of an editorial sort also seems to occur. However, this is of such a complicated character that attempts to determine by literary-critical means an "original" text are not convincing. This is most decisively true of attempts to reconstruct the chapter in poetic form. Although there are many poetic elements, especially parallelism, and even one relatively independent rhythmic section in vv. 32-34, the whole seems definitely to be more of that elevated prose which predominates in Ezekiel, rather than any restorable actual poetry. Already v. 31 demonstrates parallelism, but it serves a strange sort of transitional role. Because nothing intervenes to separate it from vv. 28-30, it serves as a kind of concluding summary of them. Yet it is linked to what follows, since it introduces the cup figure to be developed in vv. 32-34, although it is separated from those verses by a messenger formula.

The imagery of sexual misbehavior naturally brings with it some legal flavor, but actually this is less prominent than elsewhere in Ezekiel. Patterns of punishment are mentioned especially in vv. 45 and 49a, and they and the proposal of judgment in v. 36 (see also 20:4 and 22:2) make extensive use of the implications of the crime of adultery, but all of this is in the latter third of the chapter, which is apparently an elaboration based upon vv. 2-27.

The chapter must also be examined as HISTORY. It is allegorical in technique and theological in orientation, but it is nonetheless a brief venture at the analysis of the broad flow of political events into a pattern of cause and effect (von Rad, "The Beginning of Historical Writing in Ancient Israel," 166-71). Samaria's previous fall is analyzed in a PROPHETIC EXPLANATION OF PUNISHMENT (see 22:23-31) in vv. 5-10 as the result of her trusting in Assyria rather than Yahweh, and Judah's history is surveyed from a similar point of view. This is a familiar prophetic message, and it is only the larger scope of this section which qualifies it for the label HISTORY. What is most interesting is the radical character of the analysis this chapter offers. As in ch. 20, Israel's sin is traced back to Egypt, but here this is given a much sharper historical contour when the political maneuverings of Jehoiakim and Zedekiah in switching their loyalty from Babylon to Egypt are seen as a return to the days of her youth in Egypt. What the prophet can have in mind about some original misbehavior in Egypt is fully unknown to us, but it is powerfully and quite appropriately applied to her persistent attempts to win some self-achieved security through timely alliances by seeing them as infidelity.

Setting

As mentioned, Ezekiel is by no means the first either to proclaim this message or to use the image of sexual infidelity to portray it. Hosea and Jeremiah are his predecessors here, and to some extent ancient myths of sacred marriage are a part of its background. Still, the imagery here, as in Hosea and Jeremiah, is fully historicized. This is most plainly the case here where the adultery in question is almost totally of a political sort as expressed in alliances, rather than of a ritual sort as expressed in Canaanized worship. Jeremiah 3:6-11 is an especially close analogy, as is, of course, Ezekiel 16. What marks out Ezekiel's treatment as different is the way, although heavily traditional, it carries everything to an extreme. The use of sexual imagery is more crass, going even to the use of animal imagery and to references to the size of sex organs (23:20). The outcome envisaged is harsher, not divorce but death, going even to mutilation (v. 25).

A comparison of chs. 16 and 23 reveals both similarities and differences. Whorish behavior, which provokes the Lord's jealousy and which is deeply rooted in Israel's perverse rejection of her spouse and leads to destruction at the hands of an assembly of nations, is the extensive, basic similarity, but the differences are also striking. That ch. 23 deals with both Samaria and Judah is an obvious difference, but that is only a matter of the choice of what history to include. More significant is the way ch. 23 concentrates on politics rather than worship as the area of infidelity. Even Ezekiel's favorite word for idols appears only once in the basic unit of vv. 2-27. In the subsequent elaboration it appears in vv. 30, 37, 39, and 49, serving thereby as further evidence of the expansionary character of that section. (The prophet's distaste for human representation in v. 14 is largely a different matter.) Additional basic differences appear in the early phase of the development of the imagery. Unlike ch. 16, the treatment of the two sisters spends no time on either the beauty of the women or the honor inherent in being the wife of Yahweh. Instead ch. 23 stresses the attractiveness of the lovers and the craving which drove Judah to her actions.

The particular focus on Egypt as the partner to which Judah turns as an expression of disloyalty in vv. 17b-21 and in v. 27 strongly suggests that this unit may well reflect the time before 587 B.C., when Zedekiah's politics were in a state of fluctuation, but the whole of ch. 23 is so sketchy and overdone in the development of its imagery (a further partial contrast to ch. 16) that it is hard to pin it down to a particular date.

Intention

Even though the story of a divine marriage clearly reflects a long history in mythology, this chapter is so thoroughly historicized that any attempt to deal with the link to the world of nature is totally foreign to it. But at the same time any fascination with the curious aspects of human marital behavior is equally alien. In spite of the crass vividness of the imagery employed, the perspective is coldly intellectual. There is not the faintest sympathy for these two tragic women or the distinctive personal circumstances which were involved.

Instead the material gets whatever warmth it does have precisely from its gross and overdone exaggerations. Swapping partners in a way that can only be called degenerate, for it sinks below the level of human behavior to the animal, is stressed as a way of creating revulsion in the audience. The congenital aspect of this absolutely undisciplined, nymphomaniacal seeking of sexual partners is not presented as a way of creating sympathy, but just as a pictorial way of describing and identifying theologically what can only be classed as a kind of "original sin." The stress on the lustful character of the search for a partner and the switching back and forth are not presented, as they would be today, as insight into the way basically healthy human desires are corrupted by a passion for excitation apart from commitment. Instead the focus throughout is on the rebuke of Israel's desire to secure her political existence by appropriate political activity, rather than seeing in her religion a relationship of such an exclusive and absolute sort that any attempt at self-achieved security could only be inherently an utter betrayal of her heritage. Although in contrast to ch. 16 the word "trust" is not used here, that is nevertheless the exact point around which the entire chapter revolves. To unite as a partner in a bond of intimacy, allegiance, and dependence with anyone other than Yahweh would be for Israel the most deep-seated betrayal imaginable. The chapter insists on seeing and judging all political relationships in the sole light of this theological understanding. No room whatsoever is permitted for an independent, practical side to international politics. And the sexual metaphor used to degrade Israel's political activity is making a purely negative point here. In contrast to ch. 16, where the positive significance of election by Yahweh is Israel's tragically renounced privilege and destiny, here the focus is not on the failure to remember a positive distinction, but on the pillorying of a disgusting perversity intended to call forth contempt and scorn. To reach the end of this account and hear the fate of this degenerate tramp is to be moved to say, "How else could it end!" This is indeed the well-deserved fate of a psycho-social misfit whose behavior was as deliberate as it was disgusting. That is the perspective of a doxology of judgment, but carried to an extreme never before known.

Although some "lessons" may suggest themselves occasionally, the aim of the chapter is in no way primarily moral or future-oriented. The reference in v. 48 to the way "all women may take warning and not commit lewdness as you have done" is neither, as Zimmerli thinks, a didactic moralizing (*Ezekiel 1,* 492) or, as Eichrodt argues, an allegorical warning to other nations (333), but simply a way of pointing to the incomprehensible, subhuman character of Israel's behavior. In conformity to this the doom which descends upon Judah is seen both as something fully within the area of Yahweh's sovereign control of all world history (v. 22) and as the most fittingly natural consequence flowing automatically from her own acts. Affirmations that "your lewdness . . . brought this upon you" (vv. 29-30) and "your lewdness shall be requited upon you" (v. 49) are indeed secondary elaboration from the viewpoint of the literary growth of the chapter, but they are fully primary in the way they formulate the intent of the oldest material as well.

The "lessons" brought out here are indeed worth reflecting upon, but they are of a much different sort from "a moral admonition which applies to everyday life" (Zimmerli, *Ezekiel 1,* 492). As proclamation, the chapter aims at affirming the righteousness of Judah's fate, but as historiographical reflection certain intellectual affirmations are made. The major ones have to do with whorish betrayal as the root cause of Israel's doom and the way this perverse disloyalty has characterized her from the beginning. But surely an interesting sidelight is to be noted in the way the time of Yahweh's rejection of Judah is pinned down to that moment when she turned from her adulterous liaison with the Babylonians to yet another lover, i.e., in the scheming of Jehoiakim and Zedekiah with Egypt. This reminds one strongly of the way the Deuteronomistic historian fixes on Manasseh as the decisive turning point in Judah's fall as he did with Jeroboam I in the case of the Northern Kingdom. In fact, Ezek 23:18 also links the decisive moment in Judah's downfall with the similar fate of her older sister, a striking parallel in the technique of historiographical analysis.

The "lesson" most frequently drawn from nearly all OT prophetic literature is that of repentance. The Deuteronomistic historian advances that very interpretation in 2 Kgs 17:13. But such a "lesson" can scarcely be drawn here. No opening is left for any kind of future. Even though the chapter's intent for its exilic audience is to force the conclusion about 587 B.C., "The Lord had to do it," not a word of this section draws a line which extends into the future. No political future is contemplated, no line is devoted to the exiles in Babylon, and not even the idea of a shame-filled remembering, as in 16:61-63, is suggested. The focus remains the narrower one of historiographical analysis, without any element of application. Even the presence of the recognition formula, "You shall know that I am the Lord God," leaves one wondering who this "you" can be.

Bibliography

G. von Rad, "The Beginnings of Historical Writing in Ancient Israel," in *The Problem of the Hexateuch and Other Essays* (tr. E. W. Trueman Dicken; New York: McGraw-Hill, 1966) 166-204.

AN ALLEGORY: THE POT THAT CANNOT BE CLEANSED, 24:1-14

Text

The initial two words of v. 12 are corrupt and untranslatable.

Structure

I. Prophetic word formula with date	1
II. Preliminaries	2-3a
A. Address as son of man	2aα
B. Direction to write down date	2aβγb
1. The direction itself	2aβγ
2. The reason: beginning of siege	2b

The prophetic word formulas in vv. 1 and 15 make it evident that this section is presented as a textual unit, but the structure within those borders is complex and sometimes obscure. The repeated use of "therefore" plus the messenger formula in vv. 3a (messenger formula only), 6a, and 9a indicates that relatively separate sections exist in vv. 3b-5, 6-8, and 9-13. Although the figurative language about meat cooked in a pot appears in all three sections, it is used differently in each. In vv. 3b-5 the figure appears throughout without any interpretation and without a hint of anything ominous, seeming instead rather joyful. In v. 6 an interpretation speaks of the pot's uncleanness and the removal of the meat, which is followed by vv. 7-8 which have no connection to the figure at all. In vv. 9-13 the focus of attention moves from the finishing of the cooking in vv. 9b-10 to the attempt to remove uncleanness in v. 11, the failure of which is set forth in v. 12, with only this last being interpreted in v. 13.

Explanations of these structural peculiarities have not been successful, and the likelihood exists that a complicated development lies behind the text, possibly one in which the prophet and/or his disciples made repeated use of this metaphor, only particular samples of which have been preserved. The unity of the text would then consist chiefly in its attachment to the single metaphor of the pot, or at least some aspect thereof.

Genre

The passage constitutes a complex PROPHECY OF PUNISHMENT. The abundance of imperative forms moves Fohrer (138-40) to see here a REPORT OF A SYMBOLIC ACTION, but he must move v. 3a's direction to deliver an allegory to a later point in order to achieve this. It is better simply to allow the text to stand, viewing vv. 3b-5 as a song in which those preparing a meal sing joyfully to one another about their actions. Such songs are a natural accompaniment of work, and one other somewhat similar instance appears in the "song of the well" in Num 21:17f. The *māšāl* of v. 3 would then appear in vv. 3b-5 and be given two interpretations in vv. 6-8 and 9-13, each beginning with an expression of woe. Especially the second interpretation is unusual in that while vv. 9b-10 are connected to the meal preparation in vv. 3b-5, vv. 11-13 go on to deal with the only loosely related issue of the uncleanness of the pot. However, already v. 6a mentions this uncleanness, even though vv. 7-8 do not return to it. The uncertainty about the uncleanness, whether it is rust, green tarnish, ritual impurity, or scum, makes it highly difficult to trace whatever logic may exist within and between the various sections. In any case the meal metaphor is not traced to the point of the consumption of the meat, although no hint is offered about the reason for this. Instead the focus moves to the vain attempt to allow the pot to burn clean. The first two words of v. 12 are untranslatable, and it is not certain if the "not . . . anymore" of v. 13 contemplates an eventual purification or simply an abandonment in fury.

Setting and Intention

The identification and marking down of the date in vv. 1-2 as that of the beginning of the siege suggest that the text was addressed to the fantastic confidence of the

Jerusalemites earlier observed in the use of a similar metaphor in 11:3. This text seeks to reject that confidence totally and replace it with an acceptance of the certainty of Jerusalem's coming destruction. For the exiles this would mean the end of their equally fantastic and misplaced hope for a speedy return. The specific identification of the day has the purpose of finding vindication when verification arrives, as in 33:21.

The joyful confidence of the cooking song is skewed to its opposite by two different explanations. Common to both is the goal of making evident that the place of protection has now become the place of danger. Picking up the same thought as 22:2, Jerusalem's status as a bloody city (i.e., one beset by bloodguilt) makes it a threat calling God to vengeance, rather than a reliance calling to mind God's promises. The careless handling of blood, in which no attempt is made at even the simplest sort of ritual acknowledgment (see Gen 4:10; 9:5; Deut 21:1-9; Job 16:18), triggers in the priestly perspective a powerful reservoir of guilt. Such conduct is "asking for it," and in v. 8 the Lord portrays his wrath as rising to the occasion. The same point is made in v. 9, where Yahweh inserts himself into the figure, fueling the fire for his own counterpurpose. Inasmuch as metal pots were so much more durable than ceramic ones, being able to survive ceremonial accidents as well as physical ones, the text seeks to eliminate even the hope of a Jerusalem purified by fire (see Num 31:23). Thus once again there emerges the message of divine frustration and the implicitly accompanying motif of a doxology of judgment.

THE REPORT OF A SYMBOLIC ACTION: THE DEATH OF EZEKIEL'S WIFE, 24:15-27

Text

In both vv. 17 and 22 read *'ônîm* ("mourners") for *'ănāšîm* ("men"). In v. 25 delete the last two words, "their sons and their daughters."

Structure

I. Prophetic word formula		15
II. Preliminary: address as son of man		16aα
III. Direction to perform a symbolic act		16aβb-17
A. Event precipitating action: death of Ezekiel's wife		16aβ
B. Prophet's action		16b-17
1. Do not grieve outwardly		16b
2. Sigh quietly		17aα
3. Do not do funeral mourning		17aβγδb
a. Summary direction		17aβ
b. Details		17aγδb
1) Wear turban		17aγ
2) Put on sandals		17aδ
3) Do not veil face		17bα
4) Do not eat mourners' bread		17bβ

Even though section VI involves largely a new subject from I-V and a new prophetic proof saying, vv. 25 and 27bα make a manifest connection to vv. 15-24, revealing that at least from the point of view of the editing of the material the two sections are intended to be taken in immediate connection.

Genre

In vv. 15-24 the pattern of the REPORT OF A SYMBOLIC ACT provides the basis for the organization of the section, but with a few disturbing complications. The basic parts of this pattern all appear: directions to carry out the act; report of execution; and interpretation. This in itself is atypical in Ezekiel, where the usual presentation has everything drawn into the compass of the divine word, so that the latter two parts appear only in advance within God's directions to the prophet. But it is just within these latter two parts here that problems occur. The prophet's statement about speaking to the people in v. 18aα comes prematurely, being appropriate only where it appears later in v. 20a as the introduction of the prophet's response to the people's question. And yet, the "morning . . . evening" parallel in v. 18 shows the case is not one of simple misplacement. It is also surprising to find the prophet using the prophetic word formula and messenger formula when he cites the divine word communicated to him. Plainly these formulas are not solely an editorial device. But it is chiefly the alternation in speakers within vv. 21-24 that makes one raise the possibility of a severe problem in the transmission of the text. In vv. 21 and 24 the Lord interprets the act to the people, and in vv. 22-23 the prophet himself does so. Undoubtedly this awkwardness implies that the current text reflects a complex history, but the awkwardness by itself does not enable us confidently to reconstruct that history, although the idea of assuming a blending of two distinct explanation sections (one in the first person and one in the third) is a tempting conjecture. The ending of the interpretation of Ezekiel's act with a recognition formula, although unanticipated, is still fully logical and very much typical within this book.

Setting and Intention

Although the unit is not dated, its placement at the end of the prophet's message of judgment is natural and fitting. The sign is linked to Jerusalem's end, and that end is naturally linked to the report of it in v. 26. If 33:21f. had followed with the account of the fulfillment of vv. 26-27, the chronological sequence would have been excellently captured. However, questions of the overall structuring of the book dictated breaking that connection in order to use it later as an obvious link by which to resume the reporting of the prophet's words. But that would happen only after making clear, by the insertion of chs. 25–32 and the prefixing of 33:1-20, that with the report of the fulfillment in 33:21f. a new era had begun historically and, therefore, a new orientation to the prophet's preaching. Thus the combination of the arrival of the refugee and the report of the end of the prophet's dumbness has been used to create a redactional device of major importance for the arrangement of the book—and an extremely effective one at that. From the viewpoint of its functioning as the end of the collection of judgment material, it is impressively fitting that a death should provide the framework for understanding the finality of the 587 B.C. event. Further that the death be that of a loved and treasured life partner underlines most forcefully the emotional cost—first to Yahweh, and then to the people—in the destruction of both city and temple.

That this ugliest of all symbolic acts should penetrate so deeply into the life of the prophet is a matter for careful reflection. Hosea's marriage and Jeremiah's absenting of himself from all joy are important analogies, but this passage is an extreme case going beyond all analogies. As mentioned, the fact that it is Ezekiel's wife who dies does stress the painfulness of God's love in a remarkable way. And yet at this very point objections thrust themselves forward, pointing out how the cruelly sudden and matter-of-fact character of this most extreme symbolic act suggests rather the callousness of the God who would choose this technique to heighten the effectiveness of his message. Hengstenberg could not believe that God could do such a thing, and avoided facing the possibility by making it an allegory, just as he did with Hosea's marriage and the Song of Songs (Hengstenberg, 211-12). Faithful listening to the message of Ezekiel, especially its consistent going to extremes, will not permit the modern interpreter so easy an escape. The simple reading of this text makes it overwhelmingly likely that Ezekiel's wife did die. Moreover, the text yields no support for the idea that this was an otherwise accidental and unrelated death, which the prophet in a combination of desperation and bad taste tried to make of some illustrative value for his preaching. In all its crassness the reader must face the statement by the text that Ezekiel's God went this horrifyingly far in drawing the life of his messenger into the message given him. The shock and the offense we feel are not purely matters of a modern era. This whole episode would likely have been bewildering and obscenely, even blasphemously, offensive already to Ezekiel's listeners. God dare not go so far! We insist that his behavior be limited to that which we can tolerate. And yet the offensiveness of the Lord who proclaims and carries out announcements of such unbelievable extremes as the abandonment of his own holy place and the mutilation and execution of his own wife has been characteristic of Ezekiel from the beginning. But surely this death of the prophet's wife is the most offensive of all. That God should himself forsake and destroy his beloved place and people is bad enough, but that he should require another to suffer death just for the sake of the objective clarification of God's word to his unlistening people—that is too much! The thought of the God who could go this far in demonstrating the intensity of both his love and his judgment is one otherwise at home only within the context of the New Testament, where it is specifically labelled foolishness and an offense.

But 24:15-27 surprises us in yet another way. Not only is nothing said about the offensiveness of this act to Ezekiel's fellow exiles, not a word is offered about Ezekiel's own reaction. No protest in advance, no hesitation along the way, and no bitterness afterward appear. The text simply walls itself off against any biographical inquiry. The silent grief that is described is not a case of paralyzing shock or repressed feelings. These thoughts are again modern attempts to dodge the reality of the text as too offensive. Nonetheless, at the risk of being guilty of the same thing, a point not usually noticed should be made. The news of the fall of Jerusalem would be the tidings of a Babylonian victory, and to lament over the arrival of such news could be perceived as seditious in Babylon. At least to that small extent silent grief is comprehensible. That it was also a grief too great for tears is much less likely, especially in view of the expressive nature of middle-Eastern mourning customs. The keening of the women was an automatic reaction, one to be stifled only with the greatest effort.

Finally, a difficulty in the setting of vv. 25-27 must be noticed. The "day" of vv. 25 and 26 cannot be the same day, if by the taking away of "their stronghold" is meant the fall of Jerusalem in 587 B.C. The news of that event naturally did not reach Ezekiel until some months later (according to 33:21 either six months or a year and six months later, which seems amazingly long). It is conceivable that v. 25 had in view the subjective taking away of the temple, i.e., the reception of the news of its end, but other possibilities also exist. That there is some redactional confusion resulting from the connecting of passages originally referring to two different days may be likely, but the brevity of the present verses enables only the conjecture, not the reconstruction of the text. That the two days were in fact identical, since Ezekiel was actually present in Jerusalem during its fall or in a country town near enough to be reached by the news on the same day (Herntrich, 114; Bertholet, 89), is a vain attempt which is not true to "the actual nature of the text as a redactional . . . bridge" (Zimmerli, *Ezekiel 1,* 508-9).

Bibliography

E. W. Hengstenberg, *Prophecies of the Prophet Ezekiel* (tr. by A. C. Murphy and J. G. Murphy; Edinburgh: T. & T. Clark, 1869); V. Herntrich, *Ezekielprobleme* (BZAW 61; Giessen: Töpelmann, 1933).

Chapter 3

The Individual Units of Chapters 25–32: The Prophecies against Foreign Nations

THE COLLECTION AS A WHOLE, 25:1–32:32

Structure

Boundaries marked off by both subject matter and prophetic formulas reveal that chs. 25–32 are one grand literary collection of prophecies concerning foreign nations or, more precisely, a collection of collections of such materials. A closer look reveals that a total of seven nations are addressed, that seven separate prophecies are devoted to the seventh nation, Egypt, and that in the seventh of those prophecies against Egypt, seven nations are surveyed as the other inhabitants of the underworld. Clearly a fascination with the number seven has played a part in the arranging of this material. That other prophecies against foreign nations existed within the body of Ezekiel tradition is certain, because of what we find in chs. 35 and 38–39. The reasons those prophecies appear where they do will be best discussed when we come to those chapters, but the reasons underlying the ordering of chs. 25–32 are largely artificial. For example, the small stereotypical prophecy against Sidon in 28:20-24 is plainly there in order to fill out the total to seven. Similarly 29:17-21 is placed where it is, even though its date is far out of sequence, because it deals with both Tyre and Egypt, and has likely been placed after the first anti-Egyptian prophecy in order to keep it as close as possible to the anti-Tyre collection. Further, the three nations added in 32:29-30 are presented so minimally that it is apparent they too are there just to complete the number. Finally, a lesser element of artificiality is noticeable in the case of the prophecies against Moab, Edom, and the Philistines in 25:8-17, where these appear to have some individuality but are still in considerable part only stereotypical expansions parallel to 25:1-7. Other expansionary material, not affecting the total numbers but enlarging individual prophecies, is particularly noticeable in chs. 27 and 31 and to a lesser extent in 30:3-19. No real overall structural markings are present to illuminate the intention of the whole of chs. 25–32, but some do appear in 25–28, especially in 28:24-26, where a basic theological perspective is asserted.

178

Genre

The unevenness in size and variations in the patterning suggest that this COLLEC-TION of collections was not some large-scale unit planned from the outset, but instead one which took shape by an editorial process working to create an arrangement that would provide some order. Generically it is interesting to notice the way Ezekiel's most individually characteristic genre, the PROPHETIC PROOF SAYING, appears concentrated in chs. 25 and 29–32, with only one in the Tyre collection in chs. 26:1–28:19. PROPHETIC ANNOUNCEMENTS OF PUNISHMENT and DIRGES are naturally expectable genres finding representation in chs. 25–32, and in view of chs. 15–19 the prominence of lengthy figurative speech is not surprising in either chs. 27–28 or chs. 30–32.

Setting and Intention

It is when we ask about the background, social context, or mental process which might underlie this collection of collections that especially intriguing possibilities must be considered. The material in 1 Kgs 20:13 and 28 makes it highly likely that a military-cultic background originally formed the setting in which prophecies against foreign nations functioned. Military-political conditions determined who the enemy nations were, and the prophets gave expression to Yahweh's powerful word, probably in some ritual context. Bentzen (85-99) points to Egyptian execration rites and texts as a form of ritual cursing, and several factors support this conjecture, especially the frequent mood of scornful contempt, even revenge, and the many place names in these prophecies. The stereotypical language of plundering and of siege techniques strongly reminds us of magically motivated drawings in which success was visualized and dramatized. Especially the portrayal of the defeated ones being deported was a situation of personal experience for Judean exiles in Ezekiel's surroundings, as was the pattern of characterizing existence in exile as essentially a form of death (see 33:10 and 37:11). Thus the fondness for dirges and other kinds of lament patterns was to be expected.

But the creation of a literary collection of prophecies against foreign nations is a further step and implies a new setting, one which has moved from the ritual toward the rational. On a literary level, list-making was far less a powerful checking off of an enemy's roster and far more a wisdom-based activity. The delights of organizing the obscure and exhausting an area in completeness of survey are ones which we might associate with the encyclopedic compilers of onomastica. Chronological sequencing is an area where the desire to master material by its orderly arrangement is particularly clear, and chs. 25–32 are the place of the heaviest concentration of dates in the book of Ezekiel. Aspects of this mental process are illuminated when we notice how subject matter has in certain cases been given priority over chronology. The date in 26:1 is later than that in 29:1 and before those in 32:1 and 17, but the desire to keep the Tyre and Egypt materials in subcollections has inhibited any thorough chronological arrangement. Similarly 29:17-21, although the latest dated unit in the book, is placed where it is, as has been suggested above, for reasons of content.

Two matters in regard to the overall arrangement of this material take on significance when one explores the implication of placement for determining its intent. First, is there a standard presupposition that prophecies against foreign nations function as a transition from a message of judgment to one of hope? Such seems to be the case in the placement of Isaiah 13–23 as well as that of Jeremiah 46–51 in the Septuagint tradition. Is the selecting of seven such prophecies a matter of symbolic significance? The appearance of seven units in Amos 1–2 and Jer 46:1–49:33 suggests it may have been. This last observation leads to the second argument from placement to intent. According to the tradition in Deut 7:1 and elsewhere, seven nations of Canaan were to fall and be cleared away before Israel could take possession of the land. Is the selection of seven nations as the target of Ezekiel's prophecies a way of implying a typological pattern of what should take place between the new exodus and the new entry into the land (Zimmerli, *Ezekiel* 2, 3-4)? Other evidence tends to support the implications of these two arguments. For example, chs. 25–32 are obviously inserted in a break in the current text created by the gap between 24:25-27, the end of the last pericope of judgment, and 33:21-22 at the beginning of the message of consolation (see the discussion of ch. 33 for the role of 33:1-20). This insertion surely aims to make a point about how chs. 25–32 are to be interpreted as belonging to the realm of the death which is to precede life. The only other date in the remainder of the book, in 40:1 at the portrayal of the new temple in the new land, lies beyond all those in chs. 25–32, except for 29:17-21, and this too seems to express a conviction about the functional place of chs. 25–32 as a background to Israel's restoration.

Finally, in spite of the lateness of the compilation of chs. 25–32 apparent in both the date of 29:17-21 and the process by which the sets of seven were achieved, there is no reason to see any of this material as postexilic in setting. The absence of any prophecies against Babylon could be explained by Ezekiel's place of residence, but surely the formulation of some of the rest of the material, especially that specifically naming Nebuchadrezzar, e.g., 26:7-14 and 30:10-12, would look different from a perspective after 539 B.C.

Bibliography

A. Bentzen, "The Ritual Background of Amos i:2–ii:16," *OTS* 8 (1950) 85-99.

A COLLECTION OF PROPHECIES AGAINST JUDAH'S NEAREST NEIGHBORS, 25:1-17

Text

The reference to Seir in addition to Moab in v. 8b is not taken up in what follows and is most likely to be deleted as an incorrect gloss.

Structure and Genre

	a. Address as son of man	2aα
	b. Hostile orientation formula	2aβ
	c. Direction to prophesy	2b
	d. Direction to speak to the Ammonites	3aα
	e. Call to attention	3aβ
	f. Messenger formula	3bα
2.	Three-part prophetic proof saying (mainly	
	direct address, both masculine and feminine)	3bβγδ-5
	a. Reason: gloating over Judah's fall	3bβγδ
	b. Transitional "therefore"	4aα
	c. Announcement of punishment	4aβγδb-5a
	1) First intervention: delivered to the	
	people of the East	4aβ
	2) Results: occupied and plundered	4aγδb
	3) Second intervention (third person)	5a
	a) Rabbah occupied	5aα
	b) Ammon occupied	5aβ
	d. Recognition formula (2 mp)	5b
B.	Second prophecy against Ammon	6-7
1.	Resumptive "for" and messenger formula	6aαβ
2.	Three-part prophetic proof saying	
	(all direct address)	6aγb-7
	a. Reason: gloating over Israel	6aγb
	b. Transitional "therefore"	7aα
	c. Announcement of punishment (all	
	intervention): plunder and destruction	7aβγδεbα
	d. Recognition formula	7bβ
III.	Prophecy against Moab	8-11
A.	Resumptive messenger formula	8a
B.	Three-part prophetic proof saying (all third person)	8b-11
1.	Reason: gloating over Judah's experiencing a	
	fate like others	8b
2.	Transitional "therefore"	9aα
3.	Announcement of punishment	9aβb-11a
	a. First intervention: exposure of land to the	
	people of the East and Ammon	9aβb-10a
	b. Purpose: Ammon not to be remembered	10b
	c. Second intervention: judgments on Moab	11a
4.	Recognition formula	11b
IV.	Prophecy against Edom	12-14
A.	Resumptive messenger formula	12aα
B.	Three-part prophetic proof saying (all third person)	12aβb-14
1.	Reason: vengefulness against Judah	12aβb
2.	Transitional "therefore" and messenger formula	13aαβ
3.	Announcement of punishment	13aγδb-14a
	a. First intervention: total devastation	13aγδbα
	b. First result: all fall	13bβ
	c. Second intervention: vengeance through Israel	14aα

That the PROPHETIC WORD FORMULA occurs only in 25:1 and 26:1 suggests that this chapter is to be seen as a unit. The contents bear that out in that the brief, stereotyped messages in ch. 25 are in sharp contrast to the vivid, lengthy prophecy in ch. 26, and the nations treated are all Judah's immediate neighbors, arranged in clockwise geographical sequence. However, the shape of the collection in ch. 25 is a bit unusual. In one way this unusualness is the result of the manner in which the PROPHETIC WORD FORMULA is employed as a unit boundary. Because of that, the individual PROPHECIES CONCERNING FOREIGN NATIONS can no longer be marked off from one another by that formula, and so the MESSENGER FORMULA has been used for this purpose in II.B.1, III.A, IV.A, and V.A. This is a bit awkward, since it could leave the impression that each new prophecy is continuing the initial one aimed at the Ammonites. The only proper addressing of the message appears in vv. 2-3aα, the subsequent addressing having to be worked into the reason sections. Further, although all five come as three-part PROPHETIC PROOF SAYINGS, in both content and form the prophecies of ch. 25 are plainly grouped into two sub-collections: those against Moab and Ammon, and those against Edom and the Philistines. Naturally, the two prophecies against Ammon create no problem when no new address marks off the beginning of the second, since the first address can simply be assumed to carry over. The prophecy against Moab reveals its close link to the preceding in three ways: (1) the giving of the same reason, i.e., gloating; (2) the mention of Ammon in v. 10b; and (3) the delivering of each nation to the people of the East. In spite of this commonality, however, only the very first prophecy is spoken in direct address (apart from v. 5a), betraying a somewhat incomplete editorial process.

The prophecies against Edom and Philistia are particularly close in a number of ways. While the preceding three proof sayings end with the simple RECOGNITION FORMULA in second or third person, these latter two employ variations of the recognition formula adapted to this specific context. The root "revenge" (nāqam) appears five times in each prophecy and in the same pattern: three times in the reason and once each in the announcement and recognition formula. Also, only in these last two prophecies does a second messenger formula appear to introduce the announcement of punishment. As a result of this high degree of formal similarity, their overall brevity, and especially the lack of distinctive metaphorical or topographical detail, these two prophecies especially appear stereotyped and possibly are present only to round out a list.

Setting

Although no date is given for ch. 25 (in contrast to the first of the Tyre group of prophecies and several of the Egypt group which follow), its chronological setting is nonetheless clear. All the prophecies of ch. 25 presuppose the events of 587 B.C., and none implies anything of either a restoration of Judah or any fulfillment of the judgment here pronounced. If Josephus should be correct in his report (*Ant.* x.9.7 §§ 181-82) of a defeat of both Ammon and Moab in 582/1, that would narrow the time span available greatly, but his report is dubious on several grounds. Thus within the exilic period there is little which suggests any more precise time.

With the exception of the Philistines, all the peoples treated in ch. 25 are included in the list in Jer 27:3 of those whose envoys were in Jerusalem contemplating revolt against Nebuchadrezzar. While the Ammonites were reported in Ezek 21:24-25 (*RSV* 19-20) to have been the object of Babylon's attack, and their support of the murder of Gedaliah in Jeremiah 40 and 41 confirms their anti-Babylonian stance, this chapter suggests that their political position was more complicated. According to 2 Kgs 24:2 they served as Nebuchadrezzar's tool along with Moab against Judah. That here they are rebuked for having cheered Judah's fall could imply purely internecine jealousy, like that attributed to Moab and most especially Edom (see Zeph 2:8; Jer 48:27; Obad 11-14; Ps 137:7). More likely, though, the situation involved even more complicated switches in allegiance. These details of Palestinian politics may or may not have been known among the exiles, but the concentration in ch. 25 upon the reaction to the events of 587 B.C. shows how the event of Jerusalem's fall predominated over everything else in their mind. This in itself could suggest that these prophecies found their use in connection with ceremonies of lament over the fall of Jerusalem.

Intention

The desire for revenge is unmistakably a part of the mood which characterizes this entire collection of prophecies, but their very form reveals how much more than revenge is involved. The use of so-called holy war terminology with its heavy stress on Yahweh's "giving" and "stretching out" his hand, and the use of the same intervention-plus-result pattern in the announcements make it evident that these units wish to assert Yahweh's sovereignty precisely in this moment in which it seems the most threatened. The judgment of God upon Israel is not to be seen as the refutation of the sovereignty of the God of Israel. The claim that "Judah is like all the other nations" (v. 8) is not primarily a Moabite opinion to be countered. As 20:32 shows, this was a tragic option for Jewish exiles as well. When Eichrodt (359) sees Ammon as "one more example of a complete refusal to accept a specific divine sacred history which so disturbingly questions all heathen assurance of God," he obscures the fact that Israel's election was throughout Ezekiel's ministry the chief problem for his own audience, not those of other nations. Judean exiles whose view of election blinded them to Ezekiel's pre-587 B.C. message of judgment became, after the horrible truth of 587 B.C. sank in, an audience for whom such thoughts of election and sacred history had lost all their vitality. Thus these particular prophecies against foreign nations reveal the continuation of the same pastoral affirmation of Yahweh's all-causality to Ezekiel's own hearers that we have encountered so steadily before.

The affirmations of the ultimate destruction of enemies—even by Israel's own hand in the case of Edom (v. 14)—and of the recognition of Yahweh by other nations are not really the focus here. Nothing is made of these affirmations beyond their bare formulation, not just because their fulfillment was not at hand. After all, Ezekiel 35 and 36 will show how much could on occasion be implicitly made out of a prophecy against Edom. In ch. 25 the focus is deliberately not on the shape of the fulfillment but only on the Lord of the fulfillment, whose lordship is so seriously questioned by his own people.

A COLLECTION OF PROPHECIES CONCERNING TYRE, 26:1–28:19

Structure

The seven prophecies against Tyre constitute a subcollection within the larger collection of prophecies concerning foreign nations in chs. 25–32, similar to the collection concerning Egypt in chs. 29–32. The oracle against Sidon in 28:20-24 is clearly unconnected and quite dissimilar to those which immediately precede it, and apparently has been created largely to bring to seven the total of nations treated in chs. 25–32. The only link within chs. 26–28 to the preceding is the way 26:2 charges Tyre with rejoicing over Jerusalem's fall in a way corresponding to that for which each of the four nations in ch. 25 is indicted. Within the collection against Tyre the last three units are remarkably longer and more vivid than those in ch. 26. The use of the prophetic word formula in 26:1, 27:1, 28:1, and 28:11 indicates where major unit boundaries were perceived, although the resumptive messenger formula in 26:7, 15, and 19 shows subordinate boundaries in ch. 26. The occurrence of the phrase, "And I will put you in terror and you will be no more forever," as a concluding refrain in 26:21 (briefly expanded), 27:36b, and 28:19b shows that from another point of view only three units were felt to be present. The overlapping inconsistency of these patterns of organization reflects the complicated history of the development of this collection.

Genre

In marked departure from that which is standard within the book of Ezekiel, the genre of PROPHETIC PROOF SAYING is represented only once in the anti-Tyrian collection, viz., 26:2-6. Instead, PROPHETIC ANNOUNCEMENTS OF PUNISHMENT and DIRGES predominate, the three dirges (26:17-18; 27:2-36; 28:12-19) coming each as the logical follow-up to an announcement of Tyre's fall. In spite of the larger size of the units in chs. 27 and 28 there is very little basis for determining the mood of which these prophecies are an expression. The flavor of anti-commerce and anti-hubris in chs. 27 and 28 suggests a certain amount of vengeful joy may have been involved, but at the same time some formulations imply a mood of sympathetic shock. It is only with the appending of 28:24-26 that any framework of hopeful anticipation for Judah appears.

Setting

Inasmuch as Ezekiel's latest dated prophecy in 29:17-21 dealing with Nebuchadrezzar's failure to destroy Tyre is not reflected within 26:1–28:19, this material may be assumed largely to predate 571 B.C. The only date given within the Tyre prophecies is the eleventh year in 26:1, i.e., presumably soon after Jerusalem's fall. However, the complex traditio-historical heritage of some of the material, especially the mythological background of 28:11-19, makes the issue of the traditio-historical context of greater significance than the chronological one. This matter will be examined to some extent in connection with each separate unit. For a treatment of the development and changes within the sociological function of prophecies against foreign nations, the reader is directed to the treatment of chs. 25–32.

Finally, two conjectures may be offered to explain why such prominence and importance were given to Tyre making this subcollection in 26:1–28:19 seem appropriate. For one, Zimmerli (*Ezekiel 2,* 24) cites Mazar's oral supposition that there may have existed a group of Tyrian exiles located near Ezekiel's Judean deportees. For another, the way in which Tyrian sailors helped in Judah's prospering maritime ventures in 1 Kgs 9:26-28, and the way later attempts to reinstate these ventures ended in shipwreck according to 1 Kgs 22:48f., possibly due to the absence of that Tyrian help after the Jezebel episode, may have contributed to a special, long-standing feeling of commercial ill will between Judah and Tyre.

Intention

The prominence assigned to Tyre and Egypt by means of the subcollections of prophecies dealing with these nations has a certain special logic. In the prophecies against foreign nations in general there begins a movement beyond the shock of the fall of Jerusalem. Both the perspective of a restoration for Judah in security once these hostile powers were crushed, as set forth in 28:24-26, and the way in which 26:2 sees Tyre's joy over Jerusalem's fall as the ground of her own forthcoming doom reveal that these anti-Tyre prophecies now exist within a framework that makes the fall of Tyre the necessary next step in Yahweh's dealing with his people. Further, within the Tyre subcollection (26:7-14), before it (21:23-28 [*RSV* 18-23]), and after it (29:17-21), Nebuchadrezzar is seen as the one to whom Yahweh has given all the nations of the ancient Mediterranean world. Only Tyre and Egypt provided opposition serious enough to throw doubt upon that conviction, and thus these two countries became obvious candidates for special consideration by Ezekiel, most particularly within the perspective of a stress on Yahweh's total sovereignty and the prideful folly of any opposition to his will.

185

Bibliography

H. J. van Dijk, *Ezekiel's Prophecy on Tyre* (BibOr 20; Rome: Pontifical Biblical Institute, 1968).

A COLLECTION OF BRIEF PROPHECIES AGAINST TYRE, 26:1-21

Text

It is likely that at the end of v. 20 one should read *tāšūbî wĕtityaṣṣĕbî* ("you will . . . stand again") for *tēšēbî wĕnātattî ṣĕbî* ("you will . . . be inhabited and I will give glory").

Structure and Genre

Like ch. 25 this unit is marked off as such by the PROPHETIC WORD FORMULA at the beginning and again at 27:1. In between it is marked out as consisting of a grouping of four PROPHECIES CONCERNING A FOREIGN NATION by the repeated use of the MESSENGER FORMULA. Again, as in ch. 25, that messenger formula is only employed in its most proper role in v. 3, where it marks the transition within the first prophecy from the reason section to Yahweh's word in response. In the three remaining instances (vv. 7, 15, and 19), it serves essentially to show the beginning of new prophecies. Nonetheless, its function as introducing the quoted word of Yahweh means that announcements are the only possible material which can follow it. Thus, in the DIRGE in vv. 15-18, while under other circumstances the prophet or anyone else could describe the background out of which a dirge might be sung, here the use of the resumptive messenger formula in v. 15 requires that the following description of the mourners be heard as Yahweh's own word. Inasmuch as no reference to Yahweh in either first or third person appears within this entire dirge, it is possible to assume that apart from this new context it was originally formulated by the prophet not as divine speech, but with no speaker specified, like ch. 19. However, the dirges in the book of Ezekiel come in a variety of patterns. The case of 27:1-36 is exactly parallel to 26:15-18 in that it too is introduced with a messenger formula only to have Yahweh unmentioned throughout. In 28:11-19 and 32:1-16 on the other hand, the dirges are ones in which Yahweh does speak, but oddly while the messenger formula appears at the beginning of 28:12, it comes only in 32:3, after v. 2, which serves as a reason on which an announcement can be based. Thus no firm conclusion about the speaker can be drawn.

This apparent lack of a specific speaker is actually not inappropriate for the dirge genre. While some dirges, such as David's lament over Saul and Jonathan in 2 Sam 1:19-27, are eloquent expressions of the grief of a particular individual, that is not typical. One must instead think of a stock of tradition normally utilized by professional wailing women in a highly standardized way, a way in fact so standardized as to be offensive to our romantic individualism. Most of what appears in vv. 17-18 is fully typical: the 3:2 meter, the direct address of the deceased, and the initial "how!" introducing the familiar contrast between then and now. Even the fact that a city is addressed is not unusual. This technique, also known from the book of Lamentations, can be traced back to the Old Babylonian period (see the lament over Ur in *ANET*, 455-63). The only really atypical aspect here is the way the dirge meter seems to have penetrated even into the preceding descriptive material in vv. 15-16 (Zimmerli, *Ezekiel 2*, 37-38).

In spite of the minor uncertainty about the form of vv. 15-18, the editorial grouping in this chapter has managed to present an inherently logical sequence. Tyre's fall appears in the first two prophecies, the second picking up phrases from the first and adding further details, and the remaining two prophecies describe the bewailing and then the entombment of the fallen one. It is doubtful if Zimmerli is correct (*Ezekiel 2*, 33 and 37) in regarding vv. 7-14 as a secondary expansion interpreting vv. 2-6 as a targum might handle a text. The picking up of phrases from vv. 3-5 in vv. 8a, 12, and 14 is more a matter of stereotypical language than expository clarification. Similarly, not literary dependence, but the common *Topik*, or customary language associated with a theme, is responsible for the resemblances between vv. 15-18 and 27:28-36 or vv. 19-21 and 32:17-32. Further, one can hardly speak of v. 13 as "in verbal dependence on Amos 5:23" (ibid., 37). This too is only more stereotypical language, and not by any means identical words at that. In fact, both Zimmerli (ibid., 40), and even more prominently Eichrodt (371), use the criterion of greater creative skill or "difference of level" (Eichrodt, 371) in an inappropriate way here. By this late date such an extensive amount of siege portrayal, dirge, and underworld language was in circulation that the use of familiar stereotypes is only to be expected. The same is to be said about military and geographical terminology. Both the scholars in question note that the description of Tyre as "in the heart of the sea," found in both Egyptian and Assyrian sources, appears literally in Ezek 27:4 and 28:2, and loosely here in 26:5 (Zimmerli, *Ezekiel 2*, 35 and Eichrodt, 370).

Setting and Intention

Even though a month reference in the date of v. 1 is missing, there is little reason to deny that a time soon after Jerusalem's fall, near the beginning of Nebuchadrezzar's siege of Tyre, provided the chronological setting for at least much of the material in ch. 26, though the collecting of it is a process impossible to date narrowly. The existence of 29:17-21 dated sixteen years later, with its reference to the fortune of Nebuchadrezzar's siege, does suggest that even the editorial process could have been completed before 571 B.C. The way Tyre is seen in 26:2 as expressing a hostility toward Jerusalem closely similar to that of the nations in ch. 25 could explain why ch. 26 appears first, and the inner, logical sequence of fall, dirge, and entombment has already been pointed out.

Although, as mentioned in the consideration of the collection of prophecies against foreign nations as a whole, this material has moved to a new setting, the influence of the proper, original, military-cultic setting is still noticeable. The portrayal of the defeat of Tyre is a clear combination of unique references to its island location and of standard stereotypical imagery in general use and introduced here even when Tyre's uniqueness makes that inappropriate. Tyre's uniqueness is reflected in: (1) the language about the waves of the sea in vv. 3, 5, 17, and 19; (2) the prominence of commercial references in vv. 2 and 12; (3) the mention of suburbs on the mainland in vv. 6 and 8; and (4) the picturing of the defeated Tyre as only a bare rock on which fishermen might dry their nets in vv. 4-5 and 14. Inappropriate imagery appears extensively in the siege description in vv. 8b-11a, where the portrayal is plainly that of an attack upon a mainland fortress. The use of a siege wall, ramps, battering rams, horses, and chariots did not become realistic until Alexander the Great constructed a causeway from the mainland to enable for the first time the storming of fortress Tyre. Taking the standard siege imagery too literally, some scholars have concluded that the passage must come out of a setting different from Nebuchadrezzar's time, seeing in vv. 9-11 a battle song about Alexander's conquest of Tyre, or supposing that the actual reference of the passage was to a conquest of "old Tyre" on the adjacent mainland. (See the references in Zimmerli, *Ezekiel 2*, 37.) The proper recognition of the typicality of the imagery involved renders such literalistic hypotheses unnecessary.

What is essential to note about the life-setting of this material as a part of Ezekiel's ministry, and then subsequently as a part of the literary deposit of his message, is that it reflects a decisive shift from the ritual to the rational. In exile military-cultic ceremonies were nonexistent, even though still influential as memory. Now for exiles, the basic concern was a part of an entirely different mental process from prefiguring in powerful word and ritual the destruction of Israel's national enemies. Detached from, and soon deprived of, their own national existence, Ezekiel's audience listened to and recognized these familiar old patterns as a part of their heritage, but one which now triggered far more than just nationalistic nostalgia. The announcement of Tyre's fall, which once could have meant for Jerusalem the elimination of commercial competition quite similar to what Jerusalem's fall is said in v. 2 to have meant for Tyre, now triggered questions of an extremely basic sort about what possible relevance this might have for Judean exiles.

A later restored Jewish community, even one without national independence, had a perspective of faith and security of existence from which to approach the surprising announcement of the downfall of hitherto unassailable Tyre, which Ezekiel's earlier hearers lacked. While the later generation could see here touches of motifs of anti-hubris and anti-commercialism which could develop and flourish within an apocalyptic context, Ezekiel's earlier followers must have been brought to think much more of how they themselves had felt about an inviolable Zion. Although post-587 B.C. Judah was no bare rock, no "place for the spreading of nets," it certainly had become a place over which to utter dirges, and its inhabitants—including themselves—were fully justified in classifying themselves as among those within the sphere of death (33:10). To such a people this passage offers no real answers, but its affirmation of the Yahweh who was in control of all international politics was a door of potential hope that could and did open in Ezekiel's later preaching. However, at first hope was no possibility and not by any means the primary intention of this material. Instead, the words "Then they will know that I am the Lord" (v. 6b) at the end of a prophecy declaring Tyre's doom could only leave Ezekiel's early disciples wondering about who "they" could be. That Tyrian exiles would hear these words seems scarcely likely, but that Judean exiles could find themselves addressed here seems fantastically optimistic and possible only in the light of later developments. Surely those who did preserve these words in the hard days following 587 B.C. were able to do so only in the light of a more explicit message of hope.

Then, when still within Ezekiel's lifetime, the news would come of the failure of these prophecies against Tyre to be fulfilled, that fact would have been of lesser significance. Not only did, in fact, Tyre submit and accept a Babylonian commissioner, but the essential issue would then have been simply the observing and recording of how Yahweh, as so often before, changed his mind, and was nonetheless still (29:17-21) in sovereign control.

Bibliography

H. J. van Dijk, *Ezekiel's Prophecy on Tyre* (BibOr 20; Rome: Pontifical Biblical Institute, 1968) 1-47; H. Jahnow, *Das hebräische Leichenlied im Rahmen der Völkerdichtung* (BZAW 36: Giessen: Töpelmann, 1923) 211-12; C. Newsom, "A Maker of Metaphors—Ezekiel's Oracles Against Tyre," *Int* 38 (1984) 151-64; H. Wiener, "Ezekiel's Prophecy Against Tyre," *Nieuwe theologische studien* 6 (1923) 7-8.

A DIRGE OVER THE GREAT SHIP TYRE, 27:1-36

Text

Although the maritime language of this chapter makes for some uncertainty, the meaning is clear in most places. Probably in v. 3b one ought to read *'ŏnîyâ* ("ship") for *'ănî* ("I"), so that the metaphor is spelled out at the beginning. A few of the place names seem to have been incorrectly preserved, so that we should read *rōdān* ("Rhodes") for *dĕdān* ("Dedan") in v. 15, *'ĕdōm* ("Edom") for *'ărām* ("Aram") in v. 16, *wĕyayin mē'ûzāl* ("and wine from Uzal") for *wĕdān wĕyāwan mĕ'ûzzāl* ("Vedan and Javan" plus an unknown word) at the start of v. 19, linking this to the end of v. 18, and finally *wĕkol-mādai* ("and the whole of Media") for *kilmad* ("Chilmad") in v. 23.

Structure and Genre

I. Prophetic word formula	1
II. Preliminaries	2-3bα
A. Address as son of man	2a
B. Direction to conduct a dirge	2b
C. Direction to speak to Tyre	3aα

190

The entire chapter is presented as one unit, a DIRGE, introduced and labelled as such in vv. 1-3, and then presented at full length in the remainder of the chapter. Although marked as divine speech by the PROPHETIC WORD FORMULA in v. 1 and the MESSENGER FORMULA in v. 3, Yahweh does not appear anywhere in the dirge itself. This is clearly similar to the case of 26:17-18 and, as was observed there, is not to be seen as unusual. What is unusual about the dirge in ch. 27 can be summed up in two points: (1) the extended use of the ship metaphor; and (2) the lengthy prose interruption of the metaphor. Each of these requires discussion. The use of metaphors in dirges is not uncommon in the ancient world, especially when it is not an ordinary individual being mourned, but a city, nation, or dynasty. Within the book of Ezekiel the king of Egypt is portrayed as a crocodile in the dirge in 32:2-16 and the Davidic dynasty is pictured as a lioness in 19:1-9. Furthermore, pride of place for extensiveness of these metaphors must assuredly go to Ezekiel. Passing references to Jerusalem as a widow in Lamentations are dwarfed by even the medium-sized dirges in chs. 19 and 32. But ch. 27 is more than twice the size of those other two. Once again we note the most basic form-critical observation about the words of this prophet: The great distinctiveness of Ezekiel lies chiefly in the length of the units. But our investigation must then pursue how that length is achieved. The choice of the ship metaphor for Tyre is, of course, a natural one, suggested by its island location and its commercial prominence. The bulk of the metaphorical section in ch. 27 is taken up with the latter aspect, Tyre's commercial relationships. In fact, the actual movement and fate of the ship are confined to a few lines in vv. 25b-27. The rest is a rather overdone—to our tastes—presentation of Tyre's multinational contacts in vv. 5-9 and a fairly lengthy indirect expression of grief in a description of what mourners do and say in vv. 28-36.

In this apparently overbalanced use of two aspects of the metaphor, we have put our finger on the disturbing feature in the second unusual aspect of the dirge in ch. 27, the lengthy interruption of the metaphor by a nonpoetic, even pedantic, list of Tyre's trade partners and their wares. Our taste might permit an example or two to develop the idea of Tyre's glory by showing the vast extent of her ties, but a twelve-point list encompassing nearly as much space as the entire metrical part of the chapter is too much and too boring. Oddly, though, exactly this overdone development of certain aspects of the metaphor was already noticed as inherent in the poetic part of the dirge. Thus, to conclude an investigation simply by setting apart vv. 12-24 (and possibly vv. 10-11, 25a, 27, and 33) as secondary expansion is, while quite likely true, to neglect the exploration of the reason behind such expansion. The overextensive detail in vv. 5-9, for example, reflects so similar a perspective that one must ask if there is some inherent part of the mental process involved in dirge-making which typically moves toward such abnormally lengthy sections. I suggest that there is, and that it may be identified as what Mowinckel (II, 104-25) called the learned dimension of psalmography. The essential point here is to see the dirge as one of many types of poetry, one especially prone to employ metaphors, and therefore one for which aspects of the wisdom movement need to be explored. List-making is a basic element within wisdom, both within and outside the Bible (von Rad, "Job xxxviii and Ancient Egyptian Wisdom," 281-91). Lists of place names are among the most basic types of lists (Genesis 10 and Joshua 12–21), and they provided among the most obvious and natural ways to speak effectively of a foreign nation. Thus, prophecies against foreign nations, as we have seen from Amos 1 on to Jeremiah 46–51, logically reflect the exhaustive—and to our tastes exhausting—perspective of the learned geographer. No wonder that to this day geographers go eagerly to these chapters to practice their skills. Even such a minor matter as the way in which there is an avoidance of overlapping between the names in vv. 5-11 and those in vv. 12-23 finds its explanation in this learned carefulness. The use of acrostic poetry in the dirges of Lamentations is a striking parallel. What we find only a pedantic exercise ancients were able to use in their most emotion-charged literature. The lengthy descriptions of Behemoth and Leviathan in Job 40–41 are further examples.

All poetic structure involves a balance between similarity and dissimilarity. There must be enough similarity to enable the recognition that a deliberate patterning is being carried out, but enough dissimilarity to prevent monotony. Matters of taste surface when the desirability of one kind of patterning is weighed against another. But it is also precisely here that the learned aspect appears. Both Hebrew and English metrical patterns result from a combination of natural word structures with skillfully planned word choice. If an acrostic, alphabetic sequence seems too artificially and abstractly intellectual to us as a poetic pattern, what would prevent another culture from raising similar objections to the sonnet form or the dactylic hexameter of Longfellow's *Evangeline*? The cross-cultural application of standards of taste is a highly complicated venture, and the relative amount of dissimilarity needed to achieve beauty is among the most complicated parts of that venture. Poets have often regaled themselves by poking fun through exactly this kind of learned experimenting with their own craft. One has only to place alongside the labored seriousness of meter in *Evangeline* the playful delights of an Edgar Allan Poe or an Ogden Nash in order to see the scope still occupied by learned monotony within even English poetry.

Is there a logic to the arrangement of the list of nations and their products? Zimmerli points to how Rüger sees a system of four or five ancient trade routes being followed. But even then Zimmerli finds this reasoning "not really convincing," because it mixes up specific names with broad labels and does not present "a properly ordered sequence" (*Ezekiel 2*, 71). He finds it better to speak with Simons (456-57) somewhat less precisely of four trade areas: vv. 12-15, the territory roughly identified in Genesis 10 as that of Japheth; vv. 16-18, Syro-Palestine; vv. 20-22, Arabia; and v. 23,

Mesopotamia (v. 19 remaining uncertain). This indeed records what is presented, but the mere noting of these groups does not in itself bring us any further.

Perhaps a glance at word choice can take us a step further. In Ezek 27:12-24 only four main ways appear of linking each nation and its goods. The word "traded" (*RSV* usually reads "trafficked") is used in vv. 12, 15, 16, 18, and 21; the word "merchandise" in vv. 13, 17, and 19; the word "wares" in vv. 12, 14, 16, 19, and 22; and the word "exch..ge" (also *RSV* "merchandise") in vv. 13, 17, and 19. Are these patterns to be seen as skillful or mechanical, effective or tedious, varied just enough or monotonous and plodding? Is there a deliberate intent behind the way that occurrences of these four linguistic roots are grouped, for example that only in the last four verses does the same root appear twice? The answers to such questions are likely beyond us, but the mere facing of them is a humbling discipline. To impose our tastes is a dangerous business, but we really have no alternative. We must trace what is there and respond to it, but with greater modesty than is often employed. Zimmerli's literary-critical reconstruction of the dirge "in its purified form" is meaningful as an attempt based on one set of criteria (*Ezekiel 2*, 55), but each criterion is the expression of a particular mental process, and the genre of a prophetic dirge is by definition the product of the blending of several different mental processes. Thus we still find ourselves only at the beginning in our attempts at structural analysis.

Setting

A chronological background for the dirge in ch. 27 is nearly impossible to pin down. In contrast to ch. 26, no mention is made of the fall of Jerusalem. The ship metaphor predominates to the exclusion of the mention of any enemy or even of a military dimension of Tyre's downfall.

More intriguing possibilities arise when we reflect on the change in sociological life-setting the material has undergone. The dirge is rooted in funeral practices and serves to ventilate grief. The customs of self-disfigurement associated with it may at bottom have had the aim of protecting against demonic forces, but this aspect doubtless faded greatly as the development of a resource of literature came about. As mentioned earlier, to move from a dead person to a fallen city is a big step, but a very ancient one. Prophetic employment of dirges was an even bigger step, usually involving scorn and mockery, and giving the feeling of power because they treat their subject as being as good as dead. The then-now contrast often lent itself to this dimension of derision of the once mighty, as in Isa 14:4-21. Ezekiel 27 is, however, remarkably free of the scornful element. When Zimmerli sees the hissing of v. 36 as expressing a slight note of mockery (*Ezekiel 2*, 69) or contempt (ibid., 71), this misunderstands an action better seen as expressing grief (van Dijk, 91; Fohrer, 156; Eichrodt, 385). In fact, it is ironic in the extreme that this quite neutral, even sympathetic dirge over Tyre should have come to serve as the model for some of the sections in Revelation 18, especially vv. 12-13, which, though still remarkably neutral, appear in a context of the most intense hostility. There, as so often when dirges are borrowed in order to denounce foes, the focus is on the hubris of the enemy, who flaunts divine sovereignty and the commercial wealth often secured as the by-product of one's own ventures in exploitation. None of this is traceable here. Even the opening line is probably to be read as "a ship of perfect beauty" rather than as a proud self-description (→ Text above). In this, too, the prominence of a wisdom perspective which observes and orders is to be seen operating in a remarkably nontheological way.

Intention

The note of sympathy for "a particularly precious flower of human achievement" (Zimmerli, *Ezekiel 2*, 62) is clearly present. The lack of any agent active in the wreck of the ship is another instance of a remarkably nontheological form of expression. To understand the dirge in the light of its context in the surrounding chapters is to reinterpret it drastically—as was probably done at an early time in the compilation of the book. To see the horror of the mourners as made to serve "the secret counsel of the one who guides history" (ibid.) is to engage in that kind of reinterpretation, but any such perspective must be preceded by the recognition that in itself the text simply marvels over a splendor and security suddenly lost. The shocking jolt of this catastrophe can indeed lead one to make observations about the transitory character of splendor and wealth and along with that the falsity of any trust in such values, but this text does not go on to any such observations, and even the prefixing of the messenger formula in v. 3 really does not do so either (against Zimmerli, *Ezekiel 2*, 62). Thus the whole question of the failure of Nebuchadrezzar's attempts to conquer Tyre has very little bearing on the hearing of a text which contents itself with giving space for the viewing of a catastrophe apart from any evaluation of it.

Bibliography

H. J. van Dijk, *Ezekiel's Prophecy on Tyre* (BibOr 20; Rome: Pontifical Biblical Institute, 1968) 48-91; E. M. Good, "Ezekiel's Ship: Some Extended Metaphors in the Old Testament," *Semitics* 1 (1970) 79-103, especially 82-89; H. Jahnow, *Das hebräische Leichenlied im Rahmen der Völkerdichtung* (BZAW 36; Giessen: Töpelmann, 1923) 212-18; F. L. Moriarty, "The Lament over Tyre (Ez. 27)," *Gregorianum* 46 (1965) 83-88; S. Mowinckel, *The Psalms in Israel's Worship* (tr. D. R. Ap-Thomas; Nashville: Abingdon, 1962) II, 104-25; C. Newsom, "A Maker of Metaphors—Ezekiel's Oracles Against Tyre," *Int* 38 (1984) 151-64; G. von Rad, "Job xxxviii and Ancient Egyptian Wisdom," in *The Problem of the Hexateuch and Other Essays* (tr. E. W. Trueman Dicken; New York: McGraw-Hill, 1960) 281-91; J. J. Simons, *The Geographical and Topographical Texts of the Old Testament* (Leiden: Brill, 1959); E. Strömberg Krantz, *Des Schiffes Weg mitten im Meer* (ConBOT 19; Lund: Gleerup, 1982).

A PROPHECY AGAINST THE PRIDE OF THE RULER OF TYRE, 28:1-10

Structure and Genre

I. Prophetic word formula	1
II. Preliminaries	2
A. Address as son of man	2aα
B. Direction to speak to the prince of Tyre	2aβ

   The threefold occurrence of the PROPHETIC WORD FORMULA in ch. 28 makes it clear that the chapter contains three separate units. The first of these, vv. 1-10, is a fairly typical PROPHECY OF PUNISHMENT spoken to the prince of Tyre. It is actually, of course, Tyre itself as a city-state and not the person of its king which is the real object of the message, although some aspects of the ancient idea of divine kingship are employed as local color within the oracle. Thus the reason in vv. 2-5 gives first place to the affirmation of royal divinity. But the thought immediately switches to the proud security of Tyre's location "in the heart of the seas." Since wisdom belongs to and comes only from the deity, the prideful monologue affirming the king's divine status (for similar monologues see Isa 10:7-8; 14:13; 37:24; Obad 3; Ezek 29:3) moves naturally to the attribute of royal wisdom. That the precise flavoring here intended for the word "heart" is that of wisdom is established both by the usage of the word "heart" as the location of intellect and memory and by the phrase "a listening heart" as the Hebrew expression for the wisdom for which Soloman asked (1 Kgs 3:9). In a rather expansive style which is typical of the whole prophecy, vv. 3-5 go on to describe at some length the extent of the king's wisdom and consequent wealth. Zimmerli regards these verses as a secondary expansion that destroys the direct and forceful link between reason and announcement in v. 7. When he points to the awkwardly repetitious character of v. 6, made necessary by the long delay in the present text between v. 2 and v. 7, as evidence for the secondary character of vv. 3-5, he falls victim to the desire to magnify the literary skill of the original prophet. While it is indeed true that expansions occur, the basic uniqueness of the book of Ezekiel is located precisely in the length of its units. The literary style of this prophecy, not just within vv. 3-6 but in its entirety, is leisurely and repetitious. One could pare down vv. 7-10 considerably and still preserve the power and essence of this thought, and perhaps this brevity would be literarily superior to the present text, but it would no longer be Ezekiel, for it would have given up the style which is his hallmark. Already in v. 2 the interrupting objection, "yet you are a man and not god," repeated in v. 9, is powerful evidence of exactly that unhurried and expansive style characteristic of Ezekiel. It is a unique rupture of the logic of the prophecy of punishment to insert a refutation in the midst of the description of the royal pride, but it seems typical of that legal style so prominent in Ezekiel's material.

As noted, the same expansive style manifests itself in the announcement of punishment, where the fact of destruction by enemies is seen as bringing the loss of regal splendor and the consequence of the commonality of death, both of which serve as the refutation of the claims of royal divinity.

Setting and Intention

No firm basis exists for locating this unit chronologically. Presumably the anticipation of Tyre's destruction would fit best in a time before the failure of Nebuchadrezzar's efforts in his siege, but even that is not totally compelling. The very fact of the success of Tyre in resisting destruction yet one more time could well fuel the desire to see her pride smashed once and for all.

It would be, of course, totally pointless to search for a background for this oracle in the prideful personality of some particular Tyrian prince. As observed at the start, the real target is the nation of Tyre; its king and royal ideology are only vehicles for reaching that goal.

Whereas it was seen that some scholarly opinion looks upon the motif of hubris as already present in the dirge in ch. 27, it is above all in ch. 28 that this motif is developed. The manner of its development rewards closer examination. The thought of equality with God appears as the root of human sin in Gen 3:5, but it is not this universal creaturely rebellion which provides the dominant background against which our passage is to be seen. Rather it is the specially distinctive temptation of the mighty that is in view here. While in some traditions the king is seen as the realization and fulfillment of true humanity, here the focus is on the super-ordinary status of the king. His gifts and power are so far above those of the rest that he attracts the superlative praise ordinarily reserved for the deity, and comes himself to be drawn with seeming appropriateness into the sphere of the divine. Israel knew that tradition and its language in her own worship literature, the royal psalms, and it is doubtful that any wholesale polemic against that tradition is intended here. However, one may still note that in these psalms it is God who in his own speaking bestows this lofty status upon his anointed one, "You are my son" (Ps 2:7), while here it is the Tyrian king himself who employs a kind of self-introduction formula, "I am a god" (v. 2). By his use of that self-introduction formula in the recognition formula, Ezekiel makes it clear that the Tyrian king stands in sharpest contradiction to Yahweh's goals for Israel and the world. Only slightly later Deutero-Isaiah will again employ the self-introduction formula as a basic element in his affirmation of Yahweh's total sovereignty and even sole deity. All rivals are overcome both by the argument from creation and—in the exact mood of Ezek 28:1-10—by proof from history.

Bibliography

H. J. van Dijk, *Ezekiel's Prophecy on Tyre* (BibOr 20; Rome: Pontifical Biblical Institute, 1968) 92-122; C. Newsom, "A Maker of Metaphors—Ezekiel's Oracles Against Tyre," *Int* 38 (1984) 151-64; K. Yaron, "The Dirge over the King of Tyre," *ASTI* 3 (1964) 40-45.

A MYTHICAL DIRGE OVER THE KING OF TYRE, 28:11-19

Text

In v. 14 one should read *'et* ("with") for *'at* ("you," fs) and delete the copula from the first verb, connecting it with what precedes rather than what follows.

Structure

I. Prophetic word formula	11
II. Preliminaries	12abβ
A. Address as son of man	12aα
B. Direction to use a dirge against the king of Tyre	12aβ
C. Direction to speak	12bα
D. Messenger formula	12bβ
III. A mythical dirge (all direct address)	12bγδ-19
A. Description of mythical royal beauty	12bγδ-14
1. Role: a signet, full of wisdom and beauty	12bγδ
2. Locale: the garden of Eden	13aα
3. Decoration: jewels since creation	13aβγδεb
4. Companion: guardian cherub	14a
5. Activity	14b
a. Situated on God's holy mountain	14bαβ
b. Walked in midst of stones of fire	14bγ
B. Transition: blameless from your creation till your sin	15
C. Report of transgression and punishment	16-19
1. First statement	16
a. Sin: commercial violence	16a

      b. Punishment: thrown out of the garden
        (intervention)   16b
   2. Second statement   17
      a. Sin: pride   17a
      b. Punishment: thrown down to earth and exposed
        before kings (intervention)   17b
   3. Third statement   18
      a. Sin: commercial guilt and profanation   18a
      b. Punishment   18b-19
        1) Fire to ashes (intervention plus a
           bit of result)   18b
        2) Horror (result)   19a
        3) Terrifying end (result)   19b

The text is plainly a unit, marked both by the prophetic word formulas, one at its beginning in v. 11 and one at the start of the following unit in v. 20, and by its shape as consistent direct address. This apparent simplicity of structure disappears, however, as the question of genre is raised.

Genre

Although labeled a DIRGE in nearly the same way as 27:2, 28:11-19 is a far cry from any standard dirge. It does not follow the 3:2 dirge meter, otherwise so characteristic of dirges both within and outside the book of Ezekiel. The attempts of Zimmerli and others to restore that meter by drastic revision are thoroughly unconvincing. It is significant that at one place Zimmerli holds back from yet further emendation, remarking how, "One hesitates, however, to dispense with every reference to the mountain of God" (*Ezekiel 2,* 88), realizing that thereby he would have eliminated the passage's most distinctive content. In fact, throughout this metrical reconstruction the weakness of Zimmerli's method is that it pays so little attention to content. Meter is after all a feature of Hebrew parallelism, in which the parts of the line or the lines themselves exist in a kind of thought rhyme. This content aspect of parallelism receives scant attention in Zimmerli's rather mechanical reconstruction. Further, his efforts are vitiated by a refusal to accept what at least one-half of the text so plainly thrusts upon him, a series of three-part lines. The list of jewels in v. 13, for example, is undeniably so arranged. As Eichrodt concedes, the restoration of a 3:2 meter by brute force is unjustifiable (392).

All this is not to deny the immense difficulties with which the text confronts any interpreter, but it is to insist that the inner logic of the text must be found elsewhere. Appropriately, it is Zimmerli himself who points to this with his analysis of how we have here "a disintegration of the original genre" (ibid., 89). Only the contrast between then and now remains of the typical elements of a dirge. The mythological figure of the primeval man gives the text such a uniqueness of perspective that the commonality of death is simply not present. In fact, it is not so much the death of the king with which the text deals as his fall from paradise. And, of course, that Yahweh is himself throughout the speaker and presents a message of sin and punishment is also foreign to the dirge pattern.

Yet one may not simply see here a prophetic adaptation of a dirge, for unlike ch. 27, it does not climax in an announcement of a fate at hand, i.e., "you are as good as dead," but in the report of a long past primeval fall. Admittedly such primeval events were seen as of continuing power in their shaping of reality, for instance in the way that through self-centeredness, the children of Adam and Eve repeat their parents' fateful folly. But Ezek 28:11-19 has only a remote interest in how pride universally leads to a fall. Instead, by means of a primeval mythological event a pattern is implicitly applied to one unique city-state, whose commercial pride and corruption are presented by the use of this myth in such a way that its original significance is largely set aside. It is hard to resist the conclusion that this learned reworking of both dirge and myth should be examined for wisdom elements, just as was done in ch. 27. From such a perspective the technical knowledge inherent in the list of jewels and the skillful use of an international myth take on new significance. To be sure, 28:11-19 is no wisdom poem, but it does have wisdom elements, just as it has elements from dirge, myth, and prophecy of punishment. All are present, but they are all employed in the service of a prophecy against a foreign nation.

The very fact that the precise shape of this myth, of a primeval royal figure alone with a cherub in the garden of Eden and somehow also on the holy mountain of God, is otherwise largely unknown to us suggests that it is a sort of esoteric material. It clearly has contacts with Genesis 3, especially in the way that blamelessness is followed by sin and expulsion. That it is royal mythology being utilized is also clear, especially in the stress on beauty, which is proper to royalty, and in the use of the signet figure, by which a ruler is presented as the authorized representative of the deity, a device appearing in Jer 22:24 and Hag 2:23. That it is a creation myth is underlined by the twofold use of the technical term for God's creating in vv. 13 and 15. Ezekiel's use of ancient international tradition was already observed in regard to the Ugaritic Daniel in both 14:12-23 and 28:3. He speaks of the garden of Eden in 31:9 and 36:35. He is also at home with a variety of royal and dynastic terminology and imagery. And finally, in 21:35 he uses the word "create" in a message against a foreign king. In 28:11-19, then, we have what we have seen before: A learned prophet makes skillful use of traditional material, even though the brevity of his allusions—unfamiliar to us—and the complex blending of his material may leave us uncertain and even confused.

Setting and Intention

It is hard to find any basis for a precise chronological setting. Possibly the use of a dirge could imply that Tyre had already fallen, but the intention seems more to prefigure such a death than to look back upon it. While a true myth, as pointed out above, aims to affirm a fundamental reality of human existence by projecting it back into primeval time and there describing it through the actions of superhuman figures, such is not really the case here. The paradisaical king is only a device used to highlight a dimension of the actual Tyre, its pride. And Tyre is not just a typical instance in which a primeval reality is exemplified: It is a real city, unique in all the world. Thus the myth is not a genuine one with the appropriate life-setting but is simply used in and applied to a political message. All of this is clearly illustrated by the way the fire of v. 18 contrasts with the flaming sword of Gen 3:24. The latter flame is a way of describing the barrier between fallen humanity and the realm of primeval innocence, whereas the fire of 28:18 is a real, ordinary fire that can destroy a city. It stands in the tradition not of Genesis 3 but of Amos 1.

While there is much unclarity about the details within this text, its redaction-critical placement is fully evident. As so often, so here again a dirge follows an announcement of judgment. Just as 26:15-18 follows 26:1-14, and ch. 32 follows chs. 29–31, so the judgment announcement in 28:1-10 sets the stage for the dirge of vv. 11-19. And just as ch. 32 brings the oracles against Egypt to a conclusion, so 28:11-19 brings an end to those against Tyre, what follows in 28:20-26 being something entirely different.

Bibliography

H. J. van Dijk, *Ezekiel's Prophecy on Tyre* (BibOr 20; Rome: Pontifical Institute, 1968) 92-122; J. L. McKenzie, "Mythological Allusions in Ezek 28:12-18," *JBL* 75 (1956) 322-27; C. Newsom, "A Maker of Metaphors—Ezekiel's Oracles Against Tyre," *Int* 38 (1984) 151-64; A. J. Williams, "The Mythological Background of Ezekiel 28:12-19?" *BTB* 6 (1976) 49-61; K. Yaron, "The Dirge over the King of Tyre," *ASTI* 3 (1964) 40-55.

A PROPHECY AGAINST SIDON WITH SUMMARIZING APPENDICES, 28:20-26

Structure and Genre

I. Prophetic word formula	20
II. Preliminaries	21-22aαβ
A. Address as son of man	21aα
B. Hostile orientation formula	21aβ
C. Direction to prophesy	21b
D. Direction to speak using messenger formula	22aαβ
III. Prophecy against Sidon in the form of an expanded two-part prophetic proof saying with appendix	22aγδb-24
A. Announcement of punishment (direct address)	22aγδ
1. Challenge to a duel formula	22aγ
2. Intervention: I will be glorified	22aδ
B. Expanded recognition formula (third person)	22b-23
1. Recognition formula	22bα
2. Expansion	22bβγ-23
a. Summary assurance of judgment and triumph	22bβγ
b. Details of judgment: pestilence, blood, and sword	23a
c. Recognition formula	23b
C. Interpretative appendix in the form of a two-part prophetic proof saying	24
1. Announcement: result only—no more hurt to Israel from the nations	24a
2. Recognition formula	24b

In a decidedly peculiar way this unit brings the collection in chs. 25–27 to a conclusion. A completely colorless and stereotyping prophecy against Sidon is included as a device by which the number of national targets for prophecies in chs. 25–32 can be brought to a total of seven, and by which interpretative appendices can be added. The result is a rather clumsy two-part PROPHETIC PROOF SAYING in vv. 22-23, which concludes with a RECOGNITION FORMULA expanded so as to conclude in turn with another recognition formula. This same awkward construction appears in 6:13-14; 30:25-26; 34:27b-30; and according to Zimmerli also in 12:15-16 and 37:13-16 (*Ezekiel 2,* 97). In vv. 22-23 only stereotypical formulas and language about the instrumentalities of judgment are employed. With vv. 24-26 two interpretative appendices look back over 25:1–28:19 and offer a broad perspective for their understanding. Although v. 24 is structurally linked to the preceding, and vv. 25-26 are marked off by a resumptive MESSENGER FORMULA, the two appendices belong together: the first one interpreting Yahweh's judgment on Israel's neighbors as the removal of pain, and the second one seeing this judgment as the basis for Israel's future security and the fulfillment of their Lord's faithfulness. This last point about the Lord's fidelity is brought out both by a reference to his promise of the land to Jacob and by a subtle expansion of the recognition formula, "they shall know that I am Yahweh," to contain an allusion to the COVENANT FORMULA by making it conclude, "I am Yahweh their God."

Setting

The thoroughly stereotypical nature of what is said about Sidon prevents any determination of a chronological setting. However, the way in which the prophecy itself is only a foil for the interpretative appendices makes it certain that the unit is a late one, added only when the collection in chs. 25–28 was being completed. Whether all the prophecies against Tyre were yet assembled is rendered uncertain by the fact that 28:20-26 make no reference to the anti-hubris motif appearing in 27:1–28:19. Whether it comes from the hand of Ezekiel himself as the initial editor of his own material or from disciples is both impossible to decide and insignificant, since the perspective presented here is characteristic of both the prophet and his followers. The language that presents God's self-glorification as expressed in the manifestation of his holiness (vv. 22 and 25) is heavily traditional. It appears in a strongly priestly context in Lev 10:3, and is linked to the recognition formula in Exod 14:17-18. Also it is once again tied to the recognition formula modified so as to bring out its association with the covenant formula in Ezek 39:21-22, 27, 28. Even the rare word used to describe briers in 28:24 seems to be a technical priestly one. The close connection between 28:20-26 and chs. 38–39 as well as the association with the fulfillment of the land promise and accompanying security in ch. 34 makes it likely that the assembling and editing of chs. 25–28 took place at the same time as the completion of chs. 33–39, and thus perhaps of the entire book of Ezekiel.

Intention

In addition to the numerical rounding out of the nations in chs. 25–32 to a total of seven, the concentration in 28:20-26 is on providing an interpretative framework from which to regard this collection. As Zimmerli puts it, the passage serves as "a final, heightened résumé of all the preceding judgments passed on the nations" (*Ezekiel 2*, 99). While the hope for Israel's restoration to her land and in particular the longing for security from enemies in that land are a clear part of what the doom of the other nations will mean for Israel, this national hope is put within a larger and, for Ezekiel typical, boldly theological perspective. Israel's restoration is seen as the keeping of Yahweh's promise and the realization of his large-scale purpose. In familiar priestly language that purpose is described as the manifesting of glory and holiness. The mood conveyed by this vocabulary is a complex one. In part it conveys a desire for intellectual comprehension in which the sufferings of God's people can be grasped as a subordinate part of a broader aim. In part it conveys the affirmation of unstoppable, even untouchable transcendence before which no hostile nation, no matter how otherwise powerful, can stand. But the primary direction of this vocabulary is oriented toward the fulfillment of what it is to be the people of Yahweh. That is not chiefly a matter of either intellect or power but of commitment. Israel's future is to come to recognize and confess that this God is our God forever and ever. Moreover, he is that because of what he is in himself. This is the sovereign uniqueness which is his glory and his holiness, and it is also the persisting uniqueness which is his stubborn grace.

A COLLECTION OF PROPHECIES AGAINST EGYPT, 29:1–32:32

Structure

In a stroke of editorial neatness, Egypt, the seventh nation to appear in the collection of prophecies concerning foreign nations in chs. 25–32, is itself made the object of seven prophecies in chs. 29–32. Each of the prophecies is dated, with the exception of 30:1-19, and all the dates are close to the fall of Jerusalem, ranging from January 587 to March 585 B.C. (following Boadt, 152 for 32:17), with the marked exception of 29:17-21, which is dated to April 571 B.C. It seems logical that the two nonsequential units are grouped together, but it is uncertain why the pair is placed where it is.

In contrast to the preceding collection of prophecies against Tyre in chs. 26–28, no editorial structuring beyond the dates is provided, neither by way of refrains nor by a summary conclusion as in 28:24-26. It is, of course, a natural sort of logic that the account of Egypt's burial should appear in the final unit.

Genre

In all but three of the seven units Pharaoh is the addressee. The exceptions comprise the same two noted as not in order according to date, i.e., 29:17-21 and 30:1-19, plus the last unit, 32:17-32, although Pharaoh is spoken about in the final two verses of that unit.

In contrast to chs. 26–28, the PROPHETIC PROOF SAYING appears as the single most frequently attested genre in this collection, a total of seven times. However, only one of those passages offers a lengthy reason for the announced punishment, and that one, 31:2b-9, is not characterized by a mood of extensive hostility. Instead the entire collection might best be described as reflecting a mood of counterconfidence, one in which the glory and might of Egypt are confronted by a confident proclamation of how Yahweh has determined its end.

Setting

Since 29:17-21 is necessary to bring the number of prophecies to seven, the completing of the collection would have to be dated in 571 B.C. or after, but still no element of prophesying after the fulfillment appears. It is hard to be sure of the extent to which Nebuchadrezzar in his campaign in 568-567 B.C. was involved in the internal Egyptian events that led to the death of Hophra and his replacement by Amasis or what military success the Babylonian king may have had. Josephus' report of a conquest of Egypt by Nebuchadrezzar in 582 B.C. is likely mistaken. In fact, our minimal knowledge of this period would make it difficult to detail any specific allusions to events at this late time, even if they were there. Rather, most of the material is historically so nonspecific that little correlation to post-587 B.C. events should be expected.

The mental process implicit in the assembling of this collection will not differ much from that described for the entire section of prophecies against foreign nations, to which the reader is referred. There does appear, though, as in chs. 26–28, a noticeable wisdom setting in several places, especially in the "learned" material in 31:1-18 and the rationalizing in 29:17-21. It seems that literary expansion by the use of additional learned elaboration was more common, as in 31:1-18 and 32:29-32, than the next step, i.e., reflection of a summarizing sort that could lead to general conclusions. That, as mentioned, appears only in 28:24-26.

Intention

The prominence given to Egypt by devoting this much attention to it is a natural reflection of the prophetic affirmation that Yahweh's plan has given sovereignty to Babylon. As the leading opposition power, Egypt's efforts at self-assertion can only be opposition to Yahweh's decision. Egypt must fall as the major obstacle to Yahweh's plan. It is not true, however, as Boadt maintains (179), that hubris is the underlying theme in all Ezekiel's prophecies against foreign nations. That motif is still strong, but definitely less prominent with regard to Egypt than in the case of Tyre. The abasement of power is a major aim in chs. 29–32, but not all power is insolent. Chapter 31 has only a slight stress on pride and devotes rather extensive space to marveling over Egypt's glory and beauty. Even the promise of a "lowly kingdom" as Egypt's destiny after a restoration at the end of forty years (29:13-16) has its aim specifically fixed on the elimination of Egypt as a false trust for Israel rather than any explicit humiliation of the mighty.

This last aspect can be grasped more easily in terms of a modern analogy. Because of the current East-West hostility and struggle for dominance, any smaller nation is forced to choose sides between these two alternatives, the eastern and western blocs. In consequence the independence of the smaller country is automatically and significantly impaired. We are so accustomed to this that we scarcely notice it. Similarly Judah's political life was unthinkingly seen in terms of a two-party alternative, pro-Egypt or pro-Babylon. However, the prophet's counterconfidence, which speaks with utter finality of the certainty of Egypt's doom, is not at all to be seen as a pro-Babylonian stance, for it flows from an underlying affirmation of Yahweh's sovereignty that simply eliminates the whole two-party alternative. Only on the basis of this distinctively theo-political Yahwistic foundation can a valid starting point for looking beyond the current helplessness and hopelessness be found. To provide exactly that starting point is the material's central intention.

Bibliography

L. Boadt, *Ezekiel's Oracles Against Egypt* (BibOr 37; Rome: Pontifical Biblical Institute, 1980).

A COLLECTION OF BRIEF PROPHECIES AGAINST EGYPT, 29:1-16

Text

In v. 7 it is necessary to read *kap* ("hand") for *kātēp* ("shoulder") and *wĕhim-'adtâ* ("and you make . . . totter") for *wĕha'ămadtâ* ("and you make . . . stand")

Structure and Genre

I. Prophetic word formula with date		1
II. Preliminaries		2-3aβ
A. Address as son of man		2aα

Just as prophecies against Tyre began in ch. 26 with a group of brief prophecies introduced by one dated prophetic word formula, so here in 29:1-16 a similar group appears similarly introduced. There are also differences. (1) Chapter 26 has four prophecies, ch. 29 only three. (2) In ch. 26 only the first prophecy has the form of a prophetic proof saying—the only one such directed at Tyre, while all those in ch. 29 have this form—again the only ones of this form directed at Egypt. (3) In ch. 26 a resumptive messenger formula introduces each prophecy after the first, since no accusatory reasons appear in the latter three, while in ch. 29 a reason begins all three prophecies, but only in the second does a messenger formula serve as a transition to the announcement, while in the third a resumptive messenger formula introduces a second announcement— surprisingly a promise of later restoration.

Again like ch. 26 the prophecies in ch. 29 are linked to each other; as the second picks up words from the first in ch. 26, so here the third uses some of the exact language of the first two. But in contrast to ch. 26, where the logic moved from destruction to dirge to entombment, in ch. 29 three announcements of doom are suddenly supplemented by an additional announcement, this time of later restoration.

Both of the first two prophecies in ch. 29 employ a bold metaphor in denouncing their addressee. Although the king of Egypt is addressed at the beginning of the first prophecy, and all three continue with the use of the second person masculine, the content of all three makes it plain that the people of the country are included with their leader in the punishment imposed, even though the reasons presented as basis for that punishment apply only to the king, or at least—in vv. 6-7—the political leadership.

What surprises us about the figure of the crocodile in vv. 3-5 is the way it is made the vehicle for a charge of hubris, "My Nile is my own; I made it" (v. 3). When taken together with the semimythological name for this "dragon," one might expect a strong mythological element in ch. 29. However, it seems that like the Leviathan in Job 40:25–41:26 (*RSV* 41:1-34) this "dragon" has been fully demythologized, even to the point that the fate of the crocodile is quite ordinary. (For a somewhat different balancing of the mythological and the crocodile, cf. Boadt, 27-28.)

Setting

The date in v. 1 assigns the first prophecy to a time about six months before Jerusalem's fall, making it the oldest prophecy against a foreign nation in the book of Ezekiel. The second prophecy could come from about that same time, since it implies Judah's doom after being misled by Egyptian promises, but the third prophecy's promise of restoration seems to assume a restored Israel, and is likely to come from a later date. That the third prophecy cites the first one in v. 9b and refers in v. 16 to the idea behind the second, may even imply, as Zimmerli suggests (*Ezekiel 2*, 115), the reinterpreting work of the subsequent Ezekiel school. Several aspects of this promise have points of context with a wide variety of Ezekiel material. The forty years picks up on what is said about Judah in 4:4-8. The idea of the gathering of the scattered appears in 11:17; 20:34, 41; 28:25 and elsewhere. That Egypt's future is to involve a return to the land of Pathros, upper Egypt, as "the land of their origin," may imply historical recollection about Thebes, or it may simply want to stress that a future Egypt is to be far removed from the sphere of Palestinian politics. Positive pictures of the future of Egypt do appear in the OT, e.g. Jer 46:26 and Isa 19:19-25, and both of these two appear, as Zimmerli points out (ibid.), at the end of a prophecy otherwise against Egypt. Just how late a date is implied by all this is uncertain, but at least it carries us deep into the exilic period, and thereby into the time of the Ezekiel school rather than the days of the prophet himself.

The metaphors employed in the first two prophecies are both traditional, but from different varieties of tradition. Egypt as a majestic crocodile is a natural picture, known in Egyptian literature, reflecting the awareness that the Nile is Egypt's fundamental power base. The brittle reed of vv. 6b-7 appears already in Isaiah, in fact even in the mouth of the king of Assyria in 36:6, and thus is probably a conventional image at home in political rhetoric.

Intention

Common to all these prophecies is the way in which lofty Egyptian claims led Yahweh's people to a false trust. Clearly these passages operate from a "standpoint other than that of normal international politics" (Zimmerli, *Ezekiel 2*, 113). Egypt's guilt and punishment flow from its role as the tempter who led Israel to oppose Yahweh's own will and the positive purposes of his judgment. For God's people to know who he is (v. 16b), outside power must be "made small" (v. 15b). Only on the other side of such judging activity can there be restoration. To frustrate this divine purpose from outside for political profit is closely similar to the way deceptive prophets operated from within for personal profit (see Ezek 13:1-16 and Lam 2:14). Thus the guilt includes not only the proud overestimation of one's own role (vv. 3 and 9b), but also the resulting injury of those misled by such pride (vv. 6b-9a). That such double-sided folly can be brought by gracious punishment to a restoration to life for the people misled is a basic part of the prophetic message of hope, but that this restoration can include even the agent who did the misleading is an unusually powerful proclamation of the extent of the grace inherent in judgment.

A PROPHECY: EGYPT TO GO TO NEBUCHADREZZAR AS A REPLACEMENT FOR TYRE, 29:17-21

Structure

I.	Prophetic word formula with date	17
II.	Preliminary: address as son of man	18aα
III.	Announcement of "holy war" victory	18aβγδb-20
	A. Reason: Nebuchadrezzar's fruitless siege of Tyre	18aβγδb
	1. Summary in advance	18aβ
	2. Details	18aγδb
	a. Hand and shoulder labor	18aγδ
	b. No wages from his labor	18b
	B. Transitional "therefore" and messenger formula	19aαβ
	C. Announcement of victory	19aγb
	1. Intervention: I am giving Nebuchadrezzar Egypt	19aγ
	2. Result: he will plunder	19bαβγ
	3. Purpose: wages	19bδ
	D. Concluding summary: I have given him a recompense	20abα
	E. Prophetic utterance formula	20bβ
IV.	Appended prophecy of salvation in the form of a two-part prophetic proof saying	21
A.	Time specification: in that day	21aα
	B. Announcement of salvation (all intervention)	21aβγ
	1. I bring forth a horn for Israel	21aβ
	2. I give you confidence	21aγ
	C. Recognition formula	21b

Although the prophetic word formulas in 29:17 and 30:1 mark off 29:17-21 as one unit, v. 21 is clearly a separate appended unit, even though it presupposes vv. 18-20.

Genre

The passage in vv. 18-20 is rigidly, although somewhat unusually, structured. While the assurance "I have given" in v. 20a is strongly reminiscent of the "holy war" ASSURANCE OF VICTORY in Josh 6:2 and Judg 7:9 (von Rad, *Der Heilige Krieg,* 6-9) it is preceded in v. 18 by a reason for the Lord's action and in v. 19 by the participial announcement (Westermann, "The Way of Promise Through the Old Testament," 206-8), "I am giving." A "holy war" assurance is not normally preceded by any such material. Ordinarily the oracle of assurance begins immediately with the perfect tense assurance, "I have given." The reason plus announcement pattern, as we have seen repeatedly, belongs to the PROPHECY OF PUNISHMENT genre. Here, then, we see how the "holy war" assurance has been incorporated a bit awkwardly within the prophecy of punishment structure by making the assurance a kind of appended summary added on at the point where the structure of the prophecy of punishment had reached its ending. The awkwardness shows especially in the way the perfect tense of the assurance contrasts with the preceding participial announcement. The verb "give" is naturally a favorite and most appropriate one for stressing Yahweh's sovereignty in punishment, and it is frequently used in the perfect tense as a way of underlining the powerful character of Yahweh's decision, which has determined the outcome in advance. Such cases appear in Ezekiel in 7:20; 15:6; 21:20 (*RSV* 25); 22:4; 29:5; 33:27; 39:4. Interestingly, in these cases the surrounding context is largely in the future tense. But still the verb "give" appears, as here in 29:20, in this awkwardly out-of-context perfect tense. To what extent this might reflect the influence of the "holy war" assurance is impossible to determine.

The promise in v. 21 of deliverance for Israel and resulting confidence is strangely unconnected in any specific way to what has preceded, not referring expressly to the vindication of Yahweh's word or to the judgment upon Egypt. In its present, likely secondary, context it does create an implicit link with the preceding by identifying this time ("that day") as both the occasion for the actualization of the previously unfulfilled word and the dawn of deliverance for Israel. But this connection remains only implicit and editorial.

Setting

It is interesting to speculate on the mood of doubt and questioning which likely followed upon the unfulfilled oracles against Tyre in 26:1–28:19. The thirteen-year siege of Tyre by Nebuchadrezzar probably lasted from 585 to 572 B.C. and that lengthy delay and ultimate nonfulfillment of Ezekiel's oracles must have provoked an attitude comparable to and even worse than that described in 12:22 and 27, when the prophet's words against Jerusalem were seen as unfulfilled. Isaiah 5:19 and Zeph 1:12 reveal what the flavor of ancient skepticism was like. That the Babylonian siege of Tyre did result in the acceptance of Babylonian overlordship, even if not in Tyre's destruction, is interestingly not seized upon as a "way out" of the problem of an unfulfilled word. Rather, as in the case of Jonah, it is the Lord's freedom to change his plans that is asserted. Unpredictable as this freedom to change was to Jonah—and is to us in our day—it appears as an integral element within the prophetic tradition. It surfaces in its sharpest form in 1 Sam 15:11, 29, and 35 (Jeremias, 27-36) and in Dan 3:18.

The appearance of the redirection of the old Tyre prophecies in 571 B.C. presumably added new fervor to hopes for Egypt's fall, but, as Zimmerli accurately points out (*Ezekiel 2*, 119-20), we cannot in any way know what Babylonian military plans Ezekiel may have known at this time. It may even have been the case that Egyptian naval help was partly responsible for Tyre's long endurance and that this would have been extra reason for Nebuchadrezzar's hostility toward Egypt (Freedy and Redford, 483-84).

Intention

While it is totally obvious that this passage picks up the earlier pronouncements of judgment upon Tyre, the exact manner in which this resumption takes place is a matter of some dispute. This text does not withdraw, disavow, or rescind the earlier message, rather it picks it up by way of reinterpretation. This phenomenon of reinterpretation is obvious in the preservation of prophetic tradition, and is usually assigned to disciples or editors as revealing how these later generations were able to hear the old words speaking afresh to them. There is, though, no reason why this reinterpretation process is to be confined to later generations. Surely the prophet Ezekiel himself, looking back at his own words over such a lengthy span of years, would have approached the old words in the same attitude of listening expectation as disciples of a generation later. Instead of seeing something highly unusual in this passage, we are privileged to see something quite ordinary and frequent, only this time we see it from within the initial shaping of the prophetic text, rather than, as customarily, in the less easily recognizable work of later disciples—as for instance in the adaptation of the book of Hosea to a Judean audience after the fall of Samaria. As Zimmerli puts it, it is not the "withdrawal of an earlier oracle that is the dominating feature of 29:17-20; it is the new expression given to the validity of an old proclamation with reference to a new present . . . which the prophet is authorized to make" (*Ezekiel 2*, 120).

As Jer 18:1-11 had earlier treated the subject of God's freedom to change his mind about his announcements of judgment by making them contingent upon the response of the addressee, so here an even more basic issue is broached. Although not pursued systematically as in Jeremiah 18, the issue of God's freedom to change his mind for his own reasons comes plainly close to the surface. It is this freedom of God's own planning and not some overriding compulsion for just retribution that is given expression. The reference to the frustrating disappointment of Nebuchadrezzar's army is only a charming literary touch to establish a logic for the switch from Tyre to Egypt. It would not be difficult to imagine other techniques by which a similar bridge could be established, possibly even some— to our taste—mere play on words could have been used. What underlies is, as again Zimmerli formulates it, the affirmation that not every judgment is to be seen as finality, but as "a penultimate event" (ibid., 121). For, as v. 21 indicates, God's plan goes beyond judgment, whether that of Judah (chs. 1–24) or other nations (chs. 25–32) to that confident opening of the mouth which lies ahead. Of course, 33:21f. knows of one such resumption of revelatory proclamation, but in 571 B.C. and after it was yet a further one, one linked to Israel's restoration, that was anticipated.

Bibliography

L. Boadt, *Ezekiel's Oracles Against Egypt* (BibOr 37; Rome: Pontifical Biblical Institute, 1980) 13-53; K. S. Freedy and D. B. Redford, "The Dates in Ezekiel in Relation to Biblical, Babylonian and Egyptian Sources," *JAOS* 90 (1970) 462-85; Jörg Jeremias, *Die Reue Gottes* (BibS[N] 65; Neukirchen-Vluyn: Neukirchener, 1975); G. von Rad, *Der heilige Krieg im alten Israel* (ATANT 20; Zürich: Zwingli, 1951); H. F. von Rooy, "Parallelism, metre and rhetoric in Ezekiel 29:1-6," *Semitics* 8 (1982) 90-105; C. Westermann, "The Way of Promise through the Old Testament," in *The Old Testament and Christian Faith* (ed. B. Anderson; New York: Harper and Row, 1963) 200-24.

A PROPHECY: THE DAY OF THE LORD AGAINST EGYPT, 30:1-19

Text

In v. 16b read *ṣārîm* ("oppressors") for *ṣārê* ("oppressors of").

Structure and Genre

B. Announcement of punishment	13aβγδ-19a
1. Intervention	13aβγ
a. Idols destroyed	13aβ
b. Worthless idols eliminated from Memphis	13aγ
2. Interruptive results: no more leader	13aδ
3. Intervention resumed	13b-16aα
a. Fear in Egypt	13b
b. Pathros desolated	14aα
c. Fire in Zoan	14aβ
d. Judgment on Thebes	14b
e. Wrath on Sin	15a
f. Horde of Thebes cut off	15b
g. Fire on Egypt	16aα
4. Results	16aβ-18aα
a. Sin will writhe	16aβ
b. Thebes will be breached	16aγ
c. Oppressors in Memphis	16b
d. Young men of Thebes and Bubastis die	17a
e. They (fem) go into exile	17b
f. Darkness in Tahpanhes	18aα
5. Interruptive intervention: when I break the staff of Egypt	18aβ
6. Results resumed	18aγb
a. Pride cut off	18aγ
b. Covered by a cloud	18bα
c. Daughters into exile	18bβ
7. Summary intervention: judgment on Egypt	19a
C. Recognition formula	19b

Although the PROPHETIC WORD FORMULAS in 30:1 and 20 mark off vv. 1-19 as a single unit, those verses display a complicated structure, in many ways reminiscent of ch. 7. The recognition formulas in vv. 8 and 19 together with the CONCLUSION FORMULA FOR DIVINE SPEECH in v. 12 suggest the existence of three separate units (vv. 2-9, 10-12, and 13-19), but considerable continuity within all of vv. 1-19 makes it more likely to think of three subunits: two two-part PROPHETIC PROOF SAYINGS, with an ANNOUNCEMENT OF PUNISHMENT between them. Beyond this, three structural puzzles remain: (1) v. 9 seems to be a secondary extension of vv. 1-8; (2) the MESSENGER FORMULA appears quite inappropriately at the start of v. 6; and (3) the customary distinguishing of intervention in first person and results in second or third person is interrupted in a peculiar way in both IV.B and V.B.

The parallel with ch. 7 is striking. Both treat the coming of an ominous time or day, sometimes as "the day." In the beginning they both speak in surprisingly impersonal language ("a sword" in v. 4), but then go on to employ the intervention-result scheme in a rather disorganized fashion. Both introduce some elements of cosmic upheaval, here darkness and clouds (v. 18) and the drying up of the Nile (v. 12), but in both the language of war is strong, even including the element of terror or panic so frequently associated with "holy war." It seems fair to observe that this material, probably primarily because of its stereotypical content, has some definite contacts with apocalyptic, and possibly therefore has experienced a certain structural confusion, even though it is by no means to be labelled genuinely apocalyptic.

The three subunits do demonstrate a certain inner logic of connection to each other. The impersonal doom of vv. 2-7 is specified as being the Lord's doing in the two following subunits—as well as already in the elaborated recognition formula in v. 8 and the extension in v. 9. Subunit two in vv. 10-12 further specifies Nebuchadrezzar as Yahweh's agent, in a way closely similar to the manner in which 26:7-14 plays the same role for 26:1-6. The final subunit in vv. 13-19 seeks to complete the portrayal of Yahweh's judgment by specifying the names of key cities, a typical pattern of many prophecies against foreign nations. Strangely, though, no order of geography or logic is detectable among these names; repetitions and generalities leave the interpreter puzzled.

Setting

This passage is the only undated unit within the complex of prophecies against Egypt. That fact together with the considerable lack of specific points of contact with known historical events or situations makes its chronological placement quite uncertain. Since it is positioned immediately following the very late 29:17-21, that may indicate that this unit too is isolated and interruptive of what is otherwise a series of prophecies dated within a very small space of time. Eichrodt sees its generalities as a possible reason to regard it as "an introduction to the great prophecies of judgment upon Egypt, which afterwards worked out and dated more precisely each of the separate strokes of judgment" (417). He sees its present location as a result of "elaborations which have obscured the original character of the passage" (ibid.). While possible, it does not seem that speaking in "the most general terms" (ibid.) is a compelling basis for seeing the passage as a misplaced introduction.

Zimmerli argues that 30:1-4 and 6-8 were known to the author of the late unit 29:9b-16 because 29:10 presupposes 30:6, and 29:12 recapitulates 30:7 (*Ezekiel 2*, 127). But the evidence advanced seems unconvincing, especially for such stereotypical language. Other than the mention in 30:10 of Nebuchadrezzar, who after all lived until 562 B.C., and made his decisive attack on Egypt only in 568 B.C., there is little on which to base a temporal setting. To reason that the preponderance of city names from the Delta area reflects a late time within Egyptian history, perhaps even specifically the reign of Amasis, who transferred the capital to Memphis (Zimmerli, *Ezekiel 2*, 113), is forcing the evidence to yield what it cannot provide.

On the other hand, the faint apocalyptic flavor of this day of darkness and doom for an ancient foe is not strong enough to suggest that this is material from a much later time that has begun to raise expectations of universal judgment. The passage remains a somewhat vaguer than usual extension toward the future of that experience of their own judgment which dominated the lives of those exiles who persisted in affirming the powerful sovereignty of Yahweh.

Intention

The text is dominated by the emphasis upon that coming revelation of doom for Egypt which no resistance can put off. The absence of sections presenting reasons for this judgment gives the unit even more of a flavor of finality. Accusations or even arguments are not needed beyond the bald affirmation that no defense is of any avail. Incidental references to wealth, alliances, and military power are not really to be seen as indictments of false trust, as though some other more appropriate reliance was being proclaimed. Instead their collapse is more properly to be seen as a part of the portrayal of what doom and its accompanying disorder and lack of stability will involve.

The role of the recognition formula is to be understood in a similar way. That is, it is not any positive sort of knowing which is the object of this announced doom and collapse. Rather it is only the grudging renunciation of one's own attempt to exert control over one's own destiny that is expected. In v. 8b the elaboration of the recognition formula to highlight Yahweh as the bringer of the flames of destruction and the power before which all allies and rescuers are helpless makes this negative orientation clear.

This very concentration on the negative, specifically the totality of the devastation explicit in the collapse of every resource, gives the section a flavor of implicit universality. When all the customary underpinnings of national existence are removed, and nothing is described as continuing apart from defeat, terror, and darkness, one notices a similarity to the portrayals of apocalyptic doom. However, the similarity is almost completely confined to the description of military and political results. What is missing is the portrayal of any of the machinery normally associated with apocalyptic, such as the appearance of transcendent instrumentalities, a heavenly timetable, or any future beyond this destruction in rather ordinary battle. In short it is the absence of any significantly eschatological element, in the sense of universal ultimacy, which distinguishes "the day of the Lord" here from that in genuinely apocalyptic literature. (See chs. 38–39 in this regard.)

Bibliography

L. Boadt, *Ezekiel's Oracles Against Egypt* (BibOr 37; Rome: Pontifical Biblical Institute, 1980) 54-84.

A PROPHECY: THE BREAKING OF PHARAOH'S ARMS, 30:20-26

Structure and Genre

I. Prophetic word formula with date	20
II. Preliminary: address as son of man	21aα
III. Three-part prophetic proof saying	21aβb-26
A. Reason	21aβb
1. Report of past act: Pharaoh's arm broken (first person)	21aβ
2. Report of treatment not given	21bαβ
3. Result not obtained	21bγ
B. Transitional "therefore" and messenger formula	22aαβ
C. Announcement of punishment	22aγδb-25a

The entire passage is strangely redundant. Although marked off as a unit by a PROPHETIC WORD FORMULA in v. 20, this is followed by no direction to speak or prophesy. Instead v. 21a presents in perfect tense what could be either an announcement expressed with the certainty of an assurance, or a report of a past act of Yahweh as the basis for an announcement to follow. That the second is the case is made more likely by the word order here in which the verb comes at the end in contrast to the order found in assurances (Zimmerli, *Ezekiel 2,* 138).

The ANNOUNCEMENT OF PUNISHMENT in vv. 22-25 begins with the CHAL-LENGE TO A DUEL FORMULA, here expressed somewhat inappropriately in the third person. This departure from the expected direct address does, though, appear in four other instances out of a total of twenty-two: Ezek 34:10 and three times in Jer 23:30-32. The content of the announcement in v. 22a seems inconsistent in that it expects the breaking of both of Pharaoh's arms, the strong one and the broken one so that he must drop his sword. However, part of v. 21's report contained the infor-mation that satisfactory treatment of Pharaoh's broken arm had not taken place, so that he might be able to wield a sword. Awkward as this use of imagery may seem— Zimmerli opines that "one should not ask pedantically whether he now holds it in his left hand" (*Ezekiel 2,* 139)—the discussion under Setting will make clear the sensible underlying logic.

In vv. 23-24 two additional elements are included: the dispersion of Egypt and Yahweh's use of the arms of the king of Babylon to bear Yahweh's sword. Here a high level of redundancy becomes noticeable. In v. 24bα the breaking of Pharaoh's arms is repeated (see v. 22aδ), and in v. 25a the strengthening of the arms of the king of Babylon is reaffirmed (see v. 24aβ). Further, in the elaboration of the recognition formula in v. 25bβ the giving of Yahweh's sword to the king of Babylon is again expressed (see v. 24aα), and the dispersion of Egypt is restated in v. 26a (see v. 23). This extensive redundancy has tempted many (e.g., Fohrer, 173) to delete parts of vv. 24 and 25 and all of 26. Nonetheless, since this pattern of repetition is so extensive and is not confined to one spot, the improvement of the passage's style seems to rest only on an aesthetic basis, and Fohrer's result is even on these grounds not convincing, retaining as it does the repetition of the giving of Yahweh's sword to the king of Babylon in vv. 24aβ and 25bβ. Finally, that an elaborated recognition formula should eventuate in a second use of this formula has already been noted elsewhere (see 28:23b). Here Boadt argues that the recognition formula in v. 25 interrupts a scheme of double internal chiasm and is thus to be seen as an addition (Boadt, 86). However, that would be to find an extremely subtle touch of skill and beauty in a text which otherwise seems genuinely pedestrian—an attribute not infrequently characteristic of Ezekiel's style.

A different sort of question about the generic structure and development of this passage is whether v. 21 may have once been an originally independent saying later developed and expanded. This question can best be pursued after an examination of the Setting.

Setting and Intention

Behind v. 21 lies the event described in Jer 37:5 in which Pharaoh Hophra briefly raised the Babylonian siege of Jerusalem by his army's appearance in Palestine. The jubilation at this promised deliverance is mentioned by Jeremiah and denounced as a false trust. Whatever the details of Hophra's campaign, it proved ineffective, and the Babylonians returned to the siege of Jerusalem. Ezekiel, as 29:6f. and ch. 17 show, regarded reliance on Egyptian help as a vain and foolish resistance of the Lord's instrument of judgment. It may be assumed, though, that others—both in Jerusalem and in Babylon—did not share this view and hoped at the start of 587 B.C. for another, this time successful, Egyptian campaign in Palestine. In v. 21 the prophet opposes such hopes by the metaphorical argument that Egypt's arm has not recovered from its earlier injury. The arm image was a common one, as its use in Jer 48:25, Ps 10:15, and Job 38:15 shows. Hophra himself chose as a prominent part of his titulary a name meaning "possessed of a muscular arm" (Freedy and Redford, 482-83). The date of the end of April 587 B.C. given in v. 20 confirms this interpretation, but implies that the real addressee in mind was Judean exiles in their false reliance on Egyptian aid. There may in fact once have been such a prophecy of punishment addressed to exiles, and v. 21 and possibly v. 22 may have been a part of it (Zimmerli, *Ezekiel 2*, 138), but the present text, although not expressly addressed to Egypt, has a different focus in mind. The present text's unfolding structure beyond v. 21 never even implicitly raises the thought of Egypt as a false trust for Judah's deliverance. Instead the present text is a genuine PROPHECY CONCERNING A FOREIGN NATION, announcing the future doom and dispersion of Egypt. The focus on Egypt's arm and its potential for wielding a sword shifts from any possible idea of a usefulness for Judah to a concern with Yahweh's sovereign power, as expressed in the idea of his overpowering Egypt's arms, his own sword, and his utilization of the king of Babylon as the instrument for overthrowing Egypt according to his purpose. Appropriately then it is the Egyptians who shall recognize Yahweh's sovereignty in their downfall. Of course, such a proclamation is not irrelevant for the people of Yahweh, but its relevance is very similar to that of the other prophecies against foreign nations, and no longer at all linked to the issue of a false trust in political allies. Even the stress on who is truly in control and whose power is active even in apparently independent international politics is the familiar emphasis we have come to know as a standard element in prophecies against foreign nations.

Bibliography

L. Boadt, *Ezekiel's Oracles Against Egypt* (BibOr 37; Rome: Pontifical Biblical Institute, 1980) 84-89; K. S. Freedy and D. B. Redford, "The Dates in Ezekiel in Relation to Biblical, Babylonian and Egyptian Sources," *JAOS* 90 (1970) 462-85.

AN ALLEGORY: THE FALL OF PHARAOH, THE GLORIOUS TREE, 31:1-18

Text

In v. 3a it is necessary to read *tĕ'aššûr* ("a cypress") for *'aššûr* ("Assyria"). In v. 17b one should read *zōrĕ'û yōšebê* ("those who dwelt . . . were dispersed") as proposed by Driver, 179, for *ûzĕrō'ô yāšĕbû* ("and his arm they sat"). In v. 12 "upon the mountains" should most likely be taken with the first half of the verse in spite of the accents in MT.

Structure and Genre

I. Prophetic word formula with date	1
II. Preliminaries	2a
A. Address as son of man	2aα
B. Direction to speak	2aβ
C. Addressee: Pharaoh and his multitude	2aγ
III. Prophecy of punishment in allegorical language	2b-18
A. Reason: portrayal of Pharaoh's glory in allegorical language	2b-9
1. Introduction: rhetorical question showing incomparability (direct address)	2b
2. The figure of a glorious tree (third person)	3-9
a. Its characteristics in general	3-5
1) Identity: a Lebanon cypress	3aα
2) Its glory: beauty, foliage, height	3aβb
3) Its nourishment	4
a) Supplied by the subterranean depth	4a
b) Center of sustenance for other trees	4b
4) Its development: high and well-branched from abundant water	5
b. Its importance	6
1) Home for all birds	6aα
2) Shelter for all animals	6aβ
3) Shade for all nations	6b

That vv. 1-18 are a single unit is indicated by the use of the PROPHETIC WORD FORMULA only in 31:1 and 32:1, and also by the effective inclusio between v. 2b and v. 18aα. In spite of the fact that only this repeated line and v. 10aγbα are formulated in direct address, it is nonetheless evident that precisely these lines are aimed to construct the framework of a PROPHECY OF PUNISHMENT in which vv. 2b-9 form the reason and v. 10 marks the transition to the announcement of punishment. It is the allegorical nature of the bulk of the material and its particular background that are responsible for everything else being in the third person. That the entire unit is addressed to the king does not make it any less a PROPHECY CONCERNING A FOREIGN NATION, just as was the case in ch. 28 with regard to the king of Tyre.

The reason is presented in poetic form, which further distinguishes it from the prose of vv. 10-18. Although trees provide the *personae* of the chapter, it is not appropriate to label it a FABLE, for there is really no plot nor any dialogue. In fact, vv. 3-9 are totally devoid of any political references, consisting exclusively of bare description, and it is only in v. 10 that the preceding description of the tree's height is interpreted as pride responsible for the punishment then announced. That the announcement is entirely in the past tense is at first glance highly unusual, but, once the strong DIRGE perspective is noticed, the contrast between the former splendor and the tragic present state (vv. 12-13) becomes understandable as the standard then-now motif characteristic of the dirge. In fact, this same motif comes powerfully and skillfully to expression in the switch in mood between the inclusio line in v. 2b where "who are you like?" has the almost hymnic flavor of praising the incomparable, and v. 18aα where the same words bring out the bitter tragedy of the fall that has taken place. In addition the prominence of the dirge aspect is established by the use in vv. 15-18 of the motif of the journey to Sheol, frequent in prophetic dirges, e.g., 32:17-32; 26:17-21; 28:8; and Isa 14:9-11 and 15-20. It seems that the idea of the commonality of mortality at the end of v. 14 in the context of the drawing of a didactic moral lesson is made the connecting link by which the loosely attached vv. 15-18 are joined to the preceding verses.

In all, the text is essentially a prophecy of punishment, but it is one done in a botanical allegory. The reason is provided at first only implicitly by a purely descriptive section picturing the *Weltbaum,* while the announcement takes the shape of an anticipatory dirge. Thus in the blending of all these elements, as well as others soon to be examined, it is not surprising that an occasional inconsistency can arise. The idea of a *Weltbaum,* a tree that dominates the whole world, having its top in heaven and sending its roots down to the underworld and providing sustenance for all earthly life, is well known in the ancient Near East and in other cultures as well (Widengren). However, the perspective of this tree image cannot be maintained with full consistency for a number of reasons. Since lofty height and enduring power are the aspects selected to be stressed, the evergreen cypress is chosen, and thus it becomes impossible to keep the idea of the tree's fruit sustaining the inhabitants of the world. Because tall evergreens grew in the Lebanon mountains, it was natural to situate this tree there, even though this was not a spot famous for abundant water, especially that flowing forth from the depths of the earth, and even though no natural link exists between Lebanon and the garden of God in Eden in which the tree of life was classically located. Finally, even though the dirge motif was a natural one to use for a fallen mighty ruler, this clashes unpleasantly with the picture of a tree, whose wood after all only becomes available for its destined use after the killing of the tree, and the whole image of trees in Sheol is less than impressive.

It must also be noted that the *Weltbaum* is inherently a mythical figure at home within a setting in which mythical elements could carry out their intended functions. The life-sustaining transcendent character of this tree is hinted at in Ezek 17:24 and Daniel 4, but it is only in Gen 3:3 that we see how the element of conflict, inherently essential for MYTHS as stories about the gods, becomes possible. The motifs of envy and pride and potential disaster are fully demythologized already in Genesis, for God's dominion faces no ultimately serious challenge even there. A true myth could tell of the endangering of the world's order as embodied in the great tree, but to have the Lord commission people to chop it down destroys the essential fabric of the myth. With no plurality of gods, no supernatural conflict, and no opposition of ultimate import, there remain in Ezekiel 31 only broken fragments of a myth. The situation is thus reminiscent of that in 28:12-19. Probably lost from the underlying mythical apparatus behind the cosmic tree are such further elements as the figure of a divine king and the power of immortality, but it is naturally impossible to determine which elements the prophet was aware of but chose not to employ. To see the grieving of the deep in v. 15 as due to the failure of her hostile plan, as Fohrer does (170), is an overly bold conjecture with no real basis in the text.

Setting

If the passage shows no trace of the setting for a genuine myth, what other sort of setting does lie behind the use of all these diverse elements? What mental process lies behind this utilization of a botanical metaphor in such an extensive way that it has to be forced into a prophetic function by the ex post facto identification of the tree's height as a guilty pride in v. 10? The amount of learning displayed for its own sake in the portrayal of the tree in vv. 3-9 is strongly similar to the way in ch. 27 the metaphor of a ship for Tyre was elaborated by a learned listing of items of cargo and their points of origin. In similar fashion we have here too an aspect of a wisdom setting. The use of specific names for varieties of trees (for the cypress see 27:6), the insight that Egypt's greatness is totally rooted in the Nile whose resources are hidden but perennially powerful, the technique of choosing a metaphor to capture the essence of a phenomenon, and the drawing of a lesson in vv. 14 and 17, especially the lesson that pride which ignores mortality is destined for disaster by virtue of our universally inescapable mortality—all these are items which support the claim that it is a wisdom heritage that is employed here. Certainly the prophetic use of this material is decisive and controlling; but just as surely the surprisingly extensive, nonjudgmental, poetic material in vv. 3-8 and the unparalleled mortality-based morality of vv. 14 and 17 show that the prophetic use has not prevented the appearance of unusual material. Although this unusual material is really nonessential to the prophetic point, it is just this nonessential material which gives this text its distinctive flavor and its charm.

Certainly the distinctive setting of ch. 31 is more to be seen in what has just been noted than it is in the precise date in 587 B.C. provided in v. 1. The complete absence of any specific reflection of the crucial historical events of that time is all the more surprising in view of the way Ezekiel has elsewhere come back again and again to the motif of Egypt as a vain reliance for a Jerusalem facing disaster.

Intention

The element of wisdom-based reflection leads in this text—even in the days close to the moment of Jerusalem's fall—to an impressively broad kind of analysis. As Eichrodt observed, Ezekiel is able to put the events of 587 B.C. into the "setting of the world-wide judgment his God is carrying out" (429). Even the Babylon whose troops were assaulting Jerusalem's walls and whose distant land provided Ezekiel's unchosen dwelling place, could be seen as having the minor role indicated in vv. 11-12 of carrying out Yahweh's judgment on Pharaoh's pride.

But there is another dimension of this text occasioned by its imagery, which must be allowed to come to voice here. In describing the structure of the text above, the word "tragic" was used occasionally. In a rare instance that word is genuinely appropriate here. In the midst of the insistent prophetic affirmation of the Lord's total sovereignty and the familiar denunciation of the foolish pride of any nation that ventures to exalt itself against his plans, there is still an undeniable element of real sympathy here for the glory that was Egypt's. The unfailing return of the Nile's flood waters, the way the river and the king it sustained could nourish not only Egypt's people, but serve through centuries as a breadbasket for much of the world—these features are set forth in vv. 3-9 in a framework of awe-filled marveling. Truly this was an incomparable greatness which had found expression in the trappings of splendor. Yet to find in the midst of this nobility one tragic flaw, the pride that had forgotten, from the prophet's point of view, the real locus of power—that is the traditional recipe for tragedy. And to present all this in dirge language looking backward from the perspective of the great and final levelling which takes place when the former great assemble in the grave's equality, that too is fully traditional and yet somehow even today strikingly provocative.

Bibliography

L. Boadt, *Ezekiel's Oracles Against Egypt* (BibOr 37; Rome: Pontifical Biblical Institute, 1980) 90-123; G. R. Driver, "Linguistic and Textual Problems: Ezekiel," *Bib* 19 (1938) 60-69; E. Haag, "Ez 31 und die alttestamentliche Paradiesvorstellung," in *Wort, Lied und Gottesspruch* (Fest. J. Ziegler; ed. J. Schreiner; Würzburg: Echter Verlag, 1972) 171-78; H. Jahnow, *Das hebräische Leichenlied im Rahmen der Völkerdichtung* (BZAW 36; Giessen: Töpelmann, 1923) 208-10; G. Widengren, *The King and the Tree of Life in Ancient Near Eastern Religion: King and Saviour IV* (UUÅ; Uppsala: Lundequists, 1951).

A PROPHECY: THE DIRGE-BASED DOOM OF PHARAOH, THE CROCODILE, 32:1-16

Structure and Genre

This is structurally and generically a highly unusual unit. The dated MESSENGER FORMULAS in vv. 1 and 17, the homogeneous content, and the use of the DIRGE label in vv. 2 and 16 all corroborate that it is a unit. But it is not the typical dirge that the frame of vv. 2 and 16 would lead one to expect. At most v. 2b can be considered an actual dirge, for only that much is in the past tense and in the 3:2 meter normal to the genre. In sharp contrast to what one would expect in a dirge, with its looking backward—even if only in anticipation—upon the death of one bemoaned, all of vv. 3-15 look plainly ahead in the typical fashion of a PROPHETIC ANNOUNCEMENT OF PUNISHMENT. The transitional messenger formula in v. 3aα raises the possibility that v. 2b could be viewed as the reason upon which the following announcement is based, and in spite of the brevity of the portrayal of Pharaoh's former might, this does seem to be the case. A dirge would be expected to contrast former might with present ruin, but in this text only a tiny segment of a dirge-style description of former might appears, with the anticipated presentation of current ruin now set forth in announcements of future doom for Egypt. These announcements are not in 3:2 meter, and seem in several places in fact to be scarcely in poetic form at all. This metrical uncertainty is one of several factors suggesting a complicated editorial history for the text. The unmotivated switch from direct address to the use of the third person in vv. 12b-16, the use of presumably concluding PROPHETIC UTTERANCE FORMULAS in vv. 8b and 14b, and the use of a resumptive "for" with a messenger formula in v. 11a undergird this suggestion. Finally the normally strictly followed pattern within announcements, having a substantial section of Yahweh's first person interventions followed by another substantial section giving in second or third person the results thereof, is largely abandoned. Results appear only in brief sections of two items at most either interrupting a series of interventions, as in vv. 6b and 7bβ, or in a chain of alternating interventions and results, as in vv. 11b-14. Some of these result sections could more properly be seen as a part of an intervention section, although deliberately formulated as a result, still presenting a part of Yahweh's action rather than a result. The situation in v. 7b is especially clear: "I will cover the sun with a cloud, and the moon shall not give its light."

The way some of these same characteristics of the crumbling of forms have been noticed as characteristic of specific other sections in Ezekiel, namely, 7:1-27 and 30:1-19, suggests a further comparison with these sections seeking additional common elements. While 32:1-16 and the other two passages do use what may be called protoapocalyptic themes, e.g., in 32:1-16 the use of the corpse of the chaos monster as food and the darkening of the heavens, these themes are not characteristic of all three units, and the impersonal material in 7:1-27 and 30:1-19 is not present in 32:1-16. Thus, rather than being able to group these three sections as perhaps reflective of the same setting or a common editorial heritage, the most that can be said is that all three reflect how some of the same symptoms of structural crumbling recur when material moves far away from the setting responsible for its normal shape.

Setting

The date given in v. 1, whether or not emended, as is often suggested, from the twelfth to the eleventh year, indicates a time shortly after the fall of Jerusalem in 587 B.C. Nonetheless, no reference is made even implicitly to this event. The unit could in fact come from any time before the fall of Egypt to Nebuchadrezzar. The imagery of the net in v. 3 is not appropriate for the capture of a crocodile, but it is traditional in Mesopotamia, appearing even in the account of Tiamat's being captured in Marduk's net. Mountains and valleys (vv. 5-6) in any large scale are not characteristic of the Nile valley, but it is far more likely that we are simply encountering here language of a highly stereotypical sort, rather than something reflecting a specifically different original setting. Similarly, the use of lion imagery in v. 2 is only a passing reference to the "king of beasts" idea, and not a genuine alternative to the crocodile imagery of vv. 2b-6. The troubling of the waters in v. 2, appropriate to a crocodile's thrashing movement, is balanced in vv. 13-14 by a looking ahead to untroubled waters. This, however, is no switch from punishment to promise, for, as the context of vv. 13-14 shows, it is only desolation that is responsible for this future clarity.

In v. 16 there is attested the traditional use of a dirge by mourning women as a matter of professional expertise (see also 32:18). This notice is not some artful poetic inclusio, however, for although it does clearly and deliberately connect with the direction given the prophet in v. 2 to raise a dirge, both sections lie outside of the prophecy proper and constitute instead only a consistent labelling framework, appearing both before and after the material so labeled. The lack of dirge meter and the complex, even twisted structure of the unit make it highly unlikely that it ever actually functioned as any kind of professional dirge. Instead it is better seen as a literary unit which is designed more for reading than for hearing, and, though incorporating some material originally proclaimed orally, thus found its shape as the result of an editorial process.

Intention

Although the oracle's point of departure is in the figurative, dirge-style reference to the Egyptian pharaoh as a doomed crocodile in contrast to his own proud perception of himself as a lion, there is really very little rebuke of pride in the unit. Instead the major aim is the affirmation of Yahweh's sovereignty that underlies both Egypt's fall and its deliverance to the sword of Babylon. The use of "a host of many peoples" in v. 3 as the interpretation—correct, even if a gloss—of the device the Lord will employ to bring about Egypt's defeat emphasizes the extent of this sovereignty, as does the darkening of the heavens in vv. 7-8 as well as the terrifying of other nations in vv. 9-10. This was, though, not a point being made for the sake of theological accuracy, but was a part of the background upon which was based hope and trust in Yahweh's further future acts. Still, within the bounds of this unit that confidence remains only implicit and unexpressed.

Bibliography

L. Boadt, *Ezekiel's Oracles Against Egypt* (BibOr 37; Rome: Pontifical Biblical Institute, 1980) 124-50; H. Jahnow, *Das hebräische Leichenlied im Rahmen der Völkerdichtung* (BZAW 36; Giessen: Töpelmann, 1923) 228-31.

A GRIEF POEM: MIGHTY EGYPT IN THE UNDERWORLD, 32:17-32

Text

Much of this section is so highly but inexactly repetitious, as well as obscure, that it is extremely difficult to determine what is actually being said. Confusion of gender and tense as well as the use of uncertain words is only a part of the problem. (Boadt gives a good survey of the "tissue of stock phrases," 151f.) Scholars often suggest deletions and rearrangements, but the result of such steps is usually a reconstruction which is purged of that very repetition which is the text's most undeniable characteristic. Here an attempt will be made to stay as close as possible to the present text in analyzing Structure and Genre, moving to explore the history of the text's development only under Setting. In v. 18 one must likely read *'attâ* ("you") for *'ôtāh* ("it"). In v. 27 read *mē'ôlām* ("from of old") for *mē'ărēlîm* ("from uncircumcised") and *ṣinnôtām* ("their shields") for *'ăwōnōtām* ("their iniquities").

Structure and Genre

I. Prophetic word formula with date		17
II. Preliminaries		18
A. Address as son of man		18aα
B. Direction to use a grief poem		18aβγb
1. General direction		18aβ
2. Details		18aγb
a. Performers: you and women of nations		18aγbα
b. Destination: the underworld		18bβγ
III. Grief poem		19-32
A. Introduction: welcome to the underworld		19-21
1. Taunting rhetorical question		19a
2. Direction to take the proper place with the uncircumcised		19b
3. Preliminary description of the place (obscure)		20-21
a. Fall assured amid those slain by the sword		20
b. Spoken to by mighty warriors, uncircumcised and sword-pierced		21
B. Roster of residents with description		22-30
1. Assyria		22-23
a. A circle of graves around it		22a
b. All sword-pierced		22b
c. Located in the extremities of the Pit		23aα

The highly unusual character of this unit is perhaps in part the consequence of its genre. Verse 18 directs the prophet to "lament" *(nāhâ),* a term used several times in the OT, but this passage may well be the only extensive example of this category, and it is quite uncertain if the term intends to identify an actual genre. The designation *nehî* (from the Hebrew root in v. 18) is used in Jer 9:9, 19 *(RSV* 10, 20) as parallel to dirge *(qînâ)* and undoubtedly designates some closely related type of poem. If Jer 9:18 *(RSV* 19) is indeed a brief *nehî* or part thereof, the similarity to a dirge is impressive, extending even to the beginning exclamation "How!" But in Jer 9:18 *(RSV* 19) and here in Ezek 32:19-32 the meter is not the normal 3:2 of the dirge. The Jeremiah passage is so brief as to be metrically uncertain, but here in Ezekiel four-beat stichoi predominate.

While it is impossible to describe a genre on the basis of a single example, Ezek 32:19-32 does enable us to notice how this particular grief poem differs from the standard dirge. As Zimmerli points out *(Ezekiel 2,* 170-71), there is here no stress on the contrast between the glory that once was and the misery that now is. Instead, virtually the entire unit concentrates on the portrayal of the current misery, using the otherwise known motif of a journey to the underworld. This motif is utilized in genuine dirges in Isa 14:4b-11 and 12-21, and was just noticed in the preceding chapter here in Ezekiel, i.e., 31:15-18, as well as in 26:20. It is the surveying of the scene in Sheol that provides the organization of nearly the whole passage. Assyria, Elam, and Meshech-Tubal are introduced at the beginning of vv. 22, 24, and 26 as those older, now decreased powers to be seen when one glances around the nether regions. The case of v. 25 is difficult, for although it is obviously not the continuation of the description of Elam, no new power is named to explain the identity of the "her" whose bed is pictured. Surely some kind of textual corruption has taken place. In v. 27 the four preceding countries are contrasted with primeval heroes, possibly the Nephilim of Gen 6:4, if the text is revocalized. With v. 28 the switch to the second person connects effectively with the mocking rhetorical question of the introduction in v. 19 (vv. 20-21 remain obscure), functioning as what seems to be a conclusion. Perhaps indeed an early version of this unit did conclude here, as many commentators think. However, in the present text the number of nations occupying the lower regions is expanded, albeit in verses whose style and vocabulary are subtly but distinctively different (see again Boadt, 150-52). Edom appears in v. 29 and all the chiefs of the North and every Sidonian in v. 30. The addition of these three names brings the total to seven, and that seems to have been the purpose of the expansion. While the first part of v. 31 could serve as a summary conclusion, explicitly naming Pharaoh for the first time, one is startled to encounter the PROPHETIC UTTERANCE FORMULA at the end of v. 31. There has been no hint anywhere above that the composition was presented as divine speech. Even at the beginning no direction to prophesy appears, nor any messenger formula. Only in the textually suspect beginning of v. 32 does Yahweh speak, and at that verse's end there appears accordingly another somewhat more to be expected prophetic utterance formula. Thus it seems that in the final stage of its development the text was accommodated more to the pattern of the units preceding it, especially the dirges.

When compared with the other dirges, 32:17-32 comes across as quite restrained. The initial rhetorical question may be a stinging negation of hymnic boasting of the type found in Isa 44:7 (Zimmerli, *Ezekiel 2,* 172), but overall the text has little of the biting, scornful rejection of royal pride heard in Isaiah 14, and the surfeit of repetition of stock phrases gives it a distinctly pedestrian quality. Behind the fondness for "uncircumcised" as a category, there may lie a concept of those excluded from the family grave (Lods, 271-83), and behind the term "sword-pierced" may lie a legal usage designating not those slain in battle, but those murdered or executed (Eissfeldt, 73-81). In any case the overwhelming repetition of these terms turns the current text into a largely mechanical exercise rather than a sarcastic denunciation.

Setting and Intention

It is doubtful that the text ever intended to be a scornful blast of the sort in Isaiah 14. While the idea of a dishonorable burial could be used in sarcastic fury, here it appears more as a matter of sober classification. The mythological allusions that obviously lie beneath the surface here in the whole idea of a visit to the underworld and in the memory of primeval heroes, have been totally demythologized. The allusion to the vocabulary of the Tammuz myth in the word for "beauty" in v. 19 is more of a scholarly pun than anything else, and the entire focus on the idea of the assignment to the appropriate place reflects priestly precision. Instead of the horror of maggots and worms as in Isa 14:11, we detect here a technical "expulsion to the spheres of uncleanness and unrest" (Zimmerli, *Ezekiel 2*, 174). Yahweh's greater power, which is affirmed in v. 32, faces no real threat. The passage is dominated not by a confrontational mood but by the mood of the learned survey—in a word, by a wisdom perspective. As seen several times in prophecies against foreign nations, this attitude of informed observation and classification is easily detectable, especially in the elements of detailed elaboration. Particularly the idea of the frustration of all human power by the grave is a familiar thought in the perspective of those who were traditionally alert to the limits which restrict human endeavor (see Psalm 49). Zimmerli is correct when he observes that this text is no "general observation about the transitoriness of all things" (ibid., 178), but it does employ as a different kind of powerful word a learned survey of past political powers from a Babylonian point of view (vv. 22-26), expanded by a few from a Palestinian perspective (vv. 29-30), to negate any even potential resistance to God's plan by methodically and even pedantically assigning Egypt her place as one more entry in the archives, one might even say one more card in the file. That such a mood could dominate a text from the time immediately after the fall of Jerusalem is an amazing contrast to what we shall encounter in 33:21f., but it nevertheless allows us to observe some of the variety of functioning which the prophet perceived to be inherent in his calling.

Bibliography

L. Boadt, *Ezekiel's Oracles Against Egypt* (BibOr 37; Rome: Pontifical Biblical Institute, 1980) 150-68; O. Eissfeldt, "Schwerterschlagene bei Hesekiel," in *Studies in Old Testament Prophecy* (*Fest.* T. H. Robinson; ed. H. H. Rowley; Edinburgh: T. & T. Clark, 1950) 73-81; H. Jahnow, *Das hebräische Leichenlied im Rahmen der Völkerdichtung* (BZAW 36; Giessen: Töpelmann, 1923) 231-39; A. Lods, "La 'mort des incirconcis,'" *Comptes rendus des séances de l'Academie des inscriptions et belles-lettres* (Paris: 1943) 271-83.

Chapter 4

The Individual Units of Chapters 33–48:
The Message of Consolation

THE MESSAGE OF HOPE, 33:1–39:29

Structure and Genre

As in the case of chs. 1–24 and 25–32 we have here a LITERARY COLLECTION of material based on grounds of both content and chronology. While major emphasis must be placed on analysis of individual units, some things need to be said first for two reasons: (1) it is possible to detect a kind of ordering—even though minimal—which has given a shape to the collection as a whole; and (2) some summary observations can be helpful in providing a perspective for discerning the individuality of the units themselves.

Orderly progress within this editorial grouping is quite clear at the beginning and end but virtually absent elsewhere. Chapter 33 deliberately aims at serving as a transition from the message of doom to that of hope. The connection of 33:21-22 to the end of ch. 24 is only one aspect of that arrangement, the role of 33:1-20 as articulating the beginning of a new phase in the prophet's ministry being equally significant in this regard. While little if any convincing argument can be advanced for the overall arrangement of the various units gathered within 33:23–36:15, the units that follow do give the distinct impression of belonging in some sort of climactic position at or near the end of any grouping of Ezekiel's message of hope. The ultimate nature of what is promised in sections VI-IX, even though in no way ever labeled as possessing that ultimacy, comes through especially in the drastically miraculous character of what is promised. A new creation with a transformed humanity in 36:16-38, made this time for obedience, is a truly ultimate way of dealing with the question of how past failures can be prevented from destroying Israel's new beginning. Similarly, while life out of death was already the focus in 33:1-20, that metaphor is taken to the ultimate extreme in the promise in 37:1-14 of a new creation that will provide the boldest possible answer to the taunting helplessness posed in the question, "Can these bones live?" Again, no more ultimate message of political restoration is possible than the one in 37:15-28, which envisages the return of both Israel and Judah and their divinely wrought reunification in a new covenant, under a new David, and with a new sanctuary. Finally, the climactic place of chs. 38-39 is recognizable not only in the near apocalyptic character of this final and genuinely ultimate victory of the Lord over his people's enemies, but even more plainly in the way 39:21-29, especially vv. 25-29, is formulated as an overall ending to the entire message of Ezekiel, both judgment and promise. Whether this was at one time the actual ending of an earlier "edition" of the book of Ezekiel, or whether it was only a larger and more comprehensive than usual updating at the conclusion of a major section is impossible to decide and immaterial, for both of those possibilities would require precisely what these verses give us.

One could, of course, go on here quite legitimately and logically to show how chs. 40-48 could be seen as just one further aspect of this ultimacy. But, while such an analysis of the book's structure is fully possible, two points argue against it: (1) the overarching character of the ending in 39:25-29; and (2) the vast difference of chs. 40-48 in both bulk and perspective from what has gone before. Thus, even if only for the functional reason of allowing 40-48 to speak for themselves, it seems best to separate that material from our consideration of the rest of Ezekiel's message of hope.

Some interesting insights flow from an examination of the combination of varying genres in this collection. Even though the vast majority of the material within this section is organized as PROPHETIC PROOF SAYINGS, there is still a striking generic diversity. In some instances genres used for messages of punishment are employed without significant alteration in shape for the proclamation of promises. DISPUTATIONS (33:24-29 and 37:11-14) and the REPORT OF A SYMBOLIC ACT (37:15-28) are evident instances of this unproblematic use of familiar forms for new content. But in some cases a modest though still highly significant alteration in an old pattern serves to enable the proclamation of a totally different message. While announcements can be either of good or of bad news, utilizing with no difficulty in either case the substructure of intervention and results, sometimes large-scale modifications appear. The PROPHECY OF PUNISHMENT in 34:2-10 is made to serve in what follows as the foil—virtually the *reason*—for a PROPHECY OF SALVATION. The reader is referred to the individual cases for the details of these alterations in old patterns occasioned by the new message in its new setting.

In some cases it has been possible to analyze in detail the generic expression of this newness in both content and form. Starting with the treatment of ch. 34, considerable effort is devoted to an analysis of the two major techniques employed for presenting a message of God's gracious new act in a way that integrates this message into previous patterns, thereby enabling it to be comprehended in a fuller way. The first technique, presenting the new as the undoing of the old, enables a deep level of connection to the message of doom, sometimes in what is designated a "criminal centered" pattern, e.g., the shepherds in ch. 34, and other times in a "victim centered" pattern, e.g., the sheep in ch. 34. The second technique detected is that of tracing the continuity in divine action, i.e., the further acting of the same God with attention given particularly to the familiar pattern of his past acts. Here again, two subordinate aspects of this technique are analyzed, the one featuring a positive continuity of pattern of action, e.g., a new act like a known old pattern, only carried out this time better or more effectively, as in a new exodus, new David, new creation, etc. The other subordinate aspect involves a negative continuity in which God changes his mind for whatever reason, e.g., switching from curses to blessings, though still continuing to utilize material from Leviticus 26.

Setting

As is immediately apparent in ch. 33, all of this material of hope comes from the time following 587 B.C. In individual instances attempts can be made to trace how far beyond this date the individual units and their subsequent updating can be argued to take us.

More significantly, an analogy with the setting of chs. 1–24 can be established. In both collections a major dimension of the prophet's concern is the self-assessment of the people. In chs. 1–24 the people display a fantastic and unrealistic confidence, which the prophet endeavors to combat in a variety of ways, meeting with little success. In chs. 33–39 the people give expression (e.g., 33:10; 37:11) to a despair which is eminently realistic, but again the prophet seeks to combat their self-assessment in different ways, again meeting with no significant success (see especially 33:30-33). Once more the genuinely powerful word which creates history seems impotent to create acceptance. Thus the divine assessment of Ezekiel's audience in chs. 2–3 as a "rebellious house" continues to be accurate beyond 587 B.C., even though in a drastically changed situation, which might have been assumed to have brought the prophet's vindication as a true speaker of Yahweh's word. Alas, the closest he comes to vindication is appreciation and admiration! The only way even a future effectiveness of Yahweh's word can be pictured is in terms of a fantastically overpowering grace which transforms and overwhelms not only the political and geographical obstacles to its fulfillment, but even the greatest obstacle of all, the rebellious hearts of the people.

While specific examples of the updating of promises in the light of subsequent situations are best examined in the treatment of individual units, one basic aspect must at least be touched upon here. As indicated, some structural evidence suggests the presence of a large-scale organization in chs. 33–39. But within certain individual pericopes (see 34:30-31 and 37:24-28) a kind of pooling of motifs occurs which suggests an editorial activity aimed at the integration of various aspects of the message of hope. For example, the new covenant motif is introduced at the end of ch. 34, and the new temple theme at the end of ch. 37. Such a pooling of motifs, aimed at filling out one specific promise in the light of others, was most likely a literary activity and never part of an oral proclamation. The mental process it reflects is that of a learned seeking for comprehensive integration. It may be compared to the supplementing of the message of judgment in chs. 8–11, 16, and 20 with a message of hope, thereby enabling each of these large units to serve as a sample of the entire message of Ezekiel. Such an editorial activity reveals a change in setting from a concern for simply enabling the message to be heard by an unwilling audience to a concern for enabling a willing audience to integrate apparently disparate aspects of an overall message. Thus the use of this material within some sort of liturgical setting seems likely. Moreover, this concern for overall unity and integration is a learned one seeking to detect and transmit the framework for understanding. It is a concern which continues the wisdom heritage we have noticed in certain other organizing activities, e.g., chs. 25–32.

Intention

In line with what has been observed immediately above, the activity of collecting and especially arranging a collection in order has an aim which goes far beyond that reflected within the individual units. Ordering units according to a discovered pattern which has both historical, especially chronological, and theological aspects results in a tracing of the pattern of God's ways. Further, repeated use of specific techniques according to which one may recognize the inherent logic of not just some units, but all units, results in an actual grasping of God's ways. Just as in chs. 1–24 the idea of a doxology of judgment enabled the ongoing readers of this dreadful material to use it in a way that led to the liturgical response—whether vocalized or only mental—"Amen, it had to be that way," so in chs. 33–39 the grasping of the inherent logic uniting both judgment and promise leads to the parallel response, "Amen, may it be this way."

A METAPHOR: THE SENTINEL'S MESSAGE AND LIFE IN THE MIDST OF DEATH, 33:1-20

Structure and Genre

I. Prophetic word formula	1
II. Preliminaries	2aαβγ
A. Address as son of man	2aα
B. Direction to speak	2aβγ
III. Legal metaphor of a sentinel	2aδb-6
A. The background of the case: a sentinel appointed in wartime	2aδb
1. First premise: war brought (first person divine speech)	2aδ
2. Second premise: a citizen selected	2bα
3. Third premise: a sentinel appointed	2bβ
B. The case itself: the sentinel issues a warning	3
1. Perception of danger	3a
2. Response in action	3b
C. First subcase	4-5

The location of a PROPHETIC WORD FORMULA in v. 1 and the date of a new episode in v. 21 reveal that vv. 1-20 are to be seen as a single, complex unit. The use of direct address ("son of man") in vv. 2, 7, 10, and 12 indicates the subordinate sections, and the place of these smaller sections within the larger unit is indicated in turn by both content and style. Two of the four subunits function in a preparatory way, III providing the background of imagery for the commissioning of a prophet in IV, and V.A to V.D conversely providing the basis of an answer to despair, which is then supplemented in the form of a legal DISPUTATION (see Graffy, especially 72-78). In V.E to V.G the pattern of the legal disputation is especially evident in the way not one but two quotations from the people serve as foils for Yahweh's counterarguments (V.B taken up in V.D, and V.E and V.F taken up in V.G). This careful logical development serves to underline the prominence of the didactic, legal mood, in spite of which the life-and-death character of the content breaks through this apparently detached style in certain key spots. Such breakthroughs occur in v. 2a and even more powerfully in v. 6b, where the divine "I" departs from the otherwise casuistic pattern of case and subcases in order to make it evident that the verdict expressed is nothing less than a personal confrontation in condemnation. This dramatic formulation, still with the object in the metaphorical third person ("the sentinel's head," i.e., in the BLOOD RESTRICTION FORMULA) is transformed in the actual commissioning in IV to direct address ("your head"). Similarly the mood of legal argument about two cases in V.E is contrasted to affective elements in the framework around it, where V.B to V.D present the people's own despair in terms which are biting ("we are rotting away," see 4:17; 24:23; Lev 26:39; and the mood of the Deuteronomistic history of 562 B.C. in Deut 4:25-31, especially v. 26) and yet also plaintive ("how then can we live?"). But this mood shift is most noticeable of all in the divine oath in v. 11, which avows—in spite of all appearances—the priority of God's gracious love for all his people and his desire for repentance and life even now. This divine insistence climaxes in the passionate shifting of responsibility to the people in the hortatory cry, "Why will you die, O house of Israel?" Following the again didactically legal exposition of the two cases in vv. 12-16, this breakthrough of mood finds further expression in the concluding part of the framework around V.E. There once again the third person of the cases ("he shall die" in v. 18 and "he shall live" in v. 19) is switched to the momentary but climactic confrontation—open to either death or life—in the second person ("I will judge each of you").

Ezekiel's fondness for such utilization of legal language for a hortatory purpose has been noted (see especially chs. 14 and 18), and is usually designated sermonic or parenetic (Eichrodt, 445 and 451), but it is clearly reflective of the prophet's heritage in priestly law. It is also clear that no subsection of this unit ever existed separately. Zimmerli (*Ezekiel 2*, 184) is correct that vv. 7-9 are the one subsection for which original independence could conceivably be suggested, but that is true only on the level of speculation about some unit employing the metaphor of the sentinel. As it is, vv. 7-10 are firmly tied, as pointed out above, to vv. 2-6—especially the verdict in v. 6b—and to vv. 10-20, this time especially in the verdict in v. 9a as picked up in v. 14a. Thus the absence of the sentinel metaphor in vv. 10-20 is no indication of the start of an originally separate unit, but rather the picking up and elaboration of the theme of divine intervention, albeit by material whose setting lay within a different heritage.

Setting and Intention

The metaphor of a sentinel was already borrowed from city and military life by earlier prophets seeking to describe aspects of their prophetic office. Jeremiah 6:17 and Hab 2:1 are cases in point, but Ezekiel's use is fuller and more detailed. True to the implications of the metaphor, he awkwardly presents Yahweh as both the source of the danger (v. 2, "if I bring") and the source of the protection (v. 7, "I have made you"). But it is the blending together of the metaphor of the sentinel with priestly legal casuistry that is truly unique to and characteristic of Ezekiel, and it is primarily this legal aspect that needs exploration.

The legal heritage of much of the material in the unit has already been pointed out, but it is important to add that the exilic situation does not result in any speculation or categorizing about which parts or aspects of the law are still possible to keep. Instead the highest possible measure of continuity in the basis of peoplehood is both assumed and affirmed. Even though in ch. 18's lengthier treatment of this same issue a command about not eating on the mountains can still be employed at the head of a list, even for people living in a land where mountains no longer exist, here in ch. 33 we have the chance to see which commands the prophet selects as he reduces the list. Interestingly, he chooses two items of geographically universal relevance, restoring pledges and returning what has been stolen. The entire surrounding framework makes it plain that this does not constitute a discarding of ritual for ethics or any demotion of the role of apostasy as decisively destructive of peoplehood. Instead the most everyday forms of social injustice are simply seen as indicative of the underlying issues of allegiance and loyalty. When the law is seen as useless, or perhaps even as the object of contempt, being only a hindrance to personal profit, then solidarity in peoplehood is decisively denied in action, even if not in word or ritual (Eichrodt, 449). Just as the bloody city was indicted by utilizing a list of commandments in 22:1-16 in a way that climaxed in a rebuke of "dishonest gain" (22:13), so here, as constantly in Yahweh's commandments, the divine taking possession of his people is expressed in a way that centers on the relation between members of that community as the measure of their relation to their God.

When we turn to the broad questions about the redactional setting of this unit, its placement at the beginning of the consolation material in chs. 33–48 proves to be of decisive significance. The sentinel metaphor in vv. 1-9 is firmly connected to the concern about life and death in vv. 10-20. The legal casuistry lays heavy stress on the way the functioning of the sentinel, though directed at the community as a whole, must be traced into the area of individual response in order to determine its effectiveness. Strangely, not much attention has been directed to pointing out the essentially ridiculous character of that line of development. Would one need to worry about the ignoring of the sentinel's trumpet as a serious problem? There is a need for laws dealing with those who falsely and viciously, as a cruel prank, shout "Fire" in a crowded public building. There is little need for a legal treatment of the fate of those who choose in folly to ignore an alarm and remain in a burning building. Their fate is automatic and by definition prior and thus moot. One would not need at all to say their death is their own stubborn fault, unless one wished to shift the focus to the responsibility of the alarm-giver. But even here the prominence of the motif of people refusing to take warning shows how the text deliberately stresses the perverse and the unlikely. Would anyone ever be so foolish and stubborn as to ignore such an alarm? Our electronic society with its frequent malfunctions perhaps makes us miss the point. Trumpet-blowing by mistake is not anywhere hinted at in the text. Those who reject this warning are incredibly and incomprehensibly perverse and stubborn! But it is with just such people that the prophet is commissioned to work. Thus at some time soon after Jerusalem's fall this new situation provides the stimulus for expressing a kind of new call to the prophet.

Although the formulation seems to center on the prophet's responsibility to stay clear of guilt by not being delinquent in his duty (vv. 6 and 9), the call's continuation by spelling out his people's self-assessment in v. 10, in which they show themselves to be already in death, has an aim that goes far beyond the prophet's personal responsibility. The call to this prophet is indeed a matter of life and death, but not of the avoidance of a potentially threatening death. That time is now past. Now this prophet is appointed to call the dead to life! Because OT usage defined death as a realm which included what we label as only threats to life, e.g., sickness and imprisonment (C. Barth), it is necessary to express the matter just this forcefully. "Why will you die?" in v. 11, borrowed from 18:31, can now be seen for exactly what it is, the reuse in a changed situation of older material that now has a changed relevance. Whether or not ch. 18 is pre-587 B.C. is not the issue and, as was said in discussing that chapter, is nearly impossible to decide. But the significance of ch. 18 is—in the present shape of the book—redactionally determined. Placed within chs. 1–24, it takes on a coloring reflective of that placement, and now the reuse of that material from ch. 18 in ch. 33 reflects important changes in how it is to be understood. Amazingly, the prophet's people are now no less his responsibility than before. The broader understanding of death proclaimed earlier by the prophet was neither a prediction nor a proleptic declaration; it was simply an accurate, although rejected, assessment. Now the change in situation shows itself almost exclusively in the way the prophetic assessment is indeed accepted by his audience. But rather than enabling an "I told you so" approach, now this recognition of being in death requires a proclamation of how life can come out of death. Here the old legal categories are made to speak anew. The same arguments as in ch. 18 can just be repeated in condensed form, for they speak eloquently to this new situation. (Behind vv. 13-16 lie 18:21-22 and 24, although the order is reversed in ch. 33 and greater attention is devoted to the repentance of the wicked in 33:14-16 than to the backsliding righteous in 33:13. Possibly this shift in emphasis aims to stress the invitation to repent. See Zimmerli, *Ezekiel 2,* 188.) Thus any aspect of a backward-looking "I told you so" is overwhelmed by the preponderance of a forward-looking "and I tell you so again." In fact, the very metaphor of the sentinel, although rooted in the post-587 B.C. setting of this chapter, could easily be, and was, transferred to (→) 3:17-21 as reflecting a calling and responsibility characteristic of Ezekiel's entire ministry. In both places, though, its significance is not exhausted by the dimension of prophetic responsibility. That is a true and important aspect of the prophetic office, but from its setting in ch. 33 it is to be seen not just as a summons to a ministry to the perversely stubborn who will not hear. Its link to vv. 10-20 with their stress on the divine intent shown in "I have no pleasure in the death of the wicked" and "Why will you die?" (v. 11) adds a major new aspect to the understanding of the prophetic office. It has become even clearer now after 587 B.C. that the sentinel's job is nothing less than a sharing in divine frustration. Who would not heed the sentinel's trumpet? Such self-destructive folly calls forth not legal regulation; that would be like yelling "I told you so" to piles of burnt corpses. Such stubborn, self-destructive folly calls forth any possible way, including ridiculously unnecessary legal specifications, to reveal the central point of the divine tragedy of the God who loved and lost, but in his own transcendently stubborn grace refuses to allow his lost loved one to choose death without reaching out through his seeking representative.

Bibliography

See Bibliography to 33:23-33.

THE REPORT OF THE ARRIVAL OF A REFUGEE AND THE END OF EZEKIEL'S DUMBNESS, 33:21-22

Structure and Genre

I. Date	21a
II. Report of a refugee's arrival	21b
A. His arrival	21bα
B. His news	21bβ
III. Report of the removal of the prophet's dumbness	22

A. Report of previous dumbness   22aαβ
  1. Hand of Yahweh revelatory formula (pluperfect)   22aα
  2. Time specification: previous evening   22aβ
B. Report of the opening of the prophet's mouth   22aγδ
  1. Report of opening   22aγ
  2. Time specification: before morning   22aδ
C. Summary of results   22b
  1. Positive: my mouth was opened   22bα
  2. Negative: I was no longer dumb   22bβ

The lack of any prophetic word formula makes this unit unique in the book. It is simply a REPORT. Zimmerli points out accurately that the refugee's word takes the place of a divine word, and that the opening of the prophet's mouth is a divine action having sign value (*Ezekiel 2*, 191). The report of the prophet's dumbness is accomplished by the use of the HAND OF YAHWEH REVELATORY FORMULA, which elsewhere appears only at the start of the four major visions.

Setting and Intention

As noted above, these verses constitute the actual point of connection with the prophet's earlier period of activity in chs. 1–24, which concluded in 24:25-27 with the prediction of a refugee's arrival and the opening of Ezekiel's mouth. The fulfillment of both parts of that prediction is reported here in a clear redactional seam, which has only secondarily been somewhat obscured by the insertion of the prophecies against foreign nations in chs. 25–32, and the prefixing of 33:1-20 to this text as a characterization of Ezekiel's ministry in this new phase. As observed with regard to 3:25-27, the phenomenon of the prophet's dumbness came then to be viewed as a characteristic of the prophet's entire ministry, and was thus appended to the account of his call and commissioning. Thus, out of this report of a less than twelve-hour dumbness, lasting only from the onset of revelatory ecstasy in the previous evening until sometime before the morning arrival of the refugee, and out of the fourfold appearance of the hand of Yahweh revelatory formula in 1:3, 8:1, 37:1, and 40:1, there arose a general view of the nature of Ezekiel's revelatory experience. The appearance of a somewhat differently worded promise in 29:21 of an ultimate opening of the prophet's mouth and the reference in 16:63 to speechlessness as a result of shame lead Zimmerli (ibid., 193-94) to see this report of Jerusalem's fall as the vindication of Ezekiel's earlier preaching of doom that enabled him to open his mouth in a new proclamation.

Regardless of whether or not one can be so confident of the link between ashamed silence and the proof value of the refugee's words, something approximating this line of thought appears to have been intended by the arranging of the book of Ezekiel around this single, crucial pairing of prediction and fulfillment. The end to "the period of contested waiting" (Zimmerli, *Ezekiel 2*, 194) implied in 12:21-25 and 12:26-28 serves as the vindication of the prophet's whole message of Yahweh's sovereignty in history, and therefore at the same time as the authorization of a new period of prophetic activity, this time already authenticated in advance. Thus the very news of defeat becomes the empowering word of vindication.

THE SHAPE OF PIETY IN PALESTINE AND IN EXILE, 33:23-33

Structure

Two essentially separate units, III and IV, have been editorially combined by grouping them under one prophetic word formula. Both the completeness of the content in each and the new beginning in what follows—renewed address as son of man in v. 30a and a new prophetic word formula in 34:1—demonstrate the separateness of the two units. Their only connection seems to be that they both illuminate something about the post-587 B.C. religiosity of the two segments of the current Israel, the survivors in Palestine and Ezekiel's fellow exiles. In each case it is essentially a resistance to Yahweh's word which is described, but one which presents itself under the guise of a certain kind of piety.

Genre

The unit in 33:23-29 begins as a rather typical DISPUTATION, presenting both a citation of what the addressees have been saying and a countering word from Yahweh. Closer inspection reveals two important departures from the typical. In the first place, the countering word appears in two relatively separate sections, each introduced with the MESSENGER FORMULA, vv. 25-26 serving as an accusation and implicitly a reason for punishment, vv. 27-28 serving as an announcement of the punishment to come. Of these two the second is structured throughout as the customary divine speech, but the first lacks any specification of a speaker and could quite well be heard as the prophet's own word. In the second place, the presence of the RECOGNITION FORMULA in v. 29 makes it apparent that the entire unit is now to be heard as a PROPHETIC PROOF SAYING, but this formula is in turn elaborated by a statement which offers in inverted order a capsule of both announcement and reason.

Most of this first unit is also typical in formulation, as well as structure, but again with some differences. The use of the oath formula to introduce the Lord's passionate (Zimmerli, *Ezekiel 2*, 199) rejection of the claims of the survivors and the trio of instrumentalities (sword, wild beasts, and pestilence) in vv. 27-28 remind

one of material in chs. 4–24, especially 14:14-20. The employing of commandment lists as the background against which selected violations are denounced in
vv. 25-26 again reminds one of material in ch. 18 (see also 33:10-20) and 22:1-16.
This time, however, the commandments presupposed by the list of violations are
not quite so closely related to the Holiness Code legislation as before. In the first
subseries of three, eating flesh "with the blood" is forbidden in Lev 19:26, but the
formulation "upon the blood" here is unusual and is often emended to "upon the
mountains" to arrive at the indictment known from Ezek. 18:6. The term for "idols"
is Ezekiel's familiar favorite, and the shedding of blood is prominent in 22:1-16
and 24:1-14. But in the second subseries of three, while abomination and adultery
are quite familiar in H and Ezekiel, depending upon the sword is not dealt with in
any known commandment, and Zimmerli (ibid., 199) suggests that it directly
reflects the lawlessness of post-587 B.C. Judah. Similarly, the list in v. 27 of the
places where judgment will reach these survivors seems less a matter of any traditional formulation than a reflection of the actual situation of the post-587 B.C. times
(ruins, open country, strongholds, and caves).

The second unit is highly unusual from a form-critical perspective in that it
is a word directed solely to the prophet and involves no indication of any proclamation of any sort. The content of Yahweh's word to Ezekiel is so thoroughly
personal that the absence of the direction to proclaim it is not surprising, but what
is initially surprising is the way the prophet is informed of things he would surely
know. This fact, plus a comparison with Jeremiah's confessions, leads Zimmerli to
an insightful analysis (ibid., 200). Whereas in Jeremiah's confessions the prophet
himself formulates his complaints in the language and shape of the complaint
psalms, and then receives a divine response, here even the prophet's own formulation of his complaints is taken over by the Lord. One is reminded of 12:9, where
even the people's reaction to Ezekiel's symbolic action appears only in divine
speech. Thus vv. 30-32 here could be classified as the indirect presentation of the
prophet's lament, with v. 33 being the essential divine response.

Setting

Both units reflect an intimate knowledge of the post-587 B.C. circumstances, vv.
23-29, especially the quotation in vv. 24, suggesting that contacts between Judah
and the exiles were maintained more extensively than might have been suspected.
Still, as has often been pointed out in the light of World War II and subsequent
refugee experiences, exiles after any loss of a homeland strive desperately and with
amazing effectiveness in spite of barriers to keep in touch with the "old country."

The confident, even cocky (Bertholet, 117), mood of the survivors is extremely impressive. We "marvel at the will to rebuild and the strength to overcome
catastrophes" (Zimmerli, *Ezekiel 2,* 199) here and recall 11:15 and the slightly earlier mood of assurance in Jerusalem after the 597 B.C. deportation. In each case,
having been spared is not only seized upon as an indication of divine grace, but is
made the basis for a presumptuous claim. One easily detects the effort on the part
of those who have recently taken the property of others, dead or departed, to provide
divine justification for their new situation. The reference to Abraham in v. 24 shows
how the election traditions continued to be treasured and even manipulated. The
way in which at a slightly later date Abraham is referred to in Isa 41:8 and espe-

cially 51:2, with its contrast of one and "making many," tends to confirm this traditio-historical resurgence. But rather than the life-setting of "exegetical" argumentation, it appears that the confidence of the post-587 B.C. Judeans shows more in the violence Ezekiel refers to and which Jeremiah 41 details, and eventually in the apparent additional deportation by the Babylonians mentioned in Jer 52:30. In any case, the function of Ezekiel's words is to offer a far different interpretation of the patriarchal heritage and "the will of God" than the one quoted here, which Eichrodt proposed was aimed "to make the heavy labor of reconstruction more attractive" (461).

Although the second unit does not specifically indicate its chronological setting as being after 587 B.C., this is nonetheless highly likely in view of the lofty reputation Ezekiel now enjoys. The way people come eagerly, in a way relaying to each other the prophetic call to attention, implies that the validation of Ezekiel's earlier preaching had now been experienced. The picture of snatches of conversation held in the few shady spots available in that hot and sun-drenched climate is a charming vignette. But its charm is immediately soured, not just by the fact that the audiences still heard but did not heed, but by the reason given, "their heart is set on their gain" (v. 31). Such seeking for "gain" is understandable in 22:12-13 as reflecting the "business as usual" attitude which characterized a predestruction Jerusalem, but how could the profit motive be a significant factor in exile? Alas, Michael Coogan's interpretation of the cuneiform banking records of the firm of Murashu and Sons (Coogan, 6-12) offers only too likely an answer. Some of the Judean exiles did manage to prosper financially in Babylon. Their names appear as officers of the banking firm. But, as Coogan points out, it is not just any Judean names that appear. There is a concentration of those particular names which sound similar to Babylonian names, thus raising the possibility that the specific names were adopted by their bearers in that hostile, pagan environment in an effort to "pass" without their religious-national heritage being recognized. It is only to be assumed that such assimilation took place, but this illumination of the precise motive singled out here by Ezekiel is unexpected and uncomfortable corroboration.

Intention

Both units stress forcefully that God remains actively on the scene beyond the judgment already experienced. They also agree that the folly-laden attempts to build a bridge from the previous security-offering traditions of their people's election to their current situation by self-assurance and self-justifying religiosity stand under divine scrutiny. When the citizens of Judah were deprived of their possession at the hands of the Babylonians, the prophet saw God's aim as driving the exiles to return to the basis of their peoplehood and the hope of a new exodus and a new entry into the land. Instead, from the same evidence the postfall survivors of Judah deduced their own special rights in an attempt piously to maintain the continuity of God's promises to the patriarchs. Ezekiel, however, insists on the cancellation of those promises and offers no such directly continuous hope. Further, he deduces from the disobedience of the covenant law among his addressees only further evidence of their attempt to manipulate their peoplehood in disregard of allegiance. In the face of such pseudo-piety Yahweh remains active in judgment, even among those pitiful bands of survivors, whose postwar pursuit of further violence makes our age think of portrayals of the subhuman bloodiness of competition for the means of survival after a nuclear war.

While the exiles attempted to maintain their peoplehood in the subtler form of a revival of interest in prophetic proclamation, coming together as the people of God (note the occurrence of "my people" in v. 31), this too does not escape divine examination. The piety expressed here is characterized by an eagerness for, and delight in, the word from God. But, as in the case of the first unit, the text probes for the underlying intention and asks about how that intention finds expression in obedience to the Lord's will. As in the first unit, the piety is revealed to be a self-serving one that finds it easy to offer the aesthetic response of artistic appreciation, but inconvenient to offer the more revealing response of obedience. To encounter acclamation and recognition after all the previous rejection of his word must have been a heady matter for the prophet. But the account returns powerfully to thoughts expressed in his first call and reaffirmed in the account of his "second call" earlier in this chapter. That the prophetic word should be heard but go unheeded is, tragically, nothing new. But because of that word's inherent power its fulfillment will come, "whether they hear or refuse to hear" (2:5; 3:11; see also 3:27; 33:5, 31), and then there will be a true and inescapable understanding of what the prophetic office is all about. Until then this passage reveals with a special poignancy how the word of God is both powerful and yet vulnerable. It is vulnerable to many things, most obviously to being ignored (v. 5), but most of all it is vulnerable to discussion, and even appreciation (v. 32).

Bibliography

C. Barth, *Die Errettung vom Tode in den individuellen Klage- und Dankliedern des Alten Testaments* (Zollikon: Evangelischer Verlag, 1947); W. H. Brownlee, "Ezekiel's Parable of the Watchman and the Editing of Ezekiel," *VT* 28 (1978) 392-408; M. Coogan, "Life in the Diaspora: Jews at Nippur in the Fifth Century B.C.," *BA* 37/1 (March 1974) 6-12; W. Eichrodt, "Das prophetische Wächteramt," in *Tradition und Situation* (*Fest.* A. Weiser; ed. E. Würthwein and O. Kaiser; Göttingen: Vandenhoeck & Ruprecht, 1963) 31-41; A. Graffy, *A Prophet Confronts His People* (AnBib 104; Rome: Biblical Institute Press, 1984) 72-82.

A METAPHOR: THE SHEPHERDS OF YAHWEH'S FLOCK, 34:1-31

Text

In v. 16 one must emend *'ašmîd* ("I will destroy") to *'ešmōr* ("I will watch over").

Structure and Genre

I. Prophetic word formula	1
II. Preliminaries	2abαβγ
A. Address as son of man	2aα
B. Direction to prophesy against shepherds (repeated)	2aβbα

The organization of the chapter is in some respects reasonably simple, but an expansive wordiness has led to some complexities. The PROPHETIC WORD FORMULAS in 34:1 and 35:1 and commonality of content make it clear that the whole of ch. 34 is to be seen as a single unit, essentially a PROPHECY OF SALVATION, and for the most part expressed in the metaphor of the care of shepherds for their sheep. (The analysis of the chapter into two parallel texts, one regarding the word "flock" as masculine and the other treating it as feminine, by Berend Willmes, is an unconvincing attempt to solve a form-critical problem by a literary-critical approach based on an extremely small amount of evidence.) The use of editorial headings in vv. 2bβ and 17aα and of messenger formulas in vv. 2bγ, 11a, 17aβ, and 20aβ indicates that subunits are to be recognized in vv. 2-10, 11-16, and 17-31. However, the presence of a variety of formulas in vv. 7-10 reveals that the end of this first subunit has been complicated, and the presence of the conclusion formula for divine speech in v. 24b together with the abandoning of the shepherd metaphor in vv. 25-30 indicates that an additional subdivision appears in vv. 25-31. Finally, the abundance of formulas employed in vv. 30-31 reveals the complication of the final ending.

The overall pattern of the first subunit, vv. 2-10, as a PROPHECY OF PUNISHMENT is fairly clear, especially at the beginning and end, where vv. 2-6 present the reason in the form of a WOE ORACLE (see 13:3-9a and 18-19), and v. 10 the announcement of punishment. Complications resulting from expansive wordiness appear in the review of the reason in v. 8 after the transition in v. 7 which would normally lead to the announcement. Because of this backtracking in v. 8, a new transition appears in v. 9. Whether this complicating verbosity is editorial, from the hand of the prophet or later, or simply a consequence of the wordiness of style which characterizes the whole unit is difficult to determine, although the second possibility seems more likely.

The second subunit is not independent of the first (against Brownlee), for it uses the bad shepherds of vv. 2-10 as a foil for its promise of Yahweh as a good shepherd, even listing in v. 16 the duties proper to the office which Yahweh will carry out in nearly reverse order to the list in v. 4 of the same duties neglected by the bad shepherds. Further, the introduction in v. 10b of a justice-establishing dimension in the shepherd's role, requiring limiting the aggressiveness of the stronger sheep, is a deliberate anticipation of the judging to come in vv. 17-20 and 22. Thus v. 16 has been crafted to serve as a transition, looking both backward and forward.

The third subunit in vv. 17-31 prepares for the announcement of the first promise in vv. 20b-24 by prefixing a reason in vv. 17b-19, after the analogy of a pattern of a PROPHECY OF PUNISHMENT. Further, the focus of shepherding is here shifted from care of the flock as a whole in the first two subunits to the shepherd's judging (or mediatorial arbitration, which is part of what the root involves) between the stronger and the weaker sheep. But here a surprise is introduced with the unanticipated promise of a Davidic shepherd in vv. 23-24. This last item breaks down to some extent the metaphor of Yahweh as shepherd, but it does reflect a traditio-historical logic to be discussed later. A confusing alternation in the gender of suffixes in v. 23 also makes for textual and literary-critical uncertainty.

The latter half of the third subunit not only introduces a departure from the shepherd metaphor, but its conclusion becomes highly complicated through the blending of formulas. The RECOGNITION FORMULA of v. 27bα is elaborated with a second wordy recognition formula in a way occasionally encountered before (see 28:23b). Here, however, the second recognition formula becomes a fusion of recognition and COVENANT FORMULAS. That introduction of the covenant motif is further expanded in v. 31 by the return to the metaphor of the flock used in a second covenant formula, thereby bonding together both the third subunit and the entire chapter. Once again, whether this elaboration is editorial activity or just a part of the chapter's verbosity of style is hard to decide, although this time the likelihood seems to favor the first alternative.

Setting

We are almost totally uninformed about the sociological context within which an exilic message of hope like Ezekiel 34 would have been presented. In the case of Deutero-Isaiah the prophet's use of material reflecting a heritage of both complaint psalms and hymns raises the possibility of a cultic role within a community lamentation ceremony (von Waldow). Elsewhere in Ezekiel the language of disputation oracles (33:10 and 37:11) makes public or semipublic confrontation in a kind of debate seem reasonable. But here one is left completely to conjecture. Chapter 34 could be envisaged as a response to the despairing complaints within the exilic community about the folly of leaders like Zedekiah and Ishmael, the son of Nethaniah (Jeremiah 41), but that remains purely hypothetical. To keep any sort of solid basis underfoot it is necessary to turn to other aspects of the passage's setting.

Chronologically, the setting of the promise is obviously exilic, holding out hope of returning to the land for the flock now scattered "over all the face of the earth" (v. 6). The only question is whether the indictment of the bad shepherds reflects a pre-587 B.C. situation, thereby requiring an analysis of the chapter into pre- and post-587 B.C. portions. This question, however, poses a false alternative, as the analysis of the logic of an announcement of salvation reveals. When one recalls the standard genre pattern of a prophecy of punishment within which an announcement of punishment is set, there leaps to mind the function of the accusation as providing a reason upon which the appropriateness of the announcement can be based. When one asks what logic prepares the way in a prophecy of salvation for an announcement, a variety of techniques must be noted. One frequently occurring technique is the formulating of the promise by centering on the evil situation over against which the good news is presented. Naturally, this technique could function either by presenting the divine promise as the replacement of past evil by stressing the evil actions of the oppressor (criminal-centered) or by stressing the desperate plight of the oppressed (victim-centered). It is clear that both the criminal-centered and the victim-centered versions of this technique appear in this chapter. A second major means of introducing an announcement of salvation is by centering on the continuity inherent in God's action in the promised good news. Again, this technique naturally subdivides itself into positively and negatively presented continuity. There appear those positive analogies which see God's promised action as doing something one more time like that which he had done before, presumably doing it this time in a greater or more successful way. Then there are those instances of negative continuity in which God is seen as changing his mind from past punishments for whatever motive may be adduced. The introduction of the idea of a new David and of a new exodus provides immediately apparent instances of positive continuity in this chapter.

But, to return to the question which triggered this examination of reasons that undergird announcements of salvation—does an indictment of bad leadership prior to the fall of Jerusalem in 587 B.C. imply a preexilic setting for that strand of Ezekiel's preaching?—the answer should now be clear. Of course it does—as a matter of background! Ezekiel's indictment of the criminal character of the Jerusalem leadership in 34:2-4 presupposes the same situation against which the prophet had spoken frequently in chs. 4–24 before Jerusalem's final fall to the Babylonians. But this indictment in ch. 34 provides the reason for the promise of vv. 11-16 (against Fohrer, 190). This is exactly the point behind the close parallel between vv. 4 and 16. The perverse shepherds of v. 4 who violate every item in their job description are impossibly ridiculous monsters whose actions result in the elimination of their own jobs. Their motivations are not explored; they serve here only as the foil for the good shepherd of v. 16. This foil-centered character of the indictment also explains the way it treats past history as a totality of bad leadership and seems to reflect a "lack of that passion which comes from direct personal involvement," which Zimmerli notices (*Ezekiel 2*, 214). The generalizing, powerful as it is, which surveys how the rich in vv. 18-19 selfishly insist on a self-indulgence which spoils what would be left for the poor, is another example of the same structural technique. It is a passing use of the motif of degenerately subhuman behavior as an indictment, but its major role is again as a foil for the overcoming of all violence in the total security that is promised in vv. 20-31.

Traditio-historically the chapter reflects an extremely rich setting. The shepherd image for rulers can be traced back to Sumerian royal tradition, and both Mesopotamian and Egyptian texts show how the metaphor was applied also to gods. Hebrew psalms and prophets use the same metaphor in both senses as well. The closest links to Ezekiel 34 are found in Jer 23:1-6, raising the question of the precise relationship of the two passages. Both present a combination of indictment and promise using similar vocabulary, even to the point of speaking of David. Further, Jer 23:7-8 also promises a new exodus. Still, there is considerable diversity between the two passages: the verb "attend," which is of fundamental importance in Jer 23:1-4, does not appear in Ezekiel 34; the idea of God himself as the good shepherd is missing in Jer 23:1-6; and most importantly the structural setting is so different. Jeremiah 23:1-4, 5-6, and 7-8 are separate units now connected to the end of a series of prophecies about specific Judean kings by means of a wordplay on the root "righteousness" in the name Zedekiah, while Ezekiel 34 is a much more programmatic exploration of various facets of shepherding in which the word "righteousness" never appears, but instead the word "seek" is featured prominently, in contrast to Jer 23:1-6, where it does not appear. Thus it seems more accurate to see in Ezekiel 34 not literary acquaintance or dependence, but a dipping into the same broad stream of tradition, utilizing the same basic metaphor and naturally thereby much of the same vocabulary, to link past failure to future promise in such a way that there is greater similarity in the presentation of the failure than of the promise. In the light of this, to designate Jer 23:1-8 as "unmistakably the model for Ezekiel 34" (Zimmerli, *Ezekiel 2*, 214 and J. W. Miller, 106) is to put the matter too strongly, unless "model" is meant to refer only to the way old traditions are utilized.

The same process of dipping into a broad stream of tradition to pick up an item or a motif which is then actualized in a specific way is exemplified in the use of David tradition in 34:23-24. The context of shepherd imagery in Ezekiel 34 naturally suggests David's designation as a shepherd in v. 23, in contrast to the branch imagery in Jer 23:5-6, which is occasioned there by the concern for consecutive members of the Davidic house. But in both passages, as well as Hos 3:5 and Jer 30:9-10, the verb "raise up" is employed, demonstrating how even the verb used was traditional. Thus when Ezekiel refers to David as prince *(nāsî')* rather than king, we can see how bold Ezekiel could be in reinterpreting this old tradition in view of his own particular heritage. This subject will be pursued further in the treatment of chs. 44–46.

Yet another example of the reinterpretation of an old tradition occurs in the way v. 13 picks up the vocabulary of the exodus tradition in order to describe God's promised future acts as a new exodus. Even though it fits ill with the shepherd metaphor, the logic of continuity mentioned above as a way of providing a grounding for an announcement of salvation has made the analogy of a new exodus appropriate as a reason for the promised restoration. This is how Israel's God acted in the past, and thus it can serve with some legitimacy as a portrayal of how he will act in the future. But while the logic of continuity explains the presence of this analogy, it is the fixed character—even verbally—of the tradition which determines how it must be expressed. To "bring out," "gather," and "bring in" are the verbs which belong in that order to this tradition. A much larger scope of material is similarly reinterpreted in Deutero-Isaiah, but there the very extent of the material obscures the shape of its essential core. Minor motifs like going out "in haste" are reworked into the portrayal of the new saving act of God (Isa 52:12), while here we see that it is just these three verbs that are the core of the tradition. This observation receives striking confirmation by the occurrence of the same sequence in 20:34f. and again, with the first verb altered to "take," in 36:24 and 37:21. Thus Ezekiel provides us with an example of how good news was formulated as a radical—though verbally bound—witness to God's new act, like his old act only greater.

One more major instance of the utilization of old traditions in this chapter surfaces in the way vv. 25-30 reveal a close connection to Lev 26:4-13. Although more usually noticed in regard to the prophetic use of lists of curses known from treaty texts and elsewhere (Hillers), it is only to be expected that messages of hope would also make use of this highly stereotypical language about blessings. It is obvious that through the centuries oath motivation has primarily concentrated on the sphere of threatening curses, and a case can even be made for seeing some of the promised blessings listed as alternatives to the curses, being in fact simply a negating of certain curses. But in view of the essential need of every human community for fertility and security, the basic right of a list of blessings to a place in such oath motivations should not be disputed. Moreover, that Ezekiel, whose vocabulary and style elsewhere show such intimate connection with Holiness Code material, should in his proclamation of hope as well as judgment demonstrate close ties to the particular sampling of this ancient tradition evidenced in Leviticus 26, is also only to be anticipated. To attempt to trace patterns of literary dependence would be to misunderstand the whole broad range of prophetic use of traditions (against Hossfeld). To see Ezekiel's ministry as almost totally centered in the office of proclaimer of blessings and curses within the Israelite covenant festival (Reventlow) is to narrow the prophetic office excessively by overly exalting one possible, scantily attested aspect of it.

Other brief examples of dipping into streams of tradition will be passed over here with the barest mention, for they appear more prominently elsewhere. Among them are the day of Yahweh motif in the "clouds and thick darkness" of v. 12 (see the discussion of ch. 7); the "covenant of peace" motif in v. 25 (see 16:60; 37:26; and Isa 54:10); the allusion to a new covenant by inclusion of the covenant formula in the recognition formula in vv. 30-31 (see what is said about 36:26); and the theme of a single, united people of God in the "one shepherd" of v. 23 (see the treatment of 37:15-28).

Intention

In any case, out of all this diverse background of traditions there has been created a proclamation of salvation, originally oral and then editorially elaborated, which demonstrates the logic according to which God's representative dares to speak of good news. By centering on the community's leaders as instrumentalities of God's purpose, the continuity in God's purpose is allowed to come forth with special clarity. The repeated use of expressions like "my sheep" makes it plain that shepherds represent care on behalf of the owner. Their failures at this function were due to a presumptuous and careless brutality which displayed no responsibility to the owner, their duty, or the needs of those entrusted to them. God's ownership and purpose, however, are now presented as going beyond the disastrous failure of his representatives and the consequences for his people. He will not allow his purpose to be frustrated permanently.

While other chapters talk the language of life out of death and thereby stress the discontinuity between the present and future of God's people, that discontinuity is rooted in the diagnosis of the situation of the people: "Our transgressions and our sins are upon us, and we waste away because of them; how then can we live?" (33:10). Chapter 34 shifts the focus from the condition of the people to the character of the God of this people. And the divine character portrayed is not just that of an ongoing preference for life, "I have no pleasure in the death of anyone" (18:32); this presentation describes a God whose will for his sheep drives him to undertake personally the tasks he had previously entrusted to others, those of a shepherd. Similarly, God's will for justice in earlier chapters led to the rejection and disavowal of the people of the bloody city for whom their covenantal commitments expressed in laws could only serve as a framework for indictment (22:1-10). Now in ch. 34, while a similar use of the shepherds' job description appears in vv. 1-10, and the idea of justice appears as a threatening prospect, God himself makes a commitment to carry out both the negative and the positive dimensions of judging, thereby fulfilling in himself the obligations of his representatives and bringing about not just the recognition of his sovereignty but also the recognition of the covenant relationship that he has restored (vv. 30-31). As a result of that gracious persistence in his purpose for his people, without any specification of repentance as a prerequisite, or any singling out of a faithful remnant or of righteous individuals within a faithless community, the created world is portrayed as then able to function in accord with its purpose, as the sustaining framework of "peace" (vv. 25-29).

Surprisingly, within all this essentially consistent stress upon God himself as the deliverer and sustainer of his people, there appears in vv. 23-24 the scarcely integrated theme of the new David. He is indeed the care-exercising representative of God established by God himself, but neither before vv. 23-24 nor after does this chapter offer any attempt to indicate how God's own shepherding and that of David could fit together. Once again, though, no simple literary-critical assignment of these verses to another hand seems appropriate (see the discussion in Levenson, 86-91). Instead, one gets the distinct impression that here a tradition has been actualized because it was well known and, in view of David's personal background as a shepherd, exceedingly appropriate. But fascinatingly, as von Rad observed (236), the tradition of the Davidic covenant surfaces only momentarily and cannot continue without passing over into the language of the Sinaitic covenant, in this case by the odd use of one-half of the covenant formula itself, "I, the Lord, will be their God, and my servant David shall be prince among them" (v. 24). This David, though, is not king, but "prince" and even "servant." Thus, delightfully, "my servant David" occurring both in v. 23 and v. 24, while genuinely a title of privilege and intimacy, functions here to describe a task which is indeed in the form of a servant, exercised not in ruling but in feeding.

Bibliography

W. H. Brownlee, "Ezekiel's Poetic Indictment of the Shepherds," *HTR* 51 (1958) 191-203; D. Hillers, *Treaty Curses and the Old Testament Prophets* (BibOr 16; Rome: Pontifical Biblical Institute, 1964); F. Hossfeld, *Untersuchungen zu Komposition und Theologie des Ezechielbuches* (FB 20; Würzburg: Echter Verlag, 1977); J. Levenson, *Theology of the Program of Restoration of Ezekiel 40–48* (HSM 10; Missoula: Scholars Press, 1976); J. W. Miller, *Das Verhältnis Jeremias und Hesekiels sprachlich und theologisch untersucht* (Assen: Van Gorcum, 1955); G. von Rad, *Old Testament Theology* (tr. D. M. G. Stalker; New York: Harper and Row, 1965) II, 236; H. Reventlow, *Wächter über Israel* (BZAW 82; Berlin: Töpelmann, 1962); H. E. von Waldow, *Anlass und Hintergrund der Verkündigung Deuterojesajas* (Diss., Bonn, 1953); B. Willmes, *Die sogenannte Hirtenallegorie Ez 34* (BBET 19; Frankfurt: Lang, 1984).

A TWOFOLD PROPHECY: DEVASTATION FOR MOUNT SEIR BUT RESTORATION FOR THE MOUNTAINS OF ISRAEL, 35:1–36:15

Text

In spite of the many obscurities in this unit, a few emendations can be attempted with some confidence. In 35:6b it seems necessary to read *lĕdām 'āšamtā* ("you are guilty of blood") for *'im-lō' dām śānē'tā* ("surely you have hated blood"). In 35:7 one should probably read *ûmĕšammâ* ("and making it desolate") for *ûšĕmāmâ* ("and a desolation"). Finally, in 35:11b it seems the second *bām* ("in them") is a dittograph and should be changed to *bĕkā* ("in you").

Structure

      4. Announcement of punishment: jealous wrath
         like your hatred   11aδ
      5. Recognition proclaimed   11b-12aα
         a. Recognition as intervention   11b
         b. Recognition formula   12aα
      6. Review of reason   12aβγδb-13
         a. Your claim to the land heard (2 ms)   12aβγδb
         b. Your big words heard (2 mp)   13
   B. A third three-part prophetic proof saying (2 ms
      shifting to 3 mp in v. 15bβ)   14-15
      1. Resumptive messenger formula   14a
      2. Analogy of crime and punishment (serves as
         reason and announcement—intervention only)   14b-15a
         a. I will act against you like your cruel joy   14b
         b. I will act against you like your joy over
            Israel's desolated heritage   15a
      3. Announcement: Edom devastated (results only)   15bα
      4. Recognition formula (3 mp)   15bβ
IV. Resumptive preliminaries   36:1-2aα
   A. Address as son of man   1aα
   B. Direction to prophesy to the mountains of Israel   1aβ
   C. Direction to speak   1bα
   D. Address of the mountains of Israel   1bβ
   E. Call to attention   1bγ
   F. Messenger formula   2aα
V. Prophecy of salvation in the form of a three-part
   prophetic proof saying   2aβb-11
   A. Reason: enemy's claim to the land quoted   2aβb
   B. Transition   3a
      1. Transitional "therefore"   3aα
      2. Direction to prophesy   3aβ
      3. Direction to speak using messenger formula   3aγδ
   C. Review of reason: devastation leading to
      dispossession and scorn   3b
   D. Resumptive transition   4
      1. Transitional "therefore"   4aα
      2. Address of the mountains of Israel   4aβ
      3. Call to attention   4aγ
      4. Messenger formula   4bα
      5. Identification of addressee: parts of plundered
         land (serving as a review of reason)   4bβγδε
   E. Second resumptive transition   5aαβ
      1. Transitional "therefore"   5aα
      2. Messenger formula   5aβ
   F. Subsidiary announcement of punishment
      (intervention only): I have spoken (in oath language)
      against the nations and Edom for their crime   5aγδb

This passage comprises a large, extremely complex, but single unit, so identified by the single prophetic word formula at the beginning. However, the unity of the passage is the result of some relatively clear editorial activity which is best considered under Genre.

Genre

A prophecy against Mount Seir in 35:1-15 has been editorially prefixed to a PROPHECY OF SALVATION to the mountains of Israel in 36:1-15 so as to provide the reason or basis for the announcement of salvation as in ch. 34. Once again the analogy of the PROPHECY OF PUNISHMENT with its pattern of reason plus announcement appears. As in ch. 34 the technique followed in presenting the message of good news is to set it forth over against a previous evil situation. Again, as in ch. 34, the evil situation is presented in both a criminal-centered way (the hostile acts of Edom and the surrounding enemy nations) and a victim-centered one (the consequent shame of Israel). Within this constructed unit in contrast to ch. 34 little stress is laid on the continuity of divine action. Instead a pattern dominates in which God acts negatively to punish the enemy and positively to restore Israel. Only from a large-scale redaction-critical perspective does it become apparent how the element of continuity in divine action does indeed function here. Chapter 36 is presented as the reversal of ch. 6! In ch. 6 a message was delivered against the mountains of Israel; now that message is reversed in a new act of God.

But if the large-scale matters are relatively clear as to both logic and structure, that is no longer the case when we turn to look at the development within both chs. 35 and 36:1-15. Chapter 35 is made up of no less than four individual PROPHETIC PROOF SAYINGS (III.A, B, C, and D), all in strongly stereotypical language, especially in the repetition of the word "desolate." This means that ch. 35 must then be labelled a COLLECTION in itself. The complexity of the chapter's internal organization reflects what must have been a highly complex editorial process. Not only is the one two-part proof saying in 35:3-4 followed by three three-part proof sayings, but there is a distressing inconsistency between second and third person language in all three of the three-part proof sayings. In vv. 5-9 and 10-13 the reason is repeated after the announcement, while in vv. 14-15 the reason section is replaced by an analogy between crime and punishment which accomplishes much the same purpose. Since ch. 35 offers the reason behind the promise in 36:1-15, the repeated stress on reason in the latter three subsections within ch. 35 makes considerable sense, and one can speculate that this extra emphasis on the reason sections may be connected with the internal inconsistencies within only these three proof sayings.

With 36:1-15 we come to truly bewildering complexities. Time after time the sequence of subsections frustrates the reader's patience. Since the prefixed ch. 35 offers the reason behind the promise, the promise ought to appear promptly. But in fact the contrary is the case. Delay after delay is encountered, particularly in the use of transitional formulas. In vv. 1-7 no less than five "therefore's," six messenger formulas, six directions to speak or prophesy, and two calls to attention confront the confused reader. Such a concentration of formulas usually linking reason and announcement suggests that an additional consequence of using ch. 35 as a large-scale reason has been the assembling in 36:1-15 of a large group of announcements detached from their original reason sections. Retaining the transitional formulas after the reason sections were detached deprives these formulas of their original logic of place and makes them instead take on an oddly delaying function. (Reventlow, 60-64, seeks unconvincingly to trace the details of a legal procedure in these complexities.)

The long-awaited salvation can be expected to contain the announcement of Edom's doom as a negative promise as well as the actual counterbalancing announcement of good news for the mountains of Israel. But once again delay is encountered. While subsidiary announcements of Edom's punishment appear in vv. 5 and 6, in which the bare announcement of Yahweh's jealous or wrathful speaking appears, only in v. 7 does an actual statement of the enemy's fate appear. Finally, with v. 8 the positive dimension of the promise surges to the fore. The formulations of salvation in vv. 8-11 all center on the theme of undoing past evil: fertility, repopulation, and resettlement. Actually, the language is quite mild in contrast to what appears later in ch. 36. In v. 11b the offer of a future even better than the past and the allusion earlier in v. 11 to the priestly language about creation's original purpose of being fruitful and multiplying are the only items with even the faintest touch of flamboyance. This same restrained mood continues in the affixed PROPHECY OF SALVATION in vv. 13-15, where the entire message deals with undoing the shame of the land's past reputation for devouring and bereaving its inhabitants. An editorial transition in v. 12 links vv. 13-15 to the preceding by picking up the repopulation motif from vv. 10-11 and introducing the word "bereave" in an anticipation of vv. 13-15. The recognition formula at the end of v. 11 strongly suggests, nevertheless, that this transition was done secondarily to connect up to a second, presumably originally independent, unit in vv. 13-15.

Setting

It is intriguing to speculate that the literary function of the prophecy concerning a foreign nation in ch. 35 as prelude to the promise of ch. 36 may have been stimulated by some cultic ceremony in which a message of hope was introduced as the outcome of the ritual condemnation of enemy nations. This would be a second sort of possible setting, parallel to the rooting of salvation proclamation in a ceremony of public lament discussed earlier and often proposed in the light of the prominence of lament language in the salvation messages of Deutero-Isaiah. However, while the language patterns of Isaiah 40–55 do provide a sizable, tangible, and significant point of departure for such arguments, only Isaiah 46–47 could be adduced as support for this second possibility.

One can see somewhat clearly into the logic of the redactional placement of ch. 35, even if not its date. (Vogelstein argues that Edom likely fell to Nebuchadrezzar in 569 or 567 B.C., but this is by no means certain. For a greatly different approach to the setting of this material, which assigns it to the time of the Chronicler, cf. Simian.) Although ch. 35 could well have been placed alongside 25:12-14, the point of view which saw ch. 36 as the counterpart to ch. 6 has necessitated the relocation of ch. 35. It would even seem logical that ch. 35 reflects a slightly later time than 25:12-14. In the ch. 25 passage mockery over Jerusalem's fall occupies the center, while in ch. 35 it is the claim to the land which is stressed. Of course, the claim in 36:8, "they will soon come home," may well indicate a late exilic date for this passage, but it may also simply reflect the mood of confident longing and anticipation which is so prominent in 36:8-11.

As might be expected, the formulation of 35:1–36:15 as the undoing of an evil situation naturally has points of contact with the message of judgment in chs. 4–24, e.g., "the time of their final punishment" in 35:5b reminds of 21:30-34, and bloodguilt in v. 6 reminds of 22:1-12. Similarly, contacts with the blessings and curses of Leviticus 26 are not surprising, particularly the language of Lev 26:9 as picked up in 36:9. Even points of contact with the further sections of good news in 36:16–48:35 can be observed, especially the role of "inheritance" in 35:15 and 36:12 as picked up in chs. 46–48.

Intention

By labeling 35:1–36:15 as a "motivated" announcement of salvation (Zimmerli, *Ezekiel 2,* 232) parallel to motivated announcements of judgment, Zimmerli has insightfully distinguished a difference in the two kinds of motivation or reason sections. While in ch. 35 the judgment upon Edom is the direct consequence of its cruelty and presumptuous claims, in 36:1-15 "Yahweh's blessing is not to be derived as a necessary consequence of the malice of the enemies or even from Yahweh's judgment . . ." (ibid., 239). Instead Zimmerli sees here "the 'consequence' of the free divine mercy which refuses to leave in the lurch" his derided, defeated, and displaced people (ibid.). This analysis pins down in different words what has here been analyzed as Yahweh's stubborn grace. This constitutes a loyalty rooted only in his own determined love that lays purposeful claim even to the future of this otherwise hopeless people whom he persists in claiming, in a kind of renewed covenant formula, as "my people Israel," in the light of that revelation of himself whereby they come to "know that I am the Lord" (v. 11).

Again it is Zimmerli whose comment about 36:14f. catches so effectively the exact flavor of the purpose behind these words about the changed situation which is to contrast with the old slanders leveled against the Palestinian land as the bereaver of the nation. Seeing "a hidden despondency" in Ezekiel's hearers who struggle with the negative outcomes of Israel's former time in the land, he hears them asking, "Will in fact a newly bestowed history in the land work out any differently from the first history?" (*Ezekiel 2,* 239). The strength of Zimmerli's analysis in both these positions is that it centers our thoughts on just those two converse aspects of unbelief that characterize Ezekiel's addressees. On the one hand, they want desperately to be able to believe that God's promise to them is "motivated," is the necessary consequence of a past relationship which offers them the basis for a claim upon God. That unbelief refuses to hear the message of judgment canceling previous peoplehood. On the other hand, they are convinced in their own guilt that they do not have within them the power to maintain a genuine loyalty to their Lord. This is the root of their hidden despondency, unbelief that refuses to hear the message of promise that affirms the divine, one-sided reestablishment of a new peoplehood.

Chapter 35 responds to this double-sided unbelief by affirming that the natural and unavoidable political consequence of Israel's depopulation, i.e., the attempted and in part successful appropriation of her land by surrounding nations, contradicts Yahweh's own plans, and that, while he employed these nations as a part of his own vengeance on his people, he has not surrendered control to them, but maintains his own overarching purpose (cf. the somewhat different interpretation of Eichrodt, 490-91). In ch. 36 two additional affirmations deal with the same double-sided unbelief. In 36:1-15 the amazing removal of Israel's reproach and the transformation inherent in a return of the land in security and prosperity are avowed. Further, in 36:16-38 the deepest dimension of this unbelief as despondency is attacked by promises about the inward transformation of the people themselves.

Bibliography

H. Reventlow, *Wächter über Israel* (BZAW 82; Berlin: Töpelmann, 1962); H. Simian, *Die theologische Nachgeschichte der Prophetie Ezechiels* (FB 14; Würzburg: Echter, 1974); M. Vogelstein, "Nebuchadnezzar's Reconquest of Phoenicia and Palestine and the Oracles of Ezekiel," *HUCA* 23 (1950-51) II, 209-11.

A PROPHECY OF SALVATION: THE TRANSFORMATION, INNER AND OUTER, OF THE PEOPLE OF GOD, 36:16-38

Structure

In spite of a complex development in section III and the secondary character of IV and V, the passage is marked by the prophetic word formula in 36:16 as a single unit, clearly unconnected to the vision report of 37:1-14.

Genre

Here we see yet another instance of how a PROPHECY OF SALVATION can be introduced. The good news is presented again as the undoing of a previous evil situation, but this time that evil situation is not offered as an address to the people but is formulated in the unusual pattern of a private word given to the prophet alone. Nevertheless, the content of that private word is presupposed in the message to Israel which follows. The private word surveys the events of Israel's history and their consequences as resulting in the profanation of Yahweh's name, and it is upon this foundation, both in content and in formulation, that the subsequent announcement is based. That is, the historical analysis functions as a reason section, and even provides the language for the inclusio in vv. 22aδ and 32a, "not for your sake." (In a rare departure from familiar patterning, the RECOGNITION FORMULA appears in v. 23b not as the end of a PROPHETIC PROOF SAYING, but simply as part of one aspect of the positive reason undergirding the following promise.)

Fascinatingly, the perspective of "for my name's sake" also provides us with a further instance of the development of the second technique in good news formulation, the tracing of the continuity of God's action. Here it is in one sense purely a positive continuity which is seen, for as in ch. 20 all God's action is "for his name's sake." His activity in judgment is thus at least in part directly continued by his activity in restoration. Still, an element of negative continuity is also manifested in that these new acts of God will this time result in the sanctification of his name, i.e., the undoing of its profanation. Further, the prominence of the word "new" and the thought inherent in it of a second set of actions parallel to the previous "old" ones give evidence of the development of the vocabulary of prophetic eschatology (E. Rohland) as a matter of deliberate theological reflection. But with such considerations we enter the area of Setting, and thus they must be postponed.

The announcement of salvation proper in vv. 24-30 is expressed in a truly astonishing number of different images. Most of these have been encountered before: the new exodus (using "take" as the first of the three verbs, as in 37:21), the return to the land, the new covenant (as implicit in a version of the covenant formula expressed as a future relationship), and a restored fertility. Two images, however, either appear here for the first time in the book or are here put in such a unique way that they are in large measure distinct from anything earlier in the book. The image of a ritual washing to remove uncleanness (in both v. 25 and v. 29a) might well have been expected in view of the use of this metaphor in judgment messages, such as chs. 20, 22, and 23, and even its employment in 14:11 and 22:15 to describe a future purification as a part of God's judgment. But the message of a new creation in vv. 26-27 is set forth in such careful detail in the portrayal of the anthropology of salvation that it is truly surprising. Again we shall have to pursue other aspects of this amazing formulation under Setting and Intention.

The emphasis on a shame-filled memory of past misdeeds is, as we have seen, encountered elsewhere in Ezekiel (e.g., 6:8-10); here it appears uniquely as a command in v. 32. In view of the exuberant content of the preceding promises, this admonition to shame provides an oddly depressed conclusion to the section in vv. 22-32.

In sections IV and V two PROPHETIC PROOF SAYINGS are added to expand the preceding message. These two begin with phrases indicating their role as continuations: "On the day . . ." (v. 33) and "This also . . ." (v. 37). The first one is attached more closely, linking up to the previous message of cleansing (vv. 25 and 29); the second one more loosely. Both focus on the external aspect of the restoration, the first promising both fertility and repopulation, the second only the latter. Interestingly, they also differ in that the recognition formula in v. 36 aims at an acknowledgment by the nations—again a thought more in line with the preceding section's emphasis on God's name as having been profaned before the nations (vv. 21-23), while the second aims solely at recognition by "the house of Israel."

Setting

It is abundantly clear that 36:16-32 is aimed to be the continuation of the message in ch. 20. There the same sustaining factor in Israel's history was singled out, God's action "for his name's sake." We detected there a powerful element of theological reflection, still presented in a message proclaimed to an audience, but nonetheless one whose reflective and analytical dimensions strongly represented the mental process involved in its formulation. The present section in 36:16-32 and to a lesser extent vv. 33-38 demonstrate a similarly powerful reflective aspect. This shows most vividly in the way vv. 16-21 are not expressed as a message to the people, but directed solely to the prophet as divine reflection on history, facing the distress of the idea of the exile as evidence of Yahweh's impotence. (See this same struggle in Num 14:16 and Exod 32:12.) While the continuation within ch. 20 moved in the direction of a purging judgment, even though using the language of a new exodus (20:33-38), the final part of ch. 20 did shift to a promise of restoration involving the manifestation of God's holiness and even the self-loathing aspect of the people's future remembering. (Note also the way permission to "ask"—v. 37, literally "be inquired of"—constitutes the undoing of what is denied in 20:3 and 31. See also 14:3, 7, and 10.) Here, then, the technique of undoing a past evil is utilized in a way that makes even more explicit use of past proclamation than was the case in ch. 34 or 35:1–36:15. Since the latter parts of ch. 20 were likely already editorially updated after 587 B.C., 36:16-38 doubtless reflects an even later chronological setting. (Simian again sees the material reflecting the much later time of the Chronicler. See his summary, 351-58.) The closeness of much of its imagery and language to Deutero-Isaiah confirms this, e.g., "for my own sake" in Isa 43:25 and even more clearly in 48:11. Similarly the ideas of the rebuilding of Jerusalem (see Isa 44:26, 28; 54:11-12) and the repopulation of the land (see Isa 49:19 and 54:1-3) are close connections. Still, the clear tone of Ezek 36:16-38 is that of an expectation, not a realization, and most likely all of this section, even its extension, reflects an exilic setting (Zimmerli, *Ezekiel 2,* 246). In fact, in view of the notably less graphic presentation of the new exodus motif, one could argue for a time significantly prior to that of Deutero-Isaiah. In any case it is evident here how much the message of Deutero-Isaiah must be viewed as deeply influenced by that of Ezekiel (D. Baltzer and Zimmerli, *Ezekiel 2,* 250).

At the same time it is equally evident that the traditio-historical setting of

Ezekiel's message of hope is strongly influenced by the heritage of Hosea and Jeremiah, particularly in the emphasis on the repossession of the land and its fertility (see especially Hos 2:14-23 and Jer 31:1-14; 32:42-44; and 33:6-13). Even the "build and plant" language, used so extensively in Jeremiah, appears in Ezek 36:36.

It is much harder to be certain about the traditio-historical setting of the motif of the new creation of Israel. Ezekiel's priestly heritage, especially clear in its earlier use of terminology from Genesis 1 (see "firmament" in 1:22 and "increase and be fruitful" in 36:11), does not lead him to use the actual word "create," so prominent in Genesis 1 and Deutero-Isaiah, as a part of his message of hope. The passing reference to Eden (see already 28:13) is again close to Isa 51:3, but it is hard to come to any precise conclusions here. The question will be pursued further in connection with 37:1-14.

Intention

It is important to be cautious in the analysis of theological reflection, especially when bold formulations of an either/or type are being explored. The sharp formulation here "not for your sake" (vv. 22 and 32) is certainly neither a denial of Yahweh's compassion (see Eichrodt, 496) nor any warning against pride, but is instead in spite of its negative formulation a way of underlining God's graciousness as free and unmerited. This is always the point being made by such formulations, as has been seen in the exploration of the intention of ch. 20. (See also Ps 115:11 and Eph 2:1-10.) Similarly, the apparent self-interest indicated by "for the sake of my holy name" is correctly understood only when God's "reputation" is seen as simply a way of getting at his acknowledgment, invocation, and thus worship. Although not developed here, the purpose that "the nations . . . shall know" (v. 36) has significant implications for ideas of witness and universalism not unlike those in Deutero-Isaiah. But the aspect that *is* developed here needs further clarification. The survey of history in 36:15-21 faces the issue of God's impotence as implicit in Israel's exile, but the approach followed in what ensues indicates plainly that the real issue is Israel's impotence. In the earlier sections dealing with Israel's past history and present condition, the understanding of Israel's rebelliousness was always clear. It was seen as necessitating God's act of judgment (see especially 20:33-38) and resulting in retrospective self-loathing. In 36:16-38 one further logical step is taken. In order for Israel to be able to obey, it must be made new. Not just a forgiveness which cancels the guilt of the past is necessary, but one which positively transforms the people of God. What is promised is a mind that is sensitive (flesh) rather than stonily closed. One could rephrase the promise in the language of chs. 2 and 3 as the replacement of a mind which persists in not listening with a new mind, so that now obedience could be possible—recalling again that "listen" also means "obey." Once again, the totally one-sided character of these affirmations, "I will take . . . give . . . put . . . and cause you to walk," needs to be carefully assessed in order to grasp its intention. True, it does recognize that the prophetic message of repentance, particularly as expressed in the invitation in 18:31, "Get yourselves a new heart and a new spirit," is now to be evaluated as a failure, one that asks what the people of God in their rebellion are unable to give. And it promises that God himself will not only give his people a new nature so that obedience will be a possibility, but the formulation in vv. 26-27 plainly goes further to avow that disobedience will henceforth be impossible. Obedience will be automatic, or perhaps more precisely, God-determined. This has seemed to some to be a promise that goes too far, so far that it takes away the human freedom which alone could make obedience meaningful (Seilhamer, 262-70). But, again, the passage's intention is not to make an observation about the loss of freedom, but rather an affirmation about the overcoming of bondage, the bondage of disobedience, i.e., the overcoming of a past evil situation. (One can indeed speak appropriately here of God's "regenerative power," as Eichrodt does, 500.)

It is strikingly clear once more that Ezekiel's message of promise about the new heart and spirit stands in the traditio-historical line of Jer 31:31-34, facing the same problem and offering essentially the same promise as its remedy. And yet the two passages go their own ways, so that the dependence is not a literary matter of wording but one of a similarity flowing from the same extremely profound theological sensitivity.

Bibliography

D. Baltzer, *Ezechiel und Deuterojesaja* (BZAW 121; Berlin: de Gruyter, 1971); E. Rohland, *Die Bedeutung der Erwählungstraditionen Israel für die Eschatologie der alttestamentlichen Propheten* (Diss., Heidelberg, 1956); F. Seilhamer, *The New Covenant in Jeremiah 31:31-34 and its Place in the Covenant-Treaty Tradition of Israel and the Ancient Near East* (Springfield: New World Press, 1976); H. Simian, *Das theologische Nachgeschichte der Prophetie Ezechiels* (FB 14; Würzburg: Echter Verlag, 1974).

THE REPORT OF THE VISION OF DRY BONES, 37:1-14

Structure

1) Report of divine speech	4aα
2) Direction to prophesy to bones	4aβ
3) Direction to speak	4bα
4) Address of bones	4bβ
5) Call to attention	4bγ
6) Messenger formula	5aα
7) Specification of addressee	5aβ
b. Two-part prophetic proof saying	5b-6
1) Announcement, first phase: summary in advance with introductory "behold"	5b
a) Intervention: I am bringing spirit	5bα
b) Purpose: you may live	5bβ
2) Announcement, second phase: details	6a
a) Intervention	6aαβγδε
(1) Sinews to be given	6aα
(2) Flesh to be brought up	6aβ
(3) Skin to be stretched	6aγ
(4) Spirit to be given	6aδ
b) Purpose: you may live	6aε
3) Recognition formula	6b
2. Prophet's execution of the commission	7a
3. Report of resultant action in the vision	7b-8
a. Background	7b
1) Noise (with introductory "behold")	7bα
2) Bones move together	7bβ
b. Sight (with introductory "behold")	8a
1) Sinews	8aα
2) Flesh went up	8aβ
3) Skin stretched	8aγ
c. Assessment of incompleteness: no spirit	8b
F. Phase two of prophesying	9-10
1. Commission to prophesy the second time	9
a. Preliminaries	9abαβγδ
1) Report of divine speech	9aα
2) Direction to prophesy to the spirit	9aβ
3) Direction to prophesy	9bα
4) Address as son of man	9bβ
5) Direction to speak to the spirit	9bγ
6) Messenger formula	9bδ
b. Plea to the spirit	9bεζη
1) Place of origin: come from the four winds	9bε
2) Action: enter these slain	9bζ
3) Purpose: they may live	9bη
2. Prophet's execution of the commission	10a
3. Report of resultant action in the vision	10b
a. The spirit came	10bα
b. They came to life	10bβ
c. They stood as a mighty host	10bγ

Although the customary prophetic word formula at the beginning is replaced in 37:1aα by the hand of Yahweh revelatory formula, the text is presented as a unit, extending to the new prophetic word formula in 37:15. Exactly how the two parts of this text, vv. 1-10 and vv. 11-14, are to be seen as related to each other, one speaking of bones lying on the ground and the other of bodies buried in graves, is best discussed under Genre.

Genre

The HAND OF YAHWEH REVELATORY FORMULA (see 1:3; 3:22; 8:1; 33:22; 37:1; and 40:1) introduces in most cases the first person account of a vision. (For its use in 3:22, and 33:22, see the discussions of those passages.) The present passage is by far the briefest of the four visions, though certainly the most famous. The VISION REPORT itself in vv. 1-10 is of the "event" type and provides the image, while vv. 11-14 present the interpretation which contains the actual proclamation. This pattern is reminiscent of 17:1-24 and 21:1-12, but here matters are complicated by two unusual items: (1) the division of vv. 4-10 into two distinct phases of prophesying; and (2) the structuring of vv. 11-14 as a DISPUTATION. The purpose underlying each of these two matters is of critical significance for grasping the organization of the unit. There is a highly significant purpose for this apparently strange division of the miracle in vv. 4-10 into two phases, in which the restoration of the bones to life is completed only when the second phase (vv. 9-10) goes on to bring the spirit into the bodies after the lack of that spirit had been observed in v. 8b at the end of the first phase (vv. 4-8). That purpose is an instance of what has been called the second technique for the introduction of a message of salvation, the establishment of the continuity of divine action (→ 34:1-31, Setting). The new creation of the people of God in ch. 37 is deliberately structured to correspond to the old creation in Gen 2:7 by describing it as a two-phase event, in which the infusion of the invisible life-force ("breath" in Gen 2:7, "spirit" here, although elsewhere in this passage this word is used with the meaning of "wind") takes place after the shaping of the body. The analogy aims to enable the hearer trustingly to accept this promised new act because it follows the pattern of the old and thus can be regarded as attesting to the same God who will do a similar thing one more time.

The structuring of vv. 11-14 as a disputation using as the point of departure the people's self-assessment, "Our bones are dried up and our hope is lost; we are clean cut off," is a clear instance of the other technique for formulating a PROPHECY OF SALVATION, namely, wording it as the undoing of a previous evil situation. As in 33:10, the exiles after 587 B.C. view themselves as within the realm of death, existing only in "resigned despair" (Zimmerli, *Ezekiel 2*, 258), and the prophet's message is formulated as a response that takes that self-assessment with fullest seriousness. "Can these bones live?" is indeed a "monstrous . . . ludicrous question" (ibid., 260), since they were "very dry." But this is precisely the point; it is only as a resurrection of the nation, a new creation of "the whole house of Israel," that the message could reach its hearers. It is, however, too much to attempt to reconstruct the intellectual and spiritual experience of the prophet himself on the basis of the logic of the material's arrangement by claiming that the people's words in v. 11 triggered the prophetic experience in vv. 1-10. All that the material itself enables us to see is the vital transitional role of v. 11, establishing a connection both backward and forward, both in logic and in literary structure. Interestingly, though, there is, as Zimmerli notes (ibid., 262), nothing said in vv. 1-10 about communicating the vision to the people, so that one could legitimately regard the vision as "a kind of symbolic assurance for the prophet himself." Still, the way the text here once again closes itself off against all biographical inquiry makes it likely that this is an attempt to read too much out of the text's restraint.

The way the disputation leads into a PROPHETIC PROOF SAYING is not at all unexpected in Ezekiel, as 11:1-12 and 33:23-29 illustrate. Neither is it any more than a familiar kind of awkwardness that the elaboration of a RECOGNITION FORMULA in v. 13 should go on to climax in yet another recognition formula in 14bα (see 28:23b). The only structurally uncertain item in vv. 11-14 is the twofold occurrence of the phrase "O my people" in vv. 12-13. Zimmerli is entirely correct to see here "nothing less than the fully theological interpretation of covenant renewal and acceptance as the people of Yahweh" (*Ezekiel 2*, 256). While the Syriac version omits the phrase in both vv. 12 and 13, the Septuagint does contain it in v. 13, and the issue may be argued pro and con text-critically. Zimmerli's argument that it is hard to see why the word would have been omitted for the sake of compactness makes a powerful point, but it is nonetheless true that what is involved here is simply one more instance of the technique of undoing, for, as Zimmerli himself observed, what is being affirmed is "the removal of the curse pronounced in Hos 1:9" (ibid.).

Setting

It is fully obvious that this passage is set chronologically in the exilic period. The people's view of themselves in v. 11 makes that certain. Because Ezekiel's three other visions are given a date, it is often assumed that a date—presumably one before that in 40:1—has been lost by some textual accident, but this is only speculation. It is tempting to try to reconstruct a straight-line development of the content of the prophet's message, so that the role of the spirit as a motive force in this unit could be seen as prior to the more grandiose portrayal in 36:27, in which the internal transformation of God's people is described. However, such reconstruction presupposes not only that there was, in fact, some such orderly sequence of thought-development on the part of the prophet, but much more precariously that the stages in this development have been preserved without mutual influence and modification. This last is indeed highly unlikely in view of the way already chs. 11, 16, and 20 were modified in the light of Ezekiel's later preaching. In any case, this passage and 36:16-38 have several points of contact. In both instances it is first "spirit" and then "my spirit" which is involved (36:26 plus 27 and 37:9-10 plus 14; see also 39:29). In each case language of the new exodus tradition appears, the three familiar verbs in 36:24 and "bring up" plus "lead in" in 37:12. Finally, the language of restoration of covenant is present both in 36:28 and in the present text of 37:12-13.

It is often speculated that this vision of the resurrection of dead bones must have presupposed some developing belief in a physical resurrection. But in point of fact what is foretold is only a national "resurrection" in the sense of a restoration of the exilic people of God to an existence of a presumably normal sort once again in their own land. True, the imagery employed did lead later generations to reinterpret this passage, e.g., on the wall of the Dura-Europos synogogue, as a promise of a physical resurrection from the grave, but that is definitely a development which goes far beyond what this text itself says. What is strange about the view of death implicit in the use of imagery found within the text is the total lack of the usual picture of Sheol as a place of shadowy half existence, and instead the intense realism of deterioration presupposed by the scene of dry bones. Further, it is striking that the contact with these bones by the prophet in v. 2 does not raise any thought of ritual contamination, a prospect given explicit attention in 39:11-16. Clearly in 37:1-14 the focus is on life and death in their broader senses, and the imagery, although physically vivid, reflects that focus. But that thought leads us to a fuller investigation of the unit's intention.

Intention

In the OT death is very frequently viewed as a realm within which one experiences restriction. Conversely, when one is restricted or "squeezed" (the Hebrew root for "trouble" as well as the Greek word for "tribulation" both preserve and express this literal meaning), one is in death. The impotence of Israel's exilic existence is vividly captured by the imagery of bones long dead, and that impotence is bluntly faced in the ridiculous question directed to the prophet, "Can these bones live?" But, as Zimmerli has eloquently shown, both the vision and its interpretation center on showing how the prophet is "transformed from being the spokesman of human impotence into the spokesman of divine omnipotence" (*Ezekiel 2*, 260). The stress on the impossibility of any self-achieved change of the people's situation is again a foil by means of which to affirm God's unconditional will for his people's life (ibid., 265 and → ch. 18). The magnitude of the promise proclaimed is seen even more vividly when one recalls the repeated earlier message which announced death to a people whose stubborn confidence led them to deny that message. Now that the threatened death had become undeniable and presumably inescapable reality, and the hearers of the prophet were willing to confess that his earlier words had been fully validated, the prophet "proclaims life where it has become clear that the life of the one called by God is now definitely at an end" (ibid.).

Even more than this, Ezekiel speaks of life not just as a possibility but as "an imminent action on God's part" (ibid.), and of how "the revival of Israel will be God's great revelation of himself to the world" (ibid., 263). From the perspective of fulfillment, Israel—who came to know in her death the revelation of who Yahweh is—will now again come to know this same Lord yet more fully as the one whose "I am Yahweh" is once again linked to "You are my people."

Again in a way similar to what is said in 36:36 and 38, there is a kind of universalism within this hope. Although it is not, as in 36:36, "the nations" who will acknowledge Yahweh in 37:13-14, the new act of God proclaimed is presented as analogous not primarily to the exodus or covenant by which Israel came into being, although that language is a subordinate part of this unit. Instead, this new act is portrayed as a new creation, deliberately going back to the language of the creation of the whole of humanity, and thus at least implicitly what is formulated here is fantastically far-reaching. In the techniques of its formulation it expresses the undoing of an evil situation characteristic not just of Israel, although that is undeniably its primary intent, but it does so by the use of an image characteristic of all human existence, and it does so by the affirmation of a continuity with an earlier act of God whose object was again all humanity. Later reinterpretation of this text simply extended its proclamation further in a direction toward which elements within the text itself were open.

Bibliography

C. Barth, "Ezechiel 37 als Einheit," in *Beiträge zur alttestamentlichen Theologie* (*Fest.* W. Zimmerli; ed. H. Donner, R. Hanhart, and R. Smend; Göttingen: Vandenhoeck & Ruprecht, 1977) 39-52; A. Graffy, *A Prophet Confronts His People* (AnBib 104; Rome: Biblical Institute Press, 1984) 83-86; E. Haag, "Ez 37 und der Glaube an die Auferstehung der Toten,"

TTZ 82 (1973) 78-92; B. Rüdiger, "Ez 37,1-14, die Verbform *w^eqatal* und die Anfänge der Auferstehungshoffnung," *ZAW* 97 (1985) 366-89.

THE REPORT OF A SYMBOLIC ACTION WITH TWO STICKS, 37:15-28

Text

In v. 23 one must read *mĕšūbōtêhem* ("their backslidings") for *mōšĕbōtêhem* ("their dwellings").

Structure and Genre

In spite of problems in the latter verses, the pattern of the text is relatively clear. The PROPHETIC WORD FORMULAS in 37:15 and 38:1 indicate that 37:15-28 is presented as a unit. The REPORT OF A SYMBOLIC ACTION appears in vv. 16-19 in a fashion familiar from chs. 4–5, i.e., with the entire typical pattern of directions, people's questioning response, and reinterpretation all contained within Yahweh's directions to the prophet. The interpretation in III.B.3 refers to the action and gives it one meaning as a promise of reunification. After a rather awkward resumption in v. 20, a new MESSENGER FORMULA introduces another stage of interpretation shaped as a lengthy two-part proof saying, in which—starting with a wordplay on "take"—several other aspects of restoration beyond reunification are promised, climaxing in the affirmation of a restored covenant relationship in v. 23bγδ. Thereupon follows a yet further elaboration of the PROPHECY OF SALVATION, this time as a listing of items encountered elsewhere in Ezekiel 34–36 and 40–48. These items seem to be grouped as four realities now labeled "everlasting": (1) everlasting dwelling in the land (see 34:13-14, 25-29; 36:8-15); (2) David as everlasting prince (see 34:23-24); (3) an everlasting covenant (see 34:30-31; 36:28); and (4) an everlasting presence of Yahweh's sanctuary in their midst (see chs. 40–48). Once again the affirmation of a restored covenant relationship serves as a climax in v. 27aβb. The concluding elaborated recognition formula, like all of the elaboration in vv. 24-27, makes no connection to the symbolic action or the hoped-for reunification, centering exclusively on the holiness flowing from the new sanctuary.

It seems clear, then, that an original report of a symbolic action has been updated repeatedly in such a way that it has come to be a kind of summary collection of most of the major items in Ezekiel's message of hope. (C. Barth sees a special connection to 37:1-14.)

Setting

A symbolic action presents a powerful word heralding in advance the reality it announces and even initiates. But the updating of this particular action has given it a new function. In a way somewhat reminiscent of what was seen in the latter parts of chs. 11, 16, and 20, this expanded symbolic act is now a summary of most of Ezekiel's promises. Perhaps its placement is strategic and deliberate. Since chs. 38–39 and 40–48, although containing messages of hope, were viewed as relatively independent sections, 37:15-28 is thus the last pericope in the section 33–37, and a logical point for such a summary.

Chronologically it is difficult to determine the passage's setting. As the parallel hopes for reunification in Jer 3:6-25 and 30–31 show, and as Ezek 4:4-8 bears out, this theme was a subject of some expectation during the exile. To what extent the hopes for the former Northern Kingdom meant to deal with the actual former residents of that territory and to what extent they simply were a way of giving expression to an ambition for a restoration of Davidic boundaries, as was perhaps already Josiah's aim, cannot be decided for lack of evidence, but the second possibility seems much more likely. Exactly how far into the exilic period the updating elaboration of these hopes would take us could only be a matter for speculation.

As was already noted, a great many traditions have been blended and sampled to form the traditio-historical setting of this unit. Familiar connections to Leviticus 26, especially vv. 3 and 11-12, appear, and a wealth of election traditions are utilized, not just the more frequent exodus and covenant language, but also the rarer David tradition, and even a reference to Jacob and the fathers is made in connection with the promise of a new dwelling in the land. Finally the sanctuary tradition is itself employed as a kind of renewed election tradition in v. 28. The details of the way the David tradition is picked up illustrate some of the way the updating of this text has taken place. In vv. 22 and 24 David appears as king, but in v. 25 he appears as *nāśî'* ("prince"), the latter verse being likely the later and more careful formulation of the hope for the future of the Davidic dynasty within the framework of a restored confederacy. Possibly the whole theme of rulers has developed out of a play on the word "tribe" in v. 19, which also means "ruler's staff."

To conclude this brief survey, it is in place to note yet again how the two basic techniques for the formulation of good news are employed here. Technique number one, the wording of a prophecy of salvation as the undoing of a previous evil situation, provides the basic starting point. The ancient division within Israel is to be overcome in the unity of the restoration (see especially v. 22). Technique number two, the underlining of the continuity of divine action, provides the underlying logic behind all of the "new" dimensions in vv. 20-28: new exodus, new David, new covenant, new residence in the land, and new sanctuary. Even the negative aspect of continuity appears in the end of defilement by means of God's cleansing in v. 23.

Intention

The symbolic action aims at the proclamation and even initiation of the reunion of the people of God. But the elaboration develops this message in somewhat more nuanced ways. The Davidic ruler is the guarantor of this new unity, like the single shepherd in 34:23, and this implies that he will serve to protect the newly regathered people of God from the danger of a new schism (Zimmerli, *Ezekiel 2*, 276). Further, the promise of a restored sanctuary serves not only the unity of the restored people, but, according to v. 28, as the central item for Yahweh's revelation of himself to the world (ibid., 277), in a way clearly akin to a part of the message of Deutero-Isaiah. Thus once again we note a dimension of universalism in Ezekiel's words of hope. It is the nations who are to acknowledge Yahweh through his work with his people.

Bibliography

C. Barth, "Ezechiel 37 als Einheit," in *Beiträge zur alttestamentlichen Theologie (Fest. W. Zimmerli*; ed. H. Donner, R. Hanhart, and R. Smend; Göttingen: Vandenhoeck & Ruprecht, 1977) 39-52.

A COLLECTION OF PROPHECIES: THE ATTACK OF GOG AND HIS DEFEAT, 38:1–39:29

Text

In 38:14b read *tēʿōr* ("you will bestir yourself") for *tēdāʿ* ("you will know"). In 38:21a read *ḥărādâ* ("terror") for *hāray ḥereb* ("my mountains a sword"). In 39:14a delete *ʾet- hāʿōbĕrîm* ("the travelers").

Structure

I. Prophetic word formula		38:1
II. Preliminaries		2-3a
A. Address as son of man		2aα
B. Hostile orientation formula		2aβ
C. Specification of Gog's identity		2aγδ
1. From Magog		2aγ
2. Chief prince of Meshech and Tubal		2aδ
D. Direction to prophesy		2b
E. Direction to speak using messenger formula		3a

Although united under a single prophetic word formula in 38:1, the unity of 38:1–39:29 is only partially borne out by its contents. Sections III and IV, especially the former, are complicated in themselves, but the two series of appendices that follow them are only loosely attached. The first series is at least connected in thought to the Gog battle, but the latter series is of such a generalizing sort that it seems actually to be totally independent of 38:1–39:20.

Genre

To begin with these final two appendices in 39:21-29, their content reveals them to be summaries of Ezekiel's total preceding message, vv. 21-24 summarizing the message of judgment, and vv. 25-29 that of hope, although including a brief retrospective allusion to preceding judgment. These summary appendices are both given appropriately, even though somewhat artificially, the shape of two-part PRO-PHETIC PROOF SAYINGS. The major concern of the first, vv. 21-24, is to show how the proper understanding of Israel's suffering as punishment from Yahweh will serve as proof to the nations of Yahweh's lordship. Because the nations are to come to this insight in the future, vv. 21-24 are formulated in a rather unusual way as the report—in what will then be the past tense—of the fulfillment of what Ezekiel had earlier proclaimed as a PROPHECY OF PUNISHMENT. The reason can remain largely unaltered, but what was originally an ANNOUNCEMENT OF PUNISH-MENT in the future tense must now become a report of past intervention and results. The power of the old pattern to maintain itself in this new setting is nonetheless impressive.

The second summary, that dealing with the future in vv. 25-29, is broadly shaped in the familiar pattern of a two-part PROPHETIC PROOF SAYING, even though the announcement is presented in two stages. The content is naturally even more familiar, a blending of elements from Ezekiel's promises as we encounter them in chs. 34, 36, and 37, and most closely related to the summary section at the end of the first collection of PROPHECIES CONCERNING FOREIGN NATIONS, 28:25-26. One can venture to speak here again of the clear preeminence of rational, theological reflection moving even toward the area of that kind of condensed, analytical af-firmation we associate with credal formulation.

To turn now to the sections actually dealing with the battle against Gog is to move into yet more complicated material. In 38:3b-23 we can detect basically the pattern of a three-part PROPHETIC PROOF SAYING, but two large-scale incon-sistencies in this pattern emerge. For one, the reason section in 38:4-16 offers two essentially conflicting explanations: a first one in vv. 4-9, according to which Yah-weh in his total control of history moves Gog against Israel, and a second in vv. 10-13, according to which Gog himself develops his own evil scheme. Interest-ingly, especially from the perspective of editorial analysis, both explanations are summarized as the reason section is concluded in vv. 14-16. The second large-scale inconsistency shows in the way Gog changes from being directly addressed in vv. 3-16 and v. 17 to being the object of a third person announcement in vv. 18-22, which draws this complicated prophecy toward its conclusion in the recogni-tion formula in v. 23.

The second and briefer two-part PROPHETIC PROOF SAYING in 39:1-6 returns to direct address, although even here the third person reference to Magog in v. 6 could be regarded as another switch in person.

Among the first series of appendices in 39:7-20 there appears material of highly diverse sorts. The first two appendices in 39:7-8, even though they do not mention Gog or the battle, do serve rather effectively as a conclusion to the whole collection of Gog material, providing it with an interpretative framework and un-derlining the certainty of the preceding message. The remaining three appendices in the final series are much less tightly connected, providing instead in vv. 9-10 and 11-16 a pair of what can only be labeled curious afterthoughts, and in vv. 17-20 a section which would have followed far more appropriately after v. 6. In vv. 9-10 and 11-16 the afterthoughts dealt with are the product of reflection over the inherent consequences of such a mammoth battle for the Israelites on whose land it took place. Although formulated as announcements, they actually reflect a speculative mental process rather than a heralding one. Inasmuch as the corpses of the slain have already been buried in vv. 11-16, the bizarre invitation in vv. 17-20 for birds and beasts to feast on the defeated comes inappropriately late, revealing its pres-ent independence and possible original earlier placement.

Setting

The traditio-historical background of the Gog material is most plainly to be associated with the motif of a foe from the north, especially as it appears in Jeremiah 4–6. Behind the motif lies a blending of mysterious, and even possibly mythological, names from the edge of the known world of nations with the given geographical fact that the road for armies invading Palestine from anywhere other than Egypt normally came from the north. The way in which Gog is portrayed as fulfilling the role of "foe from the north" reveals significant influence from the so-called "holy war" tradition. To what extent this tradition is rooted in distinctively Israelite history and practice is a disputed matter. But that is immaterial in our case, for by the time of Ezekiel a sizable body of both historiographic and prophetic evidence makes it plain that, whatever its origin, there existed a definite theological perspective which stressed the total sovereignty of Yahweh in war. Ezekiel 38–39 gives a clear reflection of this perspective in several ways: (1) the way Yahweh himself does not merely respond, but "brings forth" Gog (38:4, see Isa 10:5-11); (2) the way Yahweh himself without any human help defeats Gog and his vast armies with mysterious superhuman force, which crumbles every possible refuge, especially by means of a divinely-induced panic (38:19-23, see Judges 6–7); (3) the way details are omitted from the description of the victory, which really permits no spectators (see Gen 19:24-26; Isa 17:12-14); and (4) the way plunder from Gog's defeat is not treated as riches for Israelite soldiers, but as belonging to the real victor, Yahweh, and therefore destined for fire (39:9-10, see Joshua 6–7; Isa 9:4 [*RSV* 5]; Ps 46:10 [*RSV* 9]) and as a feast for the non-human creation (39:18-20; see Isa 34:5-8).

But in addition to such smaller motifs, some much larger issues of a traditio-historical setting require examination. Three issues in particular need to be examined: (1) the relation of chs. 38–39 to the more customary ways in which prophecies of salvation have been formulated in Ezekiel; (2) the wisdom dimension of chs. 38–39; and (3) the relation of the Gog material to apocalyptic. Previously two main techniques have been identified as characteristic of the way good news is formulated in the book of Ezekiel: as the undoing of a past evil situation and as the expression of a continuity in style with Yahweh's past acts. The first technique, with its stress on undoing, is clearly given prominent attention of a victim-centered sort in 38:8 and especially in 39:23-29. Since this latter passage is, as was pointed out, not really part of the material dealing with the Gog battle, this means that only a very small use of the undoing technique is present in the Gog material. This is, of course, what one would expect to find in a passage centering on a promise of deliverance from a devastation not permitted to occur. The second technique of formulating a promise as characterized by evident continuity with the pattern of the Lord's former acts has already been pointed out as a major part of chs. 38–39 when we traced its utilization of "holy war" style to describe the Lord's dealing with Gog. A further dimension of this technique appears in the way Gog's being brought by Yahweh is seen as the fulfillment of former prophetic words, a dimension receiving only minor attention here, but given great prominence in much of Deutero-Isaiah, where proof from prediction becomes a major method of highlighting the continuity in divine action.

The presence of this eminently rational way of analyzing and organizing the pattern of divine activity in history forces us to ask about the second issue, the extent to which a wisdom heritage characterizes Ezekiel 38–39. Zimmerli speaks of the reference in 38:17 to the prophets of former days as "a didactic interpretative observation" (*Ezekiel 2*, 312). His assessment is accurate as far as it goes, but inadequate in the use of the label "observation." Observation is indeed the first step in the particular style of the mastering of life reflected in proverbs (von Rad, *Wisdom in Israel*, 30-33). But observation is followed by correlation, organization, and encapsulization. In Ezek 38:17 we certainly have as yet no encapsulizing of the whole picture of the onslaught by an overwhelming enemy from which the people of God receive divine deliverance. That point, though, has very likely been reached when in Rev 20:8 "Gog and Magog" can be cited as a way of referring to the content of this whole section. What is present in 38:17 is more than an observation in the sense of the gathering of data. It is, as Zimmerli's phrase indicates, already an interpretation. That is, it reflects a prior process of correlation in which the words of the prophets have been explored for related passages, resulting in a prior orderly synthesis of those passages so as to produce the classification of a particular pattern for God's future action, thereby enabling the recognition and identification of that pattern at its appearance. Zimmerli finds throughout chs. 38–39 the prophet speaking "as one who knows about the great promises" (*Ezekiel 2*, 322). He knows of the history-determining words but also of the threatening realities of political life. It is no easy intellectual achievement to understand and be able to combine this knowledge in an orderly way, blending together on the one hand the word about him of whom the prophets spoke as Yahweh's helpless instrument, and on the other hand the awareness of evil imperialistic desires for plundering the defenseless. Yet this is exactly what 38:4-16 seeks to do and even ventures to summarize in vv. 14-16. Also the attempt to summarize God's future plan in 39:25-29 reveals this aim of organizing— and thereby to some extent mastering—the future by means of an overarching perspective so as to enable the grouping of both good and bad experiences under a single concept. The concept of God's sanctifying himself (39:27, see 28:25) serves this purpose. The profaning of God's holy name made judgment necessary and also provided the past evil situation to be undone. At the same time God's sanctifying of himself (*RSV* "vindicated my holiness") in 39:27 leads logically to the purification, transformation, and restoration of God's people as the genuine partner through whom that self-revelation which is the goal of holiness can take place.

It is possible to go yet further and recognize that significant sections of ch. 39 have not been properly understood when this wisdom aspect has been overlooked. The clever way in which the leftover weapons of the enemy are made to serve as firewood in 39:9-10 seems from this perspective to be one of those neat details in which every tiny item, even the ancient tradition of burning the spoil, is made to work out with striking appropriateness. Similarly, the treatment of the bones in 39:11-16 is not to be seen as reflecting a scrupulous, priestly concern for ritual defilement. Priestly ritual concerns are eminently practical, that, is, they are rooted in the regularly recurring situations of human life. What to do with the vast burden of the bones of Gog's host is scarcely such a recurring problem. It is rather a theoretical intellectual exercise, reflecting the mental process of an adventuresome speculation—probably with a touch of humor, exactly the mental process behind many of the riddles and clever sayings with which the wisdom tradition confronts us.

The third issue, the relation of the Gog material to apocalyptic, is closely connected to an aspect of what has just been examined as wisdom tradition, namely, the idea of a future determined by the prophetic word. The intellectual exploration and utilization of past authoritative prophetic words has long been recognized as an essential aspect of wisdom, as in Jesus ben Sirach, but it is also a presupposition for apocalyptic, as in the treatment of Jeremiah's seventy years in Daniel 9. Similarly, the stress on total divine sovereignty is deeply rooted in wisdom's struggles with the prosperity of the wicked and the suffering of the righteous, as well as being the presupposition of all apocalyptic throne visions and their underlying struggle to understand how the Almighty can permit the persecution of the faithful by an impious tyrant. The answer to the dilemma is found in the complexity of the divinely determined plan, i.e., a sequence in which certain stages must follow each other (as in the statue of Daniel 2), or the inscrutable divine assignment of sovereignty to various nations until the arrival of the predestined time of consummation. It is precisely at this point, the idea of a consummation, that we see where the Gog material, in spite of all its other lesser resemblances to apocalyptic literature, stops short. Ezekiel 38–39 does not lead to a final end of history. There is indeed a cosmic shaking in 38:19-23 (B. Childs, 187-98), and it plays a key role in God's vindication of his holiness (v. 23), but this is not a true consummation. There is no real ultimate salvation for Israel here, just a climactic rescue which is to lead to a future for Israel almost identical to that promised in nearly all of Ezekiel's prophecies, the acknowledgment of Yahweh. (For the link to the covenant formula in the recognition formula of 39:22, see 28:26 and the discussion there.) What still lies ahead is also the same future, often described elsewhere in Ezekiel: a guilty memory (16:49; 39:26), the vindication of Yahweh's holiness before the nations (20:41; 28:25; 36:23; 39:27), and their acknowledgment of him (36:23, 36; 37:28; 39:21, 27). Thus, while the Gog material has superficial resemblances to apocalyptic, it differs decisively in that the salvation it promises lacks the ultimacy essentially inherent in apocalyptic eschatology. (Cf. Collins, 1-19 for a slightly different view.)

What time to decide upon as the chronological setting for such a message is a highly difficult question. As Zimmerli reminds us, in 32:17-32 Assyria, Elam, and Meshech-Tubal are seen as "the three great disrupters of the Mesopotamian world," and it seems likely that "from these three there is selected here the geographically most remote as the one who is least known" (*Ezekiel 2,* 303). Danger from this quarter could have been realistically imagined only in the time before the unification of the northern territory with the southern under Cyrus. The names Gog and Magog offer no solid basis for historical exploration. Gog may, in fact, be derived from Magog by understanding it to mean "the place of Gog." Magog in turn may be the result of an alphabetic play on the name of Babel by using in reverse order letters one step further along in the alphabet. That such far-fetched speculative devices actually were employed is known from the appearance of Sheshach in Jer 51:41 as a code for Babel by using "athbash," the replacement of the first letter in the alphabet by the last, the second letter by the second last, etc. In any case, a prophecy against Babylon, otherwise absent in Ezekiel, would be most understandable in the time of the rise of Cyrus. Since Media fell to Cyrus in 555 B.C., we are brought back very close to the time of Ezekiel himself. Others, like Eichrodt (520-21), think of the post-restoration uncertainty and feelings of helplessness attested in Isaiah 56–66 and a time around 520 B.C. The passage simply provides little by way of objective, concrete basis for any dating, and subjective matters are very hard to date. The extreme nature of the threat from Gog and the closeness of the material in some respects to apocalyptic, while indeed distinguishing chs. 38–39 from what has preceded, hardly provide a basis for more than inclinations. The problems which confront us in this unusual passage are far more responsibly handled in the present, limited state of our knowledge by restricting ourselves to facing them than by speculative attempts at their resolution.

Clearly the material within these two chapters has undergone expansion, updating, and elaboration, but that is not at all unusual, even within material widely held to be from Ezekiel's own hand. We are fascinated spectators before a section whose complexities imply an involved history, but those implications are only that, and they do not enable a reconstruction of an original core with any confidence. The efforts of Zimmerli (*Ezekiel 2*, 298-99) and Hossfeld (402-509) here are welcome as speculative attempts of considerable heuristic value in enabling the discovery of even further complexities, but they are not at all convincing as actual literary reconstructions.

Intention

The analysis of the aims of this material from the twin perspectives of organizing an overall understanding of God's promised purpose in his utilization of a great enemy, and of affirming his total sovereignty which enables ultimate confidence, appears above. The reader is referred to the sections under Setting on the relations to wisdom and apocalyptic for details. Such a comprehensive aim, together with the relative independence of 39:25-29, makes it at least possible that one "edition" of the book of Ezekiel may have ended with ch. 39, and that the ending of that chapter may have been assigned its large-scale, over-arching organizational role deliberately so that it could function as a conclusion to that book.

Bibliography

B. S. Childs, "The Enemy from the North and the Chaos Tradition," *JBL* 78 (1959) 187-98; J. J. Collins, "Introduction: Towards the Morphology of a Genre," in *Semeia 14: Apocalypse: The Morphology of a Genre* (Missoula: Scholars Press, 1979) 1-19; F. Hossfeld, *Untersuchungen zu Komposition und Theologie des Ezechielsbuches* (FB 20; Würzburg: Echter Verlag, 1977); G. von Rad, *Wisdom in Israel* (tr. J. D. Martin; Nashville: Abingdon, 1972).

THE REPORT OF A VISION OF THE NEW TEMPLE AND THE NEW COMMUNITY, 40:1–48:35

Structure and Genre

I. The new temple	40:1–42:20
II. The return of the glory of Yahweh	43:1-12
III. The measurements of the altar of burnt offerings	43:13-17
IV. The consecration of the altar of burnt offerings	43:18-27
V. The closed outer east gate	44:1-3
VI. Renewed visionary commission introducing the following ordinances	44:4-5

Although this vast block of material stands united as a single prophetic VISION REPORT, a host of matters of content and genre arise to challenge this surface impression of unity. That narrative framework of VISIONARY GUIDANCE FORMULAS, which traces the movement of the prophet and his guide and maintains an element of overall spatial continuity, disappears over relatively large spans (e.g., none between 44:4 and 46:19 or after 47:6). While most units in chs. 40–48 take the form of a description of what was seen, i.e., a VISION REPORT, that pattern tends to break down after the early chapters, when the form changes to a lengthy series of ordinances beginning in 44:6, does not return to the vision report to any full extent until 47:1-12. The conclusion is unavoidable that the initial structure of a vision report organized by a series of visionary guidance formulas has been subsequently elaborated by the incorporation of other material so that only at the beginning (40:1–44:4) is there any consistent unity, and thereafter only rarely does an occasional, almost awkward, resumption of the vision structure occur so as to maintain a faint sense of continuity. Even within the very first major section, chs. 40–42, some subsections give strong indications of departing from the surrounding pattern (e.g., 40:38-46; 41:15b-26; and 42:1-14).

Previous scholarship has attempted to trace the literary history of chs. 40–48, with certain significant positive results. Relative agreement exists about the development of the temple description itself in chs. 40–42. Sections 40:1-37, 47-49, and 41:1-4a constitute the basic nucleus, which was expanded first—soon after its composition—by 41:5-15a and 42:15-20, and then later by the remainder. Then 43:1-12 occupies a basic and strategic place in what follows in chs. 43–46. After the temple is portrayed as complete in chs. 40–42, the return of Yahweh's glory through the east gate both concludes the temple description, serving as a kind of rededication, and plays a vital role for what follows because of the permanent closing of the east gate after Yahweh's entry through it. This phenomenon of the closed east gate leads in 44:1-2 and 46:1-12 to a partial exception for the prince in regard to the use of the vestibule of the east gate for sacrificial meals. But once the prince and his role in the temple cult have been introduced, a whole series of cultic ordinances about priests, sacrifices, and property tumbles onto the scene in chs. 44–46. Much of this material is interconnected, especially in the way the roles of priests and prince fit together. Past scholarship has been fascinated with the attempt to identify literarily interconnected layers, one highlighting the role of the Zadokite priests and the other that of the prince. It is indeed the case that certain interconnections do exist and give the impression of being literarily secondary. This is especially the case with those passages, such as 40:46b, 43:19, and 48:11, which insert the point of view of Zadokite priority from 44:31 as a corrective modification into sections in which this perspective was otherwise not in evidence. But this is about all that the evidence is adequate to establish. One cannot appropriately speak of a Zadokite layer (Gese, 112-13). Even the material about the prince, having inherently a certain commonality of subject, does not really constitute a layer (Gese, 114-20 and Zimmerli, *Ezekiel 2*, 550-52). Instead, a different, more modest method of approach needs to be followed, as will be set forth below under Setting and Intention.

Chapters 47–48 not only bring a return to the form of a vision report, but with their common focus on the land outside the temple, they constitute a relatively separate section. The resumption of the vision structure functions smoothly for 47:1-12, in that the temple threshold is the source of the river these verses describe. That close connection should not, however, move one to attach 47:1-12 to 43:1-9 and 44:1-3 as somehow one continuous vision report (as Fohrer does). The interconnection of 44:1-3 with 43:1-9 is of a sort that occurs repeatedly within chs. 44–46, and there is no convincing reason to move 47:1-12 forward. In fact, to do so would destroy the link in logic by which 47:13–48:29 continues 47:1-12 with a detailed look at the land which has been hallowed by Yahweh's presence. After 48:29 a rather loosely attached appendix in 48:30-35 deals in a somewhat different way with the city which had already appeared in 48:15-20. One notices that there is no real ending to chs. 40–48. The vision is not brought to any kind of conclusion, such as by a final visionary guidance formula to complete the structural principle with which it began. Nor is there any report of the vision's impact on the prophet, as in 3:15, nor a report of the delivery of the message, as commanded in 40:4 and as given in 11:25, nor even a CONCLUSION FORMULA, such as appears in 37:14. Thus this largest of all the four major vision reports in Ezekiel is the only one whose ending is unmarked. The giving of the impressive name for the city in 48:35b serves adequately to complete the small appended section of which it is a part, but it does not fulfill that role for all of chs. 40–48, because the focus throughout is much more extensive than just the city.

Thus we are left with a definite impression of the inadequacy of the structure of chs. 40–48. Neither in genre nor in context, neither in literary-critical analysis nor in structural continuity as literature, does some impression of a positive sense of completeness emerge. Must we rest content with such a purely negative conclusion?

Setting and Intention

The distinction between negative and positive introduces the decisive factor. The search by past scholarly generations for some means of literary-critical stratification was rooted in the desire to uncover the historical situation in which the positive intentions of the material would make sense, and to which time the stratum could then be dated. To some extent Zimmerli still follows this approach (*Ezekiel 2*, 552-53), seeing the planning about a prince to reflect a time in which the return to Palestine was close at hand and a positive hope for a Davidic leader could develop. Since such hopes apparently came to a sad end with the fate of Zerubbabel, this would enable us to date one part of chs. 40–48 between 573 B.C. (in 40:1) and the early days of the return. Similarly the stress on the Zadokites as the only genuine priests would be seen as the reflection of one point of view within the struggles of exilic and post-exilic Israelite priesthood. Here, alas, our lack of historical background information makes dating more difficult, but at least the absence of any references in the book of Ezekiel to a high priest would make it certain that all the material about priests must antedate the community of 520 B.C. in which the high priest figures so prominently. This would mean, however, that the connection between Ezekiel and the Pentateuch as sources for the history of the priesthood now becomes an area of considerable complexity.

It is not the intent here to disavow the value of this method of literary-critical analysis and historical reconstruction. It is maintained, however, that this method has not proved productive in the case of Ezekiel 40–48, because the visionary material is not primarily characterized by the positive aim of proposing a new pattern, either of Davidic leadership or Zadokite priesthood. Instead the emphases within chs. 40–48 appear primarily with a negative intent. To put it crassly, the prince's value is solely to be one unlike the past kings (see 43:7-9), one whose cultic role is modest, whose property rights are so modest as to be minimal (see 45:7-8a and 48:21-22), and whose further role in connection with property is presented in a totally negative way (see 45:8b-9 and 46:16-18). Similarly all that makes Zadokites special is that they did not go astray as Levites did (see 44:15 and 48:11). These details might remain just scattered and unconnected bits, if it were not that they are a part of an already noticed pattern dominating all of Ezekiel's message of promise. As has been remarked in chs. 34–39, the major technique employed to formulate messages of hope in Ezekiel is to express them as the undoing of past evil situations. (See Levenson's references to "repairing the flaws of history," 86-87 and 94, and a similar stress by G. Ch. Macholz.) This is the essence of what is said about the prince and the Zadokite priests. The kings brought trouble for the earlier temple, as reported in 43:7-9 and repeated in many episodes of the Deuteronomistic history, climaxing in the historian's assessment of Manasseh's significance in the Lord's decision about the judgment and destruction of Jerusalem. The replacement of the king by the prince will eliminate that past evil. It should be noted that the prince's Davidic role referred to in 34:23f. and 37:24 is left unmentioned throughout chs. 40–48. (Cf. Levenson, 57-107 for a similar but somewhat different analysis.) One might even dare to see in the prince of chs. 40–48 a return to the premonarchic era of the confederacy, where the prince appears in a less lofty role (see Lev 4:22 and Numbers 7). In parallel fashion, the heritage of the worship on the high places, in which Levites were in some way involved and which was also a part of the reason for the doom of both Israel and Judah, will now be eliminated, since only Zadokites serve as priests.

But the central instance of this motif of undoing past evil in chs. 40–48 is neither the prince nor the Zadokites. In 43:1-12, the central pericope for the organization of all chs. 40–48, it is simply unmistakable that all that is being affirmed is the "negative" point that Yahweh will never leave his people again. The rules about the closed east gate, and probably a good bit of the arrangement of the temple plan so as to give preeminence to the east, are further negative statements whose essential function is to underline this undoing of past evil.

There is, of course, a positive dimension to the formulation of the messages of promise in Ezekiel, and it is present in chs. 40–48 as well. That is what is involved in the other technique by which proclamations of hope are formulated, that of a stress on the continuity of divine action. After all, what chs. 40–48 portray is a new temple with new buildings and new ordinances, all of which bear a close resemblance to the former ones. But this is not where the positive dimension is centered. That comes with the new allotment of a transformed land in chs. 47–48. But even there it is striking how the negative focus predominates. The river will eliminate an infertile wilderness and even the Dead Sea, although of course not the needed salt! And even the apportionment of the tribal land will achieve an equality which eliminates strife and the loss of former tribes.

To recognize the overwhelming centrality of this negative orientation requires that we be less ambitious in attempts at historical reconstruction which would build upon a positive intent detected behind this material. But such less ambitious attempts are not to be thought of as the sad consequence of a lack of information. There is no shortage of material here! Rather the restricting of historical reconstruction is simply the result of being faithful to the material's intention.

Bibliography

H. Gese, *Der Verfassungsentwurf des Ezechiel* (BHT 25; Tübingen: Mohr, 1957); M. Greenberg, "The Design and Themes of Ezekiel's Program of Restoration," *Int* 38 (1984) 181-208; M. Haran, "The Law Code of Ezekiel XL–XLVIII and Its Relation to the Priestly School," *HUCA* 50 (1979) 45-71; J. Levenson, *Theology of the Program of Restoration of Ezekiel 40-48* (HSM 10; Missoula: Scholars Press, 1976); G. Ch. Macholz, "Noch einmal: Planungen für den Wiederaufbau nach der Katastrophe von 587," *VT* 19 (1969) 322-52; S. Niditch, "Ezekiel 40–48 in a Visionary Context," *CBQ* (1986) 208-24; O. Procksch, "Fürst und Priester bei Hesekiel," *ZAW* 58 (1940-41) 99-133; E. A. Speiser, "Background and function of the biblical *nasi'*," *CBQ* 25 (1963) 111-17; S. Tuell, "The Temple Vision of Ezekiel 40–48: A Program for Restoration?" *PEGLBS* 2 (1982) 96-103; W. Zimmerli, "Ezechieltempel und Salamostadt," in *Hebräische Wortforschung* (*Fest.* W. Baumgartner; VTSup 16; Leiden: Brill, 1967) 389-414; idem, "Plans for Rebuilding After the Catastrophe of 587," in *I Am Yahweh* (tr. D. W. Stott; Atlanta: Knox, 1982) 111-33.

THE NEW TEMPLE, 40:1–42:20

Text

Unfortunately the text of these three chapters is among the most poorly preserved in the Hebrew Bible. Lack of space makes it impossible here even to list the major emendations necessary. Only major deletions and insertions will be mentioned in the outline of structure. The reader is referred for details to Zimmerli *(Ezekiel 2)* and to the apparatus of *BHS*.

Structure and Genre

I. Introduction	40:1-4
A. Date	1a
1. From the beginning of exile (after 597 B.C.)	1aαβγ
2. From the fall of the city (after 587 B.C.)	1aδ

Most of the material in this section is presented as a VISION REPORT, in fact as part of a vision that continues until the end of ch. 48. This overall unity of chs. 40–48 is supported by the lack of any PROPHETIC WORD FORMULA, but other factors demonstrate that a complicated history lies behind the present text. We shall return to this issue with each subsection of chs. 40–48. No sharp break appears with 43:1, but chs. 40–42 can conveniently be set apart as containing the relatively self-contained plans for a new temple. Even here, though, in certain sections the overarching visionary structure disappears over large spans (so 40:38-46 except for v. 45a, 41:15b-26 except for v. 22b, and 42:1-14 except for vv. 1 and 13aα), suggesting that material of diverse backgrounds has been secondarily molded together within a loose framework. In view, however, of the inherently fragmentary character of any such building plans, it may easily be that the secondary material is just as old as that material which preserves more of a visionary framework.

In one way 41:4, the identification of the innermost sanctuary, is the goal of all that precedes it, and all that precedes—apart from 40:38-46—is of one consistent piece, introducing each new step with a VISIONARY GUIDANCE FORMULA in which the heavenly guide's direction is reported (40:17aα, 24aα, 28a, 32a, 48aα; 41:1a). However, even within 40:1–41:4 one notices at least two formal inconsistencies: (1) the introductory "behold" normal to visions appears only rarely (40:3, 5, 17, and 24); and (2) the measuring rod described in 40:5 appears in use only in 40:6-8, returning again surprisingly in 41:8 and 42:16-19. Thus it seems impossible by any process of paring down to get effectively behind the present text to some reconstructed, problem-free original. One can only note where a decided difference in style appears, as in 40:38-46, where the purpose of items described is suddenly a matter of concern in contrast to the preceding, or in 41:5-12, where the style of a guided tour changes to what Gese called a "catalog" (*Verfassungsentwurf*, 24) and Zimmerli speaks of "sheer statistical factuality" (*Ezekiel 2*, 374). Similarly, both 41:15b-26, with a shift of focus from the basic shape of the buildings to their wall decoration and interior furnishings, and 42:1-14, with a lengthy and obscure description of the two priestly sacristies, are clearly separate and supplementary.

It is difficult even to give a proper genre label to this material. The term "plans" has been used here, and that is perhaps the best available, but it is still inadequate in certain respects. If by "plans" a blueprint is meant, that is, a sketch outlining to scale a two-dimensional cross section of a structure, the label is only partially appropriate. The term does fit the way only a two-dimensional portrayal is presented. In only an occasional instance (e.g., 40:5bδ) is the height of any structure ever given. Of course, an actual blueprint is a line drawing rather than a prose description, but only a description in words is appropriate for the spoken communication presumed by the vision's narrative framework (40:1-4) and its goal of proclamation. Strangest and most frustrating of all to modern readers is the omission of certain items essential to the understanding of what is presented. Crucial details and dimensions are omitted, so that no actual construction could ever have taken place solely on the basis of what is said in chs. 40–42. One can only conclude that this material reflects presuppositions on the basis of which such incompleteness was understandable. We shall need to return to this point under Setting and Intention, but one element implicit in it must appear in any attempt at a formulation of the genre of this material. It is above all else the *report* of a *vision* in which structures are seen and described. Presumably the seeing was comprehensive, naturally including the height of the structure seen, but the description makes no attempt to be comprehensive.

The language introducing the VISION REPORT is closely parallel to that used in connection with earlier visions, the HAND OF YAHWEH REVELATORY FORMULA appearing in 1:3, 3:14, 8:1, 37:1, the label "visions of God" in 1:1, 8:3, and 11:24, and the expression "set me down" in 37:1. The spatial aspect of the vision is responsible for the overall structure of the report, tracing as it does the gradual movement of the "man" from outside the temple complex to within the innermost part of the sanctuary. Even the details of this "tour" follow definite patterns. The sequence in which the outer gates are examined is first east, then north, and finally south, while the inner gates are then logically entered from the south, where the preceding sequence had left off, then moving to east and north. The original entrance from the east was presumably determined either because of the basic eastward orientation of the temple itself or because any return from Babylon not subject to limitations of geography, e.g., in a vision, would come from that direction. Since no west gates exist in the temple Ezekiel is shown, the sequence followed in regard to both outer and inner gates becomes unavoidable. Finally, that the prophet should be left in the nave (41:1) while his heavenly guide alone continues on to the inner sanctuary (41:3) is only the natural result of the ritual limitations about who might enter there.

However, an unavoidable consequence of this tour's linear character is a restricted focus. Tracing a "walking tour" automatically includes such matters as reporting the steps ascended: seven at the outer gates, eight at the inner gates, and ten in the vestibule leading to the nave, totalling twenty-five. But other items falling outside the purview of such a "walking tour" could only be appended in a somewhat disconnected fashion, necessitating the interruption of the logic of the description of movement. For example, the prophet is presumably left standing within the nave in 41:1-4 while he describes in 41:5-15a the measuring of external structures, which would not then have been visible to him. Rather than faulting the skill or taste of the composition of this material for such inconsistency, it is more suitable to recall as an analogy how in an actual blueprint two or more views of a structure are given in order to overcome the inherent limitations of a two-dimensional approach. Thus the expansionary sections appropriately discard for the most part the framework of a visionary tour and confine themselves to supplying information. Occasionally, as in 42:1-12, the complexities of the structures and the terminology used in their description leave us at a loss to understand exactly what is being described, an experience not at all unusual when one lacking the requisite background listens to an architect or a contractor. In any case, another natural and logical conclusion of the entire tour, in addition to the arrival at the inner sanctuary, comes in this expansionary material with the giving of final, overall measurements, first of the temple itself in 41:13-15a and then of the entire temple area in 42:15-20. Behind all this information, however, there do lie some explicit and implicit basic convictions to be explored below.

Setting

The date given in 40:1 is somewhat uncertain, depending on whether the phrase "the beginning of the year" is taken as referring to the first month or to a New Year's festival on the tenth day of the seventh month, but in any case it is the double designation of the year that is most important. The "twenty-fifth year of our exile" (573 B.C.) is seen by Zimmerli as designating the halfway point in the fifty-year period "which must elapse before the proclamation of the great year of release" mentioned in Isa 61:1 (*Ezekiel 2*, 346). Zimmerli further calls attention to the prominence of the multiples of twenty-five in the reporting of temple measurements (twenty-five as the total number of steps one must ascend in moving from the outside to the nave and as the width of each of the gates, while all the larger measurements are fifty, one hundred, or five hundred, and thus multiples of twenty-five). While there is a certain weight to this argument, the point is not by any means one to which the material explicitly directs attention, nor is the number twenty-five itself all that prominent, so that at best this interpretation could be classed as a possible subtle nicety.

However, the other date specified in 40:1, "the fourteenth year after the city was conquered," is a far less subtle way of introducing its message of hope that follows as the undoing of the past evil situation, a technique repeatedly encountered in chs. 34–39. In this case the undoing is not just a generality, but specifically the undoing of what is presented in chs. 8–11, the vision of the abominations and violations within the temple that led to the withdrawal of Yahweh's glory (see further on 43:1-12).

The more basic question of the traditio-historical setting of chs. 40–42 is an extremely large one, involving as it does the relationship of the temple described here to Solomon's preceding temple and to the one reconstructed during the Persian period. Limitations of space allow only the singling out of a few essential points. First of all, it is fully clear that the entire vision is no description of any actual temple. The "very high mountain" in 40:2 picks up language with a mythological heritage, as in Ps 48:1-2, but it is not a description of the actual geography of Jerusalem. Similar later fantastic descriptions, as in 47:1-12, reflect a parallel transcendent perspective. Nonetheless, there is also a high degree of concern for a quite literal situation in much of the material. The numbers and their totals are by no means purely symbolic, and the description abounds in details of a very practical sort. Many of these details do reflect close similarities to what is known of Solomon's temple: the three-part structure of the temple itself, windows, palm tree decoration, and two columns are some of the closest parallels. One could conclude from this that the memory of Solomon's temple supplied the necessary background, which enabled an understanding of this entire, often incomplete and unclear, description. And yet at the same time there are occasional sharp differences, e.g., the absence of any gold or flowers in the decoration, the lack of references to the nearby palace complex or towers at the gates, and the totally new descriptions of structures outside the temple building itself. Behind some of these differences there surely lie polemical purposes to which we shall return, but others simply force upon us the conclusion that this temple in 40–48 is, for unspecified reasons, new and different from its predecessor. Material in the remainder of chs. 40–48 will take us even further in this regard. And yet at the same time such an item as the pattern of the construction of the outer gates is greatly illuminated by what is known of Solomonic city gates (Zimmerli, *Ezekiel 2,* 352f.).

No real connections of a significant sort can be established between chs. 40–42 and Zerubbabel's temple or that of Herod. On the contrary, later rabbinic struggles to deal with the nonfunctional character of this material are well-known in connection with discussions of the canonicity of the book of Ezekiel. (The reference in 40:46 to a special distinguishing of the sons of Zadok is probably to be based upon the obscure tradition in 44:15-16 of an otherwise unknown event in which Zadokites demonstrated fidelity. Thus 40:44-46, which were claimed as a later expansion on other grounds, may constitute the very latest stratum of tradition within chs. 40–42.)

Finally, it is necessary briefly to explore the issue of what functional setting this section could have had. Of course, as the report of a vision it could simply function as a record of a revelatory experience. But in 40:4 the prophet is told to "declare all that you see to the house of Israel." It simply boggles our minds to contemplate the "preaching" of such dull details. Beyond a certain degree of clarity in overall intention, such as the reality of a restoration and a legitimate, divinely authorized new sanctuary, we find this wealth of minutiae extremely uncommunicative, leaving us to assume that it was, although preserved as the Lord's revelation through his prophet, doubtless "filed away" as non-functional. What a shock it is, then, to learn how this material, together with the to us equally dull details of the visions in chs. 1 and 10, became an integral part of later Jewish mysticism (see Newsom). Once again the learned use of this material appears to be a modified but nevertheless related continuation of the same fascination with esoteric learning which we have encountered in smaller degree in such places as the prophecies concerning foreign nations, and now discover here in chs. 40–48 on a far greater scale than anywhere else in the book.

Intention

The direction to the prophet to "declare all that you see to the house of Israel" must be accepted with all seriousness, and our task here is to search out precisely what is the aim of the proclamation. This aim emerges with a considerable degree of clarity when one pursues in some detail the two major techniques which the prophet employs here, as in the preceding consolation material, to link up his new message to his earlier one. This task is made a bit more difficult here because the highly objective character of the material means that similarities and contrasts to what lies in the past remain in many cases implicit. This does not mean that they are not there, only that greater care must be exercised in determining them.

As was pointed out above, the date of the vision already calls attention to the way the new temple is presented as the undoing of the past evil situation of the destruction of the old one. But, again as was already noticed, it is not just the fact of the temple's destruction that is reversed. The vision in chs. 40–42 reverses the prophet's own earlier vision in chs. 8–11, and that reversal extends further into the details of the vision than is sometimes noticed. It is fully obvious that the return of the glory of Yahweh in 43:1-5 reverses the former departure at the end of ch. 11, and this observation underlines the artificial character of the decision of convenience to break off the first subunit of chs. 40–48 at the end of ch. 42. Just as the vision of chs. 8–11 was made up of subunits with a relative degree of independence, even though none of these could have their full meaning apart from their connection to the final point of the "undedication" of the sanctuary, so here chs. 40–42 describe a new sanctuary whose newness can be explored along the way, but that newness cannot have its full significance apart from Yahweh's own rededication in 43:1-5.

The comparison with chs. 8–11 can lead us further in detecting what is undone. In overall approach both chs. 8 and 40–42 present themselves as "tours." In ch. 8 the sanctuary is approached from the north, probably reflecting both the historical awareness that it was a consequence of Jerusalem's geography that made this direction the most suitable for assault and the mythological flavor of doom associated with that direction in the tradition of a foe from the north. The approach from the east in ch. 40, as was observed earlier, probably reflects that it is from Babylon that Yahweh's chariot throne now comes, but it is surely also significant to recall that it was toward the east that the divine presence withdrew in 11:23. Further, in 8:16-18 a group of idolatrous elders is observed "with their backs to the temple of the Lord and their faces toward the east, worshiping the sun toward the east" (8:16). In the vision of the new temple not only do the prophet and his guide face west, but the very possibility of their facing east is eliminated, since there are no west gates, either outer or inner. Instead, the area to the west of the temple is filled by the building of 41:12. Since the slope toward the old Tyropoeon valley would have made any such huge structure difficult if not impossible, and since no other function is spelled out for the building, Zimmerli is surely correct in his conclusion that the sole purpose of this construction to the west is "to forbid all access to the area behind the temple, that is behind the back of the Lord of the holy of holies who is facing forward i.e. eastwards" (*Ezekiel 2,* 380).

In further contrast to ch. 8 no syncretistic or idolatrous installations or decorations are present in chs. 40–42. Instead, as 42:20 stresses at the conclusion, a major part of the goal of the construction is to "make a separation between the holy and the common" (see also 43:12). While this is a forthright undoing of the priestly failure of 22:26, it is more than that, for it is now presented as achieved more by the architecture than by priestly obedience.

This brings us to an examination of the second technique, that of the continuity of divine action between God's new act in chs. 40–42 and his former acts. Does this aspect shed any light on the intention of the material? Certainly the very beginning of the vision does force a basic question before us. Can it be accurate to regard these "plans" as intended to be carried out in the construction of an actual new sanctuary? Admittedly, there is some parallel both to the instructions about the tabernacle in Exodus 25–31, in that there Moses is shown a "pattern" (Exod 25:9; ch. 40) according to which everything is to be made, and to Solomon's temple, for which David gives Solomon the "plan," using the same Hebrew word *tabnît,* according to which everything is to be done (1 Chr 28:11-19). But the major contrast is in what is not said in Ezekiel 40–42. Not only does the word *tabnît* not appear there as the label for this description, but nothing at all is said about how this temple is to be built according to this description. This temple is simply there. It is not presented as just in the heavenly realm as a model; it is already there in the land of Israel. Clearly, this is a forceful example of negative continuity. Here the Lord himself does what previously his people were asked to do, and his action results in a radical transformation (see also 36:26f.). One may even observe that the very word *tabnît* takes on in roughly contemporary literature a strongly negative connotation. In Deut 4:16-18, 2 Kgs 16:10, and Isa 44:13 this word is used of idolatrous practices. It is tempting in view of the similar usage in Ezek 8:10 to see Ezekiel as deliberately avoiding this term in chs. 40–42, because it is now a part of the vocabulary of idolatry. However, the word is used twice in a neutral sense within the vision of chs. 8–10 to designate the shape of the hand of the guide (8:3) or of the cherubim (10:8). Thus the absence of this term in chs. 40–42 cannot be due to its idolatrous flavor, but must simply indicate that this description was never intended as a plan to be carried out by the people of God. Chapters 40–42 present instead the proleptic revelation in a transcendent way of what God gives to his people when he reestablishes his presence in their midst.

Further aspects of negative continuity will be discussed in connection with 43:6-9, but these only enhance the point being made here. Whether two other items also serve as examples of this negative continuity, as Zimmerli argues (*Ezekiel 2,* 361-62), is uncertain even though possible. The restrained decor reflected in simpler ornamentation and no mention of gold or cedar wood stands in sharp contrast to the Solomonic structure, as does the total lack of stress on the temple gates or wall as having any role as military defenses. The outer wall (40:5) is far too low to serve as protection against an attack, and its actual purpose is said in 42:20 to be for ritual separation. No mention is made of any towers upon the gates, but then, since height is never spelled out in regard to the gates, this is in large part an argument from silence. Still, in my judgment these possibilities have a definite likelihood.

There are, however, also some definite aspects of positive continuity within the vision of chs. 40–42. The functioning of the "man" of bronze in 40:3 is an evident parallel to the similar figure in 8:2, but that is a very minor item in comparison to the elements of basic structural and functional continuity that are presented. It is, after all, essentially the same sanctuary which is described as the one portrayed in the accounts of the tabernacle and of Solomon's temple. (Even the structural design of the gates is eminently Solomonic; see Zimmerli, *Ezekiel 2,* 352-53.) The pattern of three rooms (vestibule, nave, and inner sanctuary) is identical, even in size. The decor of palm trees and cherubs has strong similarities, and even though the altar and sacrifices are not specifically dealt with until 43:13-27, it is already clear from 40:39-43 and 42:13-14 that sacrifices are anticipated. The fact, though, that these last two passages are supplementary elaboration of the tour structure has led Eichrodt to see in them an alteration of the prophet's own views, which later circles found "intolerable," because "They could not envisage a new sanctuary without associating with it the performance of a cult pleasing to God" (550). While indeed not only the central tour structure, but even the supplementary material, devotes little attention to the performance of a cult, to conclude that any temple, even an eschatological one, should be thought of apart from this basic expression of communion between God and his people is to introduce a much later perspective. Thus the expansions are more likely to be seen as filling out rather than distorting the basic vision.

Bibliography

K. Elliger, "Die grosse Tempelsakristeien im Verfassungsentwurf des Ezechiel (42:1ff)," in *Geschichte und Altes Testament (Fest. A. Alt;* BHT 16; Tübingen: Mohr, 1953) 79-103; H. Gese, *Der Verfassungsentwurf des Ezechiel* (BHT 25; Tübingen: Mohr, 1957) 8-33; C. Newsom, *The Songs of the Sabbath Sacrifice: Edition, Translation and Commentary* (Atlanta: Scholars Press, 1985).

THE RETURN OF THE GLORY OF YAHWEH, 43:1-12

Text

A few minor emendations are necessary. In v. 3a read *wĕhammar'ê* ("and the vision") for the first two words ("and like the vision of the vision"), and *bĕbō'ô* ("when he came") for *bĕbō'î* ("when I came"); in v. 7b read *bĕmôtām* ("at their death") for *bāmôtām* ("their high places"); in v. 11a read *wĕhēm yikkālĕmû* ("and they will be ashamed") for the first two words ("and if they are ashamed"), *tôrōtāw* ("its laws") for the first *ṣûrōtāw* ("its forms"), and delete both the second *wĕkol-ṣûrōtāw* ("and all its forms") and *wĕkol-tôrōtāw* ("and all its laws"); in v. 11b read *tôrōtāw* ("its laws") for *ṣûrātô* ("its form").

Structure and Genre

I. Visionary guidance formula	1
A. Visionary guidance formula proper	1a
B. Specification of goal: east gate	1b
II. Vision report: the entry of the glory of Yahweh	2-4
A. Announcement of the entry, with introductory "behold"	2a
B. Description of accompanying sensations	2b
1. Sound: like mighty waters	2bα
2. Sight: earth shone	2bβ
C. Comparisons	3a
1. Like the vision of Yahweh's coming to destroy	3aαβ
2. Like the vision at the river Chebar	3aγ
D. Result: I fell on my face	3b
E. Report of the entry of the glory of Yahweh by the east gate	4
III. Transition	5
A. I was lifted by the spirit	5aα
B. Brought to the inner court	5aβ
C. Situation: glory filled the temple, with introductory "behold"	5b
IV. Interpretative prophecy of salvation	6-9
A. Preliminaries	6-7aβ
1. Report of hearing a voice	6a

Because of the absence of such clear unit markers as the prophetic word formula, it is difficult to be precise about the structure of this complicated material. In a very real way this report of the return of Yahweh's glory is the conclusion of chs. 40–42, for this alone finally undoes what happened in 587 B.C. as interpreted in the earlier vision of chs. 8–11 (→ Intention of chs. 40–42). But the fact that 43:1-12 introduces a new vision makes these verses more a parallel to 40:1-5 than a continuation.

The actual VISION REPORT (II) lasts only until v. 4, issuing in a PROPHECY OF SALVATION (IV), which, following a brief transition (III), presents both an interpretative announcement (V) exploring the meaning of the return of Yahweh's glory and a lengthier set of warnings (IV.C and IV.E) and motivations (IV.D and IV.F). This interpretative prophecy ends in v. 9 but is closely linked to the following two verses in which related motivations accompany the direction to proclaim the structure of the temple. This direction again picks up 40:4 and receives in the attached v. 12 a strange sort of double concluding summary. Talmon and Fishbane (138-49) have shown how this unusual pattern reflects the style of concluding summaries of priestly laws (Lev 7:37; 11:46; 12:7; 13:59; 14:32; and especially 14:54-57) and narrative (Num 7:84-88). While Talmon and Fishbane are a bit too mechanical in their tracing of the literary development, their observations carry forward Zimmerli's remarks aimed in the same direction (*Ezekiel 2*, 419-20).

Setting

Although this unit contributes nothing to any reconstruction of its chronological set-ting, it is—as has already been briefly pointed out—of great value in an examination of related matters of tradition history and redaction criticism. As a report of the un-doing of the "undedication" of the temple in 11:23, this passage is connected direct-ly to chs. 8–11, which began by examining in ch. 8 the ritual abominations which made necessary the withdrawal of the glory of Yahweh out the east gate in 11:22-23. Now in vv. 2-4 that same glory (so identified in v. 3aαβ) comes from the same direc-tion by which it had previously left and reenters by the same east gate (40:6), and in v. 9 reference is made to those earlier abominations which had caused that departure. Further, an additional cross reference (see 3:23 and 8:4) in v. 3aγ specifically iden-tifies the glory now seen with that of Ezekiel's call vision in chs. 1–3. This particular cross reference only formalizes what was already inherent in several preceding paral-lels in which the "many waters" of v. 2 brought to mind 1:24, and the falling upon the prophet's face of v. 3b and his hearing a voice speaking in v. 6a reminded one of 1:28 and 2:2. Also the transporting activity of the spirit makes one think of 3:12 and 14, 8:3, and 11:1 and 24. Thus a large-scale redactional purpose is undertaken by this pas-sage, and when the connections to the original dedication of both tabernacle (Exod 40:34f.) and Solomon's temple (1 Kgs 8:10f.) are taken into account, that purpose can be seen to have a grandiosely overarching perspective within Israel's entire history. Later biblical writers might continue the idea of an eschatological advent involving the glory of Yahweh (e.g., Isa 60:1; Jn 1:14; Rev 21:11, 23), but none in such a flam-boyant way. In another regard, other views of the future do transcend that of Ezekiel. Whereas Ezekiel concentrates on a holiness kept faithfully separated, others could look to an all-transforming holiness which would not require protective restrictions, but would extend forth so powerfully that in an ultimate pan-sacrality even the bells on the horses would be inscribed "Holy to the Lord" (Zech 14:20).

While the ark is not mentioned, the use of the ideas of "throne" and "place of the soles of my feet" in v. 7 does seem to be a deliberate evocation of that tradi-tion as well, even though, as in Jer 3:16-17, the character of Yahweh's promise renders the ark itself unimportant. Similarly, the use of the verb "to dwell" *(šākan)* places Ezekiel in the midst of a long stream of tradition reaching from the taber-nacle *(miškān)* to the Shekinah.

In fact, the content of 43:6-9 seems deliberately formulated so as to connect up to a maximum of other traditions. The material in v. 7 about defiling Yahweh's name and engaging in whoring makes specific reference to two other major lines of tradition in Ezekiel. The references to a contamination of the temple's holiness by the proximity of the palace and its memorials not only serve to give a priestly critique of the earlier heritage of the temple as a royal chapel, they also serve to make clear the importance and deliberate intent of the absence of any element of royal splendor in chs. 40–42.

But surely most typical of all in Ezekiel is the return in vv. 10-11 of the idea of a shame which lies beyond Israel's salvation. Just as in 16:54 and 61 and 36:32, this element of looking back in shameful recollection constitutes the final element in a section of promise.

Intention

This deliberate drawing together of so many strands of tradition seems to aim at an affirmation of finality. In fact, one powerful way of giving expression to the idea of an ultimate end would naturally be to show it as a completing of all aspects of the heritage of the past. While Ezek 43:1-12 does not have room to deal with all aspects, it certainly packs many of them into this small compass. Once again the process involves the technique of portraying the promised new reality as coming in continuity with God's past actions. In the traditio-historical analysis several examples of both positive and negative continuity were indicated.

But with all this backward look in the portrayal of a promise, is there nothing remaining which still looks ahead? At first glance it seems as though the warnings of vv. 7-9 are future-directed. Fohrer goes so far as to see in them the "condition" upon which Yahweh's continued presence with his people is dependent (244). To take this passage that way is grossly to misunderstand it. The focus of these warnings is solely to provide a contrast to what was. The new temple is designed so as to eliminate these past sins. Yahweh's eschatological presence is forever (vv. 7 and 9!). Of course, to Ezekiel's audience this vision was only a proleptic assurance, and to a certain extent any description of a sinless future embodies an element of a calling in that direction. But the basic intention of these verses is far from a summons to fidelity! It is the assurance of a future new relationship. The motivations of shame and obedience in vv. 7-9 are there, but they function not to call Yahweh's people to greater effort, but to describe that new order in which obedience is natural. Thus the only truly functional motivation at work in bringing about this future is once again Yahweh's stubborn grace. The "law of the temple" in v. 12 is not a prescription to be carried out; it is the promise of a revelation to be longed for.

Bibliography

T. Mettinger, *The Dethronement of Sabaoth* (ConBOT 18; Lund: Gleerup, 1982) 97-115; S. Talmon and M. Fishbane, "The Structuring of Biblical Books: Studies in the Book of Ezekiel," *ASTI* 10 (1975-76) 138-49.

THE MEASUREMENTS OF THE ALTAR OF BURNT OFFERINGS, 43:13-17

Text

Once again the technical character of this material has resulted in some problems in its transmission. In v. 13 read *wĕhêqōh 'ammâ* ("and its base was a cubit") for *wĕḥêq hā'ammâ* ("and the base of the cubit") and *'aḥat* ("one," feminine) for *hā'eḥād* ("the one," masculine). In v. 14 omit the article from the last word. In v. 17 it is possible that a line giving the dimensions of the lower ledge has been lost. Also in v. 17 it is necessary to read *sĕbîbôtāyw* ("around it") for the ungrammatical *sābîb 'ôtāh* ("arounding it") and *pōnôt* ("facing") for *pĕnôt* ("a facing of").

Structure and Genre

Both content and form make it clear that this is an independent unit. The content is completely unconnected to the preceding report of the return of Yahweh's glory, and while the following section 43:18-27 also deals with the altar of burnt offerings, there the form is entirely different. In that section we encounter divine speech with the appropriate formulas, while here no narrative framework of any kind is present, not even a PROPHETIC WORD FORMULA, MESSENGER FORMULA, VISIONARY GUIDANCE FORMULA, or the address as son of man. The material can only be classified as description of a totally impersonal sort. The closest analogy is the descriptive material in 41:5-15, but even that material has a rudimentary narrative framework.

Setting and Intention

In terms of content, this section supplements the observation about the altar's existence in 40:47 and provides some information useful for understanding v. 20 of the following section. It is thus doubtless to be seen as a later, secondary elaboration intended largely to satisfy curiosity. Since we do not have any detailed description of a preexilic altar of burnt offerings, scholars have been reduced to conjecture for the traditio-historical setting. The stepped shape is often compared to that of a ziggurat, and thus a Babylonian influence could be theorized (Albright, 137-42). Ahaz's Assyrian altar of 2 Kgs 16:10-16 has been argued to be the source of this pattern (de Groot, 44-52). The mysterious word for altar hearth found here also appears in Isa 29:1-2, 7. But all in all no truly significant link to preceding tradition can be found. The reference in 1 Kgs 8:64 offers no description, and 2 Chr 4:1 specifies a size of twenty cubits but no details about shape. It is surprising that the section itself, with its provision for steps, directly violates the ancient prohibition in Exod 20:25-26. Late subsequent Talmudic tradition (*b. Mid.* 3.1a and 3b) knows of an altar of similar shape, but with dimensions twice as large and a ramp in place of steps. All in all we are largely helpless before the unconnected character of this unit, able to deduce only that the final observation about the steps facing east seems to be designed to avoid the misdirected worship mentioned in 8:16. How much is intended to be of practical utility is impossible to say, although the large and relatively inaccessible work surface at the top (Fohrer, 240) makes one hesitant to find much of a functional significance in this material.

Bibliography

W. F. Albright, "The Babylonian Temple-Tower and the Altar of Burnt Offering," *JBL* 39 (1920) 137-42; J. de Groot, *Die Altäre des Salomonischen Tempelhofes* (BWANT NF 6; Stuttgart: Kohlhammer, 1924).

THE CONSECRATION OF THE ALTAR OF BURNT OFFERINGS, 43:18-27

Structure and Genre

I. Preliminaries	18aαβγ
A. Report of divine speech	18aα
B. Address as son of man	18aβ
C. Messenger formula	18aγ
II. Sacro-legal heading	18aδεb
A. Content: altar ordinances	18aδ
B. Time: day of construction	18aε
C. Purpose: burnt offerings and blood sprinkling	18b
III. Ritual procedure	19-27a
A. First day (2 ms except for 3 ms in v. 21b)	19-21
1. Agents: Zadokite priests singled out for a gift	19aαβγ
2. Interruptive prophetic utterance formula	19aδ
3. Animal: gift specified as a bull for a sin offering	19aεb
4. Use of the blood	20a
5. Purpose: cleansing and atoning as a sin offering	20b
6. Disposition: burning of the sacrifice outside	
(3 ms in v. 21b)	21
B. Second day (2 ms except for 3 mp in vv. 22b and 24b)	22-24

In this highly unusual section a set of instructions for ceremonial procedure of the sort known from priestly legislation and designated a RITUAL (R. Rendtorff, *Die Gesetze in der Priesterschrift,* 12) is framed as a prophecy. The framework consists of the preliminaries in section I, familiar from virtually all of the book of Ezekiel, an interrupting PROPHETIC UTTERANCE FORMULA in v. 19aδ, and a concluding prophetic utterance formula in v. 27bδ. It is somewhat unusual that no direction to speak appears, and that the prophet himself is the one addressed by the MESSENGER FORMULA, but for this last see 6:11. Apart from this framework we are left with what is almost a standard ritual. It has a sacro-legal heading (II) as in Exod 12:43, a body (III) which sets forth the various steps for the consecration of the altar as in Exod 29:36f., 40:9-11, and Lev 16:18f., and a conclusion (IV) describing the normal, subsequent use of the altar. Apart from the structural oddities inherent in the framing, such as the double heading (see Num 19:1-2) and the formulaic third person references to Yahweh in v. 24, one other unusual characteristic marks off the body of this ritual as unique: in much of this material the prophet continues to be addressed. Even though, as has been shown in the structural outline, the priests—presumably it is one of their number who is meant in v. 21b—

are occasionally addressed, Ezekiel remains the major addressee. This is strikingly reminiscent of the way Moses functions in some of the Pentateuchal legislation, and fits with Klaus Koch's idea that rituals lie behind the formulaic address of Exodus 25–29 (Koch, *Die Priesterschrift*, pp. 104-8).

Setting

It is easy enough to conclude that chronologically this passage reflects a situation in that part of the exilic period when the hope of a restored temple made reflection about possible rituals appropriate. It is much more difficult to integrate this passage and the mental process it reflects into the long stream of priestly tradition. Koch points out how both similarities and differences show up when comparisons are undertaken (Koch, 104-5). Only a few of the most prominent issues will be mentioned here, since fuller treatment belongs in a study of Pentateuchal traditions. The reference to Zadok in v. 19 seems clearly, like 40:46b, to reflect what is said in 44:10-16. Salt appears elsewhere in connection with cereal offerings (Lev 2:13), but only here with burnt offerings. Sprinkling blood with the finger is prominent in the altar consecration in Exod 29:12 and Lev 16:19, but that terminology is missing here in Ezekiel. Seven days as the duration of the consecration ceremony is the time span familiar from both Exod 29:37 and Lev 8:33-35, but only in vv. 25-27 of our passage does that figure appear. This, together with other factors, makes it quite possible that vv. 25-27 involve a secondary revising of vv. 19-24 (Zimmerli, *Ezekiel 2*, 435).

As indicated, further consideration of matters of the history of ritual would be out of place in a book about a prophet. Still, one final issue does appropriately demand at least to be raised, namely, is Ezekiel here seen as a new Moses? The passage seems to envisage that the prophet is personally to take the lead in a ceremony, even if the preceding sections of chs. 40–42 have no room for such an idea. In the case of Moses, Exodus 25–31 appropriately directs Moses to carry out the directions given, since that was seen as a part of his responsibility, his role as a cult founder. But nothing similar was ever specified for Ezekiel apart from this passage. Elsewhere Ezekiel only sees in a vision what the new situation will be. His participant role arises only when the form of a ritual is borrowed. And yet there is a certain appropriateness to the idea of Ezekiel as a new Moses. Not only does he describe the new sanctuary; he speaks of a new exodus, a new covenant, and later in chs. 40–48 of new boundaries and a new allocation of land. Levenson even calls attention to the way Ezekiel, like Moses, only beholds the promised land from afar (37-44).

Intention

To regard the setting of these ceremonial directions within a prophetic framework as simply the attempt "to vest these ordinances with divine authority," as Wevers does (315), is incorrect. If that were the goal, we have no evidence to suggest that it was crowned with any success. Rather than finding the appearance of such material in Ezekiel as authoritative, later generations of Jews found its departures from Pentateuchal patterns embarrassing. No, a deeper and more basic intention underlies the consecration of a new altar. The concern encountered before (→ Intention at 36:16-38) about how a new life for a restored Israel could be possible in view of her past failures demands that the Lord himself provide a way. Here—in extremely modest fashion—the way is opened for a worship of which the Lord can say, "I will accept you" (43:27). Such a way would naturally, from a priestly perspective, involve sin-removing and atoning sacrifices by appropriate representatives, but what remains surprising and without analogy—at least within the bounds of the OT—is the idea that a prophetic figure should be personally involved as a kind of new Moses in the opening of this eschatological way to a new worship by the people of God.

Bibliography

K. Koch, *Die Priesterschrift von Exodus 25 bis Leviticus 16: eine überlieferungsgeschichtliche und literarkritische Untersuchung* (FRLANT NF 53; Göttingen: Vandenhoeck & Ruprecht, 1959); J. Levenson, *Theology of the Program of Restoration of Ezekiel 40-48* (HSM 10; Missoula: Scholars Press, 1976); R. Rendtorff, *Die Gesetze in der Priesterschrift* (FRLANT NF 44; Göttingen: Vandenhoeck & Ruprecht, 1954).

THE CLOSED OUTER EAST GATE, 44:1-3

Text

In v. 3 delete *'et* (not translated) and the second *nāśî'* ("prince").

Structure and Genre

I. Visionary guidance formula: brought to the outer east gate	1a
II. Ordinance: the use of this gate	1b-3
A. Observation: it was closed	1b
B. Explanation	2
1. Report of divine speech	2aα
2. Announcement: this gate is to remain closed	2aβ
3. Reason	2aγδ
a. No one shall enter by it	2aγ
b. Because Yahweh did	2aδ
4. Conclusion: it shall be closed	2b
C. Qualification	3
1. The prince may use it for ritual meals	3a
2. Limitation: he enters and leaves by the vestibule	3b

The presence of VISIONARY GUIDANCE FORMULAS in 44:1 and 4 shows this small section to be an independent unit. Although formulated as a narrative, the narrative element exists primarily to provide the setting and reason for the articulation of a sanctuary ordinance. To an extent, thus, it is similar in shape to a cultic ETIOLOGY, such as in Genesis 32. But this is in part deceptive, for the cultic practice of maintaining a closed gate functions almost by definition as a limitation of access, i.e., a certain gate can be used only on some special occasion. Here it is

312

prescribed that this gate never be used as an entry, precisely to acknowledge the importance of what once happened there. To offer a story explaining why a certain athlete wears a particular number on his uniform would be to provide an etiology, whereas this text is more to be compared to the practice of retiring a certain uniform number from usage as a way of honoring the last one to wear that number. This takes a current practice and offers an exceptional departure from it based totally on a past event, whereas the usual etiology explains a standard practice which does continue, even if the nature of that practice is an abstention. Here again the "once for all" aspect of the divine action affirmed presupposes a different sort of mental process for its celebration and requires that it find expression in a ritual somewhat different from the customary cyclical pattern of agricultural religions.

Setting and Intention

Both the unit's placement and its content reveal its function as a transitional link within the larger structure of chs. 40–48. These verses clearly presuppose 43:1-19, and they also begin with a simple description of an existing situation. However, they also exist in order to introduce an ordinance, and in so doing serve as the beginning of the long section of such ordinances in chs. 44–46. Specifically these three initial verses anticipate 45:7-25 and 46:1-18. They perform this function somewhat awkwardly, however, for they introduce the figure of the prince without any prior preparation, only to abandon it. Perhaps some editorial activity has occasioned part of this awkwardness in two ways: (1) the use of Yahweh in the third person in vv. 2 and 3 may reveal that the angelic man of chs. 40–43 was originally the speaker in 44:1; and (2) the textual problem at the beginning of v. 3 may indicate that it is a secondary interruption between vv. 2 and 4.

The phenomenon of a closed gate has a sociological setting known in Babylon, one implied by rituals prescribing the opening of a gate, and it is a natural part of the procedure of restricting access to certain special occasions. Psalm 24 seems to imply something similar, but, as was argued above, limited access is a decisively different practice from non-access. Even the exception provided whereby the prince may eat ritual meals within this gate is, as Zimmerli points out (*Ezekiel 2*, 441), a part of the idea of the denial of the use of the gate, for in his case the gate "acquires the function of a cultic room" and no longer functions as a gate at all. Thus the major and distinctive aspect of this ordinance is to affirm the absolute finality of the restoration of Yahweh's presence to his temple. No new withdrawal parallel to the one in 11:22-23 can ever be contemplated, for Yahweh announces that he will act in such a way as to make the coming restoration an ultimate one. Thus here ritual becomes eschatology.

RENEWED VISIONARY COMMISSION INTRODUCING THE FOLLOWING ORDINANCES, 44:4-5

Text

In v. 5b read *limbô'ê habbayit ûlĕmôṣā'ê* ("to the entrances of the house and the exits of . . .") for the four words preceding the final word.

Structure, Genre, and Setting

I. Visionary guidance formula: through the north gate to the front of the temple	4aαβ
II. Report of a vision	4aγδb
A. Report of seeing	4aγ
B. Report of what is seen: the glory of the Lord, with introductory "behold"	4aδ
C. Report of response: fell on my face	4b
III. Report of divine speech	5aα
IV. Address as son of man	5aβ
V. Commission	5aγδεζb
A. Direction to attend carefully to what is said, viz., statutes and laws	5aγδεζ
B. Direction to attend to sanctuary entrances and exits	5b

Clearly a new unit at the beginning, as the new VISIONARY GUIDANCE FORMULA shows, these two verses constitute a transitional link between what has preceded and what follows. The unit is thereby much more closely tied to what follows in that it serves as a beginning in a double sense, both for 44:6-31 specifically and for 44:6–46:18 as a whole new complex. (Note that no subsequent new visionary guidance formula appears until 46:19.) The link to what has preceded shows vividly in several ways: (1) in the way v. 5 is patterned after 40:4; (2) in the way 43:1-5 is presupposed to explain how the Lord's glory got there; (3) in the way 43:11 is borne in mind as a basis for the switch from the descriptions of chs. 40–42 to the ordinances that follow here, and (4) in the way v. 4 honors the rule about the closed east gate in 44:1-2 (see also 46:1). Such a transitional link is presumably editorial, but the bare existence of the transitional link does not enable us to assign a chronological place to this one editorial step over against all other such activity. This particular editorial work is, however, especially complex, not only in the number of points of connection, but also in the subtle and skillful reformulation of previous material. Note especially the way 44:5 reverses 40:4 both in word order and in vocabulary so as to shift the focus from what was there seen to what is here heard. As in 44:2, the name Yahweh may have been secondarily introduced as speaker in v. 5, since it was presumably the angelic man who served as guide in v. 4.

Intention

The key purpose of this transitional link is to shift the orientation from what has preceded. In 43:11 the visionary plan itself was central; here the focus is on supplementary ordinances dealing with what was seen. To put it another way, 43:11 mentions exits and entrances as phenomena observed, while 44:5 mentions the same entrances and exits in order to introduce the subsequent ordinances in 44:7-14 and 46:1-10 about how these gates are to be used and who is to be denied admission.

Because this change in purpose does constitute a highly significant step, it is important to understand it from the perspective of the text itself, and to avoid reading in false or extraneous motives. To see the commission in v. 5 as concerned to give full authority to what follows is only partly appropriate. The polemical orientation of some of the following ordinances is undeniable, but this already was the case in 43:6-10. It is highly misleading to see the section of ordinances beginning here as having "no connection whatsoever with what Ezekiel originally wrote," i.e., in the preceding chapters (Eichrodt, 563). For the mind of the prophet as well as the minds of his disciples involved in the elaboration of all of chs. 40–48, there was no idea of any sharp contrast between the revealed gift of God here pictured in plans and the way the shape of that gift exposed the past guilt it was aimed to condemn. To see in the sanctuary ordinances solely a concern for future obedience is to miss the major point behind this material. As seen so many times, it is the pattern of the undoing of past evil which is mainly responsible for giving the material its shape. To draw a contrast between the bold prophet "moving forward to a new future in which the transformed community is no longer menaced by the old conditions of human imperfection and error" and "a petty-minded man who takes refuge in the old-fashioned forms of the priestly ideal of holiness" (Eichrodt, 563) is to misunderstand the eschatological character of the promises, especially 36:26-27, and to attempt to turn them into a socio-political principle. That is a serious enough error, but to upbraid the traditionist of 44:4-31 as "false to his own vocation" and misusing his ecstatic authority (ibid.) is to fall victim to a romantic delusion which exalts the vision of holiness and then strangely assigns the concrete expression of it an inferior status.

OFFICIANTS AT WORSHIP, 44:6-31

Text

In v. 6a insert *bēt* ("house of") before *merî* ("rebellion"). In vv. 8b-9a read *lākēn* ("therefore") for *lākem* ("for you") and move it to the start of v. 9. In v. 19a delete the second *'el-heḥāṣēr haḥîṣônâ* ("to the outer court") as a dittograph. In v. 28a read *wĕlō 'tihyeh lāhem naḥălâ* ("and they shall have no inheritance") for *wĕhāyĕtâ lāhem lĕnaḥălâ* ("and it will be their inheritance").

Structure and Genre

I. Preliminaries	6a
A. Direction to speak	6aα
B. Addressee: rebellious house	6aβ
C. Messenger formula	6aγ
II. Cultic ordinances in the form of a modified prophecy of punishment	6b-31
A. Accusation as reason	6b-8
1. Reproachful heading: enough abominations!	6b
2. Selected details of past cultic transgressions: use of foreigners	7-8
a. Bringing in uncircumcised foreigners profaned my house	7a
b. You broke my covenant with your abominations	7b

This is in many ways a strangely constructed unit. It is a unit because of its common content of ORDINANCES regarding priests. But these ordinances are initially presented in the pattern of a PROPHECY OF PUNISHMENT, suitably introduced with preliminaries (I) and following the standard shape of accusatory reason (II.A), transitions (II.B), and announcement (II.C). But this pattern is followed only for the first area of cultic ordinances, namely, the demoting of Levites (II.C.2) and the assignment of priestly functions to Zadokites (II.C.3). Beginning with v. 17 the entire structure of divine speech is abandoned, as a series of ordinances for priests is introduced (II.D). What facilitates this shift is the fact that in Hebrew the ORDINANCES are formulated as simple statements about the future, e.g., "they shall" or "shall not," which are identical to what appears in the results subsection of a prophetic announcement. With v. 23 begins a puzzling alternation between divine speech (vv. 23-24, 28, and 30) and further ordinances not worded as direct address. Section II.E (vv. 23-24) is also at odds with its context in that it deals with generally formulated positive priestly duties. The final section (II.G) is highly peculiar in that it contains a strange mingling of persons, and at the end prohibits for priests what was always prohibited elsewhere (Exod 22:30 [*RSV* 22:3]) for all Israelites. (But see Lev 22:8 for a similar priestly PROHIBITION.)

Two subordinate matters of genre occur here for the first time in Ezekiel, and these require attention. In v. 6 the indictment of Israel begins with "Enough now" (Zimmerli's translation, literally "much for you"). This is a rarely attested way of introducing an accusation in a hostile manner, but it does occur twice in priestly tradition in Num 16:3, 7 (coincidentally in a dispute about the relationship between Levites and priests), in Yahweh's mouth in Deut 3:26, and in the words of Jeroboam I in 1 Kgs 12:28. The other genre matter arises with the beginning of Yahweh's announcement in v. 9, "No foreigner . . . shall enter my sanctuary." This same formal pattern, i.e., "shall not enter," appears repeatedly in the law of the congregation in Deut 23:2-4 as a PROHIBITION excluding a group from participation in worship. As was the case earlier in Ezekiel, e.g., 14:1-11, the prophet adopts a legal form as a way of utilizing a familiar shape for his message. Ezekiel, however, modifies the pattern attested in Deuteronomy 23 by beginning it with "every" (*RSV* "no" because of the following negative). This usage is also found in priestly material (see Lev 6:11, 20; 11:9, 10, 20, and 42).

Setting and Intention

In view of the blending of announcement and ordinance in this section, we shall need to look at each of these types of material separately and then at their function as a combination.

The section in vv. 6-14 dealing with the transgression of the Levites makes extensive use of terminology familiar from the prophecies of judgment in chs. 4–24: "went far" (8:6 and 11:15), "going astray" (14:11), "idols" (a favorite word of Ezekiel's, 14:4), "stumbling block" (3:20; 7:19; 14:3, 4, 7; 18:30), "bear their punishment" (14:10), and "bear their shame" (16:52). It is significant that of these six expressions, four are found in 14:1-11, and two of them only there in Ezekiel apart from ch. 44. This makes all the more certain the observation that here as in 14:1-11 a prophetic message is being formulated by employing priestly legal tradition.

Zimmerli directs attention to how unusual it is that a reason should be provided not only for the message of judgment, the deposing of the Levites from priestly status, but also for the "declaration of reward" to the Zadokites. He observes that "the genuine, prophetic declarations of salvation were characterized by their lack of worldly motivation," and in a footnote refers to the refrain "not for your sake" (*Ezekiel 2*, 453). It is, of course, true that the deposing of the Levites is motivated by their previous disobedience. While it is not certain exactly what episode is in mind, it seems likely that it was connected with worship at the high places. But, whatever their sin was, it manifestly provides the reason for the announcement of their punishment. Interestingly, the other part of Zimmerli's claim, that about the use of motivation for reward, is far less clear, and in fact not even accurate. The only "reward" or "salvation" given to the Zadokites is that they are not deposed. What actually is happening in these verses is something we have repeatedly encountered in the presentation of a message of promise; it is the formulation of the "announcement of salvation" as the undoing of a past evil situation. The second technique of the continuity of divine action is not explicitly emphasized in this passage, at least not in regard to the question about Levites and Zadokites in vv. 6-16. However, the actual process of deposing the disobedient or contrariwise of assigning a priority in priestly privileges to the family of one who demonstrated faithfulness is one well known in earlier OT literature. Such episodes as the rebellion of Korah, Dathan, and Abiram and its consequences in Numbers 16–18, or the rejection of the house of Eli in 1 Sam 2:12-36 with its sequel in 1 Kgs 2:26-27 leap to mind.

Rather than stressing here the apparent exoneration of one class in contradiction to Ezekiel's earlier indictment of all in 22:23-31 and 9:4 (Zimmerli, *Ezekiel 2*, 459), it is more accurate to concentrate on the central intention of this announcement about the leaders of worship in the new temple. Earlier disobedience by leaders had brought doom, but that will not be permitted to happen again. The major focus of the earlier disobedience was the use of foreigners in the temple, presumably Canaanites (possibly Gibeonites, as in Josh 9:27, or Solomonic slaves). Now in the new temple not foreigners but Levites will be the ones to perform this servant role. The assurance that even every lowly temple servant will be from the consecrated tribe, and that every priest will be from the high priestly clan, aims to show in extreme fashion how thoroughgoing is the provision for the maintenance of proper holiness in the future temple. One might compare it to a portrayal of an eschatological Britain in which every magistrate would be a member of parliament and every member of parliament a member of the royal family. That the Chronicler should go on to celebrate Levites as bearers of a lofty office, or that P material should treat Levites less severely, is thus not likely to have been polemic against Ezekiel's views. Instead these other perspectives reflect the simple awareness that what Ezekiel offers is an eschatological promise of an extreme sort rather than a political attempt to restructure the priesthood. After all, one does not find in the Reformation claim about the priesthood of all believers or in the modern understanding of baptism as universal ordination, an attack upon seminaries. Similarly, that Leviticus 1 and 3 still provide for the slaughtering of sacrificial animals to be done by the laity bringing them, rather than by a priest, does not indicate the inability of Ezekiel's policies to be put into effect because of lay resistance, but again simply the difference between ordinary practice and eschatological transformation. Inasmuch as the rest of Ezekiel's descriptions of the new temple frequently border on the fantastic in order to make a point, is it not appropriate to expect that this section too belongs in that category, alongside a fantastically high and flat Zion (chs. 40–42), a miraculous advent (43:1-5), an amazing stream of water (47:1-12), and some most extraordinary land divisions?

The ordinances in vv. 17-31 raise an entirely different sort of issue. They seem to constitute selected samplings further indicating what appropriate holiness the stipulations for priestly behavior will require. They are taken almost entirely from the priestly tradition reflected in Leviticus: vv. 17-19 being similar to Lev 6:3-4 (*RSV* 6:10-11); v. 20 to Lev 21:5 and 10; v. 21 to Lev 10:9; v. 22 to Lev 21:7 and 22:13; and vv. 25-27 to Lev 21:1-3. Even the more general material about priestly duties in Ezek 44:23-24 also comes out of the same priestly traditio-historical setting (see Lev 10:10-11). The material in Ezek 44:28 on no inheritance of land for priests, because Yahweh is their inheritance, is a somewhat different case. This constitutes an old spiritualizing of a social situation, one encountered in Num 18:20, Deut 10:9 and 18:2, Josh 13:33, and repeatedly in the Psalms. The provisions for food for priests in Ezek 44:29-31 return again to the priestly legal stream of tradition, linking up to Lev 2:3 and 10, 6:9 (*RSV* 6:16) for the cereal offering; Lev 6:19 and 22 (*RSV* 29) for the sin offering; Lev 7:6 for the guilt offering; Lev 27:28 for the "devoted thing"; Num 18:13 for firstfruits; Num 18:25-30 for the "tithe of a tithe" given to Zadokites by the Levites; and Num 18:18-20 for the entire series.

What this explicit connection with older tradition accomplishes is nothing other than highlighting the continuity of divine action, i.e., the second technique for the formulation of a message of good news. As before, Yahweh—to whom the priests continually consecrate themselves by their observance of the appropriate cultic ordinances—remains the inheritance of his priests, and they are sustained as before from the offerings given to Yahweh. The essential point behind all of this is that, even though past sins have made necessary a transformation in cultic arrangements, the new order is like the old one and this time it will work as intended.

Once it is recognized that the presumed inner priestly polemic in this section does not reflect some historically reconstructible development within the exilic and postexilic priesthood, but rather a grandiose, eschatological affirmation of heightened holiness, dating becomes a much different sort of undertaking. Instead of sorting out layers according to the degree of their pro-Zadokite claims, seeking to arrange them in a logical sequence, and then trying to find some historical points of contact for the stages of this intramural priestly power struggle, one is left with material that can only be designated exilic. The post-exilic situation of a restored community to which foreigners were attracted as proselytes (Isa 56:3 and 6-8) would raise practical questions of a sort for which the eschatological affirmations of Ezek 44:6-31 would be totally irrelevant. To summarize, although it would be wonderful to have historical information on the details of the rise to power of Zadokites and their relationship with both the menial Levites of priestly tradition and the powerful Levitic leaders spoken of by the Chronicler, this text in Ezekiel neither provides us with such information nor helps in the reconstruction of it, for it has a far different intention. It aims not to bring about political restructuring, but to portray an ultimate transformation of a sort far transcending contemporary reality.

Bibliography

R. Abba, "Priests and Levites in Ezekiel," *VT* 28 (1978) 1-9; A. Gunneweg, *Leviten und Priester* (FRLANT NF 89; Göttingen: Vandenhoeck & Ruprecht, 1965); J. G. McConville, "Priests and Levites in Ezekiel," *TynB* 34 (1983) 3-21.

THE PROPERTY RIGHTS OF COMMUNITY LEADERS, 45:1-9

Text

In v. 1 one must read *'eśrîm* ("twenty") for *'ăśārâ* ("ten"). At the start of v. 4 the first word ("holy") must be deleted, and the next two words joined to the end of v. 3 so that the result is "it is a most holy part of the land." In v. 4b probably read *ûmigrāš lĕmiqneh* ("and a grazing space for the herds") instead of *ûmiqdāš lammiqdāš* ("and a sanctuary for the sanctuary"). At the end of v. 5 the words *'eśrîm lĕšākōt* ("twenty chambers") should be emended to *'ārîm lāšābet* ("cities for dwelling"). The first word of v. 8 ("as landed property") is to be taken with the end of v. 7.

Structure and Genre

I. Time specification as a heading: when you allocate the land	1aα
II. Prescription for a holy district	1aβγδb
A. Direction for a holy district	1aβ
B. Dimensions	1aγδ
1. Twenty-five thousand cubits long	1aγ
2. Twenty thousand cubits wide	1aδ
C. Summary assessment: all holy	1b
III. Announcement of assignments of land within the holy district	2-8a
A. For the sanctuary grounds	2
1. A five hundred cubit square	2a
2. A fifty cubit border strip around it	2b
B. For the broader sacred area	3-4aα
1. Twenty-five thousand cubits square	3a
2. Within this, the sanctuary	3b-4aα
C. For the priests	4aβγδb
1. Identification: description of priests' role	4aβγδ
2. Purpose: for houses and pasture	4b
D. For the Levites	5

This unit is another remarkable transitional section. Triggered by the question of the lack of priestly territorial possession as mentioned in 44:28, it identifies just what land is assigned to priests by setting that assignment in its due place within a framework of all such allocations excerpted in similar sequence from 48:8-22. This is done in sections I-III in a legal style addressed to Israel in vv. 1-3 which refers to the Lord in the third person. But this unit then goes on to provide a connection to the subsequent material in 45:10–46:18, in which the office of the prince figures so prominently, by means of a PRIESTLY TORAH or admonitory instruction in section IV aimed at princes. Here Yahweh speaks and Israel appears in the third person, as in fact it does already in v. 6.

The connection to the foregoing extends back as far as incorporating the sanctuary dimensions from 42:20, but mainly the link to the preceding concentrates on the language of 44:28-30. There the peculiar word for "offering" is the same as that used for "set apart" in 45:1, and in a striking inclusio it is also the word used for "cease" in 45:9.

The genre of vv. 1-8a is determined by that of 48:8-22 from which it is excerpted, and thus it will be discussed under that section. The case of vv. 8b-9 is, however, different, for here we encounter the prophetic imitation of priestly torah. (For the following see J. Begrich.) Because of the brevity of this example, we find here only the series of Yahweh's imperatives, and because of the sequence of groups being considered in the context, only the princes are here addressed. Again, because of the brevity of the section, we meet none of the other possible aspects of this genre, no statement about Yahweh's desire, not any determination of a judgment, nor any expressing of consequences. Thus we have only the barest minimum of the pattern of the priestly torah, but still it is enough to enable us to recognize its similarity to such examples as Amos 4:4-5a; 5:4b-5; 5:14-15; and Isa 1:16f.

Setting and Intention

The structural setting of the section has of necessity already been considered to a large extent, but a few matters of a redaction-critical sort still require to be noted in order to complete the picture of how this unit is set within the book as a whole. From the narrower perspective of how 45:1-9 relates to the preceding chapter, the terminological usage makes it clear that here the usage of 44:9-31 has been adopted, according to which service of the house is the Levite's duty (45:5) in contrast to service at the sanctuary (45:4) for the priests. Because this is an eschatological distinction only introduced in Ezekiel's vision of the new temple, it is naturally not one attested in older literature. Moreover, since this eschatological temple was not what was established in the restoration, we do not find it reflected in the literature of that period either.

It is, however, a far different case with the terminology of "possession." Here, as noted above, we are dealing with an old matter of the spiritualizing of what would today be called real estate law. In contrast to other tribes, whose members owned an inheritance of land (for the analysis of the terms "inheritance" and "possession," see F. Horst), the priests and Levites are repeatedly said not to have a portion in the land, but the Lord is their portion and inheritance (Num 18:20; Deut 10:9; 18:2; and Josh 13:33). This old position is reaffirmed in Ezek 44:28 for the priests, but when now in 45:4-5 a segment of the future land of Israel is assigned to both priests and Levites, this old tradition seems endangered. Actually, it is the deliberate intention of vv. 4-5 to clarify this issue. In v. 4 the segment of the holy district assigned to the priests is not said to be an inheritance, a portion, or a possession. It is simply a place for houses and cattle (if the emendation adopted is correct). On the other hand, in v. 5 the Levites' segment is said to be a possession for cities (if, again, the emendation followed is correct). It seems evident that the Levites have been eliminated from that privileged group who have no possession, for whom Yahweh is their possession. In line with 44:28 this old usage is now applicable only to the priests, in yet another instance of the perspective in chs. 40–48 according to which a stricter policy for the handling of the holy things is adopted. Now it is no longer Levites and priests who live off the sacrifices, thereby having Yahweh as their inheritance (Deut 18:1b), but only the priests, who according to Ezekiel's definition are exclusively the Zadokites. Of course, such a procedure, if ever put into practice, would require major readjustments in regard to Levitical cities, and these are in fact not mentioned in ch. 48. What we actually have here is, of course, one more instance of a way in which God's promised future is described as being in continuity with the past, but also departing to an extent from the pattern of the past so as to establish a superior new pattern—in this case one exercising better care of the holy things.

At the same time, vv. 8b-9 bring into play the other technique for formulating a promise of God's new order, that of portraying it as the elimination of a past evil situation. Princes who in 22:6, 25 are indicted for crimes involving the misuse of power, are ordered to cease such practices, replacing them with "justice and righteousness." A similar concern appears again in 46:18. What is in mind is a matter only too vividly attested in Israel's previous history, the oppression of the citizens by their kings, as in the case of Naboth's vineyard (1 Kings 21), where it should be noted it is his inheritance (Ezek 44:28) which is involved. In 1 Sam 8:14 such a pattern of behavior is viewed as characteristic of a monarchy. Now Ezekiel foretells a future new order in which kings no longer exist, and whose leaders are deliberately ordered to abstain from such behavior. The pattern of the undoing of a previous evil situation could not be clearer.

Bibliography

J. Begrich, "Die priesterliche Tora," in *Werden und Wesen des Alten Testaments* (BZAW 66; Berlin: Töpelmann, 1936) 63-88; F. Horst, "Zwei Begriffe für Eigentum (Besitz): נַחֲלָה und אֲחֻזָּה," in *Verbannung und Heimkehr* (*Fest.* W. Rudolph; ed. A. Kuschke; Tübingen: Mohr, 1961) 135-56.

PROPER WEIGHTS AND MEASURES AS THE BASIS FOR THE REQUIRED OFFERINGS, 45:10-17

Text

In v. 12b one must read *ḥămiššâ* ("five") for *'eśrîm* ("twenty"), *wa'ăśārâ* ("and ten") for *wĕ'eśrîm* ("and twenty"), and *wāḥămiššîm* ("and fifty") for *waḥămiššâ* ("and five"). In v. 13b *wĕšiššît* ("and a sixth") must be read for *wĕšiššîtem* ("and you shall give a sixth part"). In v. 14a the last three words must be deleted, and in v. 14b *hakkōr* ("the cor") be read for *ḥōmer* ("a homer"). In v. 16 the ungrammatical *hā'āreṣ* ("the land") is to be deleted.

Structure

I. Background in the area of weights and measures
   presupposed by the subsequent offering ordinance — 10-12
   A. Principle of accuracy — 10
      1. Balances, i.e., weight — 10aα
      2. Ephah, i.e., dry measure — 10aβ
      3. Bath, i.e., liquid measure — 10b
   B. Definitions of size — 11-12
      1. Content measure — 11
         a. Relative standard — 11abα

This section is only a relatively independent unit. The preceding led up to a concern with the place of the prince in the possession of land within the new community, concluding a section of divine speech with a prophetic utterance formula. That divine speech is resumed in vv. 10-17, with another prophetic utterance formula in v. 15 marking only the end of a subsection, and no formula at all marking off the end of the unit in v. 17. However, the resumptive messenger formula with which v. 18 begins does indicate that with v. 17 a certain relative conclusion has been reached. This is borne out by an examination of the content, for v. 13a plainly provides the heading for the *terumah* offering, which is then explained in vv. 13-15. The preceding subsection I serves as a parenthetical preparation for II in that it establishes the weights and measures presupposed by the prescriptions in II. Subsection III returns to the role of the prince as the one responsible for providing for the carrying out of the offerings just mentioned in II. Thus within vv. 10-17, subsection II is central, but it is subsection III which serves as the point of connection, both looking back to the preceding vv. 7-9 and looking ahead to the following, namely, the details presented in vv. 18-25 about the festivals, which were introduced in v. 17. The following sequence of units actually extends as far as 46:18, where the presentation of the prince's role is finally completed. The princely role is not the central focus in all this material, but still it provides the principle of arrangement which serves as a major part of the organizational glue holding the structure together.

Genre

Verses 13-15 constitute a complete cultic ORDINANCE, containing the framework of an initial heading and a concluding expression of purpose, and filling that framework with the two essential prescriptions of the items to be used and the functions they are to fulfill. The preceding background material in vv. 10-12 presents essentially a set of definitions in vv. 11-12, to which has been prefixed a slightly hortatory set of basic principles of accuracy which are to underlie the use of all sacral weights and measures. In vv. 16-17 the strictly essential details of the actual ordinance are extended in the formulation of a policy statement establishing the chain of responsibility for implementing the ordinances. It is presumably in the last subsection that the major new element in Ezekiel's vision is to be found.

Setting and Intention

The *terumah* offering here prescribed serves as a kind of tax imposed to provide the necessary resources for maintaining the regular sacrifices, functioning in a manner parallel to the half-shekel tax ordained as a *terumah* offering in Exod 30:11-16. While the latter passage does not indicate any chain of responsibility for carrying it out, the Ezekiel material introduces the figure of the prince for that role. Interestingly, none of the standard techniques is utilized here in the formulation of this new order. While it might be presumed that the previous chain of responsibility had led to problems, no attempt is made to describe the new pattern as the undoing of the past evil situation. Similarly, while the whole role of the prince *(nāśî')* involves the use of a term from the old tribal league and presumably the abandonment of structures of the monarchic period, no explicit establishment of any such continuity and discontinuity is set forth.

The lack of material spelling out the intention of this new ordinance makes it difficult to come to any conclusion in that area. It also makes it abundantly clear that this section cannot be understood as aimed fully at establishing a new order in any practical, realistically functional way. The absence of any accompanying ordinance about tithes leaves it totally up in the air how this tax structure would function as a coordinated part of the whole. Undoubtedly it is "up in the air," the rarified air of visionary anticipation, that this financial plan for the undergirding of worship intends to remain. Beyond the basic ordinance the prophet does not go. Does he intend that one-sixtieth of the grain production, one-hundredth of the oil production, and one two-hundredth of the flock is to replace the former one-tenth? Why is it that no provision at all is made here for the larger herd animals, e.g., the bulls, when their availability is assumed in the following vv. 18 and 22-23? The apparent reason behind all these unanswered questions is that with them we have moved into areas of the life of the new community far enough removed from the temple itself that this vision does not aim to deal with them.

THE MAJOR FESTIVALS, 45:18-25

Text

In v. 21b *šib'at* ("seven") must be read for *šebū'ôt* ("weeks").

Structure

2. Duties of the prince prescribed	25aβb
a. Summary in advance: same (as Passover)	
for seven days	25aβ
b. Details: sin, burnt, and cereal offerings plus oil	25b

As was the case in the preceding unit, this section is only a relatively independent unit. The resumptive messenger formula (I) at its beginning calls attention to an apparent change in subject from the *terumah* offering ordinance of the preceding section. In fact, the prince's obligations as already summarized in v. 17 are now detailed in vv. 21-25 (III). Again in a manner similar to the preceding unit, no actual formula of conclusion appears in v. 25. Instead, it is only a subsequent resumptive messenger formula and a shift in subject matter from major *(ḥaggîm)* to minor *(mô 'ădîm)* festivals which mark the relative ending here. Yet again in parallel to the preceding unit, it is the second major subsection—here vv. 21-25, there vv. 13-15—which occupies the central place, with the preceding providing only the necessary background.

Genre

In vv. 18-20 we encounter, as in 43:18-27, the genre of a RITUAL (see Zimmerli, *Ezekiel 2,* 482; Koch, 105-6; and the discussion above of 43:18-27). The mingling of different addressees is highly confusing. Most commentators take the singular "you" as a reference to the prophet, but it seems extremely unlikely that the prophet's presence should be counted upon for what is described as an annually recurring rite. Similarly the plural "you" in v. 20b eludes explanation.

With vv. 21-25 the genre changes to that of a festival ORDINANCE, or from an overarching perspective, that of a festival calendar (a chronologically ordered series of festival ordinances moving sequentially through the year). Some problems result from the extremely compressed character of the formulation, but that is unavoidable, given the highly selective perspective which departs drastically from that of the normal festival ordinances by setting forth little more than the actions of the prince.

Setting and Intention

Within a long tradition-history of festival calendars in the OT, this instance stands nearly in the latest position. Such matters as the fusion of Passover and the feast of unleavened bread are fully presumed. Only the developed priestly legislation in Numbers 28–29 seems later. A slight clue as to the date is sometimes found (Zimmerli, *Ezekiel 2,* 484 and Eichrodt, 574) in the way "people of the land" here no longer refers to an upper social stratum of landed gentry as in preexilic usage and even in Ezekiel's earlier preaching, e.g., 7:27, 12:19, 22:29, and 33:2. Instead this label now designates the entire cultic community. But, since that same usage occurs in Lev 4:27, and since in Ezekiel's restored community in ch. 47 each resident will in fact be an equal landowner, any conclusion about dating seems extremely uncertain.

What is instead far more certain is the amazing omission in vv. 21-25 of one of the traditional major festivals, Shavuoth (Weeks, Pentecost). All other festival calendars prescribe the observance of Shavuoth, and the corrupt text of v. 21 may reflect an attempt to insert a reference to it in Ezekiel's text. Or it is even conceivable that this corrupt text could be the only remaining fragment of an original ordinance for Shavuoth in Ezekiel, which has been lost by parablepsia. Still, no textual evidence exists to support such a theory. Of lesser significance, but still amazing, are the numerous departures from Pentateuchal legislation in Ezekiel's prescriptions about such other matters as the number of animals to be sacrificed and the use of the days involved. Space limitations here do not permit the exploration of details (see Zimmerli, *Ezekiel 2*, 485), and only the most general sort of conclusion can be drawn. While a festival calendar normally aims to prescribe the essentials for observance, still a considerable amount of background must always be assumed as presumably known to the audience. Ezekiel's ordinances carry that assumption to an extreme. Passover and Booths (the name is not even used) are presented as virtually identical in that only the priest's role is spelled out, and that is indicated to be similar for the two festivals. No explanation of any sort is provided for this drastic change. No past evil situation is seen as needing to be undone, unless it be possibly the failure to cleanse the sanctuary in an annual rite at the start of the year. It is difficult to square such an observance with either the report of the abominations in ch. 8 or the increasing prominence of calendar matters in later sectarian strife, but for whatever reason the festivals are not assigned a place of any sizable significance in Ezekiel's temple. No pattern of continuity or discontinuity in divine action is even hinted at. Instead, one must assume that the intention of the unit is only to touch in the briefest way on the subject of festivals, thereby assuming an extreme amount of previously known background (perhaps that of the standard practice of his day), and actually articulating only that one phase of the entire matter which is significantly changed, the insertion of the duty of the prince as the presenter of offerings. Nonetheless, the brevity of the material means that even such an opinion can claim no loftier status than that of conjecture.

Bibliography

K. Koch, *Die Priesterschrift von Exodus 25 bis Leviticus 16: eine überlieferungsgeschichtliche und literarkritische Untersuchung* (FRLANT NF 53; Göttingen: Vandenhoeck & Ruprecht, 1959).

THE MINOR FESTIVALS, 46:1-15

Text

In v. 14 the singular *ḥuqqat* ("an ordinance") should be read instead of the plural.

Structure

I. Resumptive messenger formula	1aα
II. Gate ordinances for the sabbath and the new moon	1aβγb-3
A. When closed and when opened	1aβγb

A. Case: when the prince offers a voluntary burnt or peace offering	12aα
B. Procedure	12aβγb
1. The east gate is opened	12aβ
2. The offering is presented as on the sabbath	12aγ
3. The gate is closed when he leaves	12b
VII. Sacrifice ordinances for the daily offering (2 ms except for 2 mp in v. 15)	13-15
A. Specification of offerings	13-14
1. Animals: lamb as a burnt offering	13a
2. Time: every morning	13b
3. Cereal	14abα
a. Heading: cereal offering	14aα
b. Time: every morning	14aβ
c. Amount	14aγδ
1) One-sixth ephah	14aγ
2) One-third hin of oil to moisten flour	14aδ
d. Designation: a cereal offering for Yahweh	14bα
4. Overall designation: a perpetual ordinance, a *tamid*	14bβγ
B. Summary ordinance	15
1. Specification of offerings: lamb, cereal, and oil	15aαβγ
2. Specification of time: every morning	15aδ
3. Designation: a *tamid* burnt offering	15b

Once again this is only a relatively independent unit. Its beginning is marked off by a resumptive messenger formula, and the following unit is similarly marked off. Still, it is closely linked to the preceding, in that it contains the ordinances for the major festivals (Passover and the festival of the seventh month) with those for the minor holidays (the sabbath and the new moon). In contrast to 45:18-25, a major area of concern in this unit's ordinances is the identification of how the gates are to be dealt with on the various occasions. Nevertheless, like the preceding unit, the central focus is directed to that material which comes in second place (not counting the resumptive messenger formula), the actual ordinances for the sacrifices on the sabbath and the new moon (III) in vv. 4-7. What precedes, the initial set of gate ordinances (II), is only a necessary set of presuppositions. Following the clear logic of temporal sequence, the actual ordinances in vv. 4-7 are continued by those further gate ordinances having to do with exit procedures (IV). After these basic sections, two more loosely linked sections follow: a review of cereal offering requirements (see 45:24 and 46:7) in V; and the gate ordinances to apply at the prince's voluntary, i.e., unscheduled, offerings (VI). As an appendix which switches to the use of direct address, as in 43:18-27 and 45:18-28, VII provides the ordinances for the daily morning sacrifice, the *tamid*.

Genre and Setting

Different styles of material are mingled together within this unit. It is not surprising that the appendix in vv. 13-15 should switch to the use of the second person, since it is clearly not the direct continuation of vv. 1-12. Nevertheless, it still has the form of a cultic ORDINANCE. Koch (107-8) shows how both vv. 1-3 and 12 are shaped as RITUALS even though v. 12 is provided with a kind of casuistic introduction (while vv. 1-3 begin rather abruptly following the messenger formula). Out of these older blocks of material reflecting a setting in more straightforward instruction about sacrificial procedure, this text creates a new, overarching unit in vv. 1-12 into which, because of the setting from within Ezekiel's eschatological vision, there are combined both the ordinances for the supervisory role of the prince as a responsible representative of the people and those for the proper functioning of the gate. In 45:17 the prince's supervisory role had been summarized, and the listing of occasions there served to prepare the way for both 45:18-25 and 46:1-12. The continuous closed status of the outer east gate was prescribed in 44:1-3 as an acknowledgment of the special significance of that gate, the one by which Yahweh entered at his return. Connecting up to that special status of the outer east gate, 46:1-3, 8-10, and 12 spell out how that special closed status bears on the use of other gates. In direct parallel to 44:1-3, the inner east gate in 46:1-3 and 12 is opened only on special occasions. Because the outer gate remains closed and there is no west gate, the ordinances in vv. 8-10 prescribing how the laity are to depart by the gate opposite to the one by which they entered must restrict people to the south and north gates only. Possibly some old tradition of not turning one's back (to Yahweh?) in the course of one's movement in the temple lay behind this ordinance.

Intention

Considerable uncertainty remains about all of this material in 46:1-15, because of inconsistencies between it and other sacrificial ordinances. Even within the temple vision in Ezekiel 40–48 this inconsistency is encountered. Different terminology for "threshold" is used here from that in 40:7. Thus it is not clear precisely where the prince stands, nor whether leaving the gate open during the festivals is aimed to let the laity watch through the open gate as the sacrifices are presented. Similarly, the differences in the sacrificial requirements between Ezek 46:1-15 and the P ordinances in Numbers 28–29 do not make explicit a purpose behind the changes. A larger number of animals is required in Ezekiel for the sabbath, but P in Num 28:11-15 has the greater requirement for the new moon. Oddest of all is the complete lack of reference in Ezekiel to the daily *evening* sacrifice. No point is made about its deliberate omission, and it is hard to imagine what could lie behind such a difference. The P ordinance is lengthy and explicit in Num 28:1-8 in parallel to Exod 29:38-42, but the practice of two daily offerings seems already to be attested in 1 Kgs 18:29, 36 and in 2 Kgs 16:15. Further, Ezek 46:14b and 15b seem deliberately to introduce the technical P label of *tamid*. At least it can be noted that unexplained inconsistencies of this sort make it clear that the intent of Ezekiel's vision does not lie in some polemical revision of the quantities of sacrificial usage. Instead, the stress on the role of the prince and the explicit tracing of the consequences of the closed outer east gate show that it is in these matters that the prophet's emphasis is centered. As Zimmerli points out, "access to the presence of God is never simply open" (*Ezekiel 2*, 494). Its limitation because of the closed east gate is commemorative, reminding of the gracious reestablishment of the possibility of temple worship. The shadowy figure of the prince is here illuminated in an interesting way. Again, Zimmerli (ibid., 493) accurately calls attention to the prerogative of the prince to stand in special proximity (as a non-priest) to God, but it is even more important that Zimmerli (ibid.) identifies the precise nature of this prerogative to be that the prince is "the first of those who bow before God." This affirmation of solidarity is not only an obvious implication of the ordinances in vv. 2-3 but it is further underlined in v. 10, where this solidarity is traced in the way the prince is to be in the people's midst as they enter and depart.

Bibliography

K. Koch, *Die Priesterschrift von Exodus 25 bis Leviticus 16: eine überlieferungsges-chichtliche und literarkritische Untersuchung* (FRLANT NF 53; Göttingen: Vandenhoeck & Ruprecht, 1959).

LEGISLATION ABOUT THE PRINCE'S PROPERTY, 46:16-18

Text

In v. 16 read *minnaḥălātô* ("from his inheritance") for *naḥălātô* ("his inheritance"), joining the word to the preceding. Also in v. 17 read *naḥălat* ("the inheritance of") for *naḥălātô* ("his inheritance").

Structure

I. Resumptive messenger formula	16aα
II. Two case laws regulating the prince's disposition of real property	16aβγb-17
A. First case	16aβγb
1. Situation: prince grants a gift of land to his sons	16aβ
2. Determination: it will belong to his sons	16aγ
3. Classification: it is theirs as an inheritance	16b
B. Second case	17
1. Situation: prince grants a gift of land to one of his servants	17aαβ
2. Determination	17aγδ
a. It shall belong to him till the year of release	17aγ
b. Then it shall return to the prince	17aδ
3. Clarification: the inheritance of sons shall be permanent	17b
III. Ordinance regulating the prince's acquisition of real property	18
A. Prohibited action: taking from the people's inheritance	18aα
B. Prohibited means: forcefully taking property	18aβ
C. Prescribed action: the sons' inheritance is to come from the prince's own property	18aγ
D. Motive clause: my people not be scattered from their property	18b

It is absolutely clear that we are dealing here with a much more independent unit than was the case in the immediately preceding sections. The use of the
first person for Yahweh in v. 18b makes it plain that the resumptive messenger
formula at the beginning functions in a way more akin to its traditional role in
prophetic literature than had been true of 45:18-25 and 46:1-15. Similarly, the
ending in 46:18 is more decisive, even though no concluding formula is employed.
The reappearance in v. 19 of a new visionary guidance formula, together with the
observation that the presentation of matters dealing with the prince is now completed, indicates that a major section has been finished.

Genre

The area to be regulated is approached from two complementary directions, so that
it thereby receives full coverage. Both the prince's disposing of land (II) and his
acquiring of it (III) are regulated. The first subject is in turn exhausted by two complementary cases covering the possible objects of the prince's beneficence, his sons
or his servants. The paired nature of the two cases is further underlined by the ending of the second, which refers back to the first. The substructure of the presentation of the laws is fully traditional, moving from the definition of the situation to
the appropriate determination of policy by integrating the issues involved into the
relevant, broader legal categories, the rules for inheritance and the rules for the year
of release respectively. The second subject, that of the acquisition of land by the
prince, is approached in III by a PROHIBITION, which is then, in a way comparable
to the preceding two cases, integrated into proper procedure in v. 18aγ. The concluding motive clause applies in negative fashion the basic underlying legal principle of the establishment by Yahweh of enduring family inheritances in Israel, i.e.,
an affirmation in this instance of continuity in divine policy rather than action. Actually this same inheritance principle has also been safeguarded in both of the cases
in II, so that the motive clause provides a fitting conclusion to the whole of what
can be regarded as a tiny legal COLLECTION.

Setting and Intention

Royal property posed a severe problem for Israel during the monarchic period
(see Noth). Part of the purpose of the upcoming presentation of the new pattern
for the restored people of Yahweh in Ezek 47:13–48:29 is to avoid the disintegration of tribal territory which took place in preexilic times as a result of the growth
and use of royal property; i.e., it is formulated so as to undo a past evil situation.
While the unit 46:16-18 could have been placed within that later section, i.e., after
48:21-22, it seems to have been placed here because the subjects of inheritance
and possession have come up in 44:28–45:9, and potential princely abuses have
already surfaced in this connection in 45:9. Further, now that the survey of the
ritual duties of the prince has been completed, this is the only remaining spot for
the treatment of this final area in his responsibility. Rather than looking for the
hand of the same "person" in 45:1-9 and 46:16-18, it is more accurate to see here
the natural process of editorial struggle for proper arrangement. This process
began with the prophet himself and continued throughout the development of the
text, not as a matter of particular individual persons and their interests, but as a

process in which impersonal principles of logic in arrangement were the dominant forces.

Bibliography

M. Noth, "Das Krongut der israelitischen Könige und seine Verwaltung," *ZDPV* 50 (1927) 211-44.

THE TWO KINDS OF SACRIFICIAL KITCHENS, 46:19-24

Structure and Genre

Once again the use of formulas marks off a clearly separated section. Two connected VISIONARY GUIDANCE FORMULAS in vv. 19 and 21, with another in 47:1, indicate a return to the pattern of boundary marking employed earlier in chs. 40–48, which had been temporarily replaced by the use of resumptive MESSENGER FORMULAS in chs. 44–45. But the existence of that long gap in the guidance sequence together with the lack of any connection in content between 45:19-24 and what immediately precedes or follows makes it evident that this section is a kind of detached appendix.

Each of the two segments, vv. 19-20 and vv. 21-24, is essentially similar in shape. They are descriptions of areas within the temple complex, each description consisting of two parts: identifying a location and then explaining its function. The second functional aspect is highlighted in the first segment while the location receives more attention in the second segment. The lack of continuity with earlier sections of temple description appears in the much smaller role assigned to measurement here.

Setting and Intention

The very placement of this material sheds considerable light on its setting within its context. In one way 46:19-24 could have been placed at 40:17, because of its spatial location in the temple plan. Even more logically it could have been presented together with 42:1-14 where the priestly chambers of 46:19 first appear. Nevertheless, the content of vv. 19-24, especially the fact of the separation of vv. 21b-23, reveals that the distinction between priests and Levites, with the latter as "temple servants," is here presupposed. Thus 46:19-24 had to come after 44:6-31 (see also 45:5), and also after the information about sacrifices in 45:10-25. Thereby it has become plain that 46:19-24 is a supplement to material which has been recognized on other grounds as constituting an expansion of the basic tour pattern. It reflects the mental process of attending to implications of otherwise unconnected matters. This is a literary activity with a distinctly editorial orientation, rather than a heralding one. It aims to satisfy curiosity rather than to communicate news. In a way closely similar to 42:1-14, this section pursues the implications of earlier material so as to provide a workable proposal for the proper separation of the holy—here especially in regard to the inner and outer courts.

THE RIVER FROM THE TEMPLE, 47:1-12

Text

In v. 4 the context requires reading *mê* ("waters of") for *mayim* ("waters"). In v. 7 the intransitive *běšûbî* ("when I returned") must be read rather than the transitive *běšûbēnî* ("when . . . returned me"). In v. 8 probably emend *hayyāmmâ* ("to the sea") to read *hammayim* ("the waters"). In v. 9 one must read the singular *hannaḥal* ("the stream") rather than the dual *naḥălayim* ("two streams").

Structure and Genre

I. Visionary guidance formula: to the temple door	1aα
II. Description of the river	1aβγb-12
A. Description of what was seen (with occasional interruptions)	1aβγb-7
1. The river's beginning	1aβγb
a. Source: temple threshold facing east (with introductory "behold")	1aβγ

336

With this new unit comes a return to the visual aspect of the temple vision of chs. 40–48, an aspect which had largely disappeared since 44:4, apart from two verses in the appendix of 46:19-24. That 47:1-12 constitutes a separate unit is above all demonstrated by the uniqueness of its content, but it is also supported by the new VISIONARY GUIDANCE FORMULA in 47:1 and the presence of a MESSENGER FORMULA in 47:13 which introduces material of an altogether different sort.

Nevertheless, 47:1-12 presents a somewhat different sort of VISION REPORT from what had gone before in chs. 40–43. There the measurements presented constituted the description, and occasionally explanations about purposes were added. Here the series of measurements serves only to lead up to the conclusion offered with the final measurement: viz., a mighty river starts here. Because of spatial limitations resulting from the river's subsequent course, the description switches from a report of what was actually seen (II.A) to a report of a verbal revelation (II.B). As that second phase of description reaches the river's destination at the Dead Sea, the description expands to include a report of the results of the river's water. This last element actually constitutes a PROPHECY OF SALVATION akin to those in 34:25-29, 36:8-12, and 36:33-36.

Because the scene described completely transcends normal physical limitations, it is sometimes classified as apocalyptic, but that label must be qualified by the observation that it does not present a cosmic ending, but rather introduces what is intended to be the basis for a new order occupied in some ways with rather ordinary ongoing activities of food production. Still there is an underlying ultimacy about this new order that makes the apocalyptic label understandable.

Setting and Intention

In both subtle and obvious ways this unit resumes the traditions underlying chs. 40–42 and 43:1-12. The subtle avoidance of the east gate indicates that it was presumed to be closed, as 44:1-3 decreed in response to the event of 43:1-5. More obviously a switch is made in 47:1-12 from the previously completed description of the temple itself, as the sanctuary consecrated by Yahweh's presence, to a concern with the consequences of that presence for the land outside the temple. In contrast to a strong stress in preceding sections on protecting the people from the life-threatening dimension of Yahweh's holiness, the focus now turns abruptly to the life-enhancing dimension of what the temple has to send forth. To accomplish that aim an aspect of the old Zion traditions hitherto unmentioned in Ezekiel is employed, that of "the river whose streams make glad the city of God" (Ps 46:5, *RSV* 4). The later usage of this theme in Joel 4:18 (*RSV* 3:18), Zech 14:8, and Rev 22:1-2 is much better attested for us, but Isa 8:6f. may provide an earlier instance of prophetic use of this tradition.

In any case the purpose of Ezekiel's utilization of this tradition is clear. It is a further instance of the formulation of the new, God-given future as the undoing of a past evil situation. In this instance implications of a truly amazing extent are presented. The undoing of the Dead Sea salt's lethal effect on entering fish becomes the vehicle for some far more extensive allusions. In the foreground we notice that a basic consequence of the geography of Palestine is overcome in this new situation, because the temple, or rather the presence of Yahweh within the temple, is now sufficient to transform the place of death into the place of life—thereby reminding us of 37:1-14. In passing, the portrayal of the abundance of life by the mention of places for net-drying picks up the very language otherwise employed to describe the doom of Tyre in 26:5 and 14. But with the language of v. 9 about the swarming living creatures, we notice that we are being deliberately reminded of Genesis 1, thereby being told that Ezek 47:1-12 depicts nothing less than a kind of new creation, a motif encountered before in chs. 36–37. This whole emphasis is, of course, the familiar second technique for the formulation of good news, the stress on the continuity in divine action. With the fruit of the trees which grow beside the stream coming from the place of God's presence another subtle nuance appears. We are reminded of that primeval disaster which involved the fruit of a tree (Genesis 3) nourished by a mighty river (Gen 2:10-14). One cannot miss the learned flavor of such allusions. Here traditions are being used and blended with the subtle creativity of an expert. The delight in hinting, in triggering in the reader's mind vast vistas of possibilities by such brief and seemingly prosaic observations as make up 47:8-12, is a style we have come to know in Israel's wisdom literature and also in some key parts of the book of Ezekiel. Finally, rather than seeing in v. 11's concern to insure a supply of salt for this new order some "later hand" which "interrupts . . . the description of the marvelous effects of the stream" in "schoolmasterly fashion" (Zimmerli, *Ezekiel 2*, 508), we notice yet one more instance of the clever practicality of one for whom even in an eschatological vision report the heritage of the sage was never far away.

THE NEW ALLOTMENT OF THE LAND, 47:13–48:29

Text

For the many emendations required in this section the reader is referred to Zimmerli, *Ezekiel 2*, 517-25.

Structure and Genre

I. Messenger formula	47:13aα
II. Instructions for the allotment (2 mp frame around an impersonal list)	13aβγb-23
A. Preliminary instructions about the division (2 mp)	13aβγb-14
1. Heading: territory for the twelve tribes	13aβγ
2. Qualification: Joseph to get two portions	13b
3. Equality: each tribe a share	14aα
4. Foundation: my oath to the fathers	14aβ
5. Role: as an inheritance	14b
B. Description of borders (impersonal)	15-20
1. Heading	15a
2. North border	15b-17
a. Heading	15bα
b. From the Sea to Hazar-enon	15bβγδ-16
c. Summary of the north border	17a
d. Concluding label: this is the north side	17b
3. East border	18
a. Heading	18aα

1. Heading	23a
2. Benjamin	23b
a. East-west extent	23bα
b. Designation: one portion for Benjamin	23bβ
3. Simeon	24
a. Northern border: alongside Benjamin	24a
b. East-west extent	24bα
c. Designation: one portion for Simeon	24bβ
4. Issachar	25
a. Northern border: alongside Simeon	25a
b. East-west extent	25bα
c. Designation: one portion for Issachar	25bβ
5. Zebulun	26
a. Northern border: alongside Issachar	26a
b. East-west extent	26bα
c. Designation: one portion for Zebulun	26bβ
6. Gad	27
a. Northern border: alongside Zebulun	27a
b. East-west extent	27bα
c. Designation: one portion for Gad	27bβ
K. South border	28
1. South of Gad	28a
2. From Tamar via Kadesh and the Brook of Egypt to the Sea	28b
L. Summary conclusion (2 mp)	29
1. This is the land for allotment	29a
2. These are the portions	29bα
3. Prophetic utterance formula	29bβ

The framework indicates that this unit is to be seen as divine speech: the MESSENGER FORMULA at the beginning; the address to a second person plural in 47:13-14, 21-23; 48:8-9, 20, and 29; and PROPHETIC UTTERANCE FORMULAS in 47:23bβ and 48:29bβ. But, although Yahweh does appear in the first person in formulaic expressions in 47:14 and 48:11, it is quite clear that the material enclosed within the unit's framework is impersonal description and not divine speech. (The same is true of the earlier excerpting from this material in 45:1-8a.) The several references to Yahweh in the third person in 48:9 (in the midst of direct address), 10, and 14, even though also formulaic, help to confirm this. The character of the content shows that within the artificial framework of divine speech is essentially a list of the borders of Canaan, 47:15-30, and a list of the tribes, 48:1-7 and 23-27, into which a description of the contents of the holy district has been inserted in 48:8-22. Thus in its entirety the unit comprises a description of the new allocation of the land.

Setting and Intention

Any attempt to suggest a chronological setting for this material depends on what its intention is assessed to be. While in some ways this unit shares with the preceding section about the river flowing from the temple a blatant disregard of geographical necessity, arranging as it does the tribal territory in parallel lattitudinal strips from the Mediterranean to the Jordan and carving out a series of shorter central strips for sacred personnel and the city, in other ways it seems to strive for genuine realism. The borders in both north and south are not mere lines of latitude, but reflect the realities of Israelite history and especially the traditions of Num 34:1-12. What could be the aim of the material which strives in such opposing directions? Once again it is the technique used in the formulation which proves to be informative. There is an obvious stress on the continuity of divine action. The parallels to Numbers 34 in both content and terminology show that what Ezekiel presents is genuinely set forth as a new allotment, parallel to the original one. It aims to fulfill Yahweh's promise to the patriarchs (see 47:14), but this time certain vital matters are changed so as to undo the failures of the previous period of occupancy.

Some of these changed matters appear only as omissions. In contrast to the admonitions to eliminate corrupting Canaanite influence which came at the end of Numbers 33, this time no such perspective is needed, for there is to be no "Conquest." That whole issue, assigned so significant a role in the Deuteronomistic history, which reached its final shape very close to the end of Ezekiel's ministry, is simply eliminated by what is not said. Similarly, in a second category, the role of the monarchy in the territorial growth and the developing of Israel's former period of occupancy is passed over in silence. Regardless of whether or not the territorial boundaries of the Davidic empire are reflected in the border listings of 47:15-20, for example in the inclusion of Philistine territory, the whole issue of the connection between monarchy and territory receives worse than no attention. Simply not to have mentioned the king would be to pay no attention, but in several ways even the possible role of the king is expressly eliminated. For one thing, the prince *(nāsî')* is a figure chosen from the days of the tribal league before the advent of the king, and it is hard not to see here in Ezekiel's usage a deliberate voiding of the royal office. Another aspect of the elimination of the monarchy's role is the way the royal property or crown land is handled. In a continuation of the intention of 45:7-9 the prince is assigned territory from the *těrûmâ* district ("contribution"), which includes the priestly, Levitical, and city land as well. The implication is, it seems, that the prince needs land to provide the offerings he is to make, but any sort of political splendor is deliberately renounced. In fact, the Davidic connections of the prince, so dramatically present in 34:23f. and 37:24, are impressively absent in this entire section. Clearly in this instance the concern to undo past evil predominates over the concern to see a continuity in which a new David could be expected. (This point is brought out by G. Ch. Macholz.) In yet a third way the stress on avoiding past evils surfaces in what is not said. Jerusalem is never mentioned. Although clearly in mind when "the city" is discussed, the very Zion traditions noticed in 47:1-12 are avoided in this new unit, apparently thereby demoting Jerusalem in order to eliminate the evils that had proved disastrous for the people of Yahweh when these Zion traditions had become a part of national ambition and false reliance. No such destructive connections are to be possible for the new community (see 43:6-9). The sanctuary is, in fact, no longer even located in the city's land. Finally, picturing a future Israel which will occupy land only west of the Jordan is both a returning to the language of the original promise to the patriarchs and an avoidance of the problems dealt with in Joshua 22 and Numbers 32.

In what is actually spelled out in 47:13–48:35 further elements of the undoing of past evils are noticeable. Listing the twelve tribes as the land is allotted is a way of promising that the division of the people of Yahweh will be overcome by this return to the pattern of a prior era (see 37:15-28). The mention of resident aliens in 47:22-23 as having a share in the future Israel is often seen (e.g., Zimmerli, *Ezekiel 2*, 532) as reflecting the presence of converts to the faith of Israel from other nations, whose existence came to modify the word *gerîm* from its original role as a technical label for a socio-legal group ("resident aliens") in the direction of a religio-legal class ("proselytes"). Reference to Isa 56:3-8 is used to show how this sort of "foreigner who has joined himself to the Lord" was included in the population of the restored community. That is, of course, an uncontested historical truth, but it is doubtful if it sheds light on the reference to resident aliens in Ezekiel's new Israel. The whole of Ezekiel 40–48 seems to have had little if any influence on the postrestoration community. Instead, is it not more likely that we have here simply a further instance of the elimination of a past evil situation? As nonlanded poor during Israel's earlier residence in Palestine, these people were subject to oppression (see Ezek 22:7, 29) and regularly singled out as necessary objects of charity. By assigning this group an inheritance in the land, the guilt inherent in their previous situation and mistreatment would now be eliminated, and Yahweh's will for his people would automatically flow from this new order (see again Levenson, 124-25).

Finally, there is an evident concern on the part of this new arrangement to safeguard the holiness of the sanctuary. Its very location is insulated from possible contamination. Only Zadokites occupy the priestly territory within which the temple is placed (see 44:6-31). Probably the ordering of tribal allotments is a part of this same aim, whereby those tribes who are descendants of the full wives of Jacob are placed closest to the territory of the sanctuary, while the offspring of the handmaidens are located farthest away. (See Levenson, 118-19 for a comparison with P's ordering of the tribes in the camp.) Quite possibly the elimination of Levitical cities in favor of a strip of Levitical territory next to the priests and even the whole idea of "offering" as the label for the central, holy portion are also parts of this new and transformed understanding of the sanctuary's role in the new land.

However individual details of these preceding proposals may be evaluated, it should not be possible to view the entire section as anything other than the tracing of an eschatological new order. Whatever elements of practicality may appear in it are not characterized by "perceptible realism" or as part of a plan "envisaged as being for the near future" (Zimmerli, *Ezekiel 2*, 539), but first of all are a part of that "new order . . . planned against the background of divine miracle" (ibid., 542). Thus the question about chronological setting becomes one to which the material affords no significant access, and the contrast with the preceding, more flamboyantly miraculous section about the river flowing from the temple becomes less than it is often seen to be (contrast Zimmerli, ibid., 526).

Bibliography

J. Levenson, *Theology of the Program of Restoration of Ezekiel 40-48* (HSM 10; Missoula: Scholars Press, 1976); G. Ch. Macholz, "Noch einmal: Planungen für den Wiederaufau nach der Katastrophe von 587," *VT* 19 (1969) 322-52.

THE CITY, ITS GATES AND NAME, 48:30-35

Structure and Genre

Although no formulas mark off this section from what precedes, the content reveals it to be an appended elaboration of 47:13–48:29 which expands upon the city of 48:15-19, but in a way that conflicts with some of what is said there. In obvious ways this unit, which constitutes a brief geographical description of the city, is deliberately dependent on the preceding material, most noticeably in the dimensions given, in the use of a heading in v. 30a parallel to those in ch. 48, and in the listing of the tribal names so that each is followed by the number "one," just as in ch. 48. Nevertheless, there are definite departures from the intent of 47:13–48:29, which require it to be seen as a modifying expansion reflecting a somewhat different setting.

Setting and Intention

Whereas in 48:1-29 the sanctuary was located in the priests' share (48:10), and the city was situated in a separate strip (48:15-19) which is classed as "profane" in contrast to the holiness of the priestly land, here it is stressed in the last half-verse that Yahweh is in the city. It is uncertain to what extent this difference is to be seen as a deliberate revision of the preceding. More likely it constitutes a kind of unresolved both/and, deliberately left unharmonized. In any case it is the Zion tradition, as in 43:1-9 and 47:1-12 (or in Isaiah's Immanuel), which has come to expression here. While it is left unchallenged that the "glory of Yahweh" has returned to the temple never more to leave, it is now also affirmed that somehow the city also has a part in Yahweh's presence. Manifestly the problem of the integration of these two different perspectives did not deter their being affirmed virtually side by side. Once again, it becomes clear that the intent of the vision is that of eschatological affirmation rather than practical clarification.

The familiar technique of the undoing of the past evil situation underlies both the avowal of Yahweh's presence "henceforth" in contrast to his previous departure in 11:22-23 (see the discussion of 43:1-6) and the listing of all twelve tribes as the names of the city's gates, thereby eliminating the earlier division. Oddly just at this point, the tribal names (48:30-35) depart from the listing in 48:1-7 and 23-28, using Levi and Joseph where the preceding unit had omitted Levi and used both Ephraim and Manasseh. However, it must be borne in mind that 48:1-7 and 23-28 have to do with tribal allotments in which Levi does not share, while the city's gates are simply aimed to express totality. Similarly, a different logic underlies the grouping of tribes here. Even though here as in 48:1-7 and 23-28 the sons of the full wives seem to be given some preference, another grouping appears according to which the Leah tribes are listed for the north and south gates and the Rachel tribes for the east and west ones (Fohrer, 263).

Although the brevity of the unit renders comparisons tenuous, it does seem certain that the at least semirealistic tenor of the descriptions throughout all of chs. 40–48 shows again in the way the eschatological city is portrayed here in less flamboyant terms than in Isa 54:12; 60:1-22, or most definitely Rev 21:12-13. Only the name is characterized by the flavor of unrestrained celebration. Greenberg effectively points to an express element of the undoing of past evil, when he recalls that Ezekiel spoke in 22:5 of Jerusalem as "polluted of name" (202).

Once again chronological placement is not possible, apart from the unit's being dependent upon and thereby to some extent later than 47:13–48:29.

Bibliography

M. Greenberg, "The Design and Themes of Ezekiel's Program of Restoration," *Int* 38 (1984) 181-208.

Glossary

GENRES

ALLEGORY (Allegorie). Not strictly a genre, but rather a speech form closely related to figurative or metaphorical language. The details of an allegory are chosen and shaped against the background of the interpretation or application so that each detail of the allegory is assigned a meaning, at least by implication, in the interpretation. The shortest form of allegory is a metaphor with just one motif calling for interpretation (Ezek 18:2); a longer form is the allegorical story where each detail has its bearing on the interpretation (frequent in Ezekiel). Allegory may be employed in many genres: prophecies of punishment (Ezekiel 16), dirges (Ezekiel 19), and prophecies of salvation (Ezekiel 34).

ASSURANCE OF VICTORY (Zusicherung eines Sieges). The formula *nātatî běyādekā* ("I have given into your hand") spoken by Yahweh and followed by the name of the enemy. This formula has its setting in an (→) oracle pronounced to the tribal militia during the opening rites of a holy war (Josh 6:2; 8:1, 18; 10:8; Judg 4:7).

COLLECTION. → LITERARY COLLECTION.

COMMISSIONING OF A MESSENGER (Aussendung eines Boten). Not an independent genre, but rather part of a narrative telling of the sending of a messenger with a message (Gen 32:3-5). The components are: instruction to the messenger concerning where to go, and—beginning with the messenger formula—instructions concerning what to say. In the prophetic tradition, this motif has become an introduction or a framing of a prophetic word (2 Sam 7:4; 24:11; 1 Kgs 12:22; 21:17; 2 Kgs 20:4). The constituent parts are: (1) the (→) prophetic word formula, identifying Yahweh as the sender of the message, (2) the (→) commissioning formula, with the imperative "Go and speak" and the identification of the addressee, and (3) the (→) messenger formula followed by the message. The message itself can assume any possible genre.

DESCRIPTION OF PUNISHMENT (Strafbeschreibung). A part of the announcement, which is in turn an element in the (→) prophecy of punishment. The punishment is normally announced as Yahweh's intervention, which is then followed by results, but occasionally the description of the results occurs as an independent genre. Its essence is the portrayal of a disaster that will come as the result of Yahweh's punishment for crimes or sins (see 1 Kgs 21:23-24; 2 Kgs 9:36; and Ezek 9:1-11).

DIRGE (Leichenlied). A funeral song bewailing the loss of the deceased and calling for further mourning. Designated as *qînâ* in Hebrew, the dirge is generally characterized by 3:2 meter, a beginning *'êk* ("how!"), a contrasting of "then" and "now," i.e., former glory and present tragedy, and imperatives summoning to grieving. Originally sung by professional wailing women in the presence of the corpse, the dirge was adapted by prophets so as to constitute an announcement of certain death for an individual or community. Often an element of mocking marks the prophetic adaptation, which commonly announced the fate of a king or a personified nation (Ezek 19:1-14; 27:1-36).

> H. Jahnow, *Das hebräische Leichenlied im Rahmen der Völkerdichtung* (BZAW 36; Giessen: Töpelmann, 1923).

DISPUTATION (Disputationswort, Streitgespräch). A prophetic genre in which the prophet presents his message by formulating it in response to the objections of his audience. The opposing views of the audience are expressed in quotations of considerable realism and often answered with such force that one must assume a setting of actual verbal encounter (Ezek 12:21-28; 18:2-4, 25), doubtless polished editorially so that the prophetic speech successfully overcomes the adversary's argument. In several cases the force of the prophetic message of response is heightened by the use of the (→) oath formula (Ezek 33:11).

> A. Graffy, *A Prophet Confronts his People* (AnBib 104; Rome: Biblical Institute Press, 1984).

ENTRANCE LITURGY (Tempeleinlassliturgie). A liturgy of inquiry and response used to determine the admissibility of worshipers to the temple precincts. Presumably all pilgrims, when arriving at the gate of the sacred grounds, had to declare their cultic purity in order not to disturb or frustrate ritual procedures. They would thus shout their query for admission from outside the holy precincts, and a functionary of the temple would answer from within, enumerating the conditions of entry. This pattern of question and answer is mirrored in three OT texts: Psalms 15 and 24 and Isa 33:14-16; they have been used to reconstruct the liturgy itself.

> K. Koch "Tempeleinlassliturgien und Dekalog," in *Studien zur Theologie der alttestamentlichen Überlieferungen* (Fest. G. von Rad; eds. R. Rendtorff and K. Koch; Neukirchen-Vluyn: Neukirchener, 1961) 45-60.

ETIOLOGY (Ätiologie). A narrative designed to explain the origins of certain elements of knowledge, experience, custom, and the like shared by a cultural group.

FABLE (Fabel). A short tale involving animals or plants as characters, usually expressing a moral point, such as the downfall of a presumptuous braggart. Normally rather brief (Judg 9:8-15), this genre easily lent itself to allegorical (→ allegory) expansion (Ezek 17:1-24).

HISTORY (Geschichtsschreibung). An extensive, continuous, written composition based upon source material, whether written or oral, devoted to the survey of some unified segment of the broad flow of political events with an analysis in terms of cause and effect. The framework of interpretation adopted seeks to organize the past in order to understand contemporary social reality. The OT contains several major examples, such as the Deuteronomistic History and the books of Chronicles. Within Ezekiel, chs. 16, 20, and 23 display many of the features of this genre, especially as it borders on (→) theological reflection.

LIST (Liste). A simple recounting in writing of names or items assembled according to a certain perspective or heading. While an elementary list ignores any ordering system, a developed list seeks to arrange its contents in an order which reconstructs an aspect of existence in reality.

LITERARY COLLECTION (Literarische Sammlung). Words of a prophet dealing with the same topic are often collected in one literary grouping which is the product of an editor. Examples are: symbolic action reports (Ezekiel 4–5 and 12:1-20); prophecies concerning Tyre (Ezekiel 26–28) or Egypt (Ezekiel 29–32). The setting of such collections is primarily the learned editorial concern for order within a large prophetic book, but presumably the worship situation of the community seeking edification and instruction also played a role.

MÄRCHEN. A traditional tale in prose, set in a mysterious world of fantasy, provoking sympathy for the principal figure. A recurring motif is the concern to show how a basic injustice was finally righted. There are no Märchen in the OT, although Märchen motifs appear from time to time (Ezekiel 16).

    A. Jolles, *Einfache Formen* (2nd ed.; Tübingen: Niemeyer, 1968).

MOTIF (Motiv). The smallest element of content with the power to persist in an oral or literary tradition. An example of a motif is that of the foundling hero. Normally a motif will be stated in an adjectival phrase like this, since the noun is not sufficiently defined to be distinct in the tradition without the adjective.

MYTH (Myth). Narrative form designed to account for patterns in the ordinary world by reference to the primeval activities of the gods in the divine world, especially in love and war.

    M. Eliade, *Cosmos and History: The Myth of the Eternal Return* (New York: Harper, 1959).

OATH (Eid, Schwur). A pronouncement, cast as either cohortative or indicative, which binds the oath taker to a particular course of action, attitude, or stance by invoking sanctions of the deity. Typically an oath is introduced with the (→) oath formula, "As the Lord lives" *(ḥay yahweh)*, e.g., Ezek 18:3. Then follows what the oath taker will or will not do. Most frequently an oath is a form of a conditional self-curse.

ORACLE (Orakel). A communication from the deity, often through an intermediary such as priest or prophet, especially in response to an (→) oracular inquiry (Ezek 14:1-3; 20:3, 31). Oracles may also come unsolicited. In all cases structure and content may vary widely. A prophet's speeches presented as God's own word may also be classed as oracles.

ORACULAR INQUIRY, REPORT OF (Erzählung eines Gottesbescheides). A type of (→) report which tells of seeking an oracle from God. The basic elements include:

(1) report that an oracle was sought; (2) the oracle in response to the inquiry. Two forms of the report occur, one associated with priests (1 Sam 23:9) and the other with prophets. Ezekiel is approached for an oracle in 14:1-3 and 20:1-3.

ORDINANCE (Ordnung). A rule prescribing authoritatively what is to be done. As a broad legal category, ordinance includes many specific types and fields of laws (e.g., cultic ordinances, festival ordinances, etc.), but an ordaining authority is normally the common element.

PRIESTLY TORAH (Priesterliche Tora). Authoritative instruction given by priests in response to a question. The word *tôrâ* designates a pointing of the way and seems to have centered in instruction about proper separations, i.e., between clean and unclean, holy and profane. Haggai 2:11-13 demonstrates both this teaching aspect of the priestly office and prophetic utilization of it. The instruction could take various shapes, and these were often imitated by prophets: a command or prohibition (Isa 1:13; Ezek 45:8b-9; Amos 5:5a); a statement of Yahweh's desire (Isa 1:11; Amos 5:21f.); the determination of a judgment (Isa 1:13); or a description of consequences (Amos 4:5). Many of the prophetic imitations are of a polemic and parodying character.

  J. Begrich, "Die priesterliche Tora," in *Werden und Wesen des alten Testaments* (ed. P. Volz, F. Stummer, and J. Hempel; BZAW 66; Berlin: Töpelmann, 1936) 63-88.

PROHIBITION (Prohibitiv). A direct forbidding of an action or thing, based upon the incontestable authority of custom, law, or decree. Its formulation as "Thou shalt not . . ." (using *lō'* with the imperfect) is self-contained, needing no accompaniment or supporting argument. A prohibition can appear alone (Exod 22:17 [*RSV* 18]), but is more commonly found in series (Ezek 20:2-17).

  J. Bright, "The Apodictic Prohibition: Some Observations," *JBL* 92 (1973) 185-204; E. Gerstenberger, *Wesen und Herkunft des "apodiktischen Rechts"* (WMANT 20; Neukirchen-Vluyn: Neukirchener, 1965).

PROPHECY CONCERNING A FOREIGN NATION (Fremdvölkerorakel). This genre is primarily identified by content. It is akin to the (→) prophecy of punishment, but presents not a message about Israel, but one about the destruction of a foreign nation by an enemy. It presents this destruction as an act of Israel's God and implicitly addresses Israel, even if for poetic effect the foreign nation or its king is directly addressed. No standard structure exists, and a large variety of genres can be utilized, especially the (→) dirge (Ezek 27:1-36; 32:1-16). Prophecies concerning foreign nations are usually transmitted in collections dealing with a particular nation (Tyre in Ezekiel 26-28; Egypt in 29-32). These collections are then combined into large sections which constitute major parts in prophetic books (Isaiah 13–23; Jeremiah 46–51; Ezekiel 25-32). The original setting probably lies in military-cultic rites of execration, but the large-scale units in Ezekiel often reflect extensive learned (27:12-24), sometimes mythological (28:11-19), elaboration.

  D. L. Christensen, *Transformations of the War Oracle in Old Testament Prophecy: Studies in the Oracles Against the Nations* (HDS 3; Missoula: Scholars Press, 1975).

351

PROPHECY OF PUNISHMENT (Gerichtsankündigung). A prophetic word announcing disaster upon a people, a group, or an individual as punishment for an offense. In lengthy examples structure can become highly complex, but in Ezekiel essentially four standard components appear. (1) Preliminaries: (→) prophetic word formula, address as "son of man," direction to speak, etc. (2) The reason: accusations or explanations establishing why the forthcoming punishment must occur. (3) Transition: "therefore" plus the (→) messenger formula. (4) The announcement of punishment proper, consisting of intervention by Yahweh in the first person and results to follow in the second or third person. Examples are: Ezek 16:3-43; 23:2b-27. Related genre: (→) Prophetic Proof Saying.

PROPHECY OF SALVATION (Prophetische Heilsankündigung). A parallel genre to the (→) prophecy of punishment, except that here good news is announced. Ordinarily, in contrast to the prophecy of punishment, no reason is presented as the ground for the announcement in terms of the behavior of the people which merits a particular response. Thus the prophecy of salvation begins, after the appropriate preliminary formulas, with the announcement itself, usually expressed as God's intervention followed by consequent results. A variety of formulations is still possible. See the discussion of Ezekiel 33–39.

PROPHETIC ANNOUNCEMENT OF PUNISHMENT (Prophetische Gerichtsankündigung). The essential element of a (→) prophecy of punishment, usually preceded by a statement of reason(s) for punishment (Ezek 16:3-34 plus 36-43), but frequently appearing by itself (Ezek 5:14-15, 16-17). In Ezekiel it is usually introduced by the (→) messenger formula and is made up of intervention and results, the former heralding Yahweh's coming acts in the first person, often introduced by *hinnēh* ("behold"), the latter presenting the consequences of those acts in second or third person.

PROPHETIC BOOK (Prophetisches Buch). The completed collection of the message of Yahweh through a particular prophet. Although the OT material reflects considerable diversity, the fact of the recognized completeness of the collection of Yahweh's speaking and/or acting through a prophet is usually indicated by the provision of a (→) superscription. Only rarely, e.g., Jer 51:64b, is an ending formula provided, but occasionally, e.g., Hos 14:9, a final verse may presuppose a completed collection. It is unclear in what circumstances and on what basis it became appropriate to regard a collection as complete. Presumably the death of an individual prophet or the cessation of his public activity could have played a role on the latter decision, but, apart from Elijah in 2 Kings 2, there are no recorded episodes specifically marking the conclusion of a prophet's ministry so as to correspond to the way a (→) vocation account often marked its beginning.

Following the superscription, almost any type of organization might be employed, but essentially a book seems to have been created as a collection of collections, be it of sayings (the commonest type), vision reports (Zechariah 1–8), disputations (Malachi), or narratives (in part Jeremiah). One clear pattern of arrangement was chronological, but this acquired major importance only for later books (Ezekiel, Haggai, and Zechariah 1–8). Sometimes chronological arrangement is less obvious, in that specific dates are not given, but nevertheless it plays a significant role in the book's structure, e.g., Isaiah 2–11 and 28–32. Theme and genre often provide a second pattern for structuring a prophetic book. This is especially clear in the case of the larger books, e.g., in the positioning of a block of prophecies concerning foreign nations between the prophecies of doom in Ezekiel 1–24 and those of consolation in Ezekiel 33–48, or in the placing of Isaiah 13–23 between the material from two different periods of Isaiah's ministry, 2–11 and 28–32, or in the locating of Jeremiah 46–51 in the LXX between 1–25 and 26–45. Smaller-scale cases of similar structuring by theme or genre exist in Amos 1–2 and 7–9 or Micah 1–3 and 4–5.

The setting in which a prophetic book functioned was presumably that of the liturgical worship of a community. Acceptance for such use would be a part of the canonization process, and an element of reinterpretation would naturally have to be assumed. Although we are largely uninformed about the details of such processes, certain aspects of the intention are probable. Prophetic books were not likely to be read in worship out of a purely archival concern to preserve the past. Instead, some factor of authority is likely to have been preeminent. The community's experience of being addressed by the preserved message may possibly lie behind the elements of "congregational response" claimed to be detectable in some instances, e.g., the doxologies of Amos or the community psalms in Isaiah 12 and 33.

PROPHETIC EXPLANATION OF PUNISHMENT (Prophetische Erklärung für Bestrafung). Divine speech in which the prophet announces the punishment God has already imposed and provides the reason for that action, rather than, as normally, announcing the action in advance.

Essentially this genre constitutes simply a modification of the familiar (→) prophecy of punishment. In that genre the prophet speaking for God announces God's punishment to come, often prefixing the reason for it. If the same pattern is followed, but with reference to a punishment now past, as in Ezek 22:23-31 and 23:5-10, and when the description of past guilt predominates, then the label "explanation" is more appropriate. If the same message were presented in some writer's own name, it would be labeled (→) history, but when set forth as divine speech it must be designated prophetic. Since the future is sometimes announced by prophets using the perfect tense to express certainty, in these cases no actual alteration of the customary genre pattern would be involved, and only the time perspective reflected would enable one to make a distinction. Thus the shift in setting undergone by a prophetic announcement once the heralded act had taken place might be reflected in minimal, if any, alteration.

PROPHETIC PROOF SAYING (Prophetisches Erweiswort). A prophetic speech in which the prophet as the one speaking for Yahweh announces punishment upon an individual, group, or nation, and argues that this punishment will convince the recipient to recognize Yahweh's sovereign identity. This genre appears in 1 Kgs 20:13 and 28, very frequently in Ezekiel, and in Isa 41:17-20 and 49:22-26.

The main elements are: (1) the announcement of punishment, and (2) the (→) recognition formula. These two combine to constitute a two-part

353

Prophetic Proof Saying (e.g., Ezek 12:19-20). When, as is often the case, a statement of the reason for punishment and a logical transition are prefixed to the announcement of punishment, the result is a three-part Prophetic Proof Saying (e.g., Ezek 25:6-7, 8b-11). Either second (e.g., Ezek 25:6-7) or third (e.g., Ezek 25:8b-11) person speech may be employed in all parts. Occasionally an announcement in a (→) prophecy of salvation can take the place of the announcement of punishment (e.g., Ezek 37:12-14). Often there is appended to the recognition formula an elaboration referring back to the preceding announcement of punishment (e.g., Ezek 25:17). More rarely such an elaboration is placed at the beginning of the recognition formula (e.g., Ezek 24:24b).

W. Zimmerli, "The Word of Divine Self-Manifestation (Proof Saying), A Prophetic Genre," in *I am Yahweh* (tr. D. W. Stott; Atlanta: Knox, 1982) 99-110; idem, *Ezekiel 1*, 38-39.

REPORT (Bericht). A brief self-contained prose narrative, usually in third person style, about a single event or situation in the past. There is no developed plot or imaginative characterization (contrast [→] story). However, insofar as there is usually action, a report is different from a statement or description. Varying in length from a very short notice to a longer, even composite account, reports can carry diverse content. Certain types of report, as defined by structure and content, take on special importance in the OT, for example, (→) theophany report, (→) vision report, (→) report of a symbolic action. The setting for reports varies according to content and purpose.

REPORT OF AN EXPRESSIVE ACTION (Bericht einer Ausdruckshandlung). A report of a gesture or simple bodily action used to express or accompany an emotion or message.

In contrast to a (→) report of a symbolic action, which is ordinarily comparatively lengthy and complex, prophets and other mediatorial figures occasionally used simpler gestures or actions, such as clapping the hands or stamping one's foot (Ezek 6:11) to embody or add power by undergirding a message. A whole host of possible intentions could be conveyed by such gestures. They do, however, occasionally constitute, as in Ezekiel 6, a type of parallel to the (→) report of a symbolic action, for they could logically follow the same pattern, i.e., direction, execution, and interpretation, and perhaps the gestures in question are all that remain of earlier, more extensive acts, possibly stemming from a background in magic. The cases in Ezekiel 6 seem, though, to have faded to the point of now constituting only incidental and virtually rhetorical accompaniment of a message whose verbal formulation in no way picks up or continues the pattern inherent in the gesture. Possibly setting one's face in a certain direction (→ hostile orientation formula; see Ezek 6:2 and eight other times in the book) was such an expressive action, but it seems in the OT to have lost any remnant of old "evil eye" thinking, as apparently lay behind Balaam's attempts to position himself properly (see Num 22:41; 23:13; 24:2).

W. Zimmerli, *Ezekiel 1*, 182-83.

REPORT OF A SYMBOLIC ACTION (Symbolische Handlung). The report of an incident in which a prophet accompanies a pronouncement with an action understood as a symbolic sign. This sign was conceived as a powerful anticipation of the coming reality announced, and it could proclaim either doom or salvation. This genre reflects a long history, possibly rooted in sympathetic magic, and ordinarily includes three main parts: (1) Yahweh's instruction to perform the action, (2) the report of its execution, and (3) a word of interpretation. In Ezekiel all such reports are in autobiographical style, and in nearly all cases the latter two parts are presented to the prophet by Yahweh, so that they are absorbed into the first part. Examples of the announcement of punishment by this genre have been collected in Ezekiel into two sections, 4:1–5:17 and 12:1-20. In addition, a message of hope is set forth via a symbolic action in 37:15-28.

G. Fohrer, "Die Gattung der Berichte über symbolische Handlungen der Propheten," *ZAW* 64 (1952) 101-20; idem, *Die symbolische Handlungen der Propheten* (2nd ed., ATANT 54; Zürich: Zwingli, 1968).

RIDDLE (Rätsel). A statement (question or proposition) that is worded in such an ambiguous or intriguing way that it provokes conjectural interpretation or solution. Its essence is the way it conceals and reveals at the same time. In the OT, *ḥîdâ* ("riddle") is often interpreted broadly (Prov 1:6; Ps 49:5), but there is a classic example in Judges 14.

The setting of the riddle is varied: a feast or celebration, a school, etc. The riddle is both a game and a test of wisdom in which there is a matching of wits, and it is often humorous.

H. P. Muller, "Der Begriff 'Rätsel' im Alten Testament," *VT* 20 (1970) 465-69; H. Torczyner, "The Riddle in the Bible," *HUCA* 1 (1924) 125-40.

RITUAL INSTRUCTIONS (Ritual). A series of compact directions prescribing individual actions inherent in the course of a cultic ceremony. The pattern known from Leviticus 1–7 is used in Ezek 43:18-27, 45:18-20, and 46:1-3, 12. While a formulaic heading or subscription, e.g., "this is . . ." or "these . . . are," often appears, the essential content of this genre is a series of stereotypical directions about presenting, killing, sprinkling, etc. The directions may be given in 2 ms or 3 ms, but at bottom they express an impersonal "whoever." Some actions may be open to laity and others only to priests. It is difficult to determine the setting of such material, but it has been thought to lack enough detail for the liturgical training of the priests themselves, and therefore possibly to reflect the public instruction of the laity by priests.

K. Koch, *Die Priesterschrift von Exodus 25 bis Leviticus 16* (FRLANT NF 53; Göttingen: Vandenhoeck & Ruprecht, 1959) 104-8; R. Rendtorff, *Die Gesetze in der Priesterschrift* (FRLANT NF 44; Göttingen: Vandenhoeck & Ruprecht, 1954) 12, 20-23.

SENTENCE (Strafurteil). The pronouncement by a court or judge of the formal and/or specific legal consequences resulting from a defendant's conviction. Conceptually, it corresponds to and rests on the "legal consequences" in the laws that are concerned with those offenses or crimes. In a wider sense sentences also occur in texts whose contexts are conceptualized judicially, although they show no actual trial setting.

Sentences can consist of the imposition of penalties such as (1) the death penalty, (2) expulsion or eviction from the community, (3) physical punishment, (4) imprisonment, (5) fines, (6) remedial restitutions or payment of damages, and (7) ransoms.

Certain accounts indicate the settings of actual sentencing and the formulations of actually pronounced sentences: "You shall surely die" (Jer 26:8; Ezek 33:14), "He shall be put to death today" (Gen 26:11), "You deserve death" (1 Kgs 2:26), "You shall die" (1 Kgs 2:37). On the other hand, the laws prescribing legal consequences for certain crimes suggest their applicability as sentences. However, one cannot assume that the formulations of legal consequences in laws are always identical to the formulations of actually pronounced sentences. Related Genre: (→) Statement of Acquittal.

H. J. Boecker, *Redeformen des Rechtslebens im Alten Testament.* (WMANT 14; Neukirchen-Vluyn: Neukirchener, 1970).

STATEMENT OF ACQUITTAL (Freisprucherklärung). The formal declaration by a judicial authority of the innocence of a person charged with a crime or offense. It is the opposite of conviction.

The forms of acquittal, some of them formulaic, are basically preserved as statements in an actual discourse and as definitions of legal consequences in the laws. In exceptional cases, a statement of acquittal can be expressed in terms of a negative (→) sentence. (1) In actual discourse, the statement of acquittal occurs: (a) as a direct address to the defendant, either by the accuser or the judge: "You are righteous" (2 Kgs 10:9; Prov 24:24; Exod 9:27; 1 Sam 24:18 [*RSV* 24:17]; 2 Sam 14:9; Neh 9:33); (b) as a declaration about the defendant, either by a judge (to the accuser): "He has not sinned" (Job 1:22; 2:10), or by the judge in reversing a previous sentence: "She is more righteous than I" (Gen 38:27), or by an advocate to the one who is both judge and accuser: "He has not sinned against you" (cf. 1 Sam 24:19 [*RSV* 18]). (2) In definitions of legal consequences, it is formulated: "He [the owner] is free from guilt/innocent" (Exod 21:28), "He is righteous" (Ezek 18:9), if the righteous "does not sin" (Ezek 3:21; 16:51), "He/she shall be exempt from punishment" (Exod 21:19; Num 5:28). (3) Statements of acquittal such as "You/he shall not die" or "You/he shall live" (Jer 38:24; Ezek 18:21, 28; 33:15), or "There is no death sentence for this man" (Jer 26:16) are pronounced or formulated in analogy to forms of a (→) sentence instead of forms of a conviction proper. See also "There shall be no bloodguilt for him" (Exod 22:2 [*RSV* 3]), and "He shall not make restitution" (Exod 22:10 [*RSV* 11]). These statements respond negatively to a specific (→) sentence implied in or expressed together with an accusation. However, this type of statement cannot be understood as a form of acquittal. It belongs to other genres such as the pronouncement of pardon or the decree of amnesty. The generic classification of these forms depends, therefore, on their contexts, and especially on the previously established guilt or innocence of a defendant.

The specific composition and setting of the legal authorities that render or define statements of acquittal vary. They can be judges in the gate, state officials in the royal court, the king, a member of the royal family, or authorities empowered with the right to establish and define law. The formulations were also used in contexts other than those pointing to a judicial setting.

The practice of acquitting (including illegitimate acquittals) through judges in courts is attested in Exod 23:7; Deut 25:1; Isa 5:23; Prov 17:5; 24:24; 2 Sam 15:4; and also in the language of Ezek 3:18; 18:21, 28; 33:13-15; Job 9:28; Exod 20:7; 1 Kgs 2:9.

STORY (Erzählung). A narrative of some literary sophistication which creates interest by arousing tension and resolving it during the course of narration. Its structure is controlled by an imaginative plot. The narrator moves from exposition (background and setting for the action) to a problem, sometimes complications in relationships (tension), to a climactic turn of events from which the resolution flows. Finally, narrative tension drains away into a concluding sense of rest.

Since literary structures are flexible and contents varied, one may not think of rigid definitions of type. Nevertheless, it proves useful to make certain distinctions. When a narrator emphasizes less the imaginative creation and artistic plot than what an event was and how it happened, we speak of a historical story. On the other hand, when a brief content is structured simply and its purpose centered on entertainment, we are dealing with a folkloristic tale. If the story dwells on the wondrous qualities and exemplary character of a person or place, it is a legend, the primary purpose of which is religious edification. Finally, a story that moves in a fantasy world unlike that of ordinary experience is a (→) Märchen; if its content centers on primordial times when gods and humans dealt with one another directly, it is a (→) myth.

With the exception of some historical stories, most OT examples of story derive from and belong to the folk. They are folktales which incorporate motifs, scenes, and narrative techniques out of popular culture and oral tradition. Settings and intentions vary widely, therefore, depending on the story type, narrator, and occasions for storytelling.

SUPERSCRIPTION (Überschrift). A statement prefixed to a literary work (book, collection, song, etc.). The term refers to the place of this statement in the structure of a work, namely, antecedent to its body (as opposed to a subscription which follows the conclusion of the body).

As such, the superscription may consist of a variety of elements, e.g., author, addressee, title, date, location. While the composition of most of these elements can vary among texts, superscriptions in the OT ordinarily indicate the character of the work, either in the concise, definitional form of a title ("This is the book of the generations of Adam," Gen 2:4a; 5:1; "A Psalm of David," Ps 101:1) or in a more elaborate form (Jer 1:1-3; Ezek 1:1-3).

G. M. Tucker, "Prophetic Superscriptions and the Growth of a Canon," in *Canon and Authority: Essays in Old Testament Religion and Theology* (ed. G. W. Coats and B. O. Long; Philadelphia: Fortress, 1977) 56-70.

THEOLOGICAL REFLECTION (Theologische Überlegung). The expression of a type of relatively abstract thinking which categorizes the concrete realities of human experience and formulates them as parts of a standardized, overarching theological structure. Examples in which OT material demonstrates this sort of mental process are: (1) the way the Deuteronomistic historian in the book of Judges schematizes Israel's behavior as (a) apostasy, (b) battering by an enemy, (c) crying out for help, and (d) deliverance; or (2) the way

Ezekiel 20 analyzes Israel's past as attesting a pattern of guilt, followed by grace, then followed by further guilt.

Also (→) history, when it stresses a theological framework of interpretation, can be a subgenre of theological reflection.

THEOPHANY REPORT (Theophaniebericht, Bericht einer Gotteserscheinung). The recounting of God's self-manifestation as distinct from epiphany, which refers more generally to the appearance of any kind of divine being, e.g., angels, cherubim, etc. Two elements are characteristic: (1) description of Yahweh's approach; (2) accompanying natural upheavals (wind, fire, storm, etc.), along with reactions of fear and awe. Ezek 1:4-28 employs several theophanic elements. The original setting may have had its roots in a cultic victory celebration.

J. Jeremias, *Theophanie, die Geschichte einer alttestamentlichen Gattung* (WMANT 10; Neukirchen-Vluyn: Neukirchener, 1965).

VISION REPORT (Visionsbericht, Visionsschilderung). The description by a prophet of what he sees (vision) or hears (audition) in an inner perception. Frequently, visual elements are introduced with an introductory "behold" *(hinnēh)* and auditory elements with "listen" *(qōl)* or a simple report of Yahweh's speaking. Three main types of vision reports are: (1) presence visions in which Yahweh is seen (Ezek 1:4-28a); (2) word-symbol visions in which the prophet sees an object that leads to the perception of a word of God (Amos 8:1-3); or (3) event visions in which the prophet witnesses an event and describes it, generally as an anticipation of future reality (Ezekiel 8–11; 37:1-11).

F. Horst, "Die Visionsschilderungen der alttestamentlichen Propheten," *EvT* 20 (1960) 193-205.

VOCATION ACCOUNT (Prophetischer Berufungsbericht). A genre in which a prophet or the prophetic tradition refers to an initiatory call, ordination, and commissioning. There are two different types: (1) connected with a vision in which the prophet sees the heavenly court of God (1 Kgs 22:19-23; Isa 6:1-12; Ezek 1:4-28); (2) instead of the visionary element, everything is subordinated to the coming of the word of God (Exodus 3–4; Jer 1:4-10; Ezek 2:1–3:15). The components of type (2) are: a personal encounter between Yahweh and the appointee, a word of initiation and commissioning, objection and answer, call-sign or ordination procedure.

N. Habel, "The Form and Significance of the Call Narratives," *ZAW* 77 (1965) 297-323.

WOE ORACLE (Wehruf). A genre that is used in the prophetic literature to criticize particular actions or attitudes of people, and sometimes to announce punishment upon them. Woe oracles are found as individual units (Isa 1:4; 3:11; 10:5) or in a series (Isa 5:8-24).

The typical woe oracle has two parts: (1) the exclamation *hôy* ("woe") followed by a participle denoting the criticized action, or a noun characterizing people in a negative way, and (2) a continuation with a variety of forms, including threats (Isa 5:9, 13-14, 24; 28:2-8), accusations (Ezek 13:3-9; 18:19), or rhetorical questions (Isa 10:3-4; Amos 6:2). This genre was like-

ly adopted by the prophets from wisdom circles (Gerstenberger, Wolff, Whedbee); according to Westermann it is a milder form of curse.
Related genre: (→) Prophecy of Punishment.

E. Gerstenberger, "The Woe Oracles of the Prophets," *JBL* 81 (1962), 249-63; G. Wanke, "אוֹי und הוֹי," *ZAW* 78 (1966) 215-18; C. Westermann, *Basic Forms of Prophetic Speech* (tr. H. C. White; Philadelphia: Westminster, 1967) 190-98; J. W. Whedbee, *Isaiah and Wisdom* (Nashville: Abingdon, 1971) 80-110; H. W. Wolff, *Amos' geistige Heimat* (WMANT 18; Neukirchener, 1964) 12-23.

FORMULAS

BLOOD RESTRICTION FORMULA (Blutbegrenzungsformel). The formula "His blood is upon him." This common legal formula (Lev 20:9, 11, 12, 13, 16, 27; Ezek 18:13; 33:4-5; see 2 Sam 1:16) does not belong to the statements of conviction, as is often said. The function of the formula is to declare that the effective sphere of the blood (normally guilt-inducing) of an executed man remains restricted to the executed, and does not affect the executor. Thus it appears as a declaratory formula after the pronouncement or prescription of the death (→) sentence, and not as a part of the forms of conviction.

K. Koch, "Der Spruch 'Sein Blut bleibe auf seinem Haupt' und die israelitische Auffassung vom vergossenen Blut," *VT* 12 (1962) 396-416; H. Reventlow, "Sein Blut komme über sein Haupt," *VT* 10 (1960) 311-27.

CALL TO ATTENTION FORMULA (Aufmerksamkeitsruf, Aufforderung zum Hören, Lehreröffnungsformel). A formula which opens a public presentation or address and intends to attract the attention of the hearers to the speech which follows. The constituent elements are an invitation to listen, mention of the addressee(s), and an indication of what is to be heard. This call would be used by, e.g., a singer (Judg 5:3), a wisdom teacher (Prov 7:24), or an official envoy (2 Kgs 18:28-29). It is frequently found in the prophetic literature in various forms, and is often expanded by relative clauses (Amos 3:1; Hos 4:1; Mic 6:1; Isa 1:10; Ezek 6:3).

This formula was developed from the short invitation, "Listen" (1 Sam 22:7; Gen 37:6), which could be used by anyone who wished to open a conversation.

CHALLENGE TO A DUEL FORMULA (Herausforderungsformel). The formula *hinĕnî 'ālayik* ("Behold, I am against you") is a short form of a longer hypothetical formula which includes the participle *ba'* ("Behold, I come against you"). It is likely that the original setting is the report of a duel (see 1 Sam 17:41-54).

The genre of a challenge to a duel is imitated by the prophets Nahum, Jeremiah, and Ezekiel, and is used particularly in words of Yahweh constituting announcements in (→) prophecies of punishment (Ezek 5:8-9; 13:8-9). In most cases the context is dominated by the imagery of battle.

P. Humbert, "Die Herausforderungsformel '*hinnenî êlêkâ*,'" *ZAW* 45 (1933) 101-8.

COMMISSIONING FORMULA (Aussendungsformel). The essential part of an authoritative charge to a subordinate to deliver a message on behalf of a superior. The standard wording is "Go and speak" plus the identification of the addressee. Normally there then follows the (→) messenger formula and the message itself, of whatever genre. In the highly developed account of Ezekiel's (→) commissioning as a messenger the commissioning formula plays a prominent role (3:1b, 4b, 11a).

CONCLUSION FORMULA FOR DIVINE SPEECH (Schlussformel eines Gottesspruchs). A formula used frequently in the book of Ezekiel to mark the end of a section of divine speech. The most common occurrence is "I Yahweh have spoken" (Ezek 5:13—here in connection with the [→] recognition formula—15, 17; 21:22 [*RSV* 21:17]; 24:14; 30:12; and 34:24). Several variations appear: (1) three times *kî* ("for") is prefixed (17:21—here in combination with the recognition formula; 21:37 [*RSV* 21:32]; and 26:14); (2) sometimes "Yahweh" is omitted (28:10; 39:5); and (3) four times "and I will do (it)" is added (17:24; 22:14; 36:36; and 37:14—here again in combination with the recognition formula).

The conclusion formula can also appear together with yet another formula at the end of a section of divine speech, the (→) prophetic utterance formula (23:34; 26:5, 14; 28:10; 37:14; 39:5). In Jer 34:5 the same combination occurs, but with "a word" prefixed as object.

The intention of the formula is to stress the power of Yahweh's word, as is borne out by the addition, "and I will do (it)."

W. Zimmerli, *Ezekiel 1* 26-27.

COVENANT FORMULA (Bundesformel). A two-part encapsulization of the relationship between Yahweh and his people, perhaps originally simply: "I am Yahweh your God; you are my people." This would have been essentially a description. In this simple form it does not appear in the OT. In a future-oriented formulation, "I will be your God, and you shall be my people," it is familiar in both prophets (e.g., Jer 7:23; 11:4; Ezek 36:28) and legal materials (e.g., Lev 26:12; Deut 29:12-13). In many instances this future-oriented formulation appears with the third person, "they shall be my people," rather than the second (e.g., Jer 24:7; 31:33; Ezek 11:20; 14:11; 37:23, 27). All of this future-oriented usage constitutes, however, a development from a purely descriptive intent to a promissory or hortatory one.

The elaboration of the formula in Deut 26:16-19 suggests that its basic setting was as an element within a covenant-making or renewing ceremony. The naturally close connection to marriage, adoption, and other legal formulas is apparent, as is the modification of the covenant formula in Hos 1:8 into an annulment.

R. Smend, *Die Bundesformel* (ThSt(B) 68; Zürich: EVZ, 1963).

Related genres: (→) Recognition Formula and (→) Prophetic Proof Saying.

HAND OF YAHWEH REVELATORY FORMULA (Hand Yahwes Offenbarungsformel). The basic form is "The hand of Yahweh was upon me." It serves to identify the experience of the ecstatic reception of revelation, most frequently in a (→) vision report (Ezek 1:3; 3:14, 21; 2 Kgs 3:15). The primary intention seems to be to portray the impact, psychological and/or physical, of the experience.

The formula is to be distinguished from the use of somewhat similar expressions to describe Yahweh's favor in Ezra-Nehemiah, e.g., "the good hand of God."

J. J. M. Roberts, "The Hand of Yahweh," *VT* 21 (1971) 244-51.

HOSTILE ORIENTATION FORMULA (Feindselige Ausrichtungsformel). The expression "set your face against X," used repeatedly in Ezekiel to introduce a prophecy against a particular group (e.g., Ezek 6:2). It is not a travel directive (contra Brownlee), but rather an expressive gesture, for it can also be used of God in Leviticus, Jeremiah, plus Ezek 14:6 and 15:7. Related genre: (→) Report of an Expressive Action.

W. Brownlee, " 'Son of Man Set Your Face,' Ezekiel the Refugee Prophet," *HUCA* 54 (1983) 83-110; W. Zimmerli, *Ezekiel 1*, 29-30, 182-83, 305.

MESSENGER FORMULA (Botenformel). The formula *kōh 'āmar* ("Thus says . . ."), which normally introduces a messenger speech. It seems to have originated in the ancient and widespread practice of the oral transmission of a message by means of a third party. The formula normally occurs twice, in the following sequence: (1) it is spoken by the sender when commissioning and instructing a messenger (Gen 32:5 [*RSV* 4]; 45:9); (2) it is reiterated by the messenger when delivering the message (2 Kgs 18:29; Num 22:15-16).

In some prophetic books the specific messenger formula, "Thus says Yahweh," frequently occurs (especially in Jeremiah and Ezekiel, but not in Hosea, Joel, Habakkuk, or Zechariah). This usage implies that a prophet delivering his message is understood in analogy with the practice of commissioning, instructing, and sending a messenger.

"NO PITY" FORMULA (Kein-Erbarmen Formel). A formula used occasionally in Deuteronomy and Ezekiel to underscore the seriousness of a crime and the necessity of appropriate punishment. To judge from the appearances in Ezekiel, the fullest wording of the formula was "your eye shall not spare and you shall not have pity." In Ezekiel the formula is used in the first person of Yahweh as determined fully to carry out an announced punishment against his people (Ezek 5:11; 7:4, 9; 8:18; 9:5, 10). But the occurrence of the formula in the second person in Deuteronomy indicates that it was originally at home in a legal context. Its placement in conjunction with instructions concerning punishments shows that its intent was to stress the drastic character of certain crimes by arguing that failure to carry out the punishment would result in the spreading of guilt throughout the community. Thus it is sometimes used together with the formulas about purging (cf. Deut 19:13; 21:21; 22:21).

OATH FORMULA (Schwurformel). The formula "As the Lord lives" (*ḥay yahweh*) with which an (→) oath is usually introduced.

PROPHETIC UTTERANCE FORMULA (Prophetische Offenbarungsformel). The phrase "the utterance of [my lord] Yahweh" (*nĕ'um ['ădōnāy] yahweh*). It labels a prophetic speech as the word of Israel's God, usually being placed at the end of a unit or a major section within a unit. The original setting may well have been the (→) vision report of a seer (Num 24:3), but by the time of Ezekiel it came to be used in any variety of prophetic speech. F. Baumgärtel, "Die Formel 'ne'um jahwe,'" *ZAW* 73 (1961) 277-90.

PROPHETIC WORD FORMULA (Prophetische Wortereignisformel). The statement that "the word of Yahweh came to me" *(wayĕhî dĕbar-yahweh 'ēlay).* Originally the narrative introduction to the report of prophetic revelation (still so in Ezek 12:8), it was used redactionally to introduce units of prophetic speech within a prophetic book (so at the beginning of nearly every unit in Ezekiel). It is often accompanied by a date or other preliminary formulas, such as the (→) messenger formula.

RECOGNITION FORMULA (Erkenntnisformel). A formula frequently used in the OT to express the purpose of Yahweh's action. The main elements are: (1) the verbal element, "and you shall know," which is rooted in the process of proving and demonstrating (Gen 42:34); and (2) the object clause, "that I am Yahweh," which employs the language of self-introduction (Exod 20:2).

The original setting was probably Yahweh's intervention in the holy war (1 Kgs 20:13, 28).

Related genre: (→) Prophetic Proof Saying.

W. Zimmerli, "Knowledge of God According to the Book of Ezekiel," 29-98.

REQUITAL FORMULA ("Vergeltungs"-formel). A formula which occurs occasionally in Ezekiel to designate the manner of punishment as corresponding to the crime committed. Essentially three words are involved: (1) the object, the "ways" of the transgressor; (2) the destination, "upon the guilty person's head," and (3) the verb, "I will put" (lit. "give"), with Yahweh as subject. The formula occurs in Ezek 7:4, 9; 9:10; 11:21; 16:43; 17:19; 22:31. In three instances (Ezek 7:4, 9; 9:10) the formula is used together with the (→) "no pity" formula.

The underlying idea of the fitting character of an action's consequences, whether as the result of the order of providence or the processes of punishment, is at home in wisdom, law, and prophecy. Especially closely related is the idiom according to which Yahweh "brings back" conduct upon a person's head.

Related formulas: (→) Blood Restriction Formula.

K. Koch, "Der Spruch 'Sein Blut bleibe auf seinem Haupt' und die israelitische Auffassung vom vergossenen Blut," *VT* 12 (1962) 396-416; idem, "Is There a Doctrine of Retribution in the Old Testament?" in *Theodicy in the Old Testament* (ed. J. L. Crenshaw; IRT 4; Philadelphia: Fortress, 1983) 57-87; P. D. Miller, Jr., *Sin and Judgment in the Prophets* (SBLMS 27; Chico: Scholars Press, 1982); H. Reventlow, "Sein Blut komme über sein Haupt," *VT* 10 (1960) 311-27.

SELF-INTRODUCTION FORMULA (Selbstvorstellungsformel). A formula by which a speaker reveals his or her identity to an addressee by announcing his or her name. While individuals occasionally use this pattern of speech in the OT, e.g., Joseph in Gen 45:4, major interest centers on Yahweh's use of this formula in the expression "I am Yahweh" or "I am Yahweh your God."

In theophanies the formula serves to reveal the otherwise uncertain identity of the deity speaking (e.g., Exod 6:2), and thus inherently expresses an element of gracious freedom, but a variety of other aspects can also be involved. Since "I am Yahweh your God" can function as the first half of a (→) covenant formula, its use at the beginning or end of paragraphs of laws can function to identify the role of these commandments as marks of Israel's peoplehood, i.e., as being a way of expressing what "you are my people" means. This usage is particularly common in Leviticus 17–26, but see also Ps 50:7 and 81:11 (*RSV* 10). In Isaiah 40–55 it functions as a part of messages of reassurance (e.g., 48:17), and in Ezekiel it plays a role in the (→) recognition formula.

K. Elliger, "Ich bin der Herr—euer Gott," in *Theologie als Glaubenswagnis* (*Fest.* K. Heim; Hamburg: Furche, 1954) 9-34; W. Zimmerli, "I am Yahweh," in *I Am Yahweh* (tr. D. W. Stott; Atlanta: Knox, 1982) 1-28.

VISIONARY GUIDANCE FORMULA (Seherische Führungsformel). A formula frequently used in the book of Ezekiel to mark off stages within a lengthy (→) vision report by identifying the beginning of a new scene. The main elements are: (1) the report of guidance by a supernatural figure, "and he brought me" (using forms of *bā', hālak,* or *yāsā'*), and (2) the specification of the place to which the seer came (e.g., "to the gate"). This formula appears in Ezek 8:7a, 14a, 16a; 40:17a, 24a, 28a, 32a, 35a, 48a; 41:1a; 42:1a, 15a; 43:1a; 44:1a, 4a; 46:19a, 21a; 47:1a, 2a, 6b.

H. Gese, *Der Verfassungsentwurf des Ezekiel* (BHT 25; Tübingen: Mohr, 1957); W. Zimmerli, *Ezekiel 2,* 343.